The Winnowing Oar – New Perspectives in Homeric Studies

The Winnowing Oar – New Perspectives in Homeric Studies

Studies in Honor of Antonios Rengakos

Edited by
Christos Tsagalis and Andreas Markantonatos

DE GRUYTER

ISBN 978-3-11-065892-7
e-ISBN (PDF) 978-3-11-055987-3
e-ISBN (EPUB) 978-3-11-055949-1

Library of Congress Cataloging-in-Publication Data
A CIP catalog record for this book has been applied for at the Library of Congress.

Bibliografic information published by the Deutsche Nationalbibliothek
The Deutsche Nationalbibliothek lists this publication in the Deutschen Nationalbibliografie;
detailed bibliografic data are available on the Internet at http://dnb.dnb.de.

© 2019 Walter de Gruyter GmbH, Berlin/Boston
This volume is text- and page-identical with the hardback published in 2017.
Cover image: Vassily Kandinsky, Blue (© Norton Simon Museum, Pasadena, California)
Printing and binding: CPI books GmbH, Leck
♾ Printed on acid-free paper
Printed in Germany

www.degruyter.com

Table of Contents

Introduction —— 1

Text

M. L. West†
Editing the *Odyssey* —— 13

Margalit Finkelberg
Homer at the Panathenaia: Some possible scenarios —— 29

Interpretation

Franco Montanari
The failed embassy: Achilles in the *Iliad* —— 43

Egbert Bakker
Hector (and) the race horse: The telescopic vision of the *Iliad* —— 57

Ruth Scodel
Homeric fate, Homeric poetics —— 75

J. S. Burgess
The *Apologos* of Odysseus: Tradition and conspiracy theories —— 95

Jonas Grethlein
The best of the Achaeans? Odysseus and Achilles in the *Odyssey* —— 121

Language and Formulas

G. O. Hutchinson
Repetition, range, and attention: The *Iliad* —— 145

A. C. Cassio
'Authentic' vs. 'artificial': Homeric ΕΠΕΕΣΣΙ(Ν) reconsidered —— 171

Christos Tsagalis
ΑΠ'/ΚΑΤ' ΑΙΓΙΛΙΠΟΣ ΠΕΤΡΗΣ: Homeric iconyms and Hittite answers —— 191

Stephanie West
Mysterious Lemnos: A note on ΑΜΙΧΘΑΛΟΕΣΣΑ (*Il.* 24.753) —— 215

Homeric Hymns

Anton Bierl
'Hail and take pleasure!' Making gods present in narration through choral song and other epiphanic strategies in the *Homeric Hymns to Dionysus* and *Apollo* —— 231

Richard Janko
Tithonus, Eos and the cicada in the *Homeric Hymn to Aphrodite* and Sappho fr. 58 —— 267

Publications by Antonios Rengakos —— 297

General Index —— 301

Index of Principal Homeric Passages —— 305

Introduction

This collection of essays by a host of eminent classical scholars on fiendishly intricate and notoriously impenetrable Homeric *zetemata* aims to pay lavish tribute to a vigorously incisive researcher of epic poetry, Antonios Rengakos, Professor of Greek in the Department of Philology at the Aristotle University of Thessaloniki, and to celebrate the happy occasion of his 60th birthday. The editors, both fortunate recipients of the honoree's wisdom and friendship, consider this the perfect opportunity to highlight the influence that Antonios Rengakos has exercised on the field of the study of Greek literature worldwide in valuable and memorable ways. His seminal work on the close interconnections between the Homeric text and Hellenistic poetry, as well as his astute and detailed contributions to our better understanding of the complex network of echoes and affinities amongst a plethora of highly interrelated Greek texts spanning a vast stretch of time from the archaic era to Alexandrian literary tradition and beyond, speaks volumes of his impeccable scholarship and sound critical judgement. It is not overbold to claim that this *Festschrift* is but a minor testimony to the great respect which Antonios Rengakos commands in the academic world of classical learning; for it would unquestionably take more than one *liber amicorum* to showcase the impressively broad range of his research interests and the strikingly profound erudition of his academic writings.

Having all this in mind one feels inadequate to pay due homage to the voluminous and versatile research work of the dedicatee, and the thought that this should be dispatched within the limited space of a preface can without doubt humble the most confident author. Be that as it may, the editors should hope that even a brief sketch of the honoree's remarkable achievement and creative intelligence will offer readers an inkling of his international stature. It is indeed beyond accident that Antonios Rengakos, an outstanding student of the prestigious German School of Athens, chose to pursue his undergraduate and postgraduate studies at the University of Freiburg; for it swiftly strikes those who have had the privilege to have known the honoree in person that the disciplined sensitivity and rock solid analytical thinking of German classical scholarship become him, especially when what is at stake is nothing less than the laborious task of both ascertaining the integrity of the text and unearthing the richness of its implications. More than that, in Germany Antonios Rengakos was fortunate enough to enjoy the enormous benefits accruing from his close collaboration with the pre-eminent scholar and distinguished classicist, Professor Wolfgang Kullmann, who has had a major impact on the honoree, motivating him towards following a distinctly neo-analytical approach to the study of Homeric epics, as well as encouraging him to forge indissoluble links to German academia. This intense schooling in the best traditions of German classical scholarship has paid dividends for Antonios Rengakos; for his well-argued and full of deep learning doctoral thesis entitled *Form und Wandel des Machtdenkens der Athener bei Thukydides* (1984), together with his tightly documented and densely deliberated *habilitation* dissertation on the remarkable ways in which the meticulous study of eminent Hellenistic poet-scholars such as Callimachus and Apollonius Rhodius can shed revealing light upon the misty beginnings of the Homeric text (1993 & 1994), has established him as an undisputed authority on Greek literature and culture.

Furthermore, with his numerous studies confirming the narrative complexity and intertextual sophistication not only of the *Iliad* and *Odyssey* but also of a wide range of Hellenistic poems, Antonios Rengakos has evaluated the current thinking on this most demanding area of knowledge, while at the same time both setting the agenda for new exciting research and making more than a few original arguments about the future direction of the continuing debate over the validity of such theoretical tools as Narratology and Intertextuality in the field of the Classics. Anyone who thinks that issues of narrational authority and intertextual empowerment are simple and easily graspable should read the dedicatee's important publications, which combine stimulating discussions of the special ways in which myth-sequences are always mediated through some kind of narrative recasting and recalibration with a wealth of useful insights into a literary work's multiple points of reference. In a series of well-considered and informative articles, as well as offering a much-needed mapping of the cultural and intellectual terrain of Hellenistic poetry, Antonios Rengakos has elegantly explored the striking intricacy of those patterns of images and motifs which one can see unabatedly building throughout poems, thereby rendering both the narrated events and the vivid descriptions overwhelming in their specific details and sensory impressions.

This first attempt at outlining the honoree's impressive scholarly accomplishments would be gravely amiss if it failed to include mention of another long series of important publications: Antonios Rengakos' remarkable edited output comprising several multi-authored volumes about a broad range of classical themes and topics, as well as numerous Modern Greek translations of fundamental reference works and academic treatises. For instance, there is something almost uncanny about how *Brill's Companion to Thucydides* (2006), proficiently edited by the dedicatee and Antonios Tsakmakis, makes the work of a long-dead historian come alive before our eyes, thereby encouraging readers to explore his life and work, as well as such perennial issues as truth, humanity, politics, and religion. The same observation applies, to move on to a different author and genre, to *Brill's Companion to Hesiod*, edited together with Franco Montanari and Christos Tsagalis. It is not incidental that interest in Hesiodic studies has been renewed after the publication of a long-needed collective work offering a rich panorama of the current *status quaestionis* in Hesiodic studies. More than this, the Modern Greek translation of Franco Montanari's influential and authoritative *Modern Dictionary of the Ancient Greek Language* (2013), expertly edited by Antonios Rengakos who was assisted by an impressive team of learned scholars from the Aristotle University of Thessaloniki, is widely recognised in his native Greece and elsewhere as a monumental achievement of scholarly sophistication and capable editorship. Last but not least, Antonios Rengakos, together with Franco Montanari, directs a large and most prestigious print publishing programme in Classical Studies Both the *Trends in Classics* scholarly journal and the corresponding series of beautifully produced and refreshingly open-minded academic monographs (*Trends in Classics Supplementary Volumes*) provide valuable access to essential research work by leading classical scholars on Greek and Latin literature and culture, thereby allowing new theoretical approaches to be reconciled with traditional modes of study.

It is fair to say that Antonios Rengakos has had his hefty share of accolades and tributes in Greece and abroad; nonetheless, his election as a tenured member of the Academy of Athens in 2011, the Academia Europea in 2013, and the Heidelberger Akademie der Wissenschaften in 2016 came as the crowning points of his professional road that began many years ago. Antonios Rengakos, as well as having transformed the historical Department of Philology at the Aristotle University of Thessaloniki through his continuous efforts to attract the most gifted Greek scholars and to create a forum for academic research of the highest order, has shown himself to be an inspiration for his colleagues and students, thereby enabling a greatly improved understanding not just of Homer's own legacy, but also of the entire Greek literature. His is a rich and important contribution to classical learning that will be central to all future discussions of ancient Greek texts.

This volume includes twelve chapters treating various themes pertaining to Homer and the Homeric Hymns. They clearly fall within the broadly defined categories of text and interpretation of the *Iliad* and the *Odyssey*, as well as the Homeric Hymns *to Hermes* and *Aphrodite*.

Part I (Editing the *Odyssey*: Homer at the Panathenaea: Some Possible Scenarios) deals with the text of the Homeric epics.

In light of his forthcoming edition of the *Odyssey* Martin West† presents some of the principles on which it is based. The fact that the *Odyssey* does not have its Venetus A and we are less well informed about it than is the case with the *Iliad* has some consequences on the use of the sources available. One cardinal case is Eustathius, who has to be consulted more often when one is preparing an edition of the *Odyssey* than when doing the same thing for the *Iliad*. The reason is that in the latter case we have two tenth-century and six eleventh-century MSS all predating Eusathius, while in the former we have one from the later tenth century, one from the eleventh, one from the twelfth, and the rest are later, Eustathius antedating all but two or three of them. West, who has consulted the largest number of manuscripts and papyri in comparison to all previous editions, has also embarked on a meticulous study of various previous editions and especially early modern editions of Homer. On this basis, he argues that there is reason to tackle various tetxual problems afresh and also reconsider some brilliant emendations made by 18th and 19th century scholars. He also draws attention to the way a modern editor has to deal with various facets of the modernization the text of Homer has suffered in antiquity.

Margalit Finkelberg surveys the basic theories pertaining to the date of the Homeric epics laying emphasis on various textual, iconographical, and performative issues. She argues in favor of a seventh-century, rather than an early eighth- or late sixth-century dating, which is strongly suggested by the iconographical evidence. Finkelberg places much emphasis on the timespan needed for the diffusion, recognition, and impact Homeric epic had in sixth-century Athens. This often neglected aspect of the performance of Homer in the Panathenaea is of prime importance for a seventh-century dating, since it gives ample time for the Homeric tradition to become influential and is in tune with vase representations of Homeric themes which become known in the seventh century. Finkelberg maintains that on balance a seventh-century dating of at least the *Iliad* 'allows for a considerably wider margin for accommodating the linguistic evidence as regards the relative chronology of the early hexameter poetry'.

Part II contains five interpretive studies, of which three pertain to the *Iliad* (The Failed Embassy: Achilles in the *Iliad*; Hector and the Race Horse: The Telescopic Vision in the *Iliad*; Homeric Fate, Homeric Poetics) and two to the *Odyssey* (The *Apologos* of Odysseus: Tradition and Conspiracy Theories; Achilles and Odysseus' Revenge).

Franco Montanari studies one of the most famous episode in the entire *Iliad*, the embassy to Achilles, with a keen eye for the deployment of the action and the later Iliadic *non sequitur* pertaining to Achilles still "waiting" for a supplication by the Achaeans. Montanari argues that the failed embassy is an invention of the poet of the *Iliad*, who is for him the person responsible for the final shaping of the epic as we know it. After embarking on a minute examination of the various aspects of the course of action after the actual embassy, Montanari suggests that its aim is to "fail". The impasse at which things find themselves heightens the dramatic tension and "asks" for – so to speak – a new plotline, which will override the previous one. In other words, no gifts, no solution of the conflict but a new wrath that will bring back a savage Achilles. The embassy fails but the unthinkable happens: the great hero returns to the fighting by means of the loss of his dearest friend Patroclus, a development partly mirrored in another unthikable event by which the poem comes to an end, i.e. the supplication of Achilles by Priam, i.e. the very father of the man he has slaughtered and brutally dishonored, Hector.

Drawing on the notion of 'traditional referentiality' a term coined by J. M. Foley describing the omnipresence of all relevant previous contexts of a repeated phrase, Egbert Bakker makes a further step arguing that this feature of Homeric epic is basically responsible for the conception and creation of the *Iliad* as a "monumental composition". Formulaic diction is not, as Bakker stresses, a by-product of oral or orally-derived poetry. It is the precise medium through which meaning is constructed and monumentality is achieved. One particular manifestation of this phenomenon is a the horse simile, the minute study of which discloses how the *Iliad* "rewrites" the story of the Trojan War. Being linked with Paris, Hector, and Achilles, this type of simile exploits similar diction so as to weave of thick web of associations between the three aforementioned heroes. The aim of this association is to unravel the poem's evolution from Trojan to Iliadic epic: liability for the besieged city's terrible situation is thus gradually transferred from Paris who is more "Trojan" and less "Iliadic" to Hector, whose haughty overconfidence makes him, as Polydamas so convincingly argues, responsible for the slaughtering of his army by an avenging Achilles who finally resumes fighting. Thus, the initial focus of the conflict that pertains to the entire war shifts from the pair Paris-Menelaus to the pair Hector-Achilles. Bakker shows that it is formulaic repetition that takes listeners "by the hand" and "invite" them to makes interpretive associations. Formulaic diction lies at the heart of epic grammar which the audience "learns" while listening to the song in performance again and again.

Ruth Scodel studies the two systems employed by the *Iliad* that show how narrated events are controlled by supernatural powers. She distinguishes between μοῖρα ('fate') and the Διὸς Βουλή ('the Plan or Will of Zeus') and argues that although they seem to co-operate their difference 'is metapoetically significant'. Whereas fate points to the fact that some aspects of the story are fixed, the Plan of Zeus indicates the particular narrative course to be followed by the *Iliad*. Zeus's power has its limitations: he cannot violate what fate predicts and his Plan is constantly curtailed or thwarted by the actions of other gods. The metapoetics of this twofold limitation of Zeus' power are telling. They partially echo the function of the poet/performer who has to strike a balance between the *Fak-*

tenkanon of the tradition and the 'pressure' exercized by audiences and patrons (mirrored, according to Scodel, onto the actions of the other gods). On the level of poetic effect, the poem alerts us to the fact that the supreme god is not as omnipotent as we would imagine him to be. After all, 'both Plan and plot remain, just barely, under control'.

Jonathan Burgess looks afresh at the *Apologos* of Odysseus in Books 9–12 and argues that it represents 'a multiform of a traditional tale of Odysseus' wanderings … [which] would have existed generally in myth and perhaps predominantly in epic form'. For Burgess some motifs and narrative devices 'may have existed in hypothetically pre-Homeric folktales', but we should not treat their Homeric version as the πρῶτος εὑρετής of their epic metamorphosis. Arguing against the widely influential theory about alternative versions of Odysseus' return, Burgess maintains that key features of the *Apologos*, such as Poseidon's wrath as a result of the blinding of his son Polyphemus and Circe the witch are traditional, though he acknowledges that certain other characteristics of the material we now find in the *Odyssey* may have originated from a reshuffling of a given sequence of tales with the addition or omission of episodes or parts of episodes. On the other hand, Burgess recognizes 'that the Homeric *Apologos* is probably distinctive in nature, whether in terms of poetics, characterization, theme, and ideology'.

Jonas Grethlein explores the interaction between the *Iliad* and the *Odyssey* on the basis of the *Odyssey*'s presentation of its main hero against the backdrop of the *Iliad*'s Achilles. While aknowledging Nagy's famous juxtaposition of Achilles and Odysseus as representatives of two distinct types of heroic valor, βίη and μῆτις respectively, which become the poetic emblems of the Iliadic and Odyssean traditions, Grethlein unearthes other aspects of this relation. Odysseus' killing of the suitors is naratively built against the backdrop of Achilles' killing of Hector. The former's rage can hardly be interpreted without knowledge of the latter's, the more so since specific verbal parallels evoke this resonance. On a more explicit level, the fates of the two heroes seem to share a form of antithetical symbiosis: Achilles gains κλέος at the expense of his *nostos*, whereas Odysseus' κλέος is his *nostos*. Oral intertextuality shows that the inbuilt antagonism between the two heroes is epically "translated" in a sophisticated form of emulation. Seen from this vantage point, an all-important questions emerges: if Odysseus' rage, stressed in the concluding and climactic part of the *Odyssey*, has been modelled on Achilles' savagery in the dramatic peak of the *Iliad*, what does this mean of the tradition's ultimate comment on the heroic code and its manifestation in its most emblematic heroes, Iliadic Achilles and Odyssean Odysseus, i.e. the "best of the Achaeans"?

Part III is devoted to language and formulas. It comprises four studies equally divided between general issues pertaining to the Homeric *Kunstsprache* (Repetition, range and attention: the *Iliad*; 'Authentic' vs. 'artificial': Homeric ἐπέεσσι(ν) reconsidered) and specific formulas that seemingly resist etymological analysis (ἀπ'/κατ' αἰγίλιπος πέτρης: Homeric iconyms and Hittite Answers; Mysterious Lemnos: A note on ἀμιχθαλόεσσα).

Gregory Hutchinson revisits the always pertinent issue of repetition of phraseology in Homer. By drawing analogies from various texts (ranging from Greco-Roman antiquity to the *Nibelungenlied* to South-Slavic oral tradition) he argues that in certain cases repetition in Homer can have an impact on the audience. A practical guide to the effect repetition may have is to study its form and scale, the latter term containing a variety of factors such as textual range, density, accumulation, and even nesting within other repetitive devices. Pointed variation, a by product of repetition, is an aesthetic principle, but also of paramount importance for drawing attention to interconnected phraseology. Traditional structural mechanisms may be also employed as platforms promoting or highlighting repetition for the audience. Hutchinson treats with hesitation the question pertaining to the oral improvisation of the poem, i.e. of a gifted singer who composes during the performance and puts some of the formulaic material he has inherited from tradition into novel use. He suggests that this possibility could be accepted only under the proviso that it allows for interpretive exploitation and planning of repetition across distant passages. Even so, repetition is not an exclusive feature of an orally composed poem. It is a literary phenomenon. It should therefore be studied as such.

Albio Cesare Cassio studies the question of authenticity vs. artificiality with respect to a particular feature of Homeric language. He persuasively argues that there is nothing intrinsically artificial in the Homeric use of the -εσσι ending for the -s- stems (δυσμενέεσσι, λεχέεσσι, βελέεσσι, ἐπέεσσι), since -εεσσι is nothing but the outcome of a banal analogical process well attested in Aeolic and Doric inscriptions and perfectly possible at a very early linguistic stage wherever -εσσι was in use. Cassio rightly stresses that poetic artificial extensions are obvious and attested (νέ-εσσι), but they are a secondary phenomenon. He also offers an explanation for the otherwise strange 'fixity' of -οις ἐπέεσσι(ν).

Christos Tsagalis revisits the arcane Homeric formula ἀπ'/κατ' αἰγίλιπος πέτρης. After a critical survey of all the previously proposed etymologies, he suggests that we should 'seek help' outside Greek culture. He, thus, draws attention to the Luwian expression *šalli lāpani' wāniya* ('great saltlick rock face'), which is attested in the Ulmi-Tesub treaty drawn either between Hattusili's son and successor Tudhaliya IV and Kurunta, nephew of Hattusili, or by Hattusili himself and Kurunta when the latter was appointed by Hattusili as ruler of *Tarḫuntašša* that is situated in a Luwian region. Tsagalis argues that this Luwian expression is analogous to the Homeric αἰγίλιπος πέτρης, since in both cases the relevant words are juxtaposed and stand in the same order. By stressing the importance of salt and salt-licking imagery in incantations and spells pertaining to Hittite ritual, the author claims that it was exactly this ritual that functioned as a 'corridor' through which the Hittite expression 'saltlick cliff' passed to Greek speakers in geographical areas where the Greeks and Hittites came together over an extended period of time. In the footsteps of Puhvel, Tsagalis tentatively suggests that as far as epic is concerned, the relevant Hittite expression has entered Greek epic diction through the Homeric simile, since it shares with Hittite spells the same twofold structure and analogical perspective. Since the formula αἰγίλιψ πέτρη was incomprehensible to the Ionian bards (having lost its denotative force pertaining to salt-licking), the licking aspect was recontextualized and associated with the familiar imagery of a mountain spring, where animals satisfy their thirst, licking with their tongues the flowing, clean water. Having being reduced to a mere iconym, this fossilized expression preserved in epic diction only some of its connotations: the rock face on which minerals are found, the image of the animals licking, the rural environment.

Stephanie West explores the etymologically obscure Homeric epithet ἀμιχθαλόεσσα. After offering a critical survey of the various suggestions made thus far, she argues that it may have been borrowed from a language other than Greek that other population groups of the island were employing at a very early stage. A connection with fire or sulphur, as a result of the island's vulcanicity and link to Hephaestus, is quite possible. Following Leumann, West argues that the poet of the *Iliad* probably did not know the exact meaning of this term but nevertheless used it in reference to Lemnos, since he believed that his audience would associate it with this particular island. In fact, ἀμιχθαλόεσσα may well be a 'pathway' to Argonautic poetry and the prehistory of the Trojan War, the more so since Lemnos featured as a transit-island in both of these two great sagas. The desire to apply ἀμιχθαλόεσσα to Lemnos must have originated from the specific association of this island with what Greeks thought this epithet meant, since the poet in his attempt to use it in his epic did not hesitate to resort even to a metrical irregularity, i.e. the violation of Hermann's Bridge.

Part IV focuses on the Homeric Hymns. It includes two studies, one dealing with the *Homeric Hymns to Dionysus and Apollo*, and the other with Tithonus, Eos and the cicada in the *Homeric Hymn to Aphrodite* and Sappho fr. 58.

Anton Bierl explores how divine presence is grafted in the narrative of the *Homeric Hymns to Dionysus and Apollo*. By targeting χορεία and stressing its importance, the author claims that both Dionysus and Apollo manifest their presence by means of their close association with this enthralling nexus of music, song, and choral dance. Hymnic narrative brings this special aspect to the limelight by reenacting the epiphany of the gods. In this way, the singer 'can self-referentially allude to his own epic production that unfolds in a poetic epiphany'. Seen from this vantage point, the Homeric Hymns display a sophistication that is often 'buried' under their survival within the closed framework of a collection. In fact, they belong to the heart, not the periphery, of modern concerns about self-referentiality in archaic epic poetry at large. Take for example, the *Homeric Hymn to Hermes* that fosters a stance that could very well be interpreted as 'polemical' versus the view associating Apollo par excellence with song and dance. The construction of the lyre sets a 'new beginning' to the living song culture 'as if Hermes, as god of literacy made the diachronic chain of performances and re-performances come to an end'.

Richard Janko revisits the text of Sappho's Tithonus Ode and suggests (after personal inspection of the relevant papyrus) the reading ἔρωι δεδάθεισαν for the *crux* of line 10. Although unattested, this participle of the verb *δάημι seems unproblematic, rendering a meaning (in agreement with Αὔων) like 'Dawn, schooled by love'. Janko offers a close analysis of Sappho's poem, which he divides into two stanzas, the first contrasting the addressees' singing and dancing and the aging speaker's inability to join the dance, the second stanza the opposition between old age and immortality. After acutely observing that the speaker does not reveal his/her gender, Janko considers the interpretive ramifications of the speaker being a man or a woman. In the former case he claims that 'if a male speaker were addressing a chorus of girls, he could easily flatter his audience by likening them to the goddess'; in the latter case, the situation becomes complex since it involves gender-reversal, which may be due to Sappho's desire to empathise with others or to her aim to reach a larger audience (given that the poem could be performed by speakers of either gender and could be addressed to audiences of either or both genders). But Janko's favorite scenario is that Sappho's self-identification with the aged Tithonus was triggered by the fact that in myth he was turned into a cicada that went on singing incessantly, more or less like the poetess herself whose fame would live forever. In the last part of his study, Janko turns to the *Homeric Hymn to Aphrodite* that also offers a version of the myth of Tithonus and antedates Sappho. Following Stehle, the author argues that the metamorphosis of Tithonus invites us to see in its treatment by Sappho the poetess' desire to be singing, cicada-like, even in her old age.

Christos Tsagalis and Andreas Markantonatos
Thessaloniki and Kalamata,
May 2017

Text

M. L. West†
Editing the *Odyssey*

When I tell a non-classicist that I am editing the *Odyssey*,[1] this is generally met with some incomprehension. The next question is always, are you translating it? Or perhaps writing a commentary? And I say no, I'm editing the Greek text. But, they say, surely that's already been done? I don't need to explain to this audience that editing a classical text is not just a once-for-all job and that it needs doing again from time to time. But I thought you might be interested in hearing more about why there is a need for a new critical edition of the *Odyssey* in particular, what is involved in the process of making it, and how I expect my edition to change things.

First some general remarks about why we need critical editions. Our texts of ancient authors are not handed down from Mt Olympos. In most cases we rely on manuscripts written in the Middle Ages or Renaissance, many centuries later than the original authors. In the case of Homer they are over 1,500 years later. These manuscripts are copies of copies of who knows how many copies. And every time a new copy was made, the text underwent changes, usually for the worse. So no two manuscripts give exactly the same text. When we read an ancient author, we don't just look at a transcript of some manuscript or other, we turn to an edition that presents us with an editor's best attempt at evaluating the manuscript sources and reconstructing an approximation to the original. This involves comparing the variant readings found in different manuscripts and deciding which one to prefer. Sometimes none of them is satisfactory and it's necessary to consider emendations proposed by scholars, or to devise a new emendation. Sometimes no satisfactory solution is apparent and the editor leaves the text as it is but marks it as corrupt. When we read a tragedy by Aeschylus or Sophocles, there will be places on every page where the manuscript tradition is certainly corrupt and has had to be emended by some scholar or other, or left as it is, adorned with a symbol signifying editorial despair. It is not nearly as bad as that with Homer, but Homer presents other problems.

---

[1] Forthcoming with Walter De Gruyter.

[After my husband died, quite unexpectedly in July 2015, I found among his papers this lecture, composed for a student group a few months earlier. He would certainly have wished to join in honouring Antonios Rengakos, and I offer this piece on his behalf: δόσις δ' ὀλίγη τε φίλη τε. S.R.W.]

A critical edition normally provides us not just with the editor's preferred form of the text, but also, at the foot of each page, with a critical apparatus containing a selection of information about the materials used, the principal manuscript variants and, where appropriate, the principal conjectural interventions by scholars. With a critical apparatus we have some basis for assessing the editor's decisions and forming our own independent views if we want to. But if we compare different editions of the same author, just as when we compare different manuscripts, we find that no two agree exactly on their text, and also that they give different selections of supporting information. Sometimes there is a consensus that one particular edition is the best one available, perhaps even a consensus that it is so good that the job won't ever need to be done again. More often the best available edition is not the best imaginable. Perhaps more work needs to be done on the manuscripts, or new evidence has become available, or finer judgment is called for. So new editions keep coming, and sometimes they represent progress.

To edit the text of any author, or to appreciate the work of someone who has, we need to have some understanding of the history of the transmission of that text: the conditions under which it has been handed down, the vicissitudes to which it has been exposed, the factors that may have brought changes to it. In the case of the Homeric epics, the story in outline goes something like this.

The poet's original manuscript, consisting probably of a collection of papyrus rolls, came into the possession of rhapsodes, or of some wealthy patron for the use of rhapsodes. These rhapsodes were accustomed to changing and improving the songs they sang from occasion to occasion; and their aim in life was personal fame and success. Even after they decided to base their recitations on the *Iliad* or *Odyssey,* they were just as ready to 'improve' it with additional verses of their own as fourth-century tragic actors were ready to 'improve' Euripides. It is generally agreed that one major interpolation is to be recognized in the *Iliad:* the *Doloneia.* For the rest, it is a reasonable view that interpolation is limited to short passages, single paragraphs or verses. In the very early stages of the transmission, when the number of copies in existence was still limited, such insertions had a chance of becoming rooted in the whole tradition. But the chance diminished as time went on, and most interpolations would have remained absent from part of the manuscript tradition. In many cases we find that an inessential, formulaic line is in fact absent from some of the medieval manuscripts. In other cases it is in all the medieval manuscripts but absent from one or more papyri. This is a pretty clear sign that it does not belong in the text.

Athens certainly played a leading part in the transmission of the Homeric poems throughout the Classical period. They were studied at school by Athenian boys, which was bound to create a continuing need for more copies. Athens was also a favourite haunt of sophists, who liked to draw material from Homer for their discourses. It is no wonder if the pre-Alexandrian tradition of Homer was largely shaped by Attic exemplars. The language of the poems as they appear in the received text is marked by many traces of Attic dialect, as Wackernagel showed in a famous book, the *Sprachliche Untersuchungen zu Homer* (Göttingen 1916). This very likely reflects Attic transmission (though in the case of the *Odyssey* I don't exclude an Attic origin). The editor must make due allowance for that.

From our knowledge of the history of Greek writing, we can assume that the Homeric text was at first written in a script that did not distinguish between short ε and the lengthened ε (later written ει) that resulted from contraction of εε or from compensatory lengthening (as in ξεῖνος < ξένϝος) nor did it distinguish between o and ō (later written ου). It is a more controversial question whether the text was ever written in a script, such as the old Attic alphabet, that did not distinguish between ε and η or between o and ω. If the poems were first written down in Ionia, it would probably have been in an Ionian alphabet in which these vowels *were* distinguished. But it remains a possibility that copies made at Athens before the adoption there of the Ionian alphabet (officially in 403) used the local alphabet familiar to the copyists. If so, errors might occasionally have arisen from later misinterpretation of ambiguous spellings in Attic copies. Alexandrian scholars postulated this as a possible source of corruption, and some modern scholars have followed them. There does seem to be a very small number of plausible instances, but the number is small because people knew the poems well from hearing them, and that generally prevented misreading of the written text.

Changes in spelling conventions and in the pronunciation of the language led to various small changes in the text. One example is the Ionian contraction of εο into a diphthong. Down to the fourth century BCE it continued to be written as εο, and so distinguished from the inherited diphthong ευ – distinguished in writing, and no doubt still pronounced differently. Then the two merged, and monosyllabic εο began to be written ευ. So transmitted spellings such as μευ, ἐκαλεῦντο must be regarded as modernizations, and if we want to recover the earlier form of the text we have to restore εο. Another example is the old long diphthong ηυ. It too came to be replaced by ευ in the late Classical period. With the dative of the word for ships, νηυσί, the correct spelling with eta prevailed in the tradition, but some papyri show νευσί with epsilon. For the augmented forms of verbs such as εὔχομαι and εὑρίσκω, the tradition overwhelmingly offers εὔχονται, εὗρον with epsilon, but some Ptolemaic papyri still give ηὖρε, ηὔχοντο with eta, and there is a good case for restoring such forms everywhere, even though ευ- with epsilon would be admissible as an unaugmented form.

The earliest papyrus fragments (third and second centuries BCE), and quotations from Homer in fourth-century authors such as Plato and Aeschines, show that many of the texts then in circulation contained a quantity of interpolated lines (usually repeated from other contexts) and that they often diverged from one another in phrasing by substitution of equivalent formulae. This had come about presumably because the poems were commonly copied by rhapsodes or by others who knew the text so well that they were able to write out whole sections from memory rather than by closely following the exemplar before them. After about the middle of the second century BCE most of the interpolations disappear. This is assumed to be due to the authority of scholars such as Aristophanes of Byzantium and Aristarchus: verses which were absent from their 'editions' were deleted from other copies, perhaps so that booksellers could advertise them as 'corrected according to Aristarchus'. But they did not go so far as to adjust the readings of the remaining verses so that they agreed with Aristarchus'. It often happens that what Didymus knew as the common reading, and what appears as such in the medieval manuscripts, differs from the reading favoured by Aristarchus.

Evidence for the text in the Roman period comes from quotations in a wide range of authors and some hundreds of papyrus fragments. Where these sources give something different from the medieval manuscripts, it is in most cases a matter of simple error, whether of memory or of copying; or the quoting author is adapting the text for his own purposes. But it is clear that a fair number of substantive variants were current. Often we can see that they go back into the Hellenistic period and probably earlier. Many of them reappear among the medieval manuscripts, sometimes but not always lifted from the scholia. So we cannot speak glibly of a medieval vulgate, as if the medieval tradition were more or less agreed on a single form of the text. Sometimes a medieval copy will offer a substantive variant, for example one speech-formula substituted for another. We then have to ask whether the substitution is just due to the Byzantine scribe who has copied a lot of Homer and knows the language, or whether it was an ancient variant that may at any time turn up on a papyrus.

There is a gap in the tradition between the sixth and the ninth century: no more papyri, and no other manuscripts either. It was a period during which interest in classical poetry evidently lay dormant. When the interest revived at Constantinople in the ninth century, scribes and scholars had to make a new start using whatever old manuscripts from late Antiquity were still to be found in their schools and monasteries. They applied themselves to this with great dedication, and some wonderful new codices were produced that contained not only the text but notes of variant readings – ancient variants – and extensive scholia deriving from ancient scholia and commentaries. The famous Venetus A of the

Iliad is a splendid example of such a codex. Unfortunately we have nothing matching it for the *Odyssey*. A few of the later manuscripts do carry important scholia and variants, but on nothing like the same scale as in the *Iliad*.

The earliest printed editions followed whatever manuscript the printer or editor had to hand. It was a long time before editors realized the importance of consulting as many manuscripts as possible, and of course they were hampered by the difficulty of finding out what manuscripts existed and then of getting access to them. Jacob La Roche in 1867 produced an edition advertised as 'ad fidem librorum optimorum', but the fifteen manuscripts he used include only one of the four oldest, and only four of the eleven that van Thiel chose as the basis of his recension. Arthur Ludwich in his important edition of 1889–1891 cites 22 manuscripts, including the oldest ones; some of them he reports fully and accurately, but of others he had only partial knowledge, as he only collated six copies in full. He admits that some of the others deserved closer study, especially the tenth-century manuscript G, which he had only been able to look at for a few days in Florence. In his edition the critical apparatus takes up a considerable space, and appears to give a great deal of detailed information. But much of it is extremely trivial, of no use to anyone.

The Oxford editor T. W. Allen undertook more extensive manuscript researches. He lists 75 manuscripts of the *Odyssey*, 64 of which he had personally looked at, though it is not clear how many he actually collated in detail. He used other people's published collations where they existed, and otherwise he seems often to have contented himself with samplings. He declares that the manuscripts (except for six that resisted classification) fall into seventeen families, and it is these families (or alleged families), and not individual manuscripts, that he mostly cites in his apparatus, using lower-case roman letters in bold. But Allen arrived at his classification into families, as he tells us, 'by a process of noting all cases of variants presented by ten or less than ten MSS., and then casting them up. The MSS. which agree most often in presenting such variants have a claim to the title of family.' Now this is a very rough and ready method, and clearly when Allen says that the **g** family has such and such a reading, we cannot take this as a warranty that all of the twelve manuscripts that he assigns to this family have that reading, only that a number of them do. So we are left not knowing which manuscripts have it and which do not. In any case, subsequent research has shown that Allen's reports of manuscript readings are often confused, and that his families have little validity. For all the effort that lies behind his apparatus, it is of small use to the serious student.

The best edition to date is the one produced by Peter Von der Mühll in 1945, later taken over into the Teubner series. He did not inspect any manuscripts for himself, he relied on published material, and he does not much concern himself with what is in which manuscript. He only occasionally refers to specific sources. He just indicates the more important variants, and reckons that it is of little importance which manuscripts they are in: they are to be assessed on their merits, not on the basis of attestation. I said this was the best edition to date. I give it that accolade because it is the most judicious. Von der Mühll applies both intelligence and knowledge of Greek in a way that neither Allen nor the more recent editor Helmut van Thiel do.

Van Thiel's edition of 1991, though a regress in critical terms, is useful because it does provide some detailed and largely accurate information about the readings of a selection of manuscripts including all of those known to be significant. He collated nineteen manuscripts, and he makes regular use of eleven. Where he mentions variants, he tells us what their manuscript support is. The trouble is that he does not mention enough variants. In general his text is too conservative and too focused on the medieval paradosis. He pays too little attention to the evidence for the text in antiquity (ancient scholars, quotations, papyri), and he ignores the need for critical revision of the text in the light of historical linguistics.

So far as the medieval manuscripts go, my policy is similar to van Thiel's, though it seems to me that a smaller selection of manuscripts is nearly always sufficient to catch the significant variants. I have chosen eight out of van Thiel's eleven and systematically collated them. On the rare occasions when I have found something of interest cited by him or by Ludwich from some other source, of course I will mention it. I have also made systematic use of Eustathius' commentary, as I did not when I edited the *Iliad*. The manuscript tradition of the *Iliad* is markedly better than that of the *Odyssey*; we have two manuscripts from the tenth century (including the excellent Venetus A) and six from the eleventh – all predating Eustathius. For the *Odyssey* we have one from the later tenth century, one from the eleventh, one from the twelfth, and the rest are later, so Eustathius antedates all but two or three of them.

If I report fewer manuscripts than van Thiel, I report them on many more points of text. I shall also have much more to offer in respect of papyri. The number of published papyri of the *Odyssey* is now, by my reckoning, 258. In addition, there are 308 unpublished fragments in the Oxyrhynchus collection, which, by the kind permission of the Egypt Exploration Society, I have collated. The total of 566 is far lower than the corresponding figure for the *Iliad*, which is about 1,550. Still, when it is all put together, it represents a significant body of evidence for the state of the text in Egypt in the Roman period and in some cases in the Hellenistic period. There are now places in the text where it is possible to cite the evidence of as many as five papyri. (In the *Iliad* it can be as many as ten.) The papyri almost never produce important new variants. But sometimes, by omitting a verse, they confirm suspicions that it is not genuine, or throw suspicion on a verse not suspected hitherto.

For evidence about the text in antiquity we must also look to quotations in literary authors, grammarians, and lexica. As in my edition of the *Iliad*, I have taken pains to collect as many testimonia as possible down to the tenth century. La Roche gathered a certain number, and Ludwich quite a lot more. I have collected many more testimonia than my predecessors, perhaps twice the number, and in my edition they will be cited in a separate register above the apparatus, specifying exactly what portion of a given verse is cited by the source.

Apart from presenting the evidence for the text more fully, how will my edition change things? One thing that will make a difference will be that after identifying the manuscript variants and establishing the weight of attestation for each, I aim to consider each problem with an open mind and without a prejudice in favour of what previous editors have printed. All too often editors of ancient texts take a follow-my-leader approach instead of applying independent thought. For example, take the passage where Telemachus remonstrates with his mother after she has told the singer Phemius to change his theme 1.346–7. In every edition from Wolf onwards the lines appear as

μῆτερ ἐμή, τί τ' ἄρα φθονέεις ἐρίηρον ἀοιδόν
τέρπειν ὅππηι οἱ νόος ὄρνυται;

'Mother, why begrudge the faithful bard giving
pleasure in whatever way he is minded?'[2]

All of the eight manuscripts that I am using give not τί τ' ἄρα but τί τ' ἄρ αὖ except for one that gives τί τ' ἄρ ἄν, which is clearly a corruption of τί τ' ἄρ αὖ. I am sure this is right, except that ταρ is to be read as one word; it is the archaic particle ταρ that occurs in Homer especially in association with an interrogative, τίς ταρ, πῶς ταρ, etc. The αὖ adds a significant nuance: 'there you go again, not letting the singer follow his inclination'. There is an exact parallel in 23.264, when Penelope insists on Odysseus' telling her about the prophecy of Tiresias that he has mentioned, and he says δαιμονίη, τί ταρ αὖ με μάλ' ὀτρύνουσα κελεύεις | εἰπέμεν; ('You strange woman, why ever do you press me so hard, demanding that I tell?) And there is a linguistic objection to τί τ' ἄρα φθονέεις. Since there is no particle ταρα, only ταρ, we should have to divide τ' ἄρα. But the τε in a question, τί τε, is indefensible. If editors had not been content to follow Wolf's lead, they might have given more weight to the predominance of the alternative reading in the tradition.

---

2 Translation by S.R.W.

I noted earlier that Von der Mühll was something of an exception among editors in paying attention to modern linguistic insights. We have to recognize that the text as it has come down to us has suffered some degree of modernization, especially before the third century BCE, after which it became more fixed. The editor in my view should not acquiesce in the transmitted form of the text but seek to counteract the modernizations where they can be identified or assumed. I am not talking about restoring some theoretical archaic form of text, resolving all possible vowel contractions, expelling particles so as to recover digamma hiatuses, and so on. I am talking about things like restoring εο in place of the later spelling ευ; Ionic κρέσσων, μέζων, etc. in place of Attic κρείσσων, μείζων; the genitive ending –οο in Αἰόλοο κλυτὰ δώματα and Αἰόλοο μεγαλήτορος; Κλυταιμήστρη for Κλυταιμνήστρη – Clytaemnestra's name in the classical period has no *nu* in it.

I shall be more active than some of my predecessors in looking out for and exposing concordance interpolations. This is much the commonest type of interpolation in Homer and the most persistent; it continues at least into the Roman period. It is the type where a scribe makes a passage agree with a longer passage that he remembers, by adding a line or lines from the longer passage that the shorter one lacks. Often the interpolated lines are shown up by the fact that they are absent in part of the manuscript tradition. An omission of a line in a single manuscript may be accidental, and certain manuscripts are prone to it. But when a line is absent from several manuscripts, it is almost always a dispensable line that occurs elsewhere in a similar context, and we can assume that it is missing not because scribes deliberately passed over a formulaic and dispensable line but because it did not belong in that context and is intrusive in that part of the tradition where it does occur. Yet many editors are just too timid to remove lines that have stood in our editions for centuries and are recognized in the standard line-numbering, which is that of Wolf's edition of 1807; there is no line-numbering in the manuscripts. In fact there are dozens of lines in Wolf's edition which are weakly attested in the manuscript tradition, are clearly concordance interpolations, and need to be thrown out. Homeric style is quite ample and leisurely, but the effect is exaggerated if we leave all these redundant verses in the text.

Often when a papyrus turns up, the suspect line proves to be missing there too. I will give you an example of a previously unsuspected interpolation shown up by one of the unpublished papyri in Oxford, which dates from the third century. Circe has just told Odysseus that before he and his men can return home they have to visit Hades to consult the soul of Tiresias, and he reacts emotionally (10.496–502):

ὣς ἔφατ', αὐτὰρ ἐμοί γε κατεκλάσθη φίλον ἦτορ,
{κλαῖον δ' ἐν λεχέεσσι καθήμενος, οὐδέ νύ μοι κῆρ   [497–9 = 4.539–41]
ἤθελ' ἔτι ζώειν καὶ ὁρᾶν φάος ἠελίοιο.
αὐτὰρ ἐπεὶ κλαίων τε κυλινδόμενος τ' ἐκορέσθην,}
καί μιν φωνήσας ἔπεα πτερόεντα προσηύδων.'
'ὦ Κίρκη, τίς γὰρ ταύτην ὁδὸν ἡγεμονεύσει;
εἰς Ἄιδος δ' οὔ πώ τις ἀφίκετο νηὶ μελαίνηι'.

So she spoke, and my heart was broken.
[I wept, sitting on the bed, and my spirit
no longer desired to live and see the sun's light.
But when I had had my fill of weeping and grovelling,]
and I addressed her with winged words:
'But Circe, who will guide us on the journey?
No one has ever reached Hades by ship'.

The bracketed lines, κλαῖον δ' ἐν λεχέεσσι . . . ἐκορέσθην, were omitted in the papyrus. They are repeated from the passage in Book 4 (539–41) that described Menelaus' reaction when he heard from Proteus about the murder of Agamemnon, except that there it was 'I wept, sitting on the sand', not 'on the bed'. If the lines are taken out, we see that 500, καί μιν φωνήσας 'and I addressed her', fits better following on from 496 than it does after the ἐπεί clause in 499. I think there is a poetic gain from the deletion. Odysseus is still dismayed by what Circe has said, but he no longer throws himself into the extravagant transports of grief that are appropriate to Menelaus on hearing of his brother's foul murder.

Overall the text of Homer is in a very good state, much better than, for example, the text of Aeschylus or Sophocles. It is easy to form the impression that there are no real corruptions, that all you have to do is choose between variants. Are there actually places where no version of the transmitted text is acceptable, where we must put an obelos or emend? Such places are few and far between, but they do exist. There is no tradition of printing obeloi in Homer, I suppose because editors have always supposed the text to be sound or easily emended, but I did print 21 obeloi in my *Iliad*,[3] expressing the hope that they might make future critics furrow their brows a little more. One place in the *Odyssey* where I think one is needed is at 8.578, where Alcinous asks why Odysseus is so upset on hearing about the fate of the Danaans and of Ilium: †Ἀργείων Δαναῶν †ἠδ' Ἰλίου οἶτον ἀκούων. The Greeks who fought at Troy are sometimes called Ἀργεῖοι, someties Δαναοί, sometimes Ἀχαιοί, but we never find two of these terms combined. A relatively easy emendation would be ἀργαλέον, agree-

---

3 See M. L. West (1988–2000). *Homeri Ilias*, 2 vols. Stuttgart and Leipzig.

ing with οἶτον, 'the hard fate of the Danaans and of Ilium', but I won't venture to put it in the text.

I have arrived at two corrections in Book 15. At line 80 Menelaus offers to take Telemachus on a tour of Greece before he goes home, to collect gifts. The line goes, according to the majority tradition, εἰ δ' ἐθέλεις τραφθῆναι ἀν' Ἑλλάδα καὶ μέσον Ἄργος,[4] but there are half a dozen variants for the infinitive: τραφῆναι, τρεφθῆναι, ταρφθῆναι, τερφθῆναι, στραφθῆναι, στραφῆναι. Seven variants, representing four different verbs: τρέω, τρέφω, τέρπω, στρέφω. Two of the seven variants are unmetrical. You might think that surely one of the other five will be the right reading, but it is not so. What we need to do is first choose the correct verb and then identify the correct form of it. The correct verb in the context is στρέφομαι, to turn this way and that, to roam from town to town (cf. 13.325–6; HHymn. to Ap. 175). The correct Homeric form of the aorist infinitive is neither στραφθῆναι nor στραφῆναι, but στρεφθῆναι. So that's what I shall print.

My other conjecture in Book 15 is, I think, a little more stimulating. Eumaeus relates how as a young boy he was abducted from his home by his Phoenician nurse, who had fallen in with some traders from her own country. She had told him of her origin from Sidon (425) ἐκ μὲν Σιδῶνος πολυχάλκου εὔχομαι εἶναι, 'I declare I am from Sidon of much bronze'. Why is Sidon called πολύχαλκος? Phoenicia has no associations with bronze. The scholiast is conscious of the difficulty. He claims that the epithet is not to be taken literally, since Sidon is not a source of bronze, ἐν αὐτῆι γὰρ χαλκὸς οὐ γίνεται: it stands rather for 'hard' (of soil) or perhaps 'wealthy', as it is a source of purple. Now one Greek word for 'purple' or 'murex' is κάλχη, which suggests the very easy emendation ἐκ μὲν Σιδῶνος πολυκάλχου, from Sidon rich in purple. After having this idea I found that one of the unpublished papyri has the same reading as the medieval manuscripts, πολυχάλκου, but another, in which only the last four letters of the word are preserved, has a chi in place of the kappa.

Now let me give you a few examples of places where the narrative is affected slightly more materially by editorial choice. The first concerns Polyphemus' arrangements for the night. When Odysseus and his men are waiting in his cave and he arrives in the evening with his sheep and goats, he brings the female animals, the ewes and the nannies, into the cave for milking but leaves the males outside, τὰ δ' ἄρσενα λεῖπε θύρηφιν, βαθείης ἔκτοθεν αὐλῆς (9.238f.). The next night he brings them *all* into the cave and leaves none of them βαθείης ἔκτοθεν αὐλῆς (338). The casual reader perhaps does not notice anything amiss here. He

---

[4] 'But if you wish to roam through Hellas and mid-Argos'.

may suppose the αὐλή to be the roomy cave. But fifty lines earlier, when the cave was first described, we were told that it had an αὐλή built round its entrance, and this was a high walled enclosure constructed of stones and timber. This is a rather unconventional adjunct to a cave, and it is obviously mentioned because it will play a role in the narrative. Clearly when Polyphemus took his ewes and nanny-goats in for milking he did not leave the rams and billies *outside* this enclosure, where they would have wandered off into the countryside, but *inside* it. That is what it was for. If you look up translations, they all say correctly 'outside in the yard' or 'out in the yard'. Some commentators tell you that ἔκτοθεν αὐλῆς can mean 'outside in the yard'. But it plainly can't. ἔκτοθεν with a genitive means 'outside of'. So ἔκτοθεν must be wrong in both passages. Ludwich prints it in his text, but he notes in his apparatus that H. Rumpf in 1850 had emended it to ἔντοθεν. In fact this had been conjectured some seventy years before Rumpf by Johann Heinrich Voss, the famous translator of Homer, who was a pupil of Heyne and an able scholar. The emendation was adopted by Bekker and most subsequent editors (with the ascription to Rumpf). Exceptions are Allen, who takes no notice of the problem, and van Thiel, who notes the conjecture but retains ἔκτοθεν in his text. So shall I be putting ἔντοθεν in my text? No. Why not? Because although the sense is right, the form is not. ἔντοθεν occurs nowhere in Homer or anywhere else in classical Greek. The Homeric form is ἔνδοθεν. The exact phrase ἔνδοθεν αὐλῆς occurs twice in the *Iliad* (6.247; 24.161) without variant. The fact that editors since 1850 have considered only ἔντοθεν is an indictment of their failure to think independently and consider problems afresh, not simply in the terms in which their predecessors have discussed them.

For another case where good critical editing clarifies what is happening consider the narrative of the escape from the Cyclops. Having reached their ship Odysseus and his surviving companions row away. Odysseus cannot resist the temptation to mock the blinded Polyphemus. This gives the ogre a bearing on where they are. He breaks off a huge rock and hurls it towards the ship. It overshoots and falls into the sea beyond the ship, creating a wave that washes it back towards the shore, 9.485–6:

τὴν δ' ἂψ ἤπειρόνδε παλιρρόθιον φέρε κῦμα,
πλημυρὶς ἐκ πόντοιο, θέμωσε δὲ χέρσον ἱκέσθαι.

The back-washing wave carried the ship,
the flood-wave from the sea, and fixed its course for reaching the dry land.

Odysseus fends them off with a pole and they desperately row out again. When they are twice as far from the shore as before – or, according to the oldest medieval manuscript, three times as far (the variant has been overlooked by all editors except van Leeuwen) – he once again calls out to Polyphemus and provokes him. Again the Cyclops hurls a massive rock, but this time it falls short, and the wave it creates carries the ship forwards, 541–2 (τὴν δὲ πρόσω φέρε κῦμα) but then again the phrase θέμωσε δὲ χέρσον ἱκέσθαι, repeated from the first passage. This is troubling, because this time they are in no danger of reaching the χέρσος, which in the context must mean the mainland on which the Cyclopes live. But instead of χέρσον the early Ptolemaic papyrus p 31 gives something different. It appears to be νηοc. But 'fixed its course for reaching the ship' makes even less sense than the other. I believe that the two round letters have been, if not misread, then miswritten, and that they should be not oc but co: it was θέμωσε δὲ νῆσον ἱκέσθαι 'fixed its course for reaching the island', the island where Odysseus' other eleven ships were moored. That's exactly the sense we need. After coming to this conclusion, I discovered that two hundred years before the papyrus was known, νῆσον had been conjectured by Richard Bentley, simply because the sense required it. His proposal didn't come to light till 1894, and no one took any notice when it did. The papyrus was published in 1925, but no one made the connection.

Another passage where there is an issue about inside and outside is in Book 23, when Penelope, still not completely sure of Odysseus' identity, puts him to the test by calling upon Eurycleia to make up his bed, bringing it out from the bedchamber that he himself constructed (23.177–80):

ἀλλ' ἄγε οἱ στόρεσον πυκινὸν λέχος, Εὐρύκλεια,
ἐκτὸς ἐυσταθέος θαλάμου, τόν ῥ' αὐτὸς ἐποίει·
ἔνθά οἱ ἐκθεῖσαι πυκινὸν λέχος ἐμβάλετ' εὐνήν,
κώεα καὶ χλαίνας καὶ ῥήγεα σιγαλόεντα.

But come, make up his bed, Eurycleia,
outside the sturdy chamber that he himself built.
Put his bed out there and put bedclothes on it.

This causes Odysseus consternation. He demands to know who has moved his bed. This ought to be an impossibility, because it was built on an old, firmly rooted olive stump, as thick as a pillar. Has someone sawn through the olive stump and taken the bed somewhere else? Now, as the text stands, Penelope has not suggested that the bed is anywhere but its original position, only that the servants should now move it from the chamber. The natural response of Odysseus to that would not be 'What? Has someone moved it?' but 'What? How are they going to move it?' This led van Leeuwen to alter ἐκτός to ἐντός and ἐκθεῖσαι to ἐνθεῖσαι. With these readings Penelope implies that the bed is currently *not* in the chamber and is to be moved back into it for Odysseus to sleep in. That makes much better sense of Odysseus' reply, and in any case it seems more rational that the bed should be put into the chamber for him to sleep in than that it should be brought out of it. Editors have been slow to accept van Leeuwen's corrections, but they seem necessary, and I shall adopt them.

Issues of greater moment may sometimes depend on the editor's judgment: for example, whether Heracles is a god. Towards the end of his excursion to Hades, Odysseus beholds Heracles, who is pursuing one of his characteristic activities, prowling about looking for enemies, aiming his arrow at frightened ghosts. He recognizes Odysseus (it's not explained how), delivers a rather peculiar speech, and then, without waiting for any response from Odysseus, goes back into Hades. Now, after the initial line 'After him I saw mighty Heracles', we read two further lines (11.602–3), εἴδωλον· αὐτὸς δὲ μετ' ἀθανάτοισι θεοῖσιν / τέρπεται ἐν θαλίῃς καὶ ἔχει καλλίσφυρον Ἥβην.[5] So the Heracles whom Odysseus sees in the Underworld and who addresses him is a phantom; well, so is everyone else whom he sees in Hades. But at the same time there is a real deified Heracles enjoying immortality among the gods. Obviously the two lines serve to reconcile the episode in Hades with the idea of his deification, which seems to have been an Athenian innovation. But were they put there by the poet of the *Odyssey*, or by someone else? They were athetized by Aristarchus, and a scholiast alleges that 'this line' (but which?) was said (by someone) to have been interpolated by Onomacritus. It certainly looks rather unlikely that a poet who regarded Heracles as a god on Olympos should have conceived the encounter in Hades. Yet it is imaginable that a poet who had described the encounter in Hades subsequently became acquainted with the Athenian story of the deification and then inserted the lines in his own poem. Ludwich, Allen, Von der Mühll, and van Thiel all leave them in the text unbracketed. Van Thiel, remarkably, does not even mention the ancient suspicion of the lines.

Information from the scholia about Alexandrian scholarship is also relevant to the question of what became of the Phaeacians after they took Odysseus home to Ithaca (8.564–71; 13.154–64). The Phaeacians are a fabulous people who play no role in any other story outside the *Odyssey*. They are located on the outer fringe of the Greek world, and in the heroic age they occasionally made excursions into Greek waters, but in the poet's contemporary world they don't exist. So what happened to them?

In Book 8 we learn that they have the custom of repatriating castaways swiftly and safely: they have marvellous ships that go at fantastic speed, never come

---

[5] His ghost; but he himself with the immortal gods delights in feasts and has (to wife) Hebe of the lovely ankles, child of great Zeus and Hera of the golden sandals.

to grief, and don't even need navigators, because they are programmed with all the sea routes, like guided missiles. Alcinous explains to Odysseus that they are going to send him home in this way (555–71), recalling, by way of conclusion, an old prophecy that he heard from his father, that one day Poseidon, angered at their safe ferrying of travellers, would smite one of their ships as it returned from such a mission and bury their city under a large mountain. Well, he says, the god may do that, or not, as he pleases.

In Book 13 they convey Odysseus to Ithaca without mishap. Poseidon sees that this has happened and is indignant. He speaks to Zeus, complaining that the Phaeacians have failed to hold him in respect. He accepts that he cannot prevent Odysseus' return home, as Zeus has approved it, but he had been determined that he should suffer many woes on the way, and now the Phaeacians have given him this easy ride, and moreover laden him with riches. Zeus is sympathetic and says all right, Poseidon can punish the Phaeacians as he pleases. But Poseidon is still nervous that Zeus might get angry, so he sets out exactly what he is minded to do: smite the ship as it returns, and bury the city under a mountain. This corresponds to the terms of the prophecy that Alcinous heard from his father. Zeus, however, does not reply 'Okay, fine, you do that', he says (154–8) 'Let me tell you what I think is best'. He advises Poseidon to turn the ship to stone when it is in sight of the shore, so that everyone is amazed. This is clearly a modification of what Poseidon had in mind. Poseidon had said he wanted to 'smite' the ship, using a word that would naturally mean to shatter and sink it, but instead of that he is to stop it in its tracks and turn it to stone. Zeus goes on, according to the text of Aristarchus, all manuscripts, and nearly all modern editions, 'and bury their city under a large mountain', μέγα δέ σφιν ὄρος πόλει ἀμφικαλύψαι, matching what Poseidon himself proposed a few lines earlier. Aristophanes of Byzantium, however, had a different reading in his text, not μέγα δέ but μηδέ: turn the ship to stone so everyone is amazed, but do *not* bury their city under a mountain. The scholium adds that Aristophanes' pupil Aristarchus opposed this reading in his commentaries: he favoured the version we have in our manuscripts.

So what happens? After hearing Zeus' advice, Poseidon goes at once to Scheria and waits for the ship to return. When it comes he gives it a great whack with his hand, turning it to stone and rooting it to the spot. The Phaeacians on shore witness the miracle and are disconcerted by it. Alcinous at once recalls the prophecy and concludes that it is in the process of fulfilment. He calls on his people to cease their ferrying activities from now on and to sacrifice twelve bulls to Poseidon in the hope that he will have mercy and not implement the second part of the prophecy by burying the city. They prepare the sacrifice – and there the poet leaves them, anxiously praying, as he turns back to Odysseus.

He deliberately leaves us in suspense and never tells us what did become of the Phaeacians. So did Poseidon wipe them off the map, or are they still there?

We have to assume that he did whatever it was that Zeus had told him to do. The poet would not have made him go and ask Zeus' advice if he was not going to follow it. So it all hinges on whether or not we accept Aristophanes' text in 158. Did Zeus tell Poseidon to cover the city with a mountain, or did he tell him not to? The answer is, I am sure, that he told him not to, and that he didn't. It is true that if the city is not buried, the old prophecy turns out to be inaccurate, and normally in stories involving prophecies the prophecy is fulfilled. But when Alcinous related the prophecy in Book 8 he did leave open the possibility that Poseidon might fulfil it or not, as he chose. There are several reasons for thinking that he spared the city.

Firstly, the ship is to be turned to stone in full view of the people. The purpose of this is to deter them from ferrying people about in future, and that is exactly the effect it has on them. There is no point in frightening them into giving up their ferryings if they are anyway about to be blotted out. Secondly, in 160 we read that Poseidon went to Scheria 'where the Phaeacians are', ὅθι Φαίηκες γεγάασιν. The present tense implies that in the poet's mind there are still Phaeacians on Scheria (and surely not in an underground city). Thirdly, in 164 we read that he turned the ship to stone and *went away,* νόσφι βεβήκει; obviously he has finished his business with the Phaeacians. When they make their propitiatory sacrifices, he has already gone. Fourthly, it is easy to see how μηδέ in 158 could be replaced by μέγα δέ through assimilation to Poseidon's preceding speech (152).

So we may enjoy the happy confidence that those nice Phaeacians were spared from extinction. Because they have given up their occasional voyages into the Aegean, nothing is heard of them any more, but they are still there in their remote island home, continuing their eirenic existence.

Works cited

Editions of the *Odyssey*

Allen, T. W. (1907), (1917–1919[2]). *Homeri Opera*, iii-iv.
Bekker, I. (1858[2]). *Carmina Homerica: Odyssea*, ii. Bonn.
La Roche, J. (1867). *Homeri Odyssea ad fidem librorum optimorum*. Leipzig.
Ludwich, A. (1889–1891). *Homeri Odyssea*. Leipzig.
van Leeuwen, J. and M. B. Mendes da Costa (1890), (1908[3]). *Homeri Odyssea cum prolegomenis et adnotatione critica*. Leiden.
van Leeuwen, J. (1917). *Odyssea*. Leiden.

van Thiel, H. (1991). *Homeri Odyssea*. Hildesheim, Zurich, and New York.
Von der Mühll, P. (1945). *Homeri Odyssea*. Basel.
Wolf, F. A. (1807). *Homeri Ilias et Odyssea item Homeri et Homeridarum reliquiae*. Leipzig.

Margalit Finkelberg
Homer at the Panathenaia: Some possible scenarios

I.

'It is now more than thirty years', E. R. Dodds wrote in 1954, 'since the old logical game of discovering inconsistencies in Homer was replaced in public esteem by the new and equally enjoyable aesthetic game of explaining them away'.[1] Although the specific issue that Dodds had in mind was the shift from the Analyst to the Unitarian approach to Homer that had taken place after World War I, his words equally apply to contemporary Homeric scholarship, in that they underscore the fact that much of what has been going on in Homeric studies – today, in Dodds' time, and before – concerns alternative assessments of the same corpus of data. This is particularly true of the scholarly assessment of what might have happened to the Homeric poems in sixth-century BCE Athens.

Raphael Sealey, who was also writing in the 1950s, presented the situation as follows:

> ... the student [of the history of the poems in the sixth century Athens] must be grateful to Professors R. Merkelbach and J. A. Davison, who have recently discussed the evidence at length and with contrasting results.[2]

Sealey refers to two different assessments of the tradition of the so-called Pisistratean Recension offered by Reinhold Merkelbach and J. A. Davison. According to the tradition in question, the sixth-century BCE Athenian ruler Pisistratus or (more likely) his son and successor Hipparchus initiated the establishment of a standard text of the Homeric poems for the sake of their regulated performance at the recently founded Panathenaic festival. According to other sources, the Homeric poems were brought to Athens at the beginning of the sixth-century on the initiative of Solon. While Merkelbach defended the tradition of the sixth-century textualization of Homer, Davison rejected it altogether.[3]

---

[1] Dodds (1954) 8.
[2] Sealey (1957) 342.
[3] Merkelbach (1952); Davison (1955). On the tradition of the Pisistratean Recension, see Andersen (2011) (with bibliography).

The situation today is not much different. On the one hand, there is a wide consensus among Homeric scholars that the performance of the poems of Homer at the Panathenaic festival, presumably introduced on the initiative of the Pisistratid Hipparchus in 522 BCE, had a pivotal role in the transmission of the poems of Homer.[4] This applies both to those scholars who, like Albio Cesare Cassio, do not associate the textualization of Homer with the establishment of the Panathenaic performance,[5] and those who, like Gregory Nagy, see the sixth-century Athenian text as only an intermediate stage on the way to the Homeric poems' assuming of their final form.[6]

Beyond this basic consensus, however, opinions as to the impact of the establishment of the Panathenaic performance of the text of the *Iliad* and the *Odyssey* differ just as radically as they did sixty years ago. While some scholars do associate the standardization of the *Iliad* and the *Odyssey* with sixth-century Athens, the majority adhere to the standard view as crystallized in the early twentieth century, according to which the texts' standardization should be located in Ionia in the eighth century BCE.

Contrary to appearances, the two views are not entirely incompatible. As the recent studies of Barbara Graziosi, Douglas Frame and Gregory Nagy have demonstrated, the Panathenaic performance of Homer was a natural successor of earlier performances at Panionian festivals, such as those at Mycale in Asia Minor or at Delos.[7] If we also take into account that, upon the conquest of Asia Minor by the Persians, Athens was rapidly gaining the status of the religious, political and cultural centre of Ionian lands,[8] we will find that, rather than two disparate historical moments at which the *Iliad* and the *Odyssey* might have been fixed, we have a continuum of epic tradition about the Trojan War, which spread with no intermission from archaic Ionia to sixth-century Athens. It is somewhere along this continuum that the Homeric poems as we know them came into being.

---

4 For the historical background, see Nagy (2011).
5 Cassio (2002) 115: 'My impression is that Peisistratus and/or the Peisistratids regulated the recitations and gave Homer an unprecedented role in Athenian public life..., but were not responsible for the final composition of the *Iliad*. The same may well be true of the *Odyssey*'.
6 Nagy (1996) 66–7: 'It is, then, in this era of the tyrants, the Peisistratidai, that we may imagine a plausible historical occasion for the transcription of the Homeric poems in manuscript form'.
7 Graziosi (2002); Frame (2009); Nagy (2009). The Panionian festivals were, in turn, preceded (as well as paralleled) by public performances of the Trojan epics in Aeolian regions of Asia Minor, such as Lesbos and the Troad; on the Panaeolian performances, see Nagy (2009) II§§272–73.
8 See esp. Nagy (2009) I§50, on 'the new Panionianism of the Peisistratidai of Athens' as triggered by the Persian occupation of old Ionian centers.

We cannot, of course, be sure that the "Homer" performed at Ionian festivals amounted to our *Iliad* and *Odyssey*; if it did, then the composition of the poems of Homer should have taken place in archaic Ionia: this would be true pertaining to both the traditional eighth-century dating and the recent tendency of placing the composition of the *Iliad* in the mid-seventh century BCE and of the *Odyssey* about a generation later (more below). Now, if the Homeric poems had been standardized already at this stage, then the Panathenaic text of Homer could hardly have been much more than a copy of already established Ionian epics. This is how this scenario is presented by Richard Janko:

> The written transcripts were preserved on Chios among the Homeridae. Guilds of rhapsodes performed parts of them from memorization, but the Homeric epics enjoyed only a limited popularity until the time when, in the sixth century, monarchs like Pisistratus, seeking to buttress their own autocratic rule against the claims of the aristocracy, revived and popularized them. The Pisistratids procured a copy in order to regulate the sequence of rhapsodic performances at Athens.[9]

Janko himself places the composition of the *Iliad* in the mid-eighth century, but the model of transmission he proposes would equally apply both to the later dating in the mid-seventh century[10] and to the earlier dating in the ninth century BCE.[11]

If, on the other hand, it is sixth-century Athens that is to be considered the birthplace of the Homeric poems, then the composition of the *Iliad* and the *Odyssey* should be attributed to the Ionian bard(s) commissioned to produce a Panathenaic text of Homer. The argument for the sixth-century Homer has been aptly articulated by Keith Stanley:

> In the absence of compelling evidence for complete textualization at this early period [i.e. the eighth century BCE], it seems more reasonable to avoid a greater credulity by retaining the possibility of a sixth-century date, especially if the setting were the reorganized Panathenaea, and a stipulation of sequential recitation the incentive for a text that exhibits the complex magnitude and unity of ours. It is under such conditions – rather than at the eighth-century Panionian or Delian festivals – that a fixed sequence of books would be most feasible...[12]

---

9 Janko (1998) 13; cf. Janko (1992) 29–32.
10 As e.g. in West (2001) 5–9.
11 Powell (1991) 187–220 and Ruijgh (1995); both favor Euboea as the place of composition.
12 Stanley (1993) 280. See also Sealey (1957); Jensen (1980); Cook (1995); Nagy (1996) 66–7; Lowenstam (1997) and (2008); Jensen (2011).

Only few tie-breaking factors have emerged throughout the years. One such factor has been Janko's 1982 monograph on diachronic development in epic diction. Janko's application of statistical methods to the analysis of linguistic phenomena resulted in the corroboration of a mid-eighth century date. Owing to the methodological rigor and high quality of Janko's research, his conclusions were favorably received and have become widely accepted.[13] In what follows, I will concentrate on what, in my opinion, has the potential of becoming a tie-breaking factor pointing in the opposite direction, namely, recent insights into the evidence provided by vase-painting.

II.

In recent decades, it has been established beyond doubt that while images evoking the poems of the Epic Cycle had started to appear on vases from the eighth century BCE, no clearly recognizable Homeric subjects were represented before the late seventh century.[14] This strongly suggests that the circulation of the traditional prototypes of the Cycle poems preceded the circulation of the poems of Homer. Furthermore, since in the Archaic Age the name "Homer" was applied indiscriminately to the entire epic tradition about the Trojan War, only a few passages in early Greek poetry, none of them predating the late seventh century BCE, can be shown to display a firmly identifiable Homeric influence.

The literary evidence thus concurs with the evidence of art. As Jonathan Burgess put it,

> It can be argued that early Greek art and literature both contain some reflexes of Homer, but the possibilities are not numerous and the first probable reflexes date from the end of the seventh century.[15]

The verdict issued by Martin West is even more straightforward:

> The fact is that there is no clear reflex of the *Iliad* in art before *c.* 630, or in literature before Alcaeus.[16]

---

13 Janko (1982) 228–33; cf. Haslam (1997); Reece (2005); Janko (2012).
14 See esp. Friis Johansen (1967) [Danish version 1934]; Snodgrass (1979); West(1995) 207 with n. 21; Lowenstam (1997) 25–7; Snodgrass (1998); Burgess (2001) 35–44, 53–114; Lowenstam (2008); Jensen (2011) 237–44; Burgess (2011, with bibliography).
15 Burgess (2001) 127. See also West (1995) 206–7; Lowenstam (1997) 58–60.
16 West (2012) 235; cf. West (2011).

This does not mean, of course, that the dates supplied by the vases should be taken as relating to the poems' composition: the evidence of vase-painting concerns the reception, not the composition, of the Homeric poems. Still, the implications of the fact that the knowledge of the Homeric poems, as evidenced by their artistic representation, did not predate the end of the seventh century are difficult to overestimate. No less illuminating is the conclusion that the Cyclic themes became influential well before the Homeric ones.[17]

Both the lateness of the first reflexes of the *Iliad* and the *Odyssey* in Greek art and the fact that they postdate the reflexes of the Cycle poems make the traditional dating of Homer in the mid-eighth century highly problematic. To quote West again,

> Of course, this [the evidence of early Greek art] need not mean that the *Iliad* was only composed around 630; but it is very hard to reconcile with the idea that it had been known and admired above all other poems since 730 or 750.[18]

Small wonder, therefore, that the evidence of the vases has become one of the main factors owing to which the standard placing of Homer in the mid-eighth century or even earlier has been questioned more than once in recent years.[19]

There is, however, an additional aspect to the early iconographical evidence, which has not yet received the attention it deserves. I mean the impact of this evidence on the diachrony of the Homeric tradition itself. The influence of the peculiarly Homeric themes in Attic vase-painting becomes clearly discernible in the early sixth century, well before the regularization of the performance of the *Iliad* and the *Odyssey* at the Panathenaic festival. Moreover, as Steven Lowenstam showed in the 1990s, the poems that circulated in late archaic and early classical Athens were not necessarily identical to the ones we have. To take only one example, in the depiction of Patroclus' funeral games represented on the François Vase (early sixth century BCE), the names of all but one of the five participants in the chariot race do not correspond to those we find in Book 23 of the *Iliad*, and two of them are not attested at all in our text of Homer (more below). Furthermore, there is good reason to suppose that the same is true of an even earlier depiction of the same games by Sophilus. 'Hence', Lowenstam wrote,

---

17 Some additional implications of this conclusion are discussed in Finkelberg, forthcoming.
18 West (1995) 207. The date proposed by West is 660–650 BCE (ibid., 218; cf. West 2012 236). Cf. also the discussion in Lowenstam (1997) 58–67.
19 See esp. West (1995) and henceforth. Cf. Lowenstam (1997) 58–67; Burgess (2001) 49–53; Lowenstam (2008) 7–10. See also Cassio (2002), who arrives at the same conclusion without resorting to the evidence of vase-painting (see below).

the fact that the two painted versions of Patroklos' funeral games differ from the Homeric narrative suggests the currency and influence of variant epic or lyric traditions in the early sixth century.[20]

This and similar examples of discrepancy between the literary and the iconographical sources are often attributed to the artists' creative independence or, alternately, to their inadequate knowledge of the Homeric poems. Both are of course important factors that should be permanently kept in mind. Yet, neither of them would satisfactorily explain the manner in which Patroclus' funeral games are depicted on the François Vase.

Consider the following. In Homer, the participants in the chariot race are Diomedes (the winner), Antilochus, Menelaus, Meriones and Eumelus (*Il.* 23.287–616). Yet, the François Vase has Odysseus (the winner), Automedon, Diomedes, Damasippos (non-Homeric) and Hippo[tho]on (non-Homeric) instead. This simple comparison shows that the reason for the discrepancy between the literary and the iconographical representation of the same event is neither the artist's offering an alternative interpretation of the event in question nor his failing to reproduce the "original" set of the participants and turning to the common stock of Iliadic characters instead. Indeed, while the introduction of both Odysseus and the model charioteer Automedon (who does not take part in the Games as described in *Iliad* 23) may still be explained along these lines, it is difficult to say what purpose the emergence of the non-entities Hippothoon and Damasippos was supposed to serve.[21] The most intriguing element of the depiction of the race is, however, the one that is conspicuous by its absence.

In *Iliad* 23, the major episode of the chariot race and of Patroclus' funeral games as a whole is the conflict between Menelaus and Antilochus over the trick perpetuated by the latter during the competition. Nestor's magnificent speech about the power of *mētis*, 'cunning', which he addresses to his son before the race; Antilochus' youthful recklessness and the anger of Menelaus; the younger man's apology and the eventual reconciliation between the two – all these turn the Menelaus-Antilochus encounter into the highpoint of the Games and one of the more memorable episodes in the entire *Iliad*. It is highly unlikely

---

20 Lowenstam (1997) 28; cf. Lowenstam (2008) 174; Jensen (2011) 238. See also Nagy (1996, 110), prompted by Lowenstam's earlier publications: 'Significant variations of Homeric themes in the iconographical evidence of vase paintings – especially variations of "Iliadic" themes – persist until around 530 B.C.E.'.
21 Cf. Wachter (1991) 96–7: 'In labelling the two losers of the race the painter obviously ran out of imagination, and gave them any "horsey names" (i.e. a kind of speaking names)'. But it is equally possible that by the moment when the François Vase was produced these "horsey names" had already been present in a traditional variant of Patroclus' funeral games.

that a painter acquainted with the *Iliad* could forget this episode or prefer to replace its protagonists with Odysseus and Automedon or moreover with Hippothoon and Damasippos. As Rudolf Wachter put it,

> But the Homeric account both in the race and in the disputes afterwards contains such unforgettably amusing scenes which mainly concern the other competitors (Eumelos, Menelaos, Antilochos, Meriones), that there is hardly any excuse: this writer did not know Homer's book 23.[22]

If we take into account that Patroclus' funeral games is a peculiarly Iliadic theme and therefore cannot be accounted for as yet another instance of early popularity of the Cycle poems, it would be hard to avoid the conclusion that the treatment of the chariot race by the painter of the François Vase could only reflect a different Iliadic tradition. As it happens, this tradition had been present in Athens even before the Panathenaic festival was established.[23] This can only mean that, whether or not previously fixed in writing, the pre-Panathenaic Homeric tradition was still a fluid one.

III.

Let us return now to the two scenarios introduced at the beginning of this chapter. According to the first scenario, our text of Homer was fixed in Ionia in the mid-eighth century BCE and in the late sixth century was either transferred to or copied in Pisistratean Athens, to serve as the basis for the Panathenaic performance. The *sine qua non* of this scenario is the preservation of the text in its pristine form, that is, exactly as it had been fixed in Ionia two centuries before. The reason is obvious: a traditional text cannot pass through the chain of performance and stay unchanged unless it had been fixed in either written or oral form.[24] This is why, according to the principle formulated by Adam Parry,

---

[22] Wachter (1991) 97.
[23] As Frame (2009, 583–4) points out, the Homeric poems must have reached Athens, an Ionian city, 'almost immediately after they took root on Chios'. Obviously, this would also be true of the Homeric tradition as such.
[24] Contrary to what many are inclined to believe, the option of oral fixation should not be automatically discarded. As comparison with the ancient Near East shows, in the case of texts that were held in especially high esteem, as e.g. the Vedas or the Avesta, memorization often was a standard model of transmission: see Shaked (2003) 65–6. Cf. also Cassio (2002) 114: 'Oral fixation may have been more of a reality than those who live in a literate society are prepared to believe'.

our "Homer" could only have been the ultimate poet in the chain of transmission, that is, the one whose performance was fixed in writing.[25] This principle has been further corroborated in an important study recently published by Jonathan Ready. Proceeding from the evidence of fieldwork experience, Ready has demonstrated that the textualization of oral performance should be regarded as a co-production of the bard, the scribe, and the textualizer ('the collector'), each contributing in his own way to the formation of the final text, and therefore as a unique event.[26]

However, as both the late appearance of Homeric themes in vase-painting and the existence of pre-Panathenaic iconographical variants demonstrate, even if an Ionian version of the Homeric poems had been fixed as early as the eighth century BCE, it did not become authoritative at that time, and thus it had to compete with alternative versions of the same tradition as late as the sixth century BCE. To be sure, some allowance should be made for the duration of the process of reception: thus, as both the literary and iconographical evidence indicates, the Panathenaic text of Homer did not become authoritative till the middle of the fifth century BCE.[27] Nevertheless, a two-hundred-year margin (or even a three-hundred-year one, if the reception of the Panathenaic text is also taken into account) still seems too wide. Rather than Homer, it would suit the reception history of the Cycle poems, which were transmitted in different versions till late antiquity without ever reaching canonical status.[28] All these make the standard eighth-century dating of Homer highly questionable.

At first sight, the second scenario, the one which associates the creation of the standardized text of the Homeric poems with the Panathenaic festival, fares better. The late emergence of the peculiarly Homeric themes in vase-painting fits in well with the hypothesis 'that', in Minna Skafte Jensen's words,

> the *Iliad* and the *Odyssey* were recorded in writing in connection with one of the Greater Panathenaea during the rule of the Pisistratids, that the singer who had won first prize in the competition was afterwards engaged to dictate his successful song to the tyrants' scribe, and that this was when the *Iliad* was born.[29]

---

[25] Parry (1966); cf. West (2001) 3 with n. 1; Jensen (2011) 245–6.
[26] This would especially be true of the period that preceded the emergence of the contemporary attitude to the recording of oral dictated texts as triggered by Parry-Lord theory of oral composition. See Ready (2015); cf. Jensen (2011) 228–9.
[27] Lowenstam (1997) 39–49 and (2008) 9.
[28] On the multiformity of the Cycle poems see Finkelberg (2000).
[29] Jensen (2011) 295.

Furthermore, the later dating would easily accommodate the existence of pre-Panathenaic variants by approaching them as raw material, as it were, out of which the Panathenaic text of Homer was created. Small wonder, therefore, that the scholars who proceed from the evidence supplied by the vases are often inclined to favor the sixth-century dating of Homer.[30]

Yet, it should not be forgotten that the iconographical evidence is not the only kind of evidence we should take into account. In a series of historical and philological arguments, Albio Cesare Cassio has built a strong case in support of the view that a fixed text of Homer existed even before the establishment of the Panathenaic competition. Firstly, Cassio refers to the evidence of Aristotle (*Rhet.* 1375b30) to the effect that the Ajax entry in the Catalogue of Ships (*Il.* 2.557–8) had been used by the Athenians against the Megarians in an arbitration over Salamis that had taken place in 560 BCE, several decades before the Panathenaic regulation was established. Secondly, he argues convincingly that the famous interpolation in the *Nekyia* (*Od.* 11.601–26), which inconsistently ascribes divine status to Heracles, goes back to the time of the Pisistratids, and therefore presupposes the existence of a written text.[31] Thirdly and most importantly, he draws attention to the fact that Theagenes of Rhegium, who was active in the 520s, that is, in the very period when the Panathenaic regulation was established, wrote an allegorical commentary on the Theomachy, the battle of the gods in Books 20 and 21 of the *Iliad*. 'Incidentally', Cassio remarks, 'are we to believe that Theagenes had to go to Athens in order to obtain the earliest available copies?'[32] I would add that the tradition of the Pisistratean Recension itself presupposes the existence of a fixed text, which should serve as a caveat to those who argue in favor of the sixth-century dating on the basis of this tradition.

Finally, it should not be forgotten that Janko's linguistic arguments in favor of the earlier dating have never been disproved, at least not from the perspective of relative chronology. This means that, in order to place Homer in the late sixth century BCE, one has to give a satisfactory answer to the following problem raised by Janko:

> ... if the artistic or historical evidence for the date of Homer did point decisively to the seventh or sixth century, then Hesiod would have to be later still by some margin or other.[33]

---

30 Notably, Lowenstam in his posthumously published book (Lowenstam 2009, 4–5); see also Jensen (2011) 244, on vase-painting as supporting the sixth-century dating.
31 Cassio (2002) 115–16.
32 Cassio (2002) 119.
33 Janko (2012) 37.

As we have seen, the artistic evidence does point decisively to a date later than the eighth century BCE. At the same time, the margin that the late sixth-century dating allows for Hesiod is certainly too narrow to comply with the linguistic data assembled by Janko. That is to say, if we place the textualization of the *Iliad* in the 520s, no timespan will be left to accommodate the *Odyssey*, Hesiod and the Hymns, all of them postdating the *Iliad* in terms of relative chronology.

Neither of the two scenarios purporting to account for the emergence of the standard text of the Homeric poems can thus be fully substantiated by extant evidence. While the widespread view according to which the composition of the Homeric poems should be placed in the eighth century BCE is at variance with the iconographical evidence, the linguistic and historical evidence do not support the late-sixth-century dating. This is not yet to say that nothing has changed since the impasse between the two alternative datings was registered by Sealey sixty years ago. Due to the new evidence accumulated in recent decades, as well as to fresh assessments of the already existing data, an additional date has emerged, the one placing the composition of the Homeric poems in the mid-seventh century BCE.

As we have seen, the seventh-century dating not only agrees with the iconographical evidence but in fact is directly suggested by it. It is true, of course, that, taken by itself, the iconographical evidence does not presuppose the existence of a fixed text (note again the evidence of the early-sixth-century iconographical variants), but, as we have seen, the presence of such a text is unambiguously required by the literary and historical sources at our disposal. Furthermore, placing Homer in the seventh rather than the eighth century BCE creates an unbroken continuity of diffusion of the Homeric tradition from the seventh-century Ionia to the sixth-century Athens and allows for a much more realistic timespan for this tradition to become influential. Last but not least, it allows for a considerably wider margin for accommodating the linguistic evidence as regards the relative chronology of the early hexameter poetry. This is not to say, of course, that the pendulum will not swing back in the future as a result of an influx of new information. In the present state of our knowledge, however, the mid-seventh century date for the composition of the *Iliad* emerges as more robust than either the mid-eighth-century or the late-sixth-century scenario.

Works cited

Andersen, Ø. (2011). 'Pisistratean Recension', in: Finkelberg, 668–70.
Andersen, Ø., and Dag T. T. Haug (eds.) (2012). *Relative Chronology in Early Greek Epic Poetry*. Cambridge.

Burgess, J. S. (2001). *The Tradition of the Trojan War in Homer and the Epic Cycle*. Baltimore.
–. (2011). 'Iconography, Early', in: Finkelberg, 391–4.
Cassio, A. C. (2002). 'Early Editions of the Greek Epics and Homeric Textual Criticism in the Sixth and Fifth Centuries BC', in: F. Montanari (ed.), *Omero tremila anne dopo*. Rome, 105–36.
Cook, E. F. (1995). *The Odyssey in Athens. Myths of Cultural Origins*. Ithaca and London.
Davison, J. A. (1955). 'Peisistratus and Homer', *TAPA* 86: 1–21.
Dodds, E. R. (1954). 'Homer', in: M. Platnauer (ed.), *Fifty Years of Classical Scholarship*. Oxford, 1–17.
Finkelberg, M. (2000). 'The *Cypria*, the *Iliad*, and the Problem of Multiformity in Oral and Written Tradition', *CP* 95: 1–11.
–. Forthcoming. 'The Formation of the Homeric Epics', in: Fritz-Heiner Mutschler (ed.), *Singing the World. The Homeric Epics and the Chinese Book of Songs Compared*. Cambridge Scholars Publishing.
–. (ed.) (2011). *The Homer Encyclopedia*. 3 vols. Malden, MA and Oxford.
Frame, D. (2009). *Hippota Nestor*. Washington, DC.
Friis Johansen, K. (1967). *The Iliad in Early Greek Art*. Copenhagen.
Graziosi, B. (2002). *Inventing Homer. The Early Reception of Epic*. Cambridge.
Haslam, M. (1997). 'Homeric Papyri and Transmission of the Text', in: I. Morris and B. Powell (eds.), *A New Companion to Homer*. Leiden, 55–100.
Janko, R. (1982). *Homer, Hesiod and the Hymns. Diachronic development in epic diction*. Cambridge.
–. (1992). 'The Text and Transmission of the *Iliad*', in: R. Janko (ed.). *The Iliad: A Commentary*, vol. 4: books 13–16. Cambridge, 20–38.
–. (1998). 'The Homeric Poems as Oral Dictated Texts', *CQ* 48: 1–13
–. (2012). 'πρῶτόν τε καὶ ὕστερον αἰὲν ἀείδειν: relative chronology and the literary history of the early Greek epos', in: Andersen and Haug, 20–43.
Jensen, M. S. (1980). *The Homeric Question and the Oral-Formulaic Theory*. Copenhagen.
–. (2011). *Writing Homer. A study based on results from modern fieldwork*. Copenhagen.
Lowenstam, S. (1997). 'Talking Vases: The Relationship between the Homeric Poems and Archaic Representations of Epic Myth', *TAPA* 127: 21–76.
–. (2008). *As Witnessed by Images. The Trojan War Tradition in Greek and Etruscan Art*. Baltimore and London.
Merkelbach, R. (1952). 'Die pisistratische Redaktion der homerischen Gedichte', *RhM* 95: 23–47.
Nagy, G. (1996). *Homeric Questions*. Austin.
–. (2009). *Homer the Preclassic*. Online edition. http://chs.harvard.edu/CHS/article/display/4377 (= Nagy, Gregory. 2012. *Homer the Preclassic*. Berkeley and Los Angeles).
–. (2011). 'Athens and Homer', in: Finkelberg, 112–16.
Parry, A. (1966). 'Have we Homer's *Iliad?*', *YCS* 20: 177–216.
Powell, B. (1991). *Homer and the Origin of the Greek Alphabet*. Cambridge.
Ready, J. L. (2015). 'The Textualization of Homeric Epic by Means of Dictation', *TAPA* 145: 1–75.
Reece, S. (2005). 'Homer's *Iliad* and *Odyssey*: From Oral Performance to Written Text', in: M. C. Amodio (ed.), *New Directions in Oral Theory*. Tempe, 43–89.

Ruijgh, C. J. (1995). 'D'Homère aux origines protomycéniennes de la tradition épique', in: J. P. Crielaard (ed.), *Homeric Questions. Essays in Philology, Ancient History and Archaeology.* Amsterdam, 1–96.

Sealy, R. (1957). 'From Phemius to Ion', *RÉG* 70: 312–55.

Shaked, S. (2003). 'Scripture and Exegesis in Zoroastrianism', in: M. Finkelberg and G. G. Stroumsa (eds.), *Homer, the Bible, and Beyond. Literary and Religious Canons in the Ancient World.* Leiden, 63–74.

Snodgrass, A. M. (1979). 'Poet and Painter in Eighth-Century Greece', *PCPS* 205: 118–30.

–. (1998). *Homer and the Artists.* Cambridge.

Stanley, K. (1993). *The Shield of Homer. Narrative Structure in the Iliad.* Princeton.

Wachter, R. (1991). 'The inscriptions on the François Vase', *MH* 48: 86–113.

West, M. L. (1995). 'The Date of the *Iliad*', *MH* 52: 203–19.

–. (2001). *Studies in the Text and Transmission of the Iliad.* München – Leipzig.

–. (2011). 'Date of Homer', in: Finkelberg, 197–8.

–. (2012). 'Towards a chronology of early Greek epic', in: Andersen and Haug, 224–41.

Interpretation

Franco Montanari
The failed embassy: Achilles in the *Iliad**

The beginning of the *Iliad* is characterised by the famous quarrel between Agamemnon and Achilles, which marks the start of the action depicted in the poem. The dispute between the two becomes increasingly exacerbated, almost reaching the point of a risk of physical aggression, and finally Achilles withdraws and abandons the war. The verbal clash was violent and in the end the split proves to be irreparable. Achilles challenges the principle of authority and, above all, he believes that Agamemnon is not worthy to represent it, while Agamemnon himself has no intention of displaying any sign of compromise or weakness concerning his authority as chief: in his mind, no one should or even could raise any doubts in this regard. The last two exchanges of dialogue represent the climax of the conflict (*Il.* 1.285–303): Agamemnon refuses to recognize that his rival has the right to threaten or undermine his power, and emphasizes that the exceptional qualities of Achilles as a warrior are due to divine favour. Achilles effectively sidesteps Agamemnon's authority, asserting that he has absolutely no intention of submitting to all of Agamemnon's demands because this would make him into a worthless man. He then makes it clear that he does not intend to fight for Briseis, given that she is being taken away from him by those who gave her to him in the first place (i.e., Agamemnon and the other Achaian chiefs). However, in no way would he accept the idea of being deprived of any other thing forming part of his possessions that are kept at his ships (*Il.* 1.293–303). This suggestion that Agamemnon's threats also extend to Achilles' belongings, quite apart from Briseis, does not appear to be justified by the earlier stages of the clash. Thus it sounds like an unwarranted amplification of the threat, a sort of exaggeration resulting from the angry response to what Achilles perceives as injustice and violence. At this point, we cannot but recognize that the situation has reached a point where no further rational interaction is possible: only the surrender of one of the two contenders can break the stalemate and resolve the dispute.

The action of the *Iliad* in the subsequent books sees the battle take place, obviously without Achilles, and in Book 8 the Achaeans are shown to be facing a situation of severe difficulty, which arouses the anxiety of Agamemnon at the beginning of Book 9 (1–78). In the assembly Agamemnon goes so far as to exhort his companions to abandon the siege, flee from Troy, and make their way back to

---

* English translation by Rachel Barritt Costa.

https://doi.org/9783110559873-004

their homeland. In contrast to the situation depicted in Book 2, this exhortation is real and authentic, the anxiety is sincere and highlights concretely the condition of defeat facing the Achaeans deprived of Achilles. It is Diomedes (having acquired influence and prestige through the great *aristeia* in Book 5 and the deeds accomplished in Book 8) who reacts vigorously against this idea of withdrawal and of an ignominious flight: he strongly attacks Agamemnon and goes so far as to tell him to depart and leave the whole affair behind him if he so wishes, but, Diomedes adds, the others are going to stay and continue the war until they have conquered Troy (*Il.* 9.30–50). Onlookers express their approval of Diomedes' statement, and Nestor puts forward a suggestion to Agamemnon: namely, Agamemnon should invite the Achaean chiefs to dinner in his tent in order to discuss the question and work out together what should be done (*Il.* 9.51–79). During the dinner, Nestor urges Agamemnon to heed good suggestions, and scolds him for the offence he committed against Achilles in taking Briseis away from him; and thus he advises Agamemnon to find a way to calm the anger that keeps the most valorous of the Achaeans far from the battlefield. And here something unexpected happens. Agamemnon undergoes a change of heart (the effect of his desperation at the defeat, evidently, along with his recognition of the favourable attitude of Zeus toward Achilles): he admits his mistake, claims he was mad and blind (ascribing the blame to the infamous *Ate*), and states his intention of trying to find a way to placate Achilles with infinite compensations. In actual fact, in *Il.* 2.377–80 there had already been an initial admission that he himself had given rise to the quarrel, but here we are faced with a total about-turn. The list of gifts that Agamemnon offers to Achilles is amazing: seven tripods never used on the fire, ten gold talents, twenty kettles, twelve prize-winning race-horses, seven beautiful women from Lesbos who were endowed with great expertise in ladies' tasks and, naturally, Briseis. With regard to the latter, Agamemnon swears that he has not engaged in sexual relations with her even though to have done so would have been quite normal. What is more, all these things are to be donated immediately, and then, Agamemnon continues, once the Achaeans have conquered Troy, Achilles will be allowed to take for himself a whole ship of gold and bronze from the loot, and moreoever to select twenty Trojan women. Finally, once Achilles is back in his homeland, he will be honoured in the same manner as Agamemnon's son Orestes and will become Agamemnon's son-in-law by choosing one of his daughters; furthermore, his bride will receive a massive endowment consisting of seven rich cities that will honour Achilles on a par with a god and will pay him rich tributes. All this, Agamemnon emphasizes, will be granted to Achilles if he sets aside his anger and once more recognizes Agamemnon's command of the Achaean army (9.121–61). Admittedly, Agamemnon does ask Achilles to submit to his authority, but this forms part of the logical unfolding of the situation: if Achilles sets aside his anger and resumes his fighting role in the army, then he effectively goes back to his place in the army of which Agamemnon is the recognized commander. But one cannot overlook the staggering extent of the gifts offered to Achilles: the return of Briseis, untouched, is in line with the motif underlying the quarrel and constitutes the reparation for the offence received, but all the rest is a grandiose addition; and finally, the offer is crowned with the proposal that Achilles should even become Agamemnon's son-in-law by marrying one of his daughters who would be given a massive dowry. Thus Agamemnon makes a truly mind-boggling offer in his endeavour to tip the scales in a favourable direction.

Nestor approves of the generous offer and advises him to send Achilles an embassy whose members would be prestigious figures, so that the proposal of reconciliation would be put forward with the appropriate solemnity. But once again, something unexpected happens – or at least, something different from what the preparation of the embassy seemed to be anticipating. Achilles, having been informed about the seriousness of the situation of the Achaeans and about the generous offer put forward by Agamemnon – which effectively corresponds to Achilles' own requests – scornfully turns the offer down and the embassy fails to achieve its objective. Achilles expresses in no uncertain terms his frustration and disappointment over what he regards as a situation that has become intolerable (*Il.* 9.307–429). What irks him is the unjust distribution of merits among those who are called upon to bear the heavy impact of the war. For instance, he grumbles that he himself, who has to bear the heaviest burden, is not recognised as deserving a reward he would consider to be appropriate, in comparison to the treatment reserved for Agamemnon, who bears a notably lighter burden yet receives a greater reward. Achilles also complains bitterly that he was the only one among the chiefs whose hard-earned prize, Briseis – whom he mentions in terms implying that she was a beloved friend (*Il.* 9.336) – was seized from him. One also senses a feeling of frustration and disappointment on the part of Achilles with regard to the behaviour of the other Achaeans, who failed to side with him but are now asking him for help. Let the ambassadors report back to Agamemnon that no one will succeed in persuading him to take up his position in the Achaean army again: on the contrary, he is planning to leave, once and for all, on very next day to go back to his homeland. That is where he wishes to live his life, and he will never accept compensatory gifts from someone who has offended him, even if he were offered a ten or twenty times greater quantity of presents. Indeed, even if Agamemnon were to raise his offer to a sky-high quantity, he would never succeed in making Achilles change his mind, and Achilles would never accept the idea of marrying a daughter of Agamemnon's, even if she were as beautiful as Aphrodite and as talented as Athena in women's activities. This, in no uncertain terms, is Achilles' sarcastic rejection of what Agamemnon interpreted as the greatest gift he could give and an offer of supreme honour. Achilles rejects everything: to his eyes everything is hateful, just as the one who is making the offer is equally hateful. Achilles asserts that riches cannot be equated with the value of a man's life: wealth can be acquired, but life cannot be regained once it has been lost. Material goods and human life cannot be compared. In conclusion, the hero recalls that his mother Thetis spoke of two possible routes for him to take towards death, two alternative destinies: either continuing the war, forsaking the idea of returning home and, accordingly, facing death but achieving immortal glory, or alternatively, abandoning the war and returning to live a long life but devoid of any heroic glory. Achilles is now thinking of leaving, and he advises the other Achaeans to do likewise: they will never capture Troy, because Zeus is protecting the city. Let the ambassadors state that the plan to bring Achilles back to the battlefield has been unsuccessful; the Achaeans should think up a better plan in order to save their lives, namely leaving the war and going back to their own homes.[1] This is an Achilles who, somewhat to our surprise, seems to prefigure the Achilles of the *Odyssey:* when Odysseus meets him in Hades, Achilles rejects the words of consolation with which Odysseus draws a parallel between the honour conferred on Achilles during his lifetime and that which now wreathes him as a lord among the deceased: rather, Achilles asserts, he would prefer to live a humble life instead of being a king in the realm of the dead (*Od*. 11.478–91).

Finally, Achilles asks his old preceptor Phoenix to separate from the others and stay with him so that they can leave together the following day. Phoenix answers that he will be unable to stay alone in Troy if Achilles returns home, and therefore he will certainly leave together with Achilles. However, Phoenix launches into a lengthy and intricately structured speech, rich in mythic examples, as a desperate final attempt to explain convincingly to Achilles how wise and useful it can sometimes be, even for those with the most unrelenting and ruthless character, to bow to pressure, to dominate their feelings, set aside their anger and calm down, accepting compensatory gifts, as sometimes happened even with the gods (*Il*. 9.432–605). But Achilles shows absolutely no change in his attitude; on the contrary, he states that Phoenix ought to follow his example and hate the one against whom Achilles himself directs his hatred. The old preceptor's peroration sounds to Achilles very much like an irritating favour granted to Agamemnon (*Il*. 9.606–19). However, the last words of Achilles'

---

[1] Hainsworth (1993) 55–7, 99–102; Mirto (1997) 1031–7, 1042–8.

reply seem to leave a glimmer of hope: 'Then with the showing of dawn we shall consider whether to return to our own land or to stay' (*Il.* 9.618–19).[2] Yet despite this final expression of doubt concerning the departure back to their homeland the next day, the essential conclusion which, at the end of the day, is clear and undisputed is that a reconciliation based on compensation is actually of no interest to Achilles. This is not what he desires, nor will he accept it. He has realized that Zeus is on his side and has granted him divine favour, and this is the only thing that can compensate his wounded honour and the grave offense committed against him. The essential aspect for the action of the *Iliad* at this point is that the embassy has failed to achieve its aim: the rejection of a reconciliation, expressed in definitive terms by Achilles, allows no space for negotiation and leads to an *impasse* which has all the characteristics of being impossible to work out. Yet while the Achilles of the *Iliad* can now no longer accept a reconciliation with Agamemnon in order to return to the battlefield and take part in the war, myth requires Achilles to fight at Troy right up to his death, and this will occur prior to the fall of the city. Therefore, with this development of the story, the poet has set his poem on a collision route, in blatant conflict with the Trojan saga regarding a codified aspect that cannot be changed, one which even the poet himself cannot change despite his extensive freedom to intervene and adapt his material. The destiny of Achilles is that he will die at Troy and achieve everlasting glory, but at this point of the *Iliad* Achilles can no longer be reconciled with Agamemnon and resume the war. The solution of an *impasse* that had become impossible and unsolvable in the terms in which it has been presented so far is provided by the character of Patroclus and his killing. We will return to this crucial aspect.

Patroclus receives little more than a bare mention in Book 1 of the poem, and subsequently reappears only in Book 8, when Zeus foresees his death (473–7). Responding vehemently to Hera, who is angry at the defeat of the Achaeans, Zeus asserts that only the return of Achilles to the battle scene will be able to repel the attack by Hector and the Trojans against the Achaean camp, when the battle starts raging around the body of Patroclus: for thus it has been established and Hera's protests are devoid of effect. This is a typical passage in which a divine prophecy fulfils the function, within the overall structure of the story, of an announcement and a preparation (*Vorbereitung*) of future events in the development of the action. A parallel can be found in 18.8–11, when Achilles calls to mind his mother's prediction that the best of the Myrmidons (i.e. Patroclus) would die before him.

---

[2] The translations of the passages from the *Iliad* are by Hammond 1987.

In Book 11 the defeat of the Achaeans takes on increasingly severe proportions, with the wounding of some of the most important chiefs: Agamemnon, Diomedes, Odysseus, Machaon, Eurypylus are injured, and Ajax is in grave danger. Achilles sends Patroclus to seek information from Nestor, who complains of Achilles' indifference to his companions' misfortunes. Nestor also reminisces about the time when Patroclus and Achilles set off to war together, and finally he asks him to intervene in such a manner that Achilles will agree to sending at least Patroclus himself as an aid to the Achaeans, who are now staring defeat in the face (*Il.* 11.794–803). Patroclus, in tears, comes back to Achilles and, reporting on the desperate situation of the Achaeans, manages to soften Achilles' heart sufficiently so that he himself is allowed to put on Achilles' armour and go with the Myrmidons to bring help to the Achaeans (16.1–100).³ Once again Achilles recalls the terrible offense and injustice he suffered from Agamemnon when he was deprived of the girl he had legitimately and rightfully been given as a tribute to his valour and successes. But at this point there follow unexpected assertions which appear somewhat problematic, at least in the context of the *Iliad* as it has unfolded so far. Achilles says (*Il.* 16.60–73) the time has come to put the whole story behind him, and that he cannot be angry forever. He had said he would not lay aside his anger unless the battle had reached the point of seriously endangering his ships (*Il.* 16.61–3); let Patroclus now wear his armour and guide the Myrmidons towards the Achaeans who are in desperate need of help, crushed as they are on the coastline and at the ships by the Trojans, who are brazenly confident because they do not see Achilles on the battlefield; 'they would soon run in flight and fill the gullies with their dead, *if lord Agamemnon would treat me kindly*' (*Il.* 16.71–3). Shortly thereafter, Achilles orders Patroclus to restrict himself to driving the Trojans away from the Achaeans' ships, but then to stop and turn back. Patroclus should not engage in full-fledged battle outside of Achilles' presence, because Achilles aims to achieve the victory for his own grandeur and does not wish his glory to be tarnished and diminished: 'but follow exactly the aim of the instruction I now put in your mind, so that you can win great honour and glory for me from all the Danaans, *and they bring me back the beautiful girl and offer splendid gifts besides*' (*Il.* 16.83–6). To this we can add that in *Il.* 11.609–10, as he prepares to send Patroclus on a fact-finding mission, Achilles had remarked: 'now I think the Achaians will crowd at my knees in supplication'. But the Achaeans had indeed already supplicated him, Agamemnon had been kind to him and had made an important move in the quest for a reconciliation, offering him precisely that which Achilles declares

---

3 Janko (1992) 309–14; Mirto (1997) 1242–6.

to be his intense desire, namely the return of Briseis, accompanied by a profusion of gifts. The decision made in Book 9 and the ensuing embassy, as we have seen, constituted a genuine and substantial change in Agamemnon's attitude, but it was Achilles who scornfully rejected the offer, whereas in Book 16 he seems to be complaining about the non-occurrence of an event which has indeed already occurred. This is an undeniable element of dissonance which cannot be erased, even though the assessment of its impact and significance may be markedly different.

After entering into the fray and achieving the result of breathing new life into the Achaeans (also killing an important Trojan hero like Sarpedon, a son of Zeus[4]), Patroclus does not obey Achilles: he continues to fight and chases the Trojans right up to the walls of the city, until the point when Hector kills him and strips his body, thereby seizing the weapons of Achilles. The final act of the dispute between Achilles and Agamemnon, of the anger and abstention from the battlefield, is found in Book 19, when Achilles lays down his anger and Agamemnon makes amends for his actions (40–300).[5] Achilles summons a meeting of the assembly of the Achaeans and pronounces the opening speech, addressing Agamemnon directly and going straight to the heart of the question, which he now delineates in a completely different manner as compared to earlier statements.

Achilles now decidedly downplays the importance of Briseis to him: despite having defined her in *Il.* 9.336 as a dear companion, he now goes so far as to say that it would have been better if Artemis had killed her on the very day when he received her as part of his war booty. He then states it had been sheer folly to quarrel over a girl, thereby causing such severe damage to the Achaeans and advantages of the Trojans. He bewails the dispute for which both parties bear responsibility, and basically wonders whether it was really worth causing such an upheaval. Finally, without mentioning even a word on the subject of the return of the girl and about the compensatory gifts – despite having so strongly emphasized this issue in *Il.* 16.83–6 – he declares that he will lay aside his anger and go back to the battlefield to fight against the common enemy, Hector and the Trojans. Agamemnon replies by blaming the gods for his blindness about the whole affair and concludes by asserting that, while he had earlier been out of his mind because of the gods' will, now he is ready to restore goodwill with all the gifts he had already offered to Achilles in the embassy, as communicated through by words of Odysseus (in *Il.* 19.140–1 there is an explicit ref-

---

4 On this character and his role in the structure of the *Iliad*, see Aceti (2008).
5 Edwards (1991) 234–5, 253–63; Mirto (1997) 1341–56.

erence to the embassy of the previous day). He also states he would like Achilles to receive all these gifts immediately, even before throwing himself into the heat of battle, so that Achilles can check whether the gifts meet his expectations (*Il.* 19.137–44). Achilles gives only cursory consideration to the proposal, as the only thing he is genuinely concerned about at this time is to return to the fight and massacre the Trojans (*Il.* 19.145–53). Odysseus intervenes to emphasize that the men need food and sustenance before fighting: let the dinner be prepared and let Agamemnon make a grand display of all the gifts and the girl herself, swearing that he never had intercourse with her. Agamemnon approves of Odysseus' suggestion, and orders that the gifts be brought in and laid out in full view. He then makes a solemn oath that spells out the commitment which has been requested (*Il.* 19.154–97), but Achilles is insistent: the attack must be launched straightway, he cannot think of food, his only desire is to massacre the enemies. Odysseus is likewise insistent, claiming to be more sensible even if less strong: they will all fight much better after having satisfied their hunger. In addition to this, Odysseus immediately begins to carry out Agamemnon's order: together with a few companions he goes over to the army commander's tent, takes Briseis with all the gifts as specified and brings them to the centre of the assembly, in full view of all who are present. Agamemnon swears with great solemnity, with a sacrifice to Zeus, that he never touched the girl; the Myrmidons bring the gifts and Briseis to Achilles' tent, where the girl is filled with desperation at the sight of the corpse of Patroclus (*Il.* 19.199–300).

Thus the affair of the quarrel and the anger of Achilles comes to an end with reconciliation, narrated in a lengthy, elaborate and complex scene, which unfolds in front of the army and endows the crucial moment with the solemnity appropriate for what evidently represents a decisive turning-point in the development of the story. It is a scene characterized by the idea that Achilles does not pay the slightest attention to the principle of compensatory gifts, or to the return of Briseis, or the vast array of presents given by Agamemnon. He does not wish to consider anything other than the battle, his own return to the fray, and his revenge for the death of Patroclus. This reconciliation completely overturns what had been the outcome of the embassy of Book 9, which resulted in the refusal by Achilles. He now perfunctorily accepts what he had been offered, and appears to be practically indifferent to the reception of Agamemnon's gifts, including Briseis – in other words, Achilles appears now indifferent to the very thing which, in Book 16, he was so fiercely insistent upon, as though he had never even been offered the prized objects. In Book 19 the attitude of Achilles has undergone a complete change: the death of Patroclus is evidently the reason for this inversion, but the narrative development also prompts an analysis of greater depth, which in actual fact we have already prefigured in its essential terms.

The figure of Achilles and the narrative structure of the *Iliad* are themes on which much – a vast amount – has been written.[6] Recently, M. L. West has made the point and drawn some relevant conclusions on the modern Homeric question, attempting, from a neo-unitarian point of view, to take into account the extremely rich and inescapable impact of the criticism dating from earlier centuries.[7] He argues that the *Iliad* and the *Odyssey* are epic poems conceived on an exceptionally vast scale, composed and written over a period of many years, each by one individual poet. A particularly new aspect of West's hypothesis consists in his re-examination not only of unitarian criticism, but at the same time also of the bulk of nineteenth- and twentieth-century analytical criticism, the results of which he uses in a different manner, remoulding them, as it were, into a unitary sense. Thus, while the analytical approach highlighted the compositional stratification of the Homeric poems and attributed it to the contribution of various different authors over a prolonged period of time, West sees the stratification as the outcome of the different phases of the artistic life and poetic activity of an individual author in each case, one for the *Iliad* and one for the *Odyssey*. In this vision of the question one of the relevant elements consists of West's total and extraordinary faith in the possibility for modern philology to reconstruct the creative processes that can be presumed to have led the two poets to compose their two masterpieces. Thus, rather than writing the poems as one single creative act respectively, he believes these two authors worked continuously on these creations throughout the years of their lives, modifying and refining them repeatedly, thereby giving rise to a veritable authorial stratification. The poems were set down in written form at the very moment of their composition (possibly by means of dictation to a professional scribe) by poets educated in the tradition of an oral form of poetry to which their predecessors belonged. According to this interpretation, the *Iliad* was written between 680 and 640 roughly, and the *Odyssey* during the last third of the 7th century BCE.

I feel it is rather difficult to share West's unshakable faith in the means of his own philology and thus to accept its results. Let us emphasize a fundamental concept that characterizes the study of the formation of the Homeric poems by repeating that the contradictions and incoherencies therein are to be ascribed to the history and process of formation of the poems, however one hypothesises the reconstruction of these phases. In contrast, the homogeneities and coherent elements are more plausibly attributable to the hand of the last author who gave the poem its final form that has come down to us. The unsolved and unsolvable

---

6 Latacz (2000) 145–57 = (2015) 151–63; West (2011) 1–68, with the relevant bibliography.
7 West (2011) 1–68.

problem obviously remains of determining the weight and role to be attributed to each of these two factors. The case we are studying forms part of this framework and of these reference parametres. I certainly do not intend to re-assess and discuss the entire problem in its innumerable aspects and problematic features, nor will I re-examine all the hypotheses (which, as far as I am concerned, remain on the level of hypotheses) put forward by West. My proposal is more limited and restricts itself to the following observations.

Achilles was the last hero to become part of the saga of Troy, in which he occupies a special position. His participation in the war is distinguished by his motivations, as he does not belong to the group of Helen's suitors associated with the oath sworn to Tyndaros: rather, he is in Troy because fighting in the war enables him to pursue his own destiny of glory. As mentioned earlier, he himself makes this point very clearly and explicitly in *Il.* 9.410–20: 'My mother, the silver-footed goddess Thetis, says that I have two fates that could carry me to the end of death. If I stay here and fight on round the Trojans' city, then gone is my homecoming, but my glory will never die; and if I come back to my dear native land, then gone is my great glory, but my life will stretch long and the end of death will not overtake me quickly. And I would advise the rest of you too to sail back home, since you will not now reach your goal in steep Ilios – wideseeing Zeus has held his hand firm above the city, and its people have taken strength'. However, it was common knowledge that Achilles died at Troy and had effectively achieved everlasting glory: therefore this alternative cannot be conceived as being real and genuinely possible. It sounds more as if it were linked to a given moment, to an *impasse* that needs to be overcome somehow because Achilles *must* go back onto the battlefield. The same can be said with regard to the possibility of leaving Troy and going back to the homeland: while this is in some sense contemplated in Book 9 (see above), the audience of archaic Greek epic knew perfectly well that this would certainly not occur.

Regardless of the moment, whenever it may have been, in which Achilles entered into the saga of Troy, he is most definitely the essential character of the *Iliad*. The conception of the poem revolves around him, regardless of all the amplifications that characterize the narrative development of the story. The most important, indeed, one might well say, the only significant action undertaken by Hector is the killing of Patroclus, Achilles' beloved friend. As the greatest defender of Troy and a hero of the war, Hector may have been invented or his figure may have been magnified and spotlighted precisely in order to ensure that Achilles had a worthy adversary, with whom to construct a grand final duel, as a consequence of Patroclus' death, for the assumption that Achilles *must* return to the battlefield, given that he will achieve his glory in Troy, is not open to doubt in any way whatsoever.

As far as his much-loved companion and friend Patroclus is concerned, in the *Iliad* itself Nestor recalls that Achilles and Patroclus set out to war together (11.780–91). If the two heroes, as it would seem, entered into the saga together as characters already recognized as a twosome, it is nevertheless hard to say whether the role and deeds of Patroclus were of the greatest importance and at the forefront of action from the very start, reflecting the portrayal in the *Iliad* as we read it now, or whether they grew over time, in the hands of the poet of the *Iliad* or of an immediate predecessor of his. In particular, it is difficult to ascertain whether the death of Patroclus at the hand of Hector is an invention by the poet of the *Iliad* or whether it already existed in a background canvas of the saga with which the poet was familiar, and he merely took it over.

Yet it seems difficult to refute the idea that the last element, the last episode to have entered into the story told in the *Iliad* was precisely the embassy of Book 9. In other words, it seems hard to deny that the embassy with its negative outcome belongs to the final level of construction of the poem as it has come down to us. We have noted that traces can be found of a development of the storyline devoid of the failed embassy, specifically in the speech by Achilles at the beginning of Book 16, as well as in 11.609 (see above). These observations are not new and involve essentially two possible explanations: either the original conception by the poet of the *Iliad* contained no embassy at all and the failed embassy was added later by another poet but the insertion left signs of incongruity; or the embassy was really an invention by the last poet himself, who remoulded his canvas inserting the embassy on a narrative framework that originally did not feature it, and this process of formation left a few imperfectly amalgamated traces.

But what is the meaning of the embassy, of its insertion into the poem? What is its function in the narrative development of the *Iliad* as we have it now? And, above all, what was the point of introducing an embassy that fails to achieve its objective? For it is above all the failed embassy that leads to the insoluble situation from which there is no way out, as described earlier: it is an *impasse* that creates unprecedented tension, which the poet has evidently built up quite deliberately. The fact that Achilles, on receiving the offer that effectively represents a climbdown by Agamemnon, definitively rejects the proposed reconciliation leads inevitably to a dead-end. At this stage Achilles cannot make his peace with Agamemnon in order to return to the battlefield according to the terms proposed in Book 9, yet the mythic story requires that Achilles should continue to fight at Troy up until the moment of his death. Thus the poet has decided to bring the action of his poem, the narrative development he himself conceived, into conflict with the established unfolding of key events in the Trojan saga as regards an aspect which absolutely cannot be changed. The destiny of Achilles is to die at Troy and acquire everlasting glory, but Achilles can no longer resume the war on the basis of a reconciliation with Agamemnon. Hence, what is needed is for him to return to the fray for a reason that is completely unrelated to the concept of reconciliation with his adversary – a motive that must be so strong and incontrovertible as to make everything else pale into insignificance. In effect, in Book 19 Achilles pours scorn on all the concrete elements that were intended to bring about a reconciliation: he spurns Briseis and the great wealth of gifts, for these have become almost irrelevant in the face of a highly pressing and cogent motive, which can be neither deferred nor repressed – namely, avenging his friend Patroclus. The paroxistic representation of Achilles' agony at the loss of Patroclus, his refusal to take food, his death wish, and then also his furious raging on the body of Hector: all this throws into sharp relief the insuppressible burden of the desire for revenge. Achilles returns to the battlefield, but not because he has been reconciled with Agamemnon: this has become inconceivable on account of an irresolvable *impasse*. Rather, what Achilles aims to do is to avenge Patroclus, independently of any concept of reconciliation with the head of the army. In short, we realise that the action of the poem has been led to a dead-end, at which point only a new event, a decisive turning point, a sort of *coup de théatre* can release him from the stranglehold of the circumstances. Here the *coup de théatre* (within the Iliadic plot) is the death of Patroclus, with the consequences it gives rise to, which continue until the end of the poem. In Aristotelian terms, we would have the structure of a tragedy culminating in the *desis* (knot, plot entanglement), after which a *lysis* (solution) is formulated which allows the storyline to continue until the end. Is this an element of "modernity" in the final conception of the *Iliad?* [8]

As we were saying, the death of Patroclus may have been an *ad hoc* invention by the poet of the *Iliad*, or it may have already existed in the saga which the poet inherited. If it did already exist, then one may suggest that the poet of the *Iliad* made special use of it, emphasizing and utilizing it as an alternative motive and eventually exploiting it as the only genuine reason underlying Achilles' return to the battlefield, once the invention of the failed embassy had decreed that any normal reconciliation according to the terms and desires of the offended party was impossible. Thus, what I would argue is that we can attribute to the poet of the *Iliad* precisely the invention of the failed embassy, which belongs to the peculiarity of the narrative construction of his *Iliad:* it fulfils an extremely significant and effective function in heightening to a remarkable degree the dramatic tension inherent in the conflict. Such strain of the confrontational atmosphere, in which no solution seems to present itself, leads to the invention of a

---

8 I discussed this idea with Fausto Montana, to whom I extend my thanks.

special type of motive for the narrative construction of the final part of the poem, namely the terrible revenge carried out by Achilles for the killing of Patroclus, with the slaughter and savagery that characterize the last part of the poem. And it is from this very same setting that there also emerges, by sublime contrast, the amazing finale in which Achilles displays his human compassion towards Priam, the old father who, as the king of Troy, deigns to kiss the hands of the man who massacred and brutalized his son, and to beg him for nothing more than a body to weep over.

Works cited[9]

Aceti, Ch. (2008). *Sarpedone fra mito e poesia*, in *Eroi dell'Iliade. Personaggi e strutture narrative*, ed. by Lara Pagani, "Pleiadi 8", Rome, 1–270.
Edwards, M.W. (1991). *The Iliad: A Commentary, vol. V: books 17–20* (General Editor: G. S. Kirk). Cambridge.
Hainsworth, B. (1993). *The Iliad: A Commentary, vol. III: books 9–12*, (General Editor: G. S. Kirk). Cambridge.
Hammond, M. (1987). Homer, *The Iliad*. Translated with an Introduction. London.
Janko, R. (1992). *The Iliad: A Commentary, vol. IV: books 13–16*. (General Editor: G. S. Kirk). Cambridge.
Latacz, J. (2000). 'Zur Struktur der *Ilias* (STR)', in: J. Latacz (ed.), *Homers* Ilias. *Gesamtkommentar: Prolegomena*, Munich – Leipzig = (2015). 'The Structure of the *Iliad* (STR)', in: A. Bierl and J. Latacz (eds.), *Homer's* Iliad. *The Basel Commentary: Prolegomena*, Berlin-Boston.
Mirto, M. S. (1997). Omero, *Iliade*, Traduzione e saggio introduttivo di Guido Paduano, commento di Maria Serena Mirto. Turin.
West, M. L. (2011). *The Making of the* Iliad. *Disquisition and Analytical Commentary*. Oxford.

---

[9] A reference bibliography for the topics addressed in these pages would have been an enormous list, yet still woefully incomplete and thus of scanty use. I have restricted myself to a very few works in which the reader can find all the references that are helpful for in-depth discussion on the themes involved.

Egbert Bakker
Hector (and) the race horse: The telescopic vision of the *Iliad*

The unity and composition of the *Iliad* has long been a fraught subject in Homeric scholarship, and within Greek philology as a whole. Ever since the inception of the Homeric Question analytic scholarship has tended to see the poem either as a cluster of accretions to a primordial "*Ur-Ilias*" commonly called *Achilleis*, or as a coalescence of a number of smaller epics ("*Einzelgedichte*"). We now know better, due in no small measure to Wolfgang Schadewaldt's *Iliasstudien*, whose value for Iliadic scholarship far exceeds the polemic with analytic scholarship for which it was originally written. The material that is seemingly extraneous to the plot revolving around Achilles' *mēnis* is not added later as "padding" of an original poem, but is the result of a deliberate strategy of compression of the entire Trojan saga: the *Iliad* wants to be the song of Troy no less than the song of Achilles' wrath, and in pursuing the latter agenda it never loses sight of the Trojan saga as a whole. The Trojan War is not "background", however, or material that is "alluded" to, much less inserted, but is an integral part of the poem's plot, and in the end the two action strings, that of the doomed city of Troy and that of the doomed short-lived Achaean hero, merge into one, in the final encounter of Achilles and the Trojan champion Hector.

In this contribution to the volume honoring Antonios Rengakos, a student of Schadewaldt's student Wolfgang Kullmann, I would like to revisit the question of the *Iliad* as a "monumental composition". Some of the observations to be presented below will not in themselves be new, but I propose to approach the question from two new angles. First, I will study the *Iliad*'s monumental composition and its large-scale design by tracking the ways in which it is "encoded" by formulaic phraseology, attempting to reconcile two branches of Homeric scholarship that have not always coexisted peacefully: oral-formulaic theory and literary analysis. And, second, in the examination of the way in which the *Iliad* subsumes and incorporates the wider narrative of the Trojan War I will shift the vantage point from Achilles and his wrath to Hector, defender of the city. Hector, I will argue, on the basis of a detailed examination of formulaic repetitions, comes to occupy the position originally held by Paris, as the one primarily responsible for the loss of Trojan life and eventually the city's destruction.

The meaning of repetition

It is impossible not to think of an oral epic poem such as the *Iliad* as characterized by repetition in many ways and at many levels. Repetition of discourse units short and long, from formulas below line-level to type scenes and entire story-patterns, is essential for the poem's composition, its comprehension, its performance, and its transmission. Repetition is more complex semantically than the pioneers of the oral poetry approach to Homer originally assumed. Earlier oral-formulaic scholarship tended to place the emphasis on *production:* formulas enable a bard to (re)produce the tale in performance without having to memorize it. Formulaic repetition in this sense becomes a natural and unavoidable consequence of oral-formulaic composition.[1] When the repeated units are larger, in the form of type-scenes or entire story-patterns, for example, they may orient and direct the poet, enabling him to oversee larger stretches of narrative.

Later oralist scholars made the important next step of seeing repetition as meaningful in and of itself, an essential element in the significance of traditional poetry. Earlier utterances of any traditional phrase, they argue, may resonate in the present and imbue the present utterance with meaning. The notion of "traditional referentiality" introduced by the late John Miles Foley is central here, a kind of generic intertextuality whereby any utterance of a traditional phrase in the present evokes the indeterminate set of its earlier utterances:

> 'Traditional referentiality (. . .) entails the invoking of a context that is enormously larger and more echoic than the text or work itself, that brings the lifeblood of generations of poems and performance to the individual performance or text. Each element in the phraseology or narrative thematics stands not simply for that singular instance but for the plurality and multiformity that are beyond the reach of textualization'.[2]

What this means is that coming fresh to an epic scene or coming to a poem—or its performance—as an outsider to the tradition in which it inserts itself is to miss a good part of the meaning, since one has access only to the syntactic and lexical surface. On this basis Adrian Kelly has shown through a detailed line-by-line

---

[1] This may lead to the at first sight paradoxical idea that repetition is in itself not what makes a phrase a formula, e.g. Parry (1971) 304: 'It is the *nature* of an expression which makes of it a formula, whereas its use a second time in Homer depends largely upon the hazard, which led a poet, or a group of poets, to use it more than once in two given poems of a limited length'. But with a less limited corpus than the Homeric poems at our disposal this issue would disappear.

[2] Foley (1991) 6–7.

analysis of *Iliad* 8 that "knowing Homeric Greek" is more than knowing the lexicon and the grammar; knowing what a given phrase does in another context is indispensable for one's understanding of what it evokes or implies now.

A given epic phrase, then, may echo "metonymically" a range of similar contexts; an important next step is made when we realize that it may also, equally "metonymically", come to stand for a *particular* scene or episode. This phenomenon is increasingly studied under the heading 'intertextuality'.[3] An often-cited example is the phrase μέγας μεγαλωστί 'great in his greatness' (*Il.* 16.776; 18.26), interpreted as evoking specifically the death of Achilles as it was conventionally told in the tradition.[4] Being aware of this association adds depth to one's understanding of the scene in which Achilles receives the news of Patroclus' death (*Il.* 18.1–64): in linking the scene to Achilles' death the hearer comes to view the death of Patroclus in strongly foreshadowing terms.

In this paper I intend to make the final step and study the repetition of specific phrases in specific contexts in a specific work, the *Iliad:* the repeated phrase brings to bear on the present context not just its meaning-in-(previous)-context, but the previous specific context as a whole.[5] Knowledge of that previous context on the part of the hearer provides essential depth to the understanding of the present context. This technique, I argue, is key to the conception and creation of the *Iliad* as a "monumental composition".

Studying the semantic and thematic potential of repetition will for some readers be stretching the concept of oral poetry beyond the breaking point and entering the realm of literary interpretation. Without denying that the benefits of the operation are decidedly "literary", and without denying that such a conception of repetition presupposes a high level of coherence and fixity of the composition, which would have to be perceived and experienced by a listening audience unambiguously as a "work", I would still maintain that reception and appreciation of an oral poem in performance is the essential dimension in which the repetition functions. Formulaic diction is not just the medium in which the monumental composer tells the tale; it is precisely the medium in and through which monumentality is achieved.

Key is the signposting and signaling for those who are familiar with the internal referentiality of the *Iliad*: those who understand what a phrase means in the present context, because they remember its previous utterance(s) earlier in

---

[3] See Burgess (2012) 168. In Bakker 2013: 157–69 I use the term "interformularity".
[4] Burgess (2012) 171–6; Barnes (2011) 2–5. For an overview of Neoanalysis in this new guise, see Burgess (2006) with much further literature (7).
[5] This type of repetition corresponds with the high point of the scale of "interformularity" proposed in Bakker (2013) 168.

the poem. Such understanding is typically achieved when one's present encounter with the poem is not the first one. The composition of the *Iliad* may be a novel conception that stands apart from more straightforwardly linear narratives, such as, presumably, the poems of the Epic Cycle; for the individual hearer, however, the *Iliad*'s treatment of the wider tradition "works" only if the poem is heard in performance many times over an individual's lifetime. The *Iliad* is replete with repetition, but the most important repetition is the poem itself.⁶

Three similes

Our point of departure and point of reference throughout the chapter is the following simile (*Il.* 6.506–11 = 15.263–8):

> ὡς δ' ὅτε τις στατὸς ἵππος ἀκοστήσας ἐπὶ φάτνηι
> δεσμὸν ἀπορρήξας θείηι πεδίοιο κροαίνων
> εἰωθὼς λούεσθαι ἐϋρρεῖος ποταμοῖο
> κυδιόων· ὑψοῦ δὲ κάρη ἔχει, ἀμφὶ δὲ χαῖται
> ὤμοις ἀΐσσονται· ὁ δ' ἀγλαΐηφι πεποιθώς
> ῥίμφά ἑ γοῦνα φέρει μετά τ' ἤθεα καὶ νομὸν ἵππων·

> Just as when a stalled horse, well fed at the manger,
> breaks his halter and runs over the plain with stamping hooves;
> he is used to washing himself in the well-flowing river,
> exulting. He holds his head high and his manes on either side
> wave over his shoulders. And he, confident in his splendor,
> lightly his legs carry him all over the haunts and the pastures of horses.

This famous simile is the longest simile to be repeated *verbatim* in the Homeric poems.⁷ The simile first occurs at the end of *Iliad* 6, when it is used for Paris as he leaves the city to rejoin the fighting, having spent time with Helen after his defeat in the duel with Menelaus. In its second occurrence the simile marks Hector's return to the battle after recovering from the blow of the giant stone thrown at him by Ajax (14.409–13) in the battle during Zeus' sleep after his seduction by

---

6 The common assumption that the "literary" quality of the *Iliad* (with respect to the Epic Cycle) must mean that the poem is novel and deliberately going against the "horizon of expectation" of the hearer is therefore in my opinion mistaken.
7 In addition to the simile under study here there are seven repeated longer similes in Homer: *Il.* 5.782–3 = *Il.* 7.256–5; *Il.* 5.860–1 = *Il.* 14.148–9; *Il.* 9.14–15 = *Il.* 16.3–4; *Il.* 11.550–5 = *Il.* 17.659–64; *Il.* 13.389–93 = *Il.* 16.482–6; *Od.* 4.335–40 = *Od.* 17.126–31 (part of a wider repeated passage); *Od.* 6.232–5 = 23.159–62. See Scott (1974) 129–30.

Hera. It is only in the concluding phrases that the similes diverge: in Paris' case the image is presented as a visualisation of pride in radiant armor, and only secondarily speed, whereas speed is primary in Hector's case:

ὡς υἱὸς Πριάμοιο Πάρις κατὰ Περγάμου ἄκρης
τεύχεσι παμφαίνων ὥς τ' ἠλέκτωρ ἐβεβήκει
καγχαλόων, ταχέες δὲ πόδες φέρον·   (*Il.* 6.512–14)

This was how Priam's son, Paris, came down from Pergamon's citadel
radiant in his armor, like the beams of the sun,
rejoicing; and fast were the feet that carried him.

ὡς Ἕκτωρ λαιψηρὰ πόδας καὶ γούνατ' ἐνώμα
ὀτρύνων ἱππῆας, ἐπεὶ θεοῦ ἔκλυεν αὐδήν.   (*Il.* 15.269–70)

Such was Hector as swiftly he moved his feet and knees,
urging on the horsemen, after he had heard the god's voice.

Scholarly opinion in antiquity tends to consider the simile's second occurrence secondary with respect to the first one. In particular, lines 265–8 are thought to fit Paris better than Hector (οἰκειότερον γὰρ ἐπὶ Ἀλεξάνδρου κεῖνται· οὐ γὰρ ἁρμόσειαν Ἕκτορι νῦν, '<these lines> do occur more properly with respect to Paris; they are not fitting for Hector here', Σ T ad 15.263–4) and are accordingly considered an interpolation to be athetized.[8]

The authorities on similes in modern scholarship are less inclined to athetize and suspect interpolation.[9] But the assumption that the race-horse after all fits Paris' stylish and carefully polished armor and weapons (6.321–2) better than Hector's awakening from a coma is indirectly apparent in the arguments made in defence of its second occurrence.[10] And the reading of the poem as oral poetry makes critics reluctant to assign primacy to either of the two occurrences.

The argument to be presented here starts from the assumption that asking whether or to what extent the image of the prize stallion breaking free from his halter is appropriate to Hector in his awakening is a less important question than asking what Hector has in common with Paris, or in what way Hector's return to the battlefield in Book 15 can be aligned with Paris' return to the battle-

---

8 Although the T scholion also records disagreement on this point, with some scholars pointing out that 'Hector too was beautiful' (τινὲς δὲ ὡς καλὸς καὶ Ἕκτωρ), adducing *Il.* 22.370–1, and that even though Hector is wounded now, he is spurred on by no fewer than two gods and can 'rejoice in his good fortune' (εἰ δὲ τέτρωται, ἀλλ' ὑπὸ δύο θεῶν ἐπίρεται. ἔστι δὲ ἐπηρμένος καὶ ἐπαγαλλόμενος ταῖς τύχαις).
9 Even Leaf (1900–1902) ad 15.263–8 resists interpolation, while calling the second occurrence of the simile 'a clear plagiarism of a passage whose beauty marked it out for plunder'.
10 Reviewed by Janko (1992) 256.

field in Book 6.[11] The usual discussion of the relevance of the simile to Hector's condition has to be mediated through the relevance of the earlier simile to Paris'. In other words, instead of asking what the image of the running prize horse does to enhance our understanding of Hector's awakening and return to the battle, we have to ask what the image of Paris as prize horse does in this regard. Our attempt at answering this question will reveal that the horse simile does not stand alone, but is part of a strategy of large-scale architecture and design.

The two horse similes for the two brothers are aligned in more ways than the mere comparison between Paris and Hector. The two similes both mark the end of an interruption of the battle narrative, the image of the galloping horse signaling a resumption of the thread of the battle narrative.[12] In the case of Paris and the race horse the interruption is Hector's and Paris' stay in the city,[13] and in the case of Hector and the race horse the interruption is the temporary reversal in the battle caused by Hera's deception of Zeus (Book 14). The two horse similes occur each in the context in which Paris/Hector is returning back to the battlefield after the intermezzo.[14]

The idea of the simile as marking the end of an interruption may bring a third, much shorter, horse simile into play. At the end of Book 21 the Achaeans would have prematurely taken Troy if Apollo had not led Achilles astray, luring him away from the battle by likening himself to Agenor. When Achilles rejoins the battle after this intermezzo, his return is described in the following simile:

---

11 There are some observations on the comparison between the two similes, e.g., Bowra (1930, 92) thinks that the repetition is deliberate and underscores the contrast between Hector and Paris; Meltzer (1990, 277 n. 34) sees Hector's recovery with divine aid as an illustration (retroactively) of 'the godlike ease of Paris' transformation' (i.e. his liberation from Hector's rebuke); and Scott (2009, 235 n. 122) observes that the repeated similes signal a similarity between Hector and Paris, linking them together as ineffectual fighters through the 'unwarlike qualities of the horse'.
12 The term 'interruption' is meant to cover the differences between the two situations: in Book 6 the battle was interrupted only in narrative time during the period in which we follow Hector's visit of the city; in Book 15 the interruption is, strictly speaking, a reversal in the battle fortunes.
13 Hector: 6.237–529; Paris: from 3.380.
14 Both battle interruptions revolve around an erotic episode: Paris and Helen, Zeus and Hera. Each time the male lover declares to his partner that his desire for her has never been greater than it is now, in remarkably similar language. Paris to Helen: ἀλλ' ἄγε δὴ φιλότητι τραπείομεν εὐνηθέντε· / οὐ γάρ πώ ποτέ μ' ὧδέ γ' ἔρως φρένας ἀμφεκάλυψεν, / οὐδ' ὅτε (. . .) ὥς σεο νῦν ἔραμαι καί με γλυκὺς ἵμερος αἱρεῖ. (Il. 3.441–2; 446); Zeus to Hera: νῶϊ δ' ἄγ' ἐν φιλότητι τραπείομεν εὐνηθέντε. / οὐ γάρ πώ ποτέ μ' ὧδε θεᾶς ἔρος οὐδὲ γυναικὸς / θυμὸν ἐνὶ στήθεσσι περιπροχυθεὶς ἐδάμασσεν, (. . .) ὥς σέο νῦν ἔραμαι καί με γλυκὺς ἵμερος αἱρεῖ. (Il. 14.314–16; 428).

σευάμενος ὥς θ' ἵππος ἀεθλοφόρος σὺν ὄχεσφιν,
ὅς ῥά τε ῥεῖα θέηισι τιταινόμενος πεδίοιο·
ὣς Ἀχιλεὺς λαιψηρὰ πόδας καὶ γούνατ' ἐνώμα. (*Il.* 22.22–4)

charging like a horse, a prize-winner with its chariot,
who runs with ease, stretching himself over the plain,
Such was Achilles as swiftly he moved his feet and knees.

The similarity with the horse simile for Paris and Hector is obvious and has often been noticed.[15] We note that the concluding formula λαιψηρὰ πόδας καὶ γούνατ' ἐνώμα (22.24) is the same as in the simile for Hector (15.269).

The three similes are placed in three distinct sections of the poem. The Paris simile takes place when Achilles and his wrath are temporarily out of focus (though not far off); the Hector simile takes place when the wrath is in full swing, resulting in Achilles' absence from the battle; and the third simile occurs when Achilles' wrath has turned, after Patroclus' death, into a murderous rage. These three sections are distinct steps in the process whereby the Trojan saga is subsumed and incorporated in the *Iliad*'s plot as well as stages in the development of Hector as an epic character.

Hector and Paris

The second simile takes place during the long day of fighting that occupies the large central part of the poem, beginning at Book 11 and ending in Book 18.[16] This is the day of the battle at the Achaean wall and ships and of the deaths of Sarpedon and of Patroclus. This day is a near-decisive victory for the Trojans, in spite of a short period of reversal during which Zeus is distracted from the battle by Hera, when Poseidon intervenes on the battlefield to the benefit of the hard-pressed Achaeans.

There are two interlocking ways to look at this crucial middle part of the *Iliad*. This is first of all the day of Hector's great error, as he misinterprets Zeus' oracularly ambiguous message that he will be victorious "until he reaches

---

15 E.g., Kirk (1990) 226.
16 The day starts (11.1–2) with Ἠὼς δ' ἐκ λεχέων παρ' ἀγαυοῦ Τιθωνοῖο / ὄρνυθ', ἵν' ἀθανάτοισι φόως φέροι ἠδὲ βροτοῖσι·, a marked two-line dawn formula that in Homer recurs only at *Od.* 5.1–2, another important new start in the narrative. The great battle day is referred to by Hector in eager anticipation (8.541 ὡς νῦν ἡμέρη ἥδε κακὸν φέρει Ἀργείοισιν). Taplin (1992, 154) sees this daybreak as the beginning of the second performance session in a tripartite *Iliad*, a vision that squares with the interpretation offered here.

the well-benched ships and the sun sets".[17] The message is a step in the Διὸς βουλή, the plan of Zeus (1.2), which will ensure great losses for the Achaeans in Achilles' absence from the battlefield.[18] Second, and in connection with the Διὸς βουλή as backbone of the poem's plot, this is the intermediate stage in the transformation of the story of the Trojan War, with Paris and Menelaus, the two husbands of Helen, as primary antagonists, into a story of Achilles and Hector as deadly opponents, whose clash will be the pivotal moment in the poem's final section.[19] The duel between the two in Book 22 mirrors that of Paris and Menelaus in Book 3 in a large-scale design of ring composition.[20]

The earlier duel is one of the scenes that properly belong to the earliest stages of the Trojan War, along with the Catalogue of Ships and the *Teichoscopia*. Paris agrees to the duel with Menelaus provoked by Hector's biting criticism of his cowering when faced with Menelaus. The stakes are precisely what is the root cause of the war: "whoever of the two of us wins and proves himself to be the stronger man, let him have all the goods and let him take the woman to his home" (ὁππότερος δέ κε νικήσηι κρείσσων τε γένηται, κτήμαθ' ἑλὼν εὖ πάντα γυναῖκά τε οἴκαδ' ἀγέσθω, 3.71–2), Paris proposes.[21] At this point, winning a duel with Menelaus will be the way for Paris to acquit himself of the debt he owes to the Trojan people, whose life he has put at grave risk by bringing Helen into the city. Losing the duel would be the end of his life, but would save his city from the grinding war.

Paris' position as *aitios* (in Herodotus' sense) of the conflict is put most trenchantly by Hector when he visits Paris and Helen in their chamber, where he finds his brother polishing his weapons, far from the battle and after making love to Helen:

τὸν δ' Ἕκτωρ νείκεσσεν ἰδὼν αἰσχροῖς ἐπέεσσι·
"δαιμόνι' οὐ μὲν καλὰ χόλον τόνδ' ἔνθεο θυμῶι,
λαοὶ μὲν φθινύθουσι περὶ πτόλιν αἰπύ τε τεῖχος

---

17 εἰς ὅ κε νῆας ἐϋσσέλμους ἀφίκη(τ)αι δύηι τ' ἠέλιος, 11.193–4, 208–9 (repeated by Zeus at 15.454–5), the temporal determiner 'until' (εἰς ὅ κε) being ambiguous between an 'inclusive' ('all the way until') and an exclusive or limitative ('till X, not any longer') understanding; cf. 17.453–5. By contrast the 'until' in Zeus' programmatic announcement at 15.70–1 (εἰς ὅ κ' Ἀχαιοὶ Ἴλιον αἰπὺ ἕλοιεν) is unambiguously inclusive.
18 As Redfield (1994, 139) puts it: 'Zeus's intention is fundamentally hostile to the Trojans. Hector is in a trap, and the Trojans with him; every success brings them closer to disaster'.
19 Cf. the general thrust in Schadewaldt (1966³).
20 Schein (1997) 346.
21 Repeated by Hector twenty lines later (3.93–4); see also Agamemnon's statement of the conditions under which the duel takes place (3.281–5).

μαρνάμενοι· σέο δ' εἵνεκ' ἀϋτή τε πτόλεμός τε
ἄστυ τόδ' ἀμφιδέδηε· σὺ δ' ἂν μαχέσαιο καὶ ἄλλωι,
ὅν τινά που μεθιέντα ἴδοις στυγεροῦ πολέμοιο.
ἀλλ' ἄνα μὴ τάχα ἄστυ πυρὸς δηΐοιο θέρηται". (Il. 6.325–31)

Hector looked at him and rebuked him with shaming words:
"Strange man, it was not good of you to put this wrath in your heart:
people are dying around the citadel and the sheer wall,
fighting. All because of you has the battle-cry and the fighting
flared up around the city. You yourself would find fault with another man
whom you would see remiss in this hateful battle.
But up now, so the city does not go up in blazing fire".

These words from Hector's mouth will turn out to be ironic when he himself, facing Achilles in direct combat, has to admit in a monologue reflecting on his situation that many Trojans have died because of him (22.104). Only by winning the fight to the death with Achilles can Hector acquit himself of the debt he owes to the Trojan people, whose life he has put at grave risk by refusing to let the Trojan troops back into the city at the end of the great day of battle.[22] The strong term that Hector uses for the severe error of judgment that led him to expose his fellow Trojans to Achilles' fury outside the walls is ἀτασθαλίηισι (ἐμῆισι), the 'recklessness' that in epic always meets with deserved punishment.[23] Hector ponders whether he should lay down his arms, approach Achilles, and offer to return Helen and all the possessions that Paris took with him from Sparta and add to it from Trojan wealth (22.114–21), but then realizes that such a deal will not work with Achilles. Returning Helen will not save Troy now. This is no longer the beginning of the war, but its culmination, and the stakes have shifted and gone up. If Paris had lost the duel with Menelaus, Helen would have been returned to Menelaus and Troy would have been saved; if Hector loses the duel with Achilles, Troy is doomed.

Hector is not Paris. But the mention of the gesture with which Paris once could have ended the conflict may invite us to compare the two in their respective positions. After Paris' duel with Menelaus, and after Hector's duel with Ajax (both times the Trojans are saved only through divine or human intervention) a proposal is made in the assembly of the Trojans to resolve the conflict without

---

22 I would not call Hector's decision to stay outside of the walls and face Achilles an 'error' (pace Redfield 1994: 128).
23 Most famously applied to the consumption of the Cattle of the Sun by Odysseus' Companions (Od. 1.7; cf. 12.300), the behavior of humans as exemplified by Aegisthus' killing Agamemnon in Zeus' theodicy (Od. 1.34), and Odysseus' reflection on the well-deserved death of the Suitors (22.317).

further fighting. Antenor proposes to give back Helen to Menelaus and the Achaeans along with all the possessions that Paris took from his host, in language of which Hector's later words will be reminiscent (underlined):

δεῦτ' ἄγετ', Ἀργείην Ἑλένην καὶ κτήμαθ' ἅμ' αὐτῆι
<u>δώομεν Ἀτρεΐδηισιν ἄγειν.</u> (*Il.* 7.350–1; cf. 22.114, 117)

Come on, then: Argive Helen and all the possessions she brought,
Let's give it all to the Atreids to lead away.

Paris' response is quick and blunt:

Ἀντῆνορ σὺ μὲν οὐκέτ' ἐμοὶ φίλα ταῦτ' ἀγορεύεις·
οἶσθα καὶ ἄλλον μῦθον ἀμείνονα τοῦδε νοῆσαι.
εἰ δ' ἐτεὸν δὴ τοῦτον ἀπὸ σπουδῆς ἀγορεύεις,
ἐξ ἄρα δή τοι ἔπειτα θεοὶ φρένας ὤλεσαν αὐτοί. (*Il.* 7.357–60)

Antenor, what you are saying there is no longer pleasing to me.
Surely you know how to think of a proposal better than this one;
and if you really put it forth with serious intentions,
then the next thing for me to do is conclude that the gods themselves have utterly destroyed your wits.

He goes on to reject returning Helen (γυναῖκα μὲν οὐκ ἀποδώσω, 7.362), but agrees to return the goods to their previous owner. These words confirm Paris' status as the ultimate *aitios* of the conflict and seal the fate of Troy in the Trojan War. But this is the *Iliad*, a poem intent on incorporating the narrative of the Trojan War and its causes and subsume it under its own narrative agenda. In the poem's plot, announced in Book 1 and picked up in earnest in Book 8, there is need for a new Paris, a Trojan whose actions and decisions seal the fate of the city.[24]

Hector's day of glory

Hector's error begins after the Trojan attack of the Achaean Wall has gained decisive momentum during the long day of fighting that turns the *Iliad* from the Song of Troy into the Song of Achilles. He attacks the Achaean camp in the company of Polydamas, who is with Hector from the beginning of the day.[25] Polyda-

---

24 On Book 8 as instrumental for preparing the transition from Trojan War poem to *Achilleïs*, see Schadewaldt (1966³) 96–127.
25 11.56; 12.88; 12.196; 14.425; 16.535–6. As various scholars note (e.g., Redfield 1994, 143; Reichel 1994, 181; Schein 1984, 185; Taplin 1992, 157), Polydamas appears in the story only in the books

mas, born in the same night as Hector, but excelling in words and councils, whereas the latter excelled in martial prowess (18.251–2), establishes some initial authority for himself when he advises his fellow Trojans to leave the horses and the chariots at the far side of the ditch around the Achaean camp and attack the wall on foot (12.61–79). Hector likes this advice (12.80). But when Polydamas interprets a portent—an eagle carrying a snake as prey that continues to be so fierce that the eagle has to drop it (12.211–29)—in a way that recommends extreme caution in warfare and a withdrawal from the siege of the Achaean Wall, Hector is less pleased. His response is quick and blunt:

Πουλυδάμα, σὺ μὲν οὐκ ἔτ' ἐμοὶ φίλα ταῦτ' ἀγορεύεις·
οἶσθα καὶ ἄλλον μῦθον ἀμείνονα τοῦδε νοῆσαι.
εἰ δ' ἐτεὸν δὴ τοῦτον ἀπὸ σπουδῆς ἀγορεύεις,
ἐξ ἄρα δή τοι ἔπειτα θεοὶ φρένας ὤλεσαν αὐτοί
ὃς κέλεαι Ζηνὸς μὲν ἐριγδούποιο λαθέσθαι
βουλέων, ἅς τε μοι αὐτὸς ὑπέσχετο καὶ κατένευσε   (*Il.* 12.231–6)

Polydamas, what you are saying there is no longer pleasing to me.
Surely you know how to think of a proposal better than this one;
and if you really put it forth with serious intentions,
then the next thing to do for me is conclude that the gods themselves have destroyed your wits,
you who order me to forget about the plans of Zeus who thunders loud,
which he himself has promised me and confirmed with his nod.

Hector's disregarding of Polydamas' advice is not yet catastrophic in itself, since Zeus had in fact promised him victory, though with restrictions that Hector does not yet understand. Nor is there immediate military gain to be had from Polydamas' advice. But Hector utters formulaic words that have already been spoken by his brother Paris as prelude to a refusal that seals the fate of the city.

The military success that Hector anticipates, an anticipation which in itself is correct, will have consequences that are unforeseen by all human parties involved. Hector's breaking through the Achaean Wall and reaching the ships is crossing the line that Achilles had drawn as the point in time at which he would rejoin the fighting (9.650–5). As it happens, Achilles will return in reverse disguise, Patroclus dressed in Achilles' armor. And after Patroclus' death Hector will be increasingly delusional about his status and the Trojans' chances in the war. The climax is reached in the assembly of the Trojans, after darkness has put

---

covering the long day of fighting, and is probably invented to be Hector's counterpart during that day. Wüst (1955) sees in the contrast between the two an opposition between the political and religious spheres. An overview of the Hector-Polydamas scenes in Reichel (1994) 175–82.

an end to the fighting. Again it is Polydamas who is the voice of reason. He understands that the tide of war has turned now that Achilles has shown himself, and urges the Trojans to withdraw into the city and continue the war from the walls. Hector's response ends the day with the same words with which he had started it:

> Πουλυδάμα σὺ μὲν οὐκέτ' ἐμοὶ φίλα ταῦτ' ἀγορεύεις,
> ὃς κέλεαι κατὰ ἄστυ ἀλήμεναι αὖτις ἰόντας.   (*Il.* 18.285–6)
>
> Polydamas, what you are saying there is no longer pleasing to me,
> who urge us to go into the city to cower there.

The exchange between Hector and Polydamas echoes that between Paris and Antenor, both occurring in Trojan assembly scenes that have a parallel function and position in their respective portions of the *Iliad*. Paris' rejection seals the fate of Troy in the conflict between the Atreids and himself on account of Helen. Hector's rejection seals the fate of Troy in the *Iliad*'s "rewriting" of the original conflict as an antagonism between Hector and Achilles. The responsible older brother, whose task it was to save the city from the consequences of Paris' folly, has now become himself the *aitios* of the city's eventual demise. As we saw, he will acknowledge this himself as he faces the grim situation the city is in after Achilles' murderous rampage, referring back to Polydamas' advice and using for himself the strongest term that epic language has for a recklessness that always has punitive consequences for the perpetrator (ἀτασθαλίηισιν ἐμῆισιν, 22.104).

Hector's day of glory, then, is a transitional phase between two roles of the defender of the city: from responsible military commander charged with the defence of the city in a conflict in which he has no part to military commander who is not only responsible for the city's defence, but also the cause of the dire situation it is in. The foil here is Paris, who provides templates for Hector in various dimensions. Just as Hector rebukes Paris (6.325–31, quoted above), so Hector himself is rebuked by the Lycian chief Glaucus for not caring about the allies who give their life for Troy:

> Ἕκτορ νῦν δὴ πάγχυ λελασμένος εἰς ἐπικούρων,
> οἳ σέθεν εἵνεκα τῆλε φίλων καὶ πατρίδος αἴης
> θυμὸν ἀποφθινύθουσι· σὺ δ' οὐκ ἐθέλεις ἐπαμύνειν.   (*Il.* 16.538–40)
>
> Hector, now you are really completely forgetful of your allies,
> who far from their near and dear and the land of their fathers
> are dying on account of you, and you do not want to defend them.

What the Trojans do for Paris, the Lycians do for Hector, and both Paris and Hector are at fault. The change in outlook is underscored when Hector rebukes Paris for a third time, repeating the address he had made to his brother before the latter's duel with Menelaus (Δύσπαρι, εἶδος ἄριστε, γυναιμανές, ἠπεροπευτά, 'You Paris-of-doom, crazy womanizer with your good looks, you cheat' (13.769; cf. 3.39). But this time the rebuke is unjustified, as Paris is fighting bravely. Ironically, Glaucus, in a second rebuke to Hector (17.142), will re-use the taunt εἶδος ἄριστε, which Hector himself had used for Paris.

Hector and Achilles

During the day of Hector's great glory the great catalyst in his growing delusion is Achilles' armor, which Hector wins and dons (16.799–800; 17.125; 17.186–97), prompting from Zeus an assessment that can be added to his earlier programmatic announcements of his plan (at 8.475–6 and 15.59–71):[26]

> ἆ δείλ' οὐδέ τί τοι θάνατος καταθύμιός ἐστιν
> ὅς δή τοι σχεδὸν εἶσι· σὺ δ' ἄμβροτα τεύχεα δύνεις
> ἀνδρὸς ἀριστῆος, τόν τε τρομέουσι καὶ ἄλλοι·
> τοῦ δὴ ἑταῖρον ἔπεφνες ἐνηέα τε κρατερόν τε,
> τεύχεα δ' οὐ κατὰ κόσμον ἀπὸ κρατός τε καὶ ὤμων
> εἵλευ· ἀτάρ τοι νῦν γε μέγα κράτος ἐγγυαλίξω,
> τῶν ποινὴν ὅ τοι οὔ τι μάχης ἐκνοστήσαντι
> δέξεται Ἀνδρομάχη κλυτὰ τεύχεα Πηλεΐωνος. (Il. 17.201–8)

> Wretched man, death is not at all on your mind,
> while it is really very close. You don the immortal armor
> of a man of unique excellence, for whom others tremble as well.
> You have now killed his companion, brave and strong;
> It was not right for you to take the armor from his head and shoulders;
> still, I will give you great strength, at least for now, in compensation
> for the fact that Andromache will not receive the famed armor of Peleus' son from you
> safely back from the battle.

Wearing Achilles' armor is not merely an act of hybris on the part of Hector, but also a disposition of personal vanity and exultation. As Thetis puts it when she explains to Achilles that he cannot immediately, without armor, rejoin the fighting:

---

[26] Zeus' increasingly detailed announcements of what is to come is what Schadewaldt (1966³, 112–13) called *stückweise Enthüllung des Kommenden* 'piecemeal revelation of what is to come'.

> ἀλλά τοι ἔντεα καλὰ μετὰ Τρώεσσιν ἔχονται
> χάλκεα μαρμαίροντα· τὰ μὲν κορυθαίολος Ἕκτωρ
> αὐτὸς ἔχων ὤμοισιν <u>ἀγάλλεται</u>· οὐδέ ἕ φημι
> δηρὸν <u>ἐπαγλαϊεῖσθαι</u>, ἐπεὶ φόνος ἐγγύθεν αὐτῶι.   (Il. 18.130–3)

> But your beautiful armor is now with the Trojans,
> bronze and flashing. Hector of the glimmering helmet
> has them on his shoulders and he <u>exults</u> in it. But I say
> that he will not <u>rejoice in his splendor</u> for very long, since his murder is upon him.

The verbal forms ἀγάλλεται and ἐπαγλαϊεῖσθαι stand out. They tend to be, in the *Iliad*, equine terms, being used both for the proud animal itself in its exultation (20.222) or for its proud human master, such as the Trojan ally Asios, who in excessive pride in his horses and chariot disregarded Polydamas' advice to leave the horses and chariots at the ditch (12.110–15). Hector's looks and demeanor, then, when exulting in Achilles' armor, is reminiscent of the horse simile, an association that is strengthened by Thetis' use of the verb ἐπαγλαϊεῖσθαι, yet another verb for equine pride (cf. 10.331), and directly derived from the noun ἀγλαΐη 'splendor', which we find in the horse simile (ἀγλαΐηφι πεποιθώς).

It appears, then, that the horse simile in Book 15 not only links Hector to Paris, but also prepares the way for Hector's futile exulting in Achilles' armor. That armor was meant to make Patroclus look like Achilles (11.799; 16.41), a function that only underlines Patroclus' lesser status: wearing Achilles' armor marks him out as doomed.[27] It does so equally to Hector, who in donning Achilles' armor not only formally encodes himself as Patroclus' slayer, but also as a man doomed to die. Achilles' armor is the material extension of Achilles' person, indissolubly connected with him, and so with Patroclus. Taking the armor off Patroclus' corpse is severing two organically linked items, as is systematically encoded in the poem's formulaic system:

[carrying to Achilles/bringing back to the ships/fighting over Patroclus' body]

γυμνόν, ἀτὰρ τά γε τεύχε' ἔχει κορυθαίολος Ἕκτωρ (Il. 17.122, 693; 18.21)

stripped; the armor is in the hands of Hector of the glimmering helmet.

Without the armor Patroclus is not 'whole', and in appropriating Achilles' armor Hector partly becomes Achilles. In this context we may return to the third horse simile quoted earlier, the simile accompanying Achilles' return to the battle:

---

27 Cf. Taplin (1992) 181–5.

σευάμενος ὥς θ' ἵππος ἀεθλοφόρος σὺν ὄχεσφιν,
ὅς ῥά τε ῥεῖα θέηισι τιταινόμενος πεδίοιο·
ὣς Ἀχιλεὺς λαιψηρὰ πόδας καὶ γούνατ' ἐνώμα. (*Il.* 22.22–4)

charging like a horse, a prize-winner with its chariot,
who runs with ease, stretching himself over the plain,
Such was Achilles as swiftly he moved his feet and knees.

The formula λαιψηρὰ πόδας καὶ γούνατ' ἐνώμα in the last line, which was uttered previously in the longer simile (15.269) to express Hector's swiftness of foot, is properly, we now realize, an illustration of Achilles' essential epithet, πόδας ὠκὺς Ἀχιλλεύς 'Achilles swift of foot'. And swiftness of foot will be an important element in the scenes preceding Hector's last stand.[28] Hector and Achilles will in fact both be swift-footed horses as they run three times around the city, competing in speed for the prize of Hector's life:

πρόσθε μὲν ἐσθλὸς ἔφευγε, δίωκε δέ μιν μέγ' ἀμείνων
καρπαλίμως, ἐπεὶ οὐχ ἱερήϊον οὐδὲ βοείην
ἀρνύσθην, ἅ τε ποσσὶν ἀέθλια γίγνεται ἀνδρῶν,
ἀλλὰ περὶ ψυχῆς θέον Ἕκτορος ἱπποδάμοιο.
ὡς δ' ὅτ' ἀεθλοφόροι περὶ τέρματα μώνυχες ἵπποι
ῥίμφα μάλα τρωχῶσι· τὸ δὲ μέγα κεῖται ἄεθλον
ἢ τρίπος ἠὲ γυνὴ ἀνδρὸς κατατεθνηῶτος·
ὣς τὼ τρὶς Πριάμοιο πόλιν πέρι δινηθήτην
καρπαλίμοισι πόδεσσι· θεοὶ δ' ἐς πάντες ὁρῶντο (*Il.* 22.158–66)

Ahead was fleeing someone valiant; pursuing him was someone far greater,
with great speed, since it was not for a sacrificial victim or an ox-hide
that they were competing, which are the prize for footraces of men;
no, they ran for the <very> soul of horse-taming Hector.
Just as when prize-bearing one-hooved horses run
lightly around the goal post of the course – a big prize lies ready,
either a tripod or a woman, wife of a man who is now dead –
just so were the two of them whirling thrice around the city of Priam
with swift feet. And all the gods were looking on.

This race is the occasion of the real funeral games in honor of Patroclus, ahead of the ritual battles that will follow in the next book. The rage at the calamity of death that drives the competition is real, not symbolic, and the prize is not a precious object or a token of prestige, but the very life of one of the two competitors. Achilles is battling his new *alter ego*, Hector who wears Achilles' armor.[29]

---

[28] 22.166 καρπαλίμοισι πόδεσσι; 22.173, 230 ποσὶν ταχέεσσι;
[29] See Devereux (1978–1979) on Achilles' killing of Hector as a form of suicide.

The footrace is the culmination of a series of horse similes that form a thread in the texture of the plot. The horse starts as a proud prize horse, exulting in its own beauty and a proud possession of its owner; the exultation then turns into joy at supernaturally restored, but temporary, strength; and finally it has to run for a prize that is not the possession of its owner, but its own life. In this way it links Paris, Hector, and Achilles in a triangle of resemblance and death. Occupying the middle position, the simile, applied to Hector when wakened out of his coma and restored to strength, brings out the vital links between Hector and Paris on the one hand and Hector and Achilles on the other. The link between the two "outer" members of the triad, Paris and Achilles—the death of the latter at the hands of the former—remains outside the *Iliad*'s narrative purview, though it looms large and is the object of a series of prophecies culminating in Hector's dying words:[30]

> φράζεο νῦν, μή τοί τι θεῶν μήνιμα γένωμαι
> ἤματι τῶι ὅτε κέν σε Πάρις καὶ Φοῖβος Ἀπόλλων
> ἐσθλὸν ἐόντ' ὀλέσωσιν ἐνὶ Σκαιῆισι πύληισιν.   (*Il.* 22.358–60)
>
> Look out now, lest I will become a cause of the gods' wrath,
> on that day when Paris and Phoebus Apollo
> will destroy you, the valiant warrior, in the Scaean Gates.

Instead of including the death of Achilles in its plot and bringing Paris (back) into agency, the *Iliad* uses it to underscore the vital connection between Achilles' death and Hector's, as well as between Hector's and Patroclus' deaths, as encoded by phraseology used exclusively for these two events, which was meant to evoke the death of Achilles:[31]

> ψυχὴ δ' ἐκ ῥεθέων πταμένη Ἄϊδος δὲ βεβήκει
> ὃν πότμον γοόωσα λιποῦσ' ἀνδροτῆτα καὶ ἥβην.   (*Il.* 22.362–3 = 16.856–7)
>
> And his soul, from the limbs flying it went toward Hades,
> lamenting its fate after leaving vigor and youth.

The horse simile, then, plays a pivotal role in the *Iliad*'s "rewriting" of the story of the Trojan War. In the poem's initial segment (roughly the first nine Books) elements of the traditional story are picked up and modified, and it is Paris who is primarily liable for the city's dire situation. The second segment, in par-

---

[30] See also 19.416–7 (the prophecy of a horse!); 21.277–8 (prophecy of Thetis, recalled by Achilles).
[31] See Barnes (2011, 2–5), who points out a further essential feature that the two scenes have in common: the speech of dismissal of the slain opponent's dying prophetic words.

ticular the Books of the long battle day (11–18) brings the transfer of liability from Paris to Hector, as part of the plan of Zeus, the Διὸς βουλή. Hector becomes here the functional equivalent of his brother as the one who has put his city in grave danger, as encoded by the horse simile. The focal point of the conflict between the Trojans and the Achaeans is transferred from Paris-Menelaus to Hector-Achilles. In reaching the pinnacle of glory—and delusion—Hector dons Achilles' armor, thus turning into the living embodiment of Achilles' rage as the catalyst of his city's demise. In the telescopic vision of the *Iliad* Paris is at the same time a background figure (watching, like everyone else, the gods included, the duel between Hector and Achilles as the event that will decide the war) *and* a protagonist in the poem's plot as the template for what Hector will become as he achieves temporary glory in Achilles' absence.

If this is a compelling interpretation of the *Iliad*, then we are perhaps justified in seeing it confirmed by the formulaic repetitions this chapter has been exploring. For an audience listening to the poem in performance the idea of an interpretation confirmed by formulas works the other way: the formulas suggest and guide the interpretation. Parry and Lord taught us that epic formulas form a system, a system that not only enables the poet to compose in performance, but that also facilitates the audience to create meaning out of traditional phraseology. What this chapter has been suggesting is that this formulaic encoding (indeed, Lord spoke of a formulaic 'grammar')[32] can be poem-specific: the repetition of key phrases or sequences of verses, within the system of a single poem that constitutes its own grammar, can guide knowledgeable audiences to the interpretation intended by the poet(s).

In closing I suggest that the interpretation presented here may provide a rationale for the notable breach in Parryan economy constituted by the doublet Ἕκτορος ἀνδροφόνοιο 'man-murdering Hector' and Ἕκτορος ἱπποδόμοιο 'Hector the horse-tamer'. The former is almost three times as frequent as the latter (11 against 4 occurrences) and can perhaps be seen as the default, unmarked case. But more to the point is that it refers to Hector precisely in his quality of the murderous warrior who is irresistible in Achilles' absence.[33] Of the latter phrase two instances (22.161, 211) are used precisely for Hector in his horse-race and final confrontation with Achilles. And it is perhaps no coincidence that the final word of the poem's final line sets up the death and 'funeral of Hec-

---

32 Lord (1960) 35–6.
33 Various instances are focalized by Achilles himself: 1.242 (anticipating Hector's rampage in his absence), 9.351, 16.77, 16.840 (Hector's projected self-image through the eyes of Achilles). The two last instances (24.509, 24.724) highlight the dramatic contrast between Hector's dead body and the murderous warrior he was.

tor the horse-tamer' as a catastrophic loss for a doomed, horse-taming culture (*Il.* 24.804):

ὣς οἵ γ' ἀμφίεπον τάφον Ἕκτορος ἱπποδάμοιο.
That was how they were occupied with the funeral of Hector the horse-tamer.

Works cited

Bakker, E. J. (2013). *The Meaning of Meat and the Structure of the* Odyssey. Cambridge.
Barnes, T. G. (2011). 'Homeric ΑΝΔΡΟΤΗΤΑ ΚΑΙ ΗΒΗΝ', *JHS* 131: 1–13.
Bowra, C. M. (1930). *Tradition and Design in the Iliad*. Oxford.
Burgess, J. S. (2006). 'Neoanalysis, Orality, and Intertextuality: An Examination of Homeric Motif Transference', *Oral Tradition* 21: 148–89.
–. (2012). 'Intertextuality without Text in Early Greek Epic', in: Ø. Andersen and D.T.T. Haug (eds.), *Relative Chronology in Early Greek Epic Poetry*. Cambridge, 168–83.
Devereux, G. (1978–1979). 'Achilles' "Suicide" in the *Iliad*', *Helios* 6: 3–15.
Fränkel, H. (1921). *Die homerischen Gleichnisse*. Göttingen.
Janko, R. (1992). *The* Iliad: *A Commentary, vol. IV: Books 13–16*. Cambridge.
Kelly, A. (2007). *A Referential Commentary and Lexicon to Homer,* Iliad *VIII*. Oxford.
Kirk, G. S. (1990). *The* Iliad: *A Commentary, vol. I: Books 5–8*. Cambridge.
Leaf, W. (1900–1902). *The Iliad: Edited with Apparatus Criticus, Prolegomena, Notes, and Appendices*. London. Repr. Amsterdam 1971.
Lord, A. B. (1960). *The Singer of Tales*. Cambridge, MA.
Meltzer, G. S. (1990). 'The Role of Comic Perspectives in Shaping Homer's Tragic Vision', *CW* 83: 265–80.
Moulton, C. (1977). *Similes in the Homeric Poems*. Göttingen.
Parry, M. (1971). *The Making of Homeric Verse: The Collected Writings of Milman Parry*, ed. A. Parry. Oxford.
Reichel, M. (1994). *Fernbeziehungen in der Ilias*. Tübingen.
Schadewaldt, W. (1966³). *Iliasstudien*. Berlin.
Schein, S. (1984). *The Mortal Hero: An Introduction to Homer's* Iliad. Berkeley and Los Angeles.
–. (1997). 'The *Iliad:* Structure and Interpretation', in: I. Morris and B. Powell (eds.), *A New Companion to Homer*. Leiden, 345–59.
Scott, W. C. (1974). *The Oral Nature of the Homeric Simile*. Leiden.
–. (2009). *The Artistry of the Homeric Simile*. Hanover, NH.
Taplin, O. (1992). *Homeric Soundings: The Shaping of the* Iliad. Oxford.
Wüst, E. (1955). 'Hektor und Polydamas. Von Klerus und Staat in Griechenland', *RhM* 98: 335–49.

Ruth Scodel
Homeric fate, Homeric poetics

The *Iliad* employs two different systems to indicate that supernatural powers control the narrated events. On one side stands μοῖρα, 'fate', along with its synonyms or quasi-synonyms (αἶσα, πεπρωμένον), and on the other, the Διὸς Βουλή, the Plan or Will of Zeus as it operates within the narrative. Although these often function together, so that the audience of the poem hardly needs to distinguish them, this paper will suggest that the difference between them is metapoetically significant. Both fate and Zeus' Plan can work to signal this particular version's relation to tradition.[1] Metapoetically, fate-language indicates that some aspects of the story are fixed (even if not everything said to be fated really was included in a fixed canon of facts), while the Plan of Zeus marks the narrative trajectory of this particular song.[2] Yet Zeus does not entirely control events.[3] Indeed, Zeus' intentions are constantly in danger of being thwarted, either by opposition from other powers or through his own negligence. This suggests that the epic was not composed at a distance from the many contingencies of performance that were not only unscripted, but were open to interference. It perhaps reflects a compositional practice in which the poet-performer responded to the interventions of audience members.

Along with the language of fate—μοῖρα, αἶσα, πεπρωμένον—the *Iliad* speaks of the Will or Plan of Zeus, the Διὸς Βουλή, as a determinant of the course of the poem's story. The Plan of Zeus is announced in the proem:

> Μῆνιν ἄειδε θεὰ Πηληϊάδεω Ἀχιλῆος
> οὐλομένην, ἣ μυρί' Ἀχαιοῖς ἄλγε' ἔθηκε,
> πολλὰς δ' ἰφθίμους ψυχὰς Ἄϊδι προΐαψεν
> ἡρώων, αὐτοὺς δὲ ἑλώρια τεῦχε κύνεσσιν
> οἰωνοῖσί τε πᾶσι, Διὸς δ' ἐτελείετο βουλή
> ἐξ οὗ δὴ τὰ πρῶτα... (*Il.* 1.1–6)

Sing the rage, goddess, of Achilles son of Peleus, accursed, which laid innumerable sufferings on the Achaeans, and hurled to Hades many mighty spirits of heroes, but made themselves prey for dogs and all birds and the Plan of Zeus was accomplished, from when first...

---

1 Currie (2006) 34–6.
2 Murnaghan (1997); Fowler (2004).
3 The Zeus of this paper is not the supreme patriarch with whom we are familiar, as in Erbse (1986) 209–18.

Since antiquity scholars have debated exactly what this Plan of Zeus is.[4] Within the poem, Zeus plans how he will fulfill the request of Thetis, and this must be the primary reference of the proem.[5] The *Cypria*, however, apparently presented two Plans of Zeus. The first sought to alleviate the overburdened Earth by killing many at Troy, while the second simply offered a respite to the Trojans through Achilles' anger.[6] Kullmann in particular argues that Zeus' Plan in the *Iliad* reflects the theme of the overburdened Earth.[7] Indeed, a Plan of Zeus invoked at the very beginning of the poem can evoke not only the Plan Zeus forms within this poem, and his larger Plan for the Trojan War, but even his control of the cosmos as a whole.[8] Still, the proem emphasizes the events resulting from Achilles' anger. All these belonged within the control of Zeus, and so this poem must follow Zeus' Plan. In this chapter, 'Zeus' Plan' refers to the Plan for this poem (which begins with the promise to Thetis but is ultimately not entirely identical with it).

The Plan of Zeus for the plot of the poem, however, appears to be improvised, and can be temporarily circumvented by the improvisations of other gods. So there are at least three levels of narrative events: those that are fixed in the tradition; those that are part of the core plot of this song; and those that are retardations or deviations within that core plot. The narrative presents only the first as immutable. So the *Iliad* itself implies fluid narrative possibilities, a world in which almost anything can happen as long as the story ends as it must.

The resistance of the other gods to Zeus' Plan is more striking because it has no real parallel elsewhere in the Trojan or Theban epic traditions. In the *Odyssey*, Zeus goes behind Poseidon's back rather as other gods circumvent Zeus in the *Iliad*, but he also allows Poseidon to persecute Odysseus up to a point, and when Zeus and Poseidon meet, they negotiate without hostility. In the *Iliad*, Zeus himself, as David Elmer has shown, resembles Agamemnon in not seeking to establish a consensus before choosing a course of action.[9] As a result, the *Iliad* is distinguished by reiterated attempts to frustrate the Plan of Zeus that resemble either the early stages of Zeus' rule or the struggles between Zeus and Hera over

---

4 So Σ D *Il*. 1.5 (the Mythographus Homericus).
5 So Latacz (2000) on *Il*. 1.5 (p. 20); Kirk (1990) on *Il*. 1.5 (p. 53).
6 Currie (2015) 296–7.
7 Kullmann (1956) and (1960) 212–14, 225–6, 358–9. Cf. Murnaghan (1997) 23–7.
8 Allan (2008).
9 Elmer (2013) 146–73.

Heracles.[10] The *Iliad* alludes to such earlier struggles, but always in the vaguest of terms: at *Il.* 1.396–406, Achilles says that Athena, Hera, and Poseidon sought to bind Zeus, who was rescued by Thetis (but why did they seek to overthrow him?); Hephaestus tried to defend Hera and was thrown out of Olympus (*Il.* 1.590–3; again, why was he angry with her on that occasion?).[11] At *Il.* 14.242–62, Sleep is afraid to interfere with Zeus because he escaped the last time only by fleeing to Night, and in this passage we learn that it was about Heracles. All the stories of divine resistance look as if the details have been adapted to the *Iliad*'s context.[12] Neither in the *Iliad* nor in the Cycle do the gods who favor Troy resist the fundamental decision of Zeus to destroy it.

Insofar as the Plan of Zeus represents the plot of this poem, the epic presents its own narrative as the product both of an inherited and immutable tradition, and of an improvisation by Zeus that includes his responses to the improvised opposition of other gods. So the resistance of Athena, Hera, and Poseidon constitutes a delay within a delay. Furthermore, because Achilles' anger and Zeus' decision to support it defy the basic tendency of the broader story, the *Iliad*'s plot potentially threatens the entire sequence. The interventions of other gods threaten the Plan, but they also seem to force Zeus to work out how he can make Achilles' anger and the Achaeans' defeat serve the fated ends of Achilles' death and Troy's fall. Although Hera, Athena, and Poseidon work towards what is actually the fated outcome, the fall of Troy, once the Plan of Zeus has begun, Zeus cannot simply return the action to some simpler line of development. Instead, their opposition to the Plan forces Zeus not only to suppress their revolts in order to keep developments on track, but to work out his Plan so that the end will be traditionally correct.

Of course the *Iliad* is not improvised. Like Zeus' Plan, however, the epic needs to fit its plot into the wider story. If Achilles could be mollified with gifts, this would not be a serious problem. His anger would be an episode without further consequences. However, it seems to be a precondition of this plot that he, like Meleager, cannot be mollified, and Zeus knows it.

---

10 Yasamura (2011) is a general study of the theme of opposition to Zeus. Rousseau (2001, 145–9), argues that the detours of the story ultimately serve Zeus' plan, which is really manifest only in retrospect.
11 Most Homerists seem to accept the argument of Slatkin (1991) that this passage evokes the place of Thetis in the succession myth. But even if its components are older than the *Iliad*, details seem to be adapted for this context. Latacz (2000 on 590) points out that the text is not explicit that Hephaestus was defending Hera, but Aristarchus already connected these lines with *Il.* 15.18–24 (Σ *Il.* 1.591a, Σ *Il.* 15.18a). See Schironi (forthcoming).
12 Lang (1983) turns all these into a single more-or-less coherent narrative.

Whatever else fate, μοῖρα, is in the epic world, metapoetically it can represent fixed points in inherited tradition. Homerists who agree about little else agree that fate, for the poet, can represent what actually happened.[13] At *Il.* 2.155 the Achaeans would have gone home (without taking Troy) ὑπέρμορα. This would be truly impossible not only because the powers governing the world had ordained otherwise but because the real events were known and essential to the epic narrative. A number of counterfactual comments in the epics function this way.[14] Similarly, when Apollo warns Patroclus that neither Patroclus nor Achilles is fated to take Troy (*Il.* 16.707–9), he evokes a general knowledge of how Troy was taken. Such passages indicate that the audience assumed that some 'facts' were truly fixed.[15] The fates of individuals do not generally belong quite in this category—while each individual's death was presumably fated, only a few heroes had to die at a certain time, in certain circumstances that were essential for the whole story. Sometimes, though, a counterfactual approaches this fixity, for even if no word for 'fate' appears, when the audience hears that Menelaus would have killed Paris had not Aphrodite intervened (*Il.* 3.373–82), everyone must be reminded that the larger story means that Paris cannot die at this point. Some prophecies have a similar effect, as when Odysseus reminds the Achaean army of Calchas' interpretation of the omen at Aulis (*Il.* 2.299–330).

Still, claims (implicit or explicit) that an event is 'fated' may not always refer to universal 'facts' of Greek tradition. A poet could manipulate audience beliefs about fate for his own purposes. Since the *Iliad* notoriously refuses to allow heroes to be immortalized, μοῖρα marks the poem's particular view of the inescapability of the mortal condition.[16] When Achilles at *Il.* 18.119 attributes the death of Heracles to μοῖρα and Hera's anger, this 'fate' directly and polemically denies alternate versions.[17]

In many respects, there is no real difference between fate and Zeus' Plan. The epics often seem to use μοῖρα, Zeus, and the gods interchangeably. Achilles claims honor from the 'apportionment of Zeus', Διὸς αἴσηι (*Il.* 9.608). The narrator speaks of a fate that leads a particular individual to his death (*Il.* 4.517, 5.613, 13.602), but asks Patroclus whom he killed 'when the gods called you to death', ὅτε δή σε θεοὶ θάνατόνδε κάλεσσαν (*Il.* 16.693), although the gods have never discussed the death of Patroclus and it has been planned by Zeus alone. Although

---

[13] Janko (1992) 6; de Jong (2004) 263 n. 76; Fränkel (1965) 57–8; Redfield (1994) 133; Whitman (1958) 228.
[14] Lang (1989); Morrison (1992a); Nesselrath (1992) 5–38; Louden (1993); de Jong (2004) 68–81.
[15] Marks (2008) 6–7. This is often called by Kullmann's term, the *Faktenkanon*.
[16] Currie (2006) 32–5.
[17] Griffin (1980) 166.

Apollo is personally involved in Patroclus' death, Zeus has not directed him to attack Patroclus. Zeus is directly responsible for Patroclus' folly in forgetting the warning of Achilles:

> καὶ μέγ' ἀάσθη
> νήπιος· εἰ δὲ ἔπος Πηληϊάδαο φύλαξεν
> ἤ τ' ἂν ὑπέκφυγε κῆρα κακὴν μέλανος θανάτοιο.
> ἀλλ' αἰεί τε Διὸς κρείσσων νόος ἠέ περ ἀνδρῶν·
> ὅς τε καὶ ἄλκιμον ἄνδρα φοβεῖ καὶ ἀφείλετο νίκην
> ῥηϊδίως, ὅτε δ' αὐτὸς ἐποτρύνῃσι μάχεσθαι·
> ὅς οἱ καὶ τότε θυμὸν ἐνὶ στήθεσσιν ἀνῆκεν.   (*Il.* 16.685–90)

And he experienced great *atē*, the fool. If he had guarded the word of Peleus' son, he would truly have escaped the cruel doom of black death. But the mind of Zeus is always more powerful than the minds of men. He puts to flight the valiant man and easily takes away victory when he himself arouses a man to fight. He also then roused the spirit in his chest.

For good reasons, then, we cannot always make a sharp distinction between fate and Zeus' plan or between the actions of Zeus and those of the gods generally, even outside the cases of 'Jörgensen's Rule' that characters refer to Zeus or 'the gods' where the poet names a specific god. Each individual's fate, however, is apparently set at the moment of birth (*Il.* 16.441 and 22.179, πάλαι πεπρωμένον αἴσῃ, 'fated long ago by the allocation') and both poets and audience surely assumed that larger events that are fated have been determined long before they happen. An individual's fate may be partially open, as with Achilles' famous choice between glory at Troy and a long but inglorious life, or Euchenor's fate of an early death, whether at Troy or by disease at home, but even in these cases, fate is fixed once the character chooses a particular path. The hero's life can resemble a flow chart, where he can select which branch he will follow, but the endpoint of each is determined. Since mortals, unless given a prophecy, cannot recognize fate before it is fulfilled, and even gods, even Zeus, seem to know it only in part, fate does not diminish the importance of human motivation and decision.

Zeus' Plan for the *Iliad*, in contrast, is improvised: in response to Thetis' plea that he honor Achilles by granting the Trojans success, Zeus develops a plan that leads the Trojan story back to its appointed end in a way that nobody within the story would have predicted from the beginning. It was not fate, but the Will of Zeus that ensured that Achilles' anger led to the deaths of many heroes (even if the deaths of those heroes were individually fated). Zeus' will, then, marks the storyline of this poem, a storyline that cannot violate μοῖρα but is also surely not identical to it. While the poet implies that events said to be fated are both inevitable and known from past tradition, the Plan of Zeus is a narrative impulse that the poet himself controls. Zeus is responsible for the *atē* of Patroclus. His death within this narrative is his personal μοῖρα, but it is impossible to know whether it was a universal in the tradition. The Plan of Zeus, then, could mark what may be different from other versions.[18]

The Plan drives the plot of the epic as fate does not, although it is not really essential for a Wrath of Achilles. The anger of a hero was evidently a regular generator of epic narrative (and for this argument, it is not relevant whether individual references to a hero's anger point to a familiar story or a common motif).[19] The narrative of Phoenix about the anger of Meleager is the most important, because it demonstrates that a plot similar to the *Iliad*'s, in which an army loses because its outstanding fighter withdraws in anger, did not require divine intervention. The outcome of Achilles' anger is overdetermined: Zeus' Plan ensures that the outcome of Achilles' withdrawal is what we might expect it to be.[20] The plot seems to require it only for the deceptive dream that leads Agamemnon to initiate a full-scale attack at a time when it would be inherently less likely to succeed. At the same time, the proem attributes to Zeus the many Achaean deaths caused by the anger of Achilles, and it perhaps implies that Achilles' anger might have played out differently had Zeus been differently inclined.[21] The narrator thereby shifts to Zeus the blame for the unwelcome Achaean losses of his tale, as Telemachus blames Zeus for Phemius' sad song (*Od.* 1.347–9).

This is, however, an excessively rational approach, because a poem in which Achilles' withdrawal led directly to Trojan victory might not have pleased Greek audiences. The Plan of Zeus helps make it possible for the Trojans to succeed without any suggestion that the Greeks are inferior to them without Achilles. Even though the Trojans drive the Achaeans to their ships and set fire to one ship, named Trojan casualties, even in 13–16, are absurdly disproportionate, 119 Trojans or Trojan allies to 36 Achaeans.[22] Although both sides retreat when the other has a strong advantage, the Trojans are much more likely to flee. Only Trojans are taken prisoner or supplicate for mercy, and only Trojans are res-

---

18 So e.g. de Jong (2004, 263 n. 76) contrasts fate with the plot identified with the Διὸς Βουλή, 'which has presumably been invented by the poet'.
19 Patzer (1972) 46.
20 The famous discussions of 'double motivation' or 'overdetermination' by Dodds (1951, 1–18) and Lesky (1961) emphasize psychological interventions, but for this 'superfluous' intervention (Snell 1953, 30; Whitman 1958, 227–8).
21 Edwards (1987, 175) says that Zeus, not being responsible for the quarrel, is not responsible for its consequences, but surely through his Plan he is responsible.
22 These numbers and the points following are from Stoevesandt (2005) 337–40.

cued by gods. Sixteen Achaeans are compared in similes to ferocious animals, but only Hector, Sarpedon, and Aeneas on the other side. Only Achaeans have real *aristeiai*. To be sure, the general narrative technique of moving between 'long-shot' views, where the Achaeans can lose, and 'close-up',[23] where they typically win, contributes to this peculiar result, and so does the apparent bad luck of the wounding of the leaders in Book 11. Yet without the Plan, however, it would be very hard to contrive that the better army would be decisively defeated, and that better warriors could not lose their prestige in losing. Achilles does not really need Zeus' Plan, but the audience does.

The Plan has other important narrative functions. It is, perhaps most of all, a mechanism for generating conflict among gods. There is at least one salient difference between μοῖρα and Zeus' Plan—the other gods never resist or complain about fate, but they resent and oppose Zeus' Plan. Their opposition is obviously essential in delaying the Achaean defeat and making the poem as long as it is. Indeed, it is probably not accidental that the gods who most resent the Plan of Zeus, Hera, Athena, and Poseidon, even though they have personal motives for their resentment, all act at some point to maintain μοῖρα. Hera and Athena speak against Zeus' fantasies of rescuing Sarpedon and Hector, while Poseidon rescues Aeneas. Here, as elsewhere, it appears likely that the narrator is deliberately marking the limits of Zeus' control. Without the intervention of others, fate would be endangered.

While the *Iliad* may well reflect plans of Zeus broader then his agreement with Thetis, the poem's narrative implicitly denies that Zeus has any such plan. Zeus is conspicuously absent from the *Iliad* until Thetis supplicates him. His absence is a notorious problem, because when Achilles asks his mother to seek help from Zeus, she explains that Zeus went 'yesterday' to visit the Aethiopians *(Il.* 1.423–4), and the gods followed. If Zeus is inaccessible when he is among the Aethiopians, the other gods should be also, but Hera has suggested to Achilles that he call an assembly, Athena, prompted by Hera, has intervened to stop Achilles from killing Agamemnon, and Apollo responds to the intercession of Chryses. The contradiction is apparent. The delay between Achilles' request of his mother and her approach to Zeus allows the narrator to construct a thematically strong sequence by inserting the journey to placate Apollo between the meeting of Achilles and Thetis and the meeting of Thetis and Zeus (the Achaeans first escape the anger of Apollo, but then are victims of Zeus' en-

---

23 On this cinematic aspect of the epic, see de Jong and Nünlist (2004); Bonifazi (2007); Tsagalis (2012) 63, 78, 82.

dorsement of Achilles' anger).²⁴ Still, Zeus is gone for ten days, and the length of his absence seems to have no function unless it serves to balance the ten days of preparation for Hector's funeral at the end, a very remote echo for so long a text whose audience would receive it in performance. It makes more sense as an instance of the general rule of Homeric narrative that delay before an event signals the event's importance.²⁵ The visit to the Aethiopians, at the cost of some incoherence about the other Olympians, strongly marks that Zeus is not engaged with the quarrel between Achilles and Agamemnon.

The *Iliad* begins in a space in which other gods act freely, without direction from Zeus. This freedom, for example, implies that when Athena promises Achilles triple compensation at *Il.* 1.213–14, she is not speaking from genuine foreknowledge. While such an outcome is likely, the end of this quarrel has not yet been determined. Its beginning is, indeed, remarkably sensitive to particular conditions. When the army suffers Apollo's plague, Hera inspires Achilles to summon the assembly. Presumably she works through Achilles because Agamemnon would not be receptive to the suggestion, but it seems to be an obvious mistake—why would Hera not work by having Athena prompt Odysseus, for example, who would have acted more tactfully than Achilles does? There is little interpretive value, though, in attributing a misjudgment to the goddess.²⁶ There is, however, considerable point if the poet marks the absence of Zeus by signaling the activity of Hera in summoning the assembly, and the intervention of both Hera and Athena to prevent Achilles from killing Agamemnon. These are impromptu efforts to address immediate problems, not part of any long-term strategy. Zeus did not cause the situation that his Plan addresses.

When Thetis supplicates Zeus to help Achilles, he is initially silent. Thetis has a powerful argument, because she rescued him from a conspiracy by Poseidon, Hera, and Athena (although she tactfully refers to it only vaguely when she supplicates him). This narrative itself, especially the gods who seek to bind Zeus, appears to have been put together from traditional materials to fit precisely this context.²⁷ Finally, she urges him to say yes or no (applying some emotional blackmail):

ἢ ἀπόειπ', ἐπεὶ οὔ τοι ἔπι δέος, ὄφρ' ἐῢ εἰδέω
ὅσσον ἐγὼ μετὰ πᾶσιν ἀτιμοτάτη θεός εἰμι.   (*Il.* 1.515–16)

---

24 Scodel (2007).
25 Austin (1966).
26 Redfield (1994) 95.
27 Willcock (1994) 143–4.

Or say no, since you have nothing to fear, so that I may know well the extent to which I am the most dishonored divinity among them all.

When he finally answers, he says that he is not happy about her request, because it will lead to quarreling with Hera:

> τὴν δὲ μέγ' ὀχθήσας προσέφη νεφεληγερέτα Ζεύς
> 'ἦ δὴ λοίγια ἔργ' ὅ τέ μ' ἐχθοδοπῆσαι ἐφήσεις
> Ἥρηι ὅτ' ἄν μ' ἐρέθηισιν ὀνειδείοις ἐπέεσσιν·
> ἣ δὲ καὶ αὔτως μ' αἰεὶ ἐν ἀθανάτοισι θεοῖσι
> νεικεῖ, καί τέ μέ φησι μάχηι Τρώεσσιν ἀρήγειν'.   (*Il.* 1.517–20)

Greatly upset, cloud-gathering Zeus addressed her: 'Truly miserable will the events be, since you will drive me to enmity with Hera, when she provokes me with abusive words. As it is, she constantly quarrels with me before the immortal gods, and claims that I help the Trojans in battle'.

The narrator confirms that he is distressed, so there is no reason for the audience to think that Zeus is being disingenuous. Zeus, interestingly, does not say whether there is any truth in Hera's accusation that he helps the Trojans. While he at first suggests that Thetis leave furtively, a moment later he offers to nod in agreement:

> ἀλλὰ σὺ μὲν νῦν αὖτις ἀπόστιχε, μή τι νοήσηι
> Ἥρη· ἐμοὶ δέ κε ταῦτα μελήσεται ὄφρα τελέσσω·
> εἰ δ' ἄγε τοι κεφαλῆι κατανεύσομαι ὄφρα πεποίθηις·
> τοῦτο γὰρ ἐξ ἐμέθεν γε μετ' ἀθανάτοισι μέγιστον
> τέκμωρ· οὐ γὰρ ἐμὸν παλινάγρετον οὐδ' ἀπατηλόν
> οὐδ' ἀτελεύτητον ὅ τι κεν κεφαλῆι κατανεύσω.   (*Il.* 1.522–7)

But you for now go back again, so that Hera does not notice anything. I will concern myself with fulfilling all this. Or come—let me nod with my head, so you can be confident. For this is the greatest sign from me among the immortals. What I nod to is not revocable or deceitful or unaccomplished.

The nod shakes Olympus, so that it not only confirms that Zeus will do what he has promised—it is what economists call a 'commitment device'—but renders it impossible that Hera could fail to notice what has happened. So Zeus must have changed his mind, realizing that he could not fulfill the request of Thetis without Hera's knowledge anyway. Unless his reluctance has been entirely feigned, Zeus has not intended the temporary defeat of the Achaeans until Thetis asks him for it. Achilles' anger is an unexpected problem, and the solution that Zeus finds for it constitutes the plot of the *Iliad*.

The Plan of Zeus within the poem stands in distinct contrast with his implicit future Plan to destroy the favorite cities of Hera, because he negotiates it with Hera in advance (*Il.* 4.39–54). In the scene following his meeting with Thetis, he makes no effort to conciliate Hera. On the contrary, he gives the impression that he has decided to use this decision, which he knows Hera will dislike, as an opportunity to quarrel with her and display his power. He does not explain until *Il.* 15.69–71 that his Plan will ultimately lead to the fall of Troy, and Poseidon, who has not heard Zeus' prediction, at *Il.* 15.213–17 expresses his worry that Zeus may spare Troy. Although Menelaus and Agamemnon refer to the crime of Paris and to the Trojans' violation of their oath when they call on Zeus (*Il.* 3.351–4, 13.636–7; 4.163–8, 234–9), Zeus does not address the crimes of the Trojans.[28]

Perhaps Zeus is a remarkably incompetent manager, who does not even try to win his subordinates' support by explaining from the start that the temporary Achaean defeat will lead to Hector's death. He explains the Plan only at moments when he is enraged with Hera. The narrator thereby implies that Zeus would not have declared his intentions without this emotional stimulus, and raises the question of why he declares them in this way when he did not choose to explain them earlier. If he has already formulated the Plan, he must be concealing it only because he wants to annoy Hera, as an expression of his resentment of her attempts to control him, but when he is enraged he declares his intentions in order to insist that he will do as he chooses. But it is just as reasonable to infer that Zeus has not formulated his Plan until the moment he speaks it.

Zeus' Plan requires that Achilles reject the Embassy:

οὐ γὰρ πρὶν πολέμου ἀποπαύσεται ὄβριμος Ἕκτωρ
πρὶν ὄρθαι παρὰ ναῦφι ποδώκεα Πηλεΐωνα,
ἤματι τῶι ὅτ' ἂν οἱ μὲν ἐπὶ πρύμνηισι μάχωνται
στείνει ἐν αἰνοτάτωι περὶ Πατρόκλοιο θανόντος·
ὣς γὰρ θέσφατόν ἐστι· σέθεν δ' ἐγὼ οὐκ ἀλεγίζω,
χωομένης... (*Il.* 8.473–8)

> For mighty Hector will not stop from war until he rouses the swift-footed son of Peleus by the ships, on the day when they fight by the sterns, in the most dreadful strait over dead Patroclus. For it is so decreed. I do not care about you in your anger...

This prediction is misleading, giving the impression that Patroclus will die near the ships and that Hector will directly 'rouse' Achilles. ἤματι τῶι also sounds as

---

28 See van Erp Taalman Kip (2000).

if it refers to a relatively remote future rather than 'tomorrow'. Scholars since Aristarchus have often thought that the prophecy is inaccurate, but however we evaluate its accuracy, for the audience it is a misdirection.[29] When Achilles at *Il.* 18.203–21 appears by the ditch, the corpse has been brought back near the ships, though not apparently right against them (the battle is past the wall and ditch). This summary implies a simpler series of events, in which Patroclus is killed soon after he goes out to rescue the Achaeans and Achilles immediately intervenes. There is no indication that Zeus intervenes to ensure that Achilles will reject Agamemnon's offer, or that he will feel compassionate enough towards his comrades to let Patroclus rescue the ships while refusing to fight himself. Perhaps the narrative implies that Zeus does not intervene because intervention is unnecessary. Zeus knows roughly what will happen. His scornful claim not to care about Hera's resentment, though, shows that he underestimates her resistance.

Zeus calls this series of events θέσφατον. That does not mean that it is 'fated'.[30] It is divinely determined because Zeus has declared it to be so. The inaccuracy can be explained, if we choose, entirely by the *Ungenauigkeitsprinzip*, the rule that predictions are never too precise.[31] It is surely because of the *Ungenauigkeitsprinzip* that Zeus says only that Hector will rouse Achilles when Patroclus dies, failing to explain the actual causal chain of events, or to state either that Hector will slay Patroclus or that Achilles will then kill Hector. But it is also possible that, even if the poet has planned the Embassy and Achilles' responses, the suggestion of Nestor that Patroclus wear Achilles' armor, and Patroclus' failure to remember that Achilles warned him not to attack Troy, Zeus has not planned all these events in their detail, at least not yet. Zeus either does not control the action meticulously, and he must react to the unexpected, or he prefers to exert only limited control. Just as his Plan can be delayed by the intervention of other gods, and is therefore not a complete blueprint of the action, so it develops as the narrative develops. Fate may constrain what Zeus can determine, and Zeus constrains what the poet or his characters can determine, but there is much that is not constrained.

When he speaks angrily to Hera again, after the *Dios Apatē*, there can be no question that his prediction is inaccurate.

---

29 Σ (A) *Il.* 8.475–6; Van der Valk (1963–1964) 2.417 (poet wants to stress how critical the Greek situation will be); Diller (1965) 142 (rejecting the entire episode); Reinhardt (1960) 167–8. Its accuracy is defended by Kelly (2007) 64 n. 308. For misdirection here and in 15, see Morrison (1992b) 80–3.
30 Despite the definition in *LfgrE* (Nordheider). See Kirk (1990) ad loc.
31 Schadewaldt (1966³) 110, 140.

> αὐτὰρ Ἀχαιοὺς
> αὖτις ἀποστρέψῃσιν ἀνάλκιδα φύζαν ἐνόρσας,
> φεύγοντες δ' ἐν νηυσὶ πολυκλήϊσι πέσωσι
> Πηλεΐδεω Ἀχιλῆος· ὃ δ' ἀνστήσει ὃν ἑταῖρον
> Πάτροκλον· τὸν δὲ κτενεῖ ἔγχεϊ φαίδιμος Ἕκτωρ
> Ἰλίου προπάροιθε πολέας ὀλέσαντ' αἰζηοὺς
> τοὺς ἄλλους, μετὰ δ' υἱὸν ἐμὸν Σαρπηδόνα δῖον.
> τοῦ δὲ χολωσάμενος κτενεῖ Ἕκτορα δῖος Ἀχιλλεύς.
> ἐκ τοῦ δ' ἄν τοι ἔπειτα παλίωξιν παρὰ νηῶν
> αἰὲν ἐγὼ τεύχοιμι διαμπερὲς εἰς ὅ κ' Ἀχαιοὶ
> Ἴλιον αἰπὺ ἕλοιεν Ἀθηναίης διὰ βουλάς. (*Il.* 15.62–71) [32]

But he will turn back the Achaeans, rousing cowardly panic, and fleeing they will fall upon the many-benched ships of Achilles son of Peleus. He will rouse his companion Patroclus. Brilliant Hector will kill him with the spear in front of Troy when he has destroyed many young men, others, but among them my own son, godlike Sarpedon. In anger over him godlike Achilles will kill Hector. From that point, I will then bring out a continual counterattack from the ships, until the Achaeans take steep Troy through the counsels of Athena.

The Achaeans do not fall onto Achilles' ships, and Achilles does not initially rouse Patroclus, although he eventually urges him on. Although the "counsels of Athena" doubtless alludes to the Wooden Horse, anyone who did not know how Troy ultimately fell would interpret Zeus' prophecy as predicting a straightforward military defeat.

The request of Thetis requires that Zeus give victory to the Trojans so that Agamemnon will realize that he needs Achilles. It does not require the death of Patroclus, which Thetis, despite her prophetic knowledge, does not anticipate or even know about until Achilles is in mourning. It does not require the death of Sarpedon. Indeed, nothing in the plot requires the death of Sarpedon. Although other rescued Trojans are taken to the city or to the rear of battle, when Zeus considers rescuing his son, he wants to set him down in far-off Lycia (*Il.* 16.433–8). That would remove him from the war almost as effectively as his death does. Sarpedon apparently must be killed by Patroclus so that Patroclus will have a true *aristeia*, which requires that he kill an important hero. Patroclus could require a true *aristeia* for various reasons. From Zeus' point of view, Patroclus' success may placate the gods who have been angry about the Trojan victory. From the poet's, it may satisfy audiences who similarly want Achaean triumph. The *aristeia* also increases the pathos of Patroclus' death. Finally, Patroclus has assumed

---

[32] Aristophanes and Aristarchus athetized 56–77, and Zenodotus' text did not include 64–77; see Janko (1992) on 56–77, Schironi (forthcoming).

the armor and a part of the heroic nature of Achilles. His *aristeia* and death imitate those of Achilles.³³

The death of Sarpedon is explicitly part of the Plan of Zeus as he has announced—not necessarily part of fixed tradition, but essential to this version. While interpreters have discussed how he considers interfering with fate, they have given less attention to how Zeus' fantasies of rescuing both Sarpedon and Hector require that he overturn his own Plan.³⁴ Here the poet-narrator may be particularly close to Zeus. Like Zeus, he feels pity for his own characters. He may wish that the story were different. However, not only the existing poetic traditions, but his own narrative scheme may requires him to kill characters that his sympathies would urge him to spare.

But there are other actions that take place within the Plan but are explicitly not part of it at all and are not prompted by Zeus. The narrator emphasizes that Patroclus' body would not have been recovered had not Iris roused Achilles:

οὐδέ κε Πάτροκλόν περ ἐϋκνήμιδες Ἀχαιοὶ
ἐκ βελέων ἐρύσαντο νέκυν θεράποντ' Ἀχιλῆος   (*Il.* 18.151–2)
...
καί νύ κεν εἴρυσσέν τε καὶ ἄσπετον ἤρατο κῦδος,
εἰ μὴ Πηλεΐωνι ποδήνεμος ὠκέα Ἶρις
ἄγγελος ἦλθε θέουσ' ἀπ' Ὀλύμπου θωρήσσεσθαι
κρύβδα Διὸς ἄλλων τε θεῶν. πρὸ γὰρ ἧκέ μιν Ἥρη.   (*Il.* 18.165–8)

Nor would the Achaeans with the fine shin-armor have dragged out from under the spears the corpse, the companion of Achilles
...
And he would have dragged him and won unquenchable splendor, if windfooted quick Iris had not come running from Olympus as a messenger to the son of Peleus, for him to put on armor, secretly from Zeus and the other gods. For Hera sent her.

Iris even tells Achilles that Hera has sent her without the knowledge of Zeus or the other gods (*Il.* 18.185–6), although when Achilles actually appears Athena protects him with the aegis, makes him gleam with fire, and joins his shout. This secrecy is mysterious. To be sure, Zeus has not formally given the other gods permission to intervene, but he showed concern to save Patroclus' body

---

33 This is a central proposal of Neoanalysis: Pestalozzi (1946) 26, 32, 42; 16, Kakridis (1949) 65–75; Schadewaldt (1965) 166. See Burgess (2006) 160–1. It is also found outside Neoanalytic scholarship, e.g. Whitman (1958) 200–3, and it also dovetails with the argument that Patroclus is a ritual substitute for Achilles, Nagy (1999) 292–3. Kelly (2012) argues that no motif transference is required to understand Thetis' mourning for Patroclus.
34 On fate, see Erbse (1986) 273–93; Jones (1996) 114–16; Haubold and Graziosi (2005) 91.

from mutilation at *Il.* 17.270 – 3. Iris has been consistently loyal to Zeus, and she would hardly participate in a scheme that violated his intentions. For Hector to take Achilles' armor from the dead Patroclus but not to get the corpse should fit both Zeus' Plan and the poet's. Zeus, however, although he should want the body saved, does not act. At *Il.* 18.356 – 67, Zeus congratulates Hera on rousing Achilles, with sarcastic comment on her affection for the Achaeans and she takes credit. It is as if Zeus disavows crucial elements of his own plan.

Zeus' failure to mind his own affairs is truly remarkable. At the opening of *Iliad* 13 he looks away from the battlefield, believing that no other god will interfere:

ἐς Τροίην δ' οὐ πάμπαν ἔτι τρέπεν ὄσσε φαεινώ·
οὐ γὰρ ὅ γ' ἀθανάτων τινα ἔλπετο ὃν κατὰ θυμὸν
ἐλθόντ' ἢ Τρώεσσιν ἀρηξέμεν ἢ Δαναοῖσιν. (*Il.* 13.7– 9)

He did not turn his bright eyes to Troy at all, since he did not expect in his mind that any of the immortals would come and help either Trojans or Danaans.

He is wrong, of course—Poseidon notices that Zeus is not paying attention and immediately prepares to intervene. In this instance, Poseidon opposes Zeus, but in the rescue of Aeneas, he acts precisely so that Zeus will not be angered (μή πως καὶ Κρονίδης κεχολώσεται, *Il.* 20.301). Poseidon's intervention has concerned critics, since he is hostile to the Trojans, and indeed the narrator strongly marks the peculiarity of his intervention. Scholars, though, have tended to ask why Apollo, who prompted Aeneas to confront Achilles, does not save him, but it is just as surprising that the poet has Poseidon say that Zeus cares about Aeneas although Zeus shows no evidence of caring.[35] Zeus, that is, seems very peculiarly detached from his own concerns. In order to ensure that Achilles will not sack Troy contrary to fate (and in this context fate is surely the established tradition), he gives all the gods permission to intervene in battle (*Il.* 20.20 – 30), while remaining aloof himself, until he authorizes Athena to assist Achilles in killing Hector (*Il.* 22.185)—that is, until a core element of his Plan is again at issue.

The *Iliad*-poet repeatedly stresses contingency. Zeus does not seem to have a real plan for how he will move events back to the proper course, the plan he announces does not move smoothly, and important events seem to be out of his control. That does not, of course, suggest that the poet had no plan. If the poet identifies with Zeus, there is an element of self-mockery in this identifica-

---

35 Scheibner (1939) 6. It is possible that it reflects a cult of Poseidon among Aeneidae; see Nagy (1999) 268 – 9.

tion. Zeus may be almost a parody of the poet in performance, struggling to return his narrative to the right path. The poet-narrator may even be displaying his own superiority to Zeus, for Zeus may fail to ensure that the events of the Trojan War do not progress correctly, but the narrator, calling on the other gods, brings everything to its proper outcome. This evident distance between Zeus and the poet-narrator means that one is not a simple model for the other. At the same time, Zeus' repeated frustration with the other gods' resistance to his plan again makes Zeus a possibly comic foil for the poet. The rebellious gods want a different version of the story that reaches the conclusion more directly. Ironically, though, they only render the version of Zeus even more indirect and entangled, but it finally prevails. Zeus successfully improvises. This aspect of the epic's metapoetics, with its focus on the single organizer at the center, suggests a composer who must accommodate outside pressures.

Within the Homeric poems, intervention in an ongoing song takes the form of interruption: the arrival of the Embassy ends Achilles' song (*Il.* 9.189–95), and Alcinous stops Demodocus from starting a new song (*Od.* 8.37–103) and interrupts an ongoing song (*Od.* 8.533–43). Demodocus, being blind, cannot observe his audience as other singers might. Audience members may request a particular theme, as Odysseus challenges Demodocus to sing the Wooden Horse (*Od.* 8.486–98), or request a complete change of theme, as Penelope asks Phemius not to perform the return of the Achaeans (*Od.* 1.337–44). However, in a performance that is bard-like, Alcinous asks Odysseus not just to continue his story, but also to narrate meetings with his Trojan comrades (*Od.* 11.370–6). While the external narrator needs Agamemnon's tale for thematic reasons, the narrative sequence implies that Odysseus would not have included this material if it had not been requested.

As Parry pointed out, 'the poet is at the convenience of his hearers'.[36] Although Homer depicts audiences as enraptured, he is surely idealizing, and audiences in Homer exert considerable control despite their enchantment. We simply do not know the norms that governed early Greek epic performance, which probably differed depending on the performance situation. Audience intervention is always a possibility in face-to-face narration, since audience members may show their pleasure of displeasure even by their posture or facial expression.[37] A. B. Lord stressed how audience response determined in particular the

---

[36] Parry (1971) 441 (this chapter is a selection from a longer, unfinished work of 1933–1935). Jensen (2011, 88–91) discusses audience engagement in various traditions.
[37] Ryan (2004) 41.

length of performances in the South Slavic tradition.³⁸ In the Arabic Bani Hilal, audience members may request particular episodes or complain of details that they believe a performer has gotten wrong, and after a break, a performer may adapt his performance to what he has heard from the audience.³⁹

If the difficulties Zeus must confront in fulfilling his Plan and then bringing the plot back to its necessary and traditional end echo those of poet/performer, the metapoetic level implies a single composer in constant negotiation with both the tradition and present audiences and patrons. It does not resemble a process of gradual convergence on an authorized version.⁴⁰ The other gods represent all the pressures and demands on the poet. His audience has preferences, and he cannot entirely ignore them. His tradition offers varied and variant stories, and some, at least, must be accommodated even if they present problems for his plot. Of course, the figure of Zeus as a reflection of the compositional process is only partial at best—the poet cannot gaze on faraway places and allow his plot to take care of itself (*Il.* 13.1–9). The problems of Zeus could hardly stand for the problems faced by the composer of this very unusual performance text. It is unlikely that any audience member rescued the *Iliad*-poet from his own forgetfulness about the narrative. Rather, Zeus' Plan represents the regular difficulties of the practicing performer, transferred to the divine plane and spread over the extraordinarily long text.

The real point of this metapoetic level, however, is its poetic effect. By giving Zeus all the difficulties in creating a story that will satisfy all constituencies, the poem offers a picture of a supreme god who cannot manage every thread of his story himself. The result is both funny and telling. A supreme god who is tempted to interfere in ways that would ruin his own scheme generates both pathos and amusement. Both Plan and plot remain, just barely, under control.

Works cited

Allan, W. (2008). 'Performing the Will of Zeus: the Διὸς Βουλή and the Scope of Early Greek Epic', in: M. M. Revermann and P. Wilson, (eds). *Performance, Iconography, Reception: Studies in Honour of Oliver Taplin*. Oxford, 204–16.
Austin, N. (1966). 'The Function of Digressions in the *Iliad*', *GRBS* 7.4: 295–311.

---

38 Lord (1960) 16–17.
39 Reynolds (1999) 164–6; Slyomovics (1987) 73.
40 So I agree with our *laudandus*, Rengakos (2011) 167.

Bonifazi, A. (2007). 'Memory and Visualization in Homeric Discourse Markers', in: E. A. Mackay (ed.), *Orality, Literacy, Memory In the Ancient Greek And Roman World* Boston, 35–64.

Burgess, J. (2006). 'Neoanalysis, Orality, and Intertextuality: an Examination of Homeric Motif Transference', *Oral Tradition* 21: 143–89.

Currie, B. (2006). 'Homer and the Early Epic Tradition', in: M. Clarke, *Epic Interactions: Perspectives On Homer, Virgil, and the Epic Tradition: Presented to Jasper Griffin by Former Pupils*. Oxford, 1–45.

–. (2015). 'Cypria', in: M. Fantuzzi and C. Tsagalis (eds.), *The Greek Epic Cycle and Its Ancient Reception: A Companion*. Cambridge, 281–305.

de Jong, I. J. F. (2004²). *Narrators and Focalizers: The Presentation of the Story in the Iliad*. Bristol.

de Jong, I. J. F. and Nünlist, R. (2004). 'From Bird's-eye View to Close-Up: the Standpoint of the Narrator in the Homeric Epics', in: A. Bierl, A. Schmitt, and A. Willi (eds.), *Antike Literatur in neuer Deutung*. Munich, 63–84.

Diller, H. (1965). 'Hera und Athena im achten Buch der *Ilias*', *Hermes* 93: 137–47.

Dodds, E. R. (1951). *The Greeks and the Irrational*. Berkeley and Los Angeles.

Edwards, M. (1987). *Homer, Poet of the Iliad*. Baltimore.

Elmer, D. F. (2013). *The poetics of consent: collective decision making and the Iliad*. Baltimore.

Erbse, H. (1986). *Untersuchungen zur Funktion der Götter im homerischen Epos*. Berlin.

Fowler, R. F. (2004). 'The Homeric Question', in: R. F. Fowler (ed.), *The Cambridge Companion to Homer*. Cambridge, 220–32.

Fränkel, H. (1975). *Early Greek poetry and philosophy: a history of Greek epic, lyric, and prose to the middle of the fifth century*. Trans. M. Hadas and J. Willis. New York.

Gaisser, J. H. (1979). 'A Structural Analysis of the Digressions in the *Iliad* and the *Odyssey*', *HSCP* 73: 1–43.

Griffin, J. (1980). *Homer on Life and Death*. Oxford.

Haubold, J. and Graziosi, B. (2005). *Homer: the Resonance of Epic*. London.

Janko, R. (1992). *The Iliad: A Commentary, vol. IV: books 13–16*. Cambridge.

Jensen, M. (2011). *Writing Homer: A Study Based on Results from Modern Fieldwork*. Copenhagen.

Jones, P. V. (1996). 'The independant heroes of the *Iliad*', *JHS* 116: 108–18.

Jörgensen, O. (1904). 'Das Auftreten der Götter in den Büchern ι-μ der *Odyssee*', *Hermes* 39: 357–82.

Kakridis, J. (1949). *Homeric Researches*. Lund.

Kelly, A. (2007). *A referential commentary and lexicon to Iliad VIII*. Oxford.

–. (2012). 'The Mourning of Thetis: "Allusion" and the Future in the *Iliad*', in: F. Montanari, A. Rengakos, and C. Tsagalis (eds.), *Homeric Contexts: Neoanalysis and the Interpretation of Oral Poetry*. Berlin.

Kirk, G. S. (1990). *The Iliad: A Commentary, vol. II: books 5–9*. Cambridge.

Kullmann, W. (1956). 'Zur Διὸς βουλή des Iliasproömiums', *Philologus* 100: 132–9.

–. (1960). *Die Quellen der Ilias. Troischer Sagenkreis*. Wiesbaden.

–. (1984). 'Oral Poetry Theory and Neoanalysis in Homeric Research', *GRBS* 25: 307–23.

–. (1985). 'Men and Gods in the *Iliad* and the *Odyssey*', *HSCP* 89: 1–23.

Lang M. L. (1983). 'Reverberation and Mythology in the *Iliad*', in: C. Robino and C. Shelmerdine (eds.), *Approaches to Homer*. Austin, 140–64.
–. (1989). 'Unreal Conditions in Homeric Narrative', *GRBS* 30: 5–26.
Latacz, J. (2000). *Homers Ilias: Gesamtkommentar (Basler Kommentar/BK)*. 1.2. Munich.
Lesky, A. (1961). *Göttliche und menschliche Motivation im homerischen Epos*. Heidelberg:.
Lord, A. B. (1960). *The Singer of Tales*. Cambridge.
Louden, B. (1993). 'Pivotal Counterfactuals', *CIA* 12: 181–98.
Marks. J. (2008). *Zeus in the* Odyssey. Washington, DC.
Morrison, J. (1992a). 'Alternatives to the Epic Tradition: Homer's Challenges in the *Iliad*', *TAPA* 122: 61–71.
–. (1992b). *Homeric Misdirection. False Predictions in the* Iliad. Ann Arbor.
Murnaghan, S. (1997). 'Equal Honor and Future Glory: The Plan of Zeus in the *Iliad*', in: D. H. Roberts, F. Dunn, and D. Fowler (eds.), *Classical Closure: Reading the End In Greek and Latin Literature*. Princeton, 23–42.
Nagy, G. (1999). *The Best of the Achaeans: Concepts of the Hero In Archaic Greek Poetry*. Rev. ed. Baltimore:.
Nesselrath, H.-G. (1992). *Ungeschehenes Geschehen: Beinahe-Episoden im griechischen und römischen Epos von Homer bis zur Spätantike*. Stuttgart.
Parry, M. (1971). *The Making of Homeric Verse. The Collected Papers of Milman Parry*. Ed. Adam Parry. Oxford.
Patzer, H. (1972). *Dichterische Kunst und poetisches Handwerk im homerischen Epos*. Wiesbaden.
Pestalozzi, H. (1945). *Die Achilleis als Quelle der* Ilias. Erlenbach-Zürich.
Redfield, J. (1994²). *Nature and Culture in the* Iliad. Durham, NC.
Reinhardt, C. (1938). 'Das Parisurteil', in: *Tradition und Geist: Gesammelte Essays zur Dichtung*. Göttingen, 16–36 (originally published as *Das Parisurteil*. Frankfurt. In English, 'The Judgement of Paris', in: G. M Wright, P. V. Jones (eds.), *Homer: German Scholarship in Translation*. Oxford, 170–91.
Rengakos, A. (2011). 'Die Überlieferungsgeschichte der homerischen Epen', in: A. Rengakos and B. Zimmermann (eds.), *Homer Handbuch. Leben-Werk-Wirkung*. Stuttgart, 167–75.
Reynolds, D. (1999). 'Problematic Performances, Overlapping Genres, and Levels of Participation in Arabic Oral Epic-Singing', in: M. Beissinger, J. Tylus, S. L. Wofford (eds.), *Epic Traditions in the Contemporary World: The Poetics of Community*. Berkeley, 155–68.
Ryan, M.-L. (2004). *Narrative Across Media: the Languages of Storytelling*. Lincoln.
Rousseau, P. (2001). 'L'intrigue de Zeus', *Europe: revue littéraire mensuelle* 79, n° 865: 120–58.
Scodel, R. (2007). 'The Gods' Visit to the Ethiopians in *Ilias* 1', *HSCP* 103: 83–98.
Schadewaldt, W. (1965⁴). *Von Homers Welt und Werk*. Stuttgart.
Schadewaldt, W. (1966³). *Iliasstudien*. Darmstadt.
Scheibner, G. (1939). *Der Aufbau des 20. und 21. Buches der Ilias*. Borna and Leipzig.
Schironi, F. (2018). *The Best of the Grammarians: Aristarchus of Samothrace on the* Iliad. Ann Arbor.
Slatkin, L. (1991). *The Power of Thetis. Allusion and Interpretation in the* Iliad. Berkeley and Los Angeles.
Slyomovics, S. (1987). *The Merchant of Art: An Egyptian Hilali Oral Epic Poet in Performance*. Berkeley.

Snell, B. (1953). *The Discovery of the Mind: the Greek Origins of European Thought*. Translated by T. G. Rosenmeyer. Oxford: (originally published 1955, *Die Entdeckung des Geistes*. Hamburg).
Stoevesandt, M. (2004). *Feinde – Gegner – Opfer: zur Darstellung der Troianer in den Kampfszenen der Ilias*. Basel.
Tsagalis, C. (2012). *From Listeners to Viewers: Space in the* Iliad. Washington, DC.
Van der Valk, M. (1963–1964). *Researches on the Text and Scholia of the* Iliad. Leiden.
Van Erp Taalman Kip, A. M. (2000). 'The Gods of the *Iliad* and the Fate of Troy', *Mnemosyne* 53.4: 385–402.
Whitman, C. H. (1958). *Homer And the Heroic Tradition*. Cambridge.
Willcock M. M. (1964). 'Mythological Paradeigma in the *Iliad*', *CQ* 14: 141–54.
Yasumura, N. (2011). *Challenges to the power of Zeus in early Greek poetry*. London.

J. S. Burgess
The *Apologos* of Odysseus: Tradition and conspiracy theories

My argument is that the Homeric story of Odysseus' wanderings at sea, the *apologos* of Odysseus, is traditional.¹ The *Odyssey*'s account would naturally vary in scale, arrangement, and complexity from preceding and/or contemporaneous versions. But we should assume what ancient audiences would expect, that the basic material in the Homeric wanderings is traditional. Homerists have resisted this view. There are multiple theories that claim radical Homeric invention for the *apologos*, whether by plagiarism (e.g., of Argonautic myth), inversion (fantastic for real-world travel), or collection (of folktales or sailors' yarns). The poetics of the *apologos* may be distinctive, but it is hard to believe that it filled an empty slot with random material. I would side with Italo Calvino's judgment that the journey of Odysseus was 'the most archaic stratum' of the epic.²

But how to conceive of the traditional, pre-Homeric wanderings of Odysseus? For cyclic myth, my method has been to augment meager evidence about the Epic Cycle with cyclic material in ancient literature and art.³ The results suggest that cyclic traditions preceded the Homeric poems and remained popular even after the *Iliad* and *Odyssey* became influential.⁴ The Homeric epics themselves refer to cyclic myth outside of their narrative boundaries, which is best taken as acknowledgement of pre-existing traditions, not idle invention.⁵ The *Odyssey* contains much cyclic material, notably songs of the Trojan War by Demodocus (8.73–82, 499–520; cf. the Cyclic *Little Iliad* and *Iliou Persis*), the *nostos* of the Achaeans sung by Phemius (1.325–7), and the *nostoi* narrated by Nestor and Menelaus in Books 3 and 4 (cf. the Cyclic *Nostoi*).⁶ Odysseus' retrospective account of his *nostos* in Books 9–12 also falls outside the boundaries of direct narrative in the *Odyssey* and should similarly be regarded as traditional, pre-Homeric material—i.e., cyclic.

---

1 By *apologos* I refer to Odysseus' account of his experiences at sea in Books 9–12; by "wanderings" I refer to a non-Homeric tradition of the same journey.
2 Calvino (1986) 57–8 (n. 57), disputing under-valuation of the wanderings in Heubeck (1988–1992).
3 By "Cyclic", I refer to the specific epics eventually collected into the Epic Cycle; uncapitalized "cyclic" refers to mythical tradition of their narratives, preceding and subsequent.
4 Burgess (2001), (2016a).
5 See especially Kullmann (1960). Implicit "mirroring" of cyclic material: Burgess (2009).
6 Burgess (2001) 142–3: the *Nostoi* may have included Odysseus' return.

https://doi.org/9783110559873-007

The earliest iconography relevant to the wanderings of Odysseus, from the first half of the seventh century, represents the blinding of the Cyclops.[7] Our most natural reaction, given our familiarity with the *Odyssey* and awareness of its great influence down through time, is that the painters have been inspired by the Homeric poem. It would then seem to follow that the *Odyssey* and therefore a preceding *Iliad* not only existed by the seventh century but also were already famous.[8] But I have argued, after surveying relevant literary and iconographic material, that the Homeric poems were not widely influential before the late seventh or early sixth centuries.[9] I consider the early images a reflection of traditional myth about Odysseus, not Book 9 of the *Odyssey* specifically. Representations of Polyphemus and escape from his cave are isolated until the end of the seventh century, when other "Odyssean" figures begin to appear. That these images also concern the journey of Odysseus suggests that its tradition was celebrated before the *Odyssey* itself became well known.[10]

For the early Cyclops iconography, I was happy to cite often and approvingly Anthony Snodgrass' *Homer and the Artists*.[11] Our approach is open to criticism, of course.[12] A rigid distinction between Homeric and non-Homeric imagery dis-

---

[7] Surveys of Odysseus imagery: Touchefeu-Meynier (1968), (1992a); Brommer (1983). Cyclops iconography: Touchefeu-Meynier (1992b), (1997).
[8] Reference to "Nestor's cup" on an inscription in a late eighth-century Ischian vessel has inspired similarly large claims based on little evidence: Burgess (2001) 114, with extensive bibliography at 233 n. 236. In Homeric studies it is generally agreed that the inscription does not allude to the *Iliad* specifically.
[9] Burgess (2001) 47–131 (early Cyclops iconography at 94–115). Cf. Lowenstam (2008) 13: 'The romantic interpretation... is to regard these painters, spread around the Mediterranean, as heralding the birth of Homer's *Odyssey*, but in fact neither do these four images nor do those that follow during the next hundred and fifty years reveal any particular knowledge of that poem'. See also Gonzalez (2013), section I.2; my position is more moderate.
[10] Images of Circe, the Sirens, and Scylla: cf. Snodgrass (1998) 58–61; Small (2001) 28–9; Dougherty (2001) 40–1; Lowenstam (2008) 43–51, 136–9; Giuliani (2013) 156–71.
[11] Snodgrass (1998) 89–100 (for Cyclops imagery). I first presented on Homer and art in 1995, and then again at a conference in Leeds in 1996, where Anthony Snodgrass graciously provided support in the question period and in private; we were independently inspired by R. Cook (1983). For the independence of iconographical and literary traditions, see also Small (2001) 21–31 (on methodology); Lowenstam (2008) 1–12 (on methodology); 13–17 (on the early Cyclops images); Gonzalez (2013), section I.2.
[12] Giuliani (2013) 70–88 makes an elegant case for Homeric inspiration of the early Cyclops iconography (methodology: 243–53, notably on "oraliture", aural reception of performed texts). Squire (2009, 124–6) critiques Snodgrass' approach (see also 300–56 for a masterful study of Polyphemus and Galatea imagery in later art). Grethlein (2015, 203–4) critiques my arguments (in an interesting study of sensory perception in the *apologos* and early iconography) and cautiously sides with 'the majority of earlier scholarship, and, more recently, Giuliani and

counts the necessities of different media.¹³ And some insist that drinking vessels in the blinding images must allude to the strong Maronian wine that Odysseus offers Polyphemus in *Odyssey* Book 9. But the most authoritative commentary on the *Odyssey* judges the wine's function in Book 9 so opaque as to be a vestige of pre-Homeric versions.¹⁴ Odysseus claims he brought some wine with him because of an intuition that he would come across a strong and unjust man (213–15). This may imply that that the wine will serve as a weapon, as Polyphemus after the fact concludes (454, 516). Yet the sleep of Polyphemus suffices for the blinding.¹⁵ Some conclude that inebriation is actually intended to facilitate the name-trick, as Odysseus himself implies (362–7).¹⁶ What the hero tells Polyphemus is that he brought the wine as a libation (349), which must be devious flattery. The Cyclops seems to regard it as a gift, for which he deviously promises an exchange (355–6).¹⁷ No single or obvious function seems to be articulated for the wine in *Odyssey* Book 9.

Does this conclusion imply that Homer was a shoddy composer? Hard Parryists of yore were wont to emphasize mistakes in Homeric poetry as proof of oral composition. Denys Page, joining oralist to analytical methodology, was particularly negative when searching for mishaps in the Polyphemus episode.¹⁸ In my view Homeric poetry is both oral and wonderfully sophisticated; polysemy is valued over sequence of action. Our early vase painters seem to signal wine (synchronically represented) as central to the blinding of Polyphemus. Since Book 9 of the *Odyssey* does not, it seems that the artists are influenced by a non-Homeric narrative. That should not be surprising; in the performance culture of the early Archaic Age, even a great epic like the *Odyssey* would not have extensive impact immediately. Of course, uncertainty about the origins of the Homeric poems—not least, their date, publication, and preservation—allows for multiple hypotheses. Worthy of consideration is the supposition that the Polyphemus episode was independently performed,¹⁹ or that "oraliture" reception

---

Squire' (204). At Burgess (2001, 56–7) I critiqued, rather too brusquely the method of Karl Schefold, Giuliani's teacher.
13 Hansen (2002) 298–9. At Burgess (2001, 97) I stated that medium plausibly explains 'a number of differences between the images and text'.
14 Heubeck (1989) 32, as noted at Burgess (2001) 230, with further bibliography.
15 Page (1955) 8: '[T]here is no need whatever to make the giant drunk'.
16 Hansen (2002) 295, deeming inebriation not 'really necessary to Homer's story'.
17 Podlecki (1961) focuses on the wine's function as a gift exclusively. For Danek (1998, 176–8, 188) wine functions as guest gift and (unnecessary) soporific; it may be Homeric invention.
18 Page (1955) 1–20.
19 Burgess (2001) 111, (2012) 286 n.49.

of Homer explains non-correlation.[20] Also imaginable, on the other hand, is that there was no literary or artistic reception of Homer before the later sixth century because the *Iliad* and *Odyssey* were first created then.[21] On the whole, the argument that the Polyphemus imagery is *necessarily* non-Homeric because of medium but *essentially* Homeric seems like having your cake and eating it too.

There are also folktale *comparanda* to consider. When speculating about a pre-Homeric version of the Polyphemus episode, scholars have long referenced modern folk tales involving the blinding of an ogre.[22] Though some are not willing to retroject a tale type from post-antiquity into the pre-Homeric past,[23] I agree with the consensus that there was a pre-Homeric ogre-blinding tale type. How similar was it to the modern one? The modern tale type tends to have the ogre blinded with metal spits, not a wooded stake as in the Homeric episode and apparently in the early blinding images. But the modern tale type favors escape by hiding under sheep skins, as opposed to hiding under live sheep or rams in Homer and Greek iconography. And the wine present in both Homer and the blinding images is not common in the modern folktales.[24] Now I seem to have an eaten cake in hand: the images are *essentially* folktale-ish but not folktale-ish *in details*.[25]

But I do not equate the modern folktales with a hypothetical pre-Homeric tale type. The Polyphemus episode is comparable (but not exactly) to the ogre-blinding tale type, and its name-trick is comparable (but not exactly) to completely different modern tale types.[26] The early blinding images are also comparable (but not exactly) to the ogre-blinding tale type. No monolithic pre-Homeric tale type can be reconstructed on the basis of the modern folktales.

---

20 Giuliani's concept of "oraliture" reception plausibly explains, for example, images of the games of Patroclus in the sixth century that are dissimilar in details from the Homeric episode in *Iliad* 23 (Giuliani (2013) 115–18; cf. Burgess (2001) 81–2: 'Homeric-derived'; Snodgrass (1998) 117–20: possibly non-Homeric variants.
21 Jensen (2011), described as 'just possible' at Burgess (2015) 102.
22 Hansen (2002) 289–301, with bibliography. Folkloric aspects of the Homeric epics: Davies (2002); methodology of folkloristics for Homer: Edmunds (2016) 10, 30–6.
23 Bibliography at Hansen (2002) 293–4, 301 nn.10–11, with Bremmer (2002).
24 Some modern folktales contain wine, but without intoxication: E. Cook (1995) 96 n.7. Page (1955) 8: '[T]he common folk-tale, in which the giant goes naturally to sleep after a heavy dinner, has some advantage in economy and coherence'. This disjunction between Homer and the folktales has featured in arguments about the independence of the folktales from Homer: Hansen (2002) 292.
25 Giuliani (2013) 281 n. 61; Grethlein (2015) 203.
26 Hansen (2002) 295–7. Commonly in the ogre-blinding tale type, a speaking magic ring given to the protagonist reveals his location; in a completely different tale type, the protagonist's false name "Myself" prevents aid for the antagonist.

Also, my argument is that the Homeric episode and the early iconography reflect traditional myth about Odysseus, not folktales.²⁷ With some help from the comparative folktale material, we can conclude that the Polyphemus episode complicates simpler myth about Odysseus, whereas the blinding iconography would seem to reflect this traditional myth more directly.²⁸ This conclusion is not denigration of the artists but rather respect for the independence of their medium. Early artists themselves documented such independence by using non-epic forms of Odysseus' name. Whereas Ὀδυσσεύς is regular in early Greek epic, vase inscriptions beginning in the late seventh century employ forms of the Ithacan hero's name with a lambda instead of a delta. The delta form first appears on Greek art in the mid-sixth century and becomes dominant only in the mid-fifth. Whatever the early artists were listening to, it does not seem to be Homer or even epic. Several other variations of the hero's name in antiquity point to Odysseus' extensive fame in non-Homeric and non-epic traditions.²⁹

The traditional wanderings

What would be the basic elements of the traditional wanderings of Odysseus? I would isolate three: A) departure for home from Troy by sea, B) long duration of wandering beyond Greek civilization, and C) arrival home as sole survivor. Element A identifies his journey as a type, the *nostoi* of the Greek heroes from the war. The length of the hero's absence (Element B) spurs the suitors' interest in Penelope and Odysseus' property. Odysseus' *nostos* is distinct from all the other heroic returns in that it is the longest. Lost, adventurous, or detained, Odysseus must be away for a considerable period of time, and so far away that nobody in Ithaca learns of his whereabouts, or whether he is dead or alive. Element C, sole survival, necessitates plotting against the suitors: there are too many for Odysseus to face alone.³⁰ The crisis at Ithaca is wholly predicated on the wanderings.³¹

Narratives of the wanderings containing my three basic elements would have a lot of room for variation. I will review the possibilities for form first before mov-

---

27 At Burgess (2001) 95 I properly raised but rejected the possibility that the Polyphemus images reflected a pre-Homeric folktale.
28 On simple narrative versus Homeric narrative, see Danek 1998, who builds on Hölscher (1989) 25–34.
29 Wüst (1935–1937); M. L. West (2014) 6–7; Kanavou (2015) 98–9.
30 The issue is announced early at 1.78–9 and then is a frequent theme (de Jong 2001 393).
31 Bakker (2013) 3, 17–35.

ing onto content. Take quantitative aspects, for example. In the *Odyssey* the hero is missing for something over eight years (for those keeping track),[32] with Odysseus with Calypso for seven years. Our *Odyssey* indicates that the suitors imposed themselves on Penelope and her home about three years before Odysseus returned.[33] For what it is worth, absence away from home by a husband in the "homecoming husband" tale type commonly lasts "a long time, seven or nine years".[34] One could imagine a more compact story of wandering and courtship, with Odysseus returning just in time after discovery of Penelope's delaying web trick forces her to choose a new husband.[35] It is often suspected that Odysseus' detention by Calypso, which constitutes by far the longest part of Odysseus' absence from Ithaca, is a Homeric invention.[36] Arguably, the eighteen months or so of the famous adventures that precede Odysseus washing up at Calypso's island would be a long enough absence, providing that other heroes return first.

Episodes within the wanderings might vary in duration. Some challenges are just passed by (Sirens, Scylla, Charybdis the first time), and some episodes involve a day or less (Lotus-eaters, Laestrygonians, journey to the Underworld, Charybdis by Odysseus alone). The Ciconian episode takes at least two days, and the Polyphemus episode lasts for several days. Odysseus is hosted by Aeolus for a month, followed by nine days of sailing to Ithaca before the bag of winds is opened, and the Greeks stay at Thrinacia episodes for over a month. Odysseus and his men stay with Circe for a year. Then there is the time sailing at sea, sometimes specified, sometimes not. Other versions of the wanderings might easily represent the duration of some of these episodes differently.

The twelve ships that Odysseus commands in the *apologos* matches the number in the Catalogue of Ships (*Il.* 2.631–7). But a fleet is awkward for many episodes in the wanderings. For example, in the Polyphemus episode the fleet must be stationed at Goat Island before Odysseus proceeds to the land of the Cyclopes with his own ship, and in the Aeolus episode Odysseus somehow steers the fleet by himself before the twelve ships are all blown back to Aeolia together as a unit. All but one ship are destroyed in the Laestrygonian episode. It may be that traditionally the loss of most of the fleet occurred

---

[32] E. Cook (1995) 68–9; Burgess (2015) 25–36.
[33] So, Athena at 13.377.
[34] Hansen (2002) 202; the amount of time the protagonist expects to be absent varies (207).
[35] Woodhouse (1930) 132; S. West (1988) 51 n. 3; M. L. West (2014) 3, 102–4, 115–17 (three years of wandering); Currie (2016) 50 ('considerably shorter').
[36] E.g., M. L. West (2014) 29–30, 108–9, 115–16, 163–4: extension caused by the duration of Menelaus' journey, harmonized with Orestes' vengeance on Aegisthus.

earlier in the journey.³⁷ Or Odysseus traditionally may have had a smaller fleet. In the *Odyssey* only twelve of the more than one hundred suitors are from Ithaca (16.247–51; cf. 1.245–8, 1.394–6, 21.346–7); in an alternative and more plausible version of Odysseus' homecoming he would plot against only a dozen or so Ithacan suitors.³⁸ One could also imagine Odysseus commanding just a single ship to Troy, on which he would embark on his wanderings after the war.³⁹ That is mere speculation, but it does seem that the *Odyssey* favors quantity over logic. The motivation for the hyperbole may be a desire to emphasize the status of Odysseus, as well as the number of companions lost and suitors vanquished.

Aristotle famously distinguished the Homeric poems from episodic epic, citing poems from the Epic Cycle as examples.⁴⁰ Odysseus' journey is an episodic narrative that might, in accordance with oral composition, be readily expanded or contracted.⁴¹ The repetition and doubling found in the *apologos* reflects this essential nature of the story. Both the Cyclopes and the Laestrygonians are large cannibals, for example, and both Circe and Calypso are island-dwelling goddesses. In its episodic and duplicating manner, the *apologos* might be described as cyclic in nature.⁴² But Homerists have argued that the *apologos* is distinguished by sophisticated patterning.⁴³ Books 9, 10, and 12 narrate two smaller episodes (Cicones, Lotus-eaters; Aeolus, Laestrygonians; Sirens, Scylla and Charybdis) before featuring a longer one (Polyphemus, Circe, Thrinacia). Arguably there is cross-reference between episodes within these triads; alternation of tempting utopias and dangerous dystopias also seems to occur. The Underworld, the furthest episode, surrounded by Circe, can be considered a capstone for preceding and subsequent series of episodes. Patterning may be normal for oral composition, but one suspects that the Homeric *apologos* is extraordinary in the arrangement of its inherently episodic material.

The wrath of Poseidon provides a rationale for the duration of the *apologos*; in a sense, it is the plot of the *apologos*. The sea god's anger also provides a di-

---

37 Cf. Danek (1998) 174, 197–9; M. L. West (2014) 12, 114–15, 117. Woodhouse (1930) 133–4: Odysseus returned ship-less and alone from the start!
38 Cf. Danek (1998) 198–9; M. L. West (2014) 3–4, 104, 138.
39 Reinhardt (1996) 69–71; Danek (1998) 170, 174, 197–9; M. L. West (2014) 114.
40 See Burgess (2001) 18, 143–4.
41 Martin (1989) 216–19.
42 Repetition and doublets in the Epic Cycle: Burgess (2001) 144–5; Sammons (2013), (2017) 126–154; Rengakos (2015) 159–160. Wanderings of Odysseus as cyclic: cf. Tsagalis (2012) 310–11; Burgess (2016a) 29–30, with bibliography.
43 Cf. E. Cook (1995) 49–92, (2014) 82–100; Burgess (1999); Bakker (2013) 13–35. Newton (1987) argues that the patterning constitutes Aristotelian unity.

vine dimension to the story.⁴⁴ But though Athena claims she avoided helping Odysseus out of respect for Poseidon (13.341–3), we only see the sea god notice Odysseus and intervene in two places (5.282 ff., 13.125 ff.). And Helios' wrath in the Thrinacian episode might seem to duplicate Poseidon's.⁴⁵ Could the wanderings be narrated without the anger of Poseidon? It seems to me that the god's wrath is securely situated in the traditional wanderings.⁴⁶ That we find it outside of Books 9–12 suggests its traditionality. Zeus cites the existing wrath of Poseidon at the very beginning of the poem, and the "inland journey" implicitly alludes to a continuing need to appease Poseidon after Odysseus' return (11.129–31).⁴⁷ The wrath would seem to be in effect tacitly, even when actions of Poseidon are not specified. Its immediate effect after the Polyphemus episode is demonstrated by Odysseus' hindsight conclusion that Zeus rejected his sacrifice (9.553–4) shortly after the prayer of Polyphemus to Poseidon (9.526–35). Odysseus assumes that Zeus was already then planning the destruction of his companions and fleet, a detail of the prayer. Aeolus surmises in the very next episode that Odysseus is hated by the gods (10.74–5). The repetition of wording in Polyphemus' prayer to Poseidon in Tiresias' prophecy (cf. 9.534–5; 11.114–15) confirms that the wrath has become Odysseus' ongoing fate.⁴⁸

If the wrath of Poseidon is the narrative engine of the traditional wanderings, a cause of his anger should be traditional (the problem with such guessing games is that each judgment commits one to consequential ones). Why not a son of Poseidon harmed by Odysseus?⁴⁹ And if so, why not a Cyclops?⁵⁰ Though the Homeric version of the Cyclopes is unusual,⁵¹ by nature a Cyclops is strong and one-eyed: perfect for a bully who is blinded.⁵² In *Odyssey* 9 Odysseus is curiously lax about specifying a single eye, perhaps because a Cyclops was the hero's traditional antagonist. Myth about Odysseus requires more than an anonymous

---

44 Theology and the *Odyssey:* Clay (1983); E. Cook (1995); Marks (2008); Bakker (2013) 124–34.
45 Possibly invented: Danek (1998) 261–4. Traditional, identifying Odysseus in the proem before he is named: Scodel (2002) 115. Since the Thrinacia scene is featured in the narrator's invocation to the Muse, I would hesitate to label it an innovation.
46 Invented and inconsistently employed: Reinhardt (1996) 84–7; M. L. West (2014) 203, 215–16. Explicated in *Od.* 1 because it is not traditional: Scodel (2002) 115–16.
47 If death from the sea comes to Odysseus (11.134; see Burgess 2014c), then Odysseus fails to appease the god.
48 See E. Cook (1995) 55, 94–5, 178–80; Bakker (2013) 118–24, 126–7.
49 Not: Danek (1998) 189.
50 Differently, Scott (2016); Reece (1993) 127 ('Polyphemus is made to be the son of Poseidon in order to adapt the folktale to the overarching Odyssean theme of the curse').
51 Mondi (1983).
52 Hansen (2002) 293: a blinded Cyclops precedes other manifestations of Cyclopes.

folktale ogre, and the son of Poseidon blinded by Odysseus may have traditionally been named "Polyphemus". If the name means "much-famous", this would refer to fame derived from the Cyclops' key role in the traditional wanderings.[53]

Many also suppose Circe to be a traditional part of the wanderings, with suspicion cast on the Homeric Calypso as a pale doublet.[54] Circe appears relatively early in iconography, so I am inclined to agree. And her role in the *apologos*, at least, is important. She serves as a sort of master of ceremonies: reinvigorating the Greeks enervated by a harrowing series of episodes, sending them off to the Underworld, and then advising Odysseus for a further series of challenging episodes. She has her finger on the pulse of the narrative, possessing foreknowledge of the hero's arrival (10.330–2; cf. 457–9), an unexplained certainty that he must consult Tiresias (10.490–3), and information required for survival in his subsequent adventures (12.37 ff.). Since the goddess' advice is necessary for survival in many episodes, my assumption of their traditionality implies hers as well. But have episodes and characters in the *apologos* been invented? Some, like the Ciconian, Laestrygonian, and Thrinacian episodes, are often thought Homeric innovation.[55] Other episodes, however traditional, may have been greatly modified, as when Odysseus returns to Aeolus and to Charybdis.[56] But removing or changing episodes in order to perceive the pre-Homeric wanderings often causes as many problems as it solves. At a certain point speculation is idle; my position is that most of the material in the *apologos* is traditional, though some variation is normal for traditional myth.

Though one might be forgiven for forgetting this at times, the *apologos* is a first-person narrative. The hero's speech is necessarily presented by the epic as hexameter, with attendant formulae, and Odysseus employs bardic techniques like similes and character speech. One Analyst theory even argued that a non-Homeric third-person narrative has been transposed into a first-person one, with consequential awkwardness, as when Odysseus explains how he knew what Helios said to Zeus (12.389–90).[57] Unitarians tend to credit Homer with embedding the wanderings in character speech, deeming embarrassment or creativ-

---

[53] E. Cook (1995) 94–5 argues, by reference to πολύφημος Phemius (22.376), that the Cyclops causes the hero's *kleos*; Bakker (2001) links the name to Polyphemus' prayer to Poseidon. These views are harmonious with my argument.
[54] The opposite was once thought; see Reinhardt (1996) 90–9 for bibliography and rebuttal.
[55] Reinhardt (1996) 71; Danek (1998) 165, 198–9, 261–3 (as exemplary discussions; there is no point to cite those who think all of the *apologos* is invented).
[56] Reinhardt (1996) 87–90, 102–3; Danek (1998) 194–6, 257–8, (2002).
[57] See Heubeck (1989) 5–6.

ity to be his motive.[58] The different approaches assume that a first-person account of the adventures is unusual. In my view, the wanderings would have normally been narrated as a first-person travel tale. In the "homecoming husband" tale type, the narrative usually focuses on the husband's experiences, narrated either chronologically or analeptically.[59] The *in medias res* composition of the *Odyssey*, supposedly characteristic of Homeric epic, is also found in South Slavic "homecoming husband" tales.[60] One example, at least, provides a first-person retrospective of absence from home by the husband, structurally comparable to the *apologos*.[61]

Odysseus' narrative abilities are so good that he is explicitly or implicitly compared to a bard several times.[62] But his Muse-less prose is substantially different from the Muse-inspired verse of the main narrator.[63] In particular, it is noticeable that Odysseus as a secondary narrator adapts his tale rhetorically to his internal audience, the Phaeacians. For example, the *apologos* features the theme of bad hospitality, whether hyper- (delaying) or hypo- (hostile), apparently as a message to his listening hosts.[64] Another theme of the *apologos* is the growing antagonism between Odysseus and his companions. Here we find some coordination with the main narrator, who deemed the companions foolish soon into the proem (1.7–9).[65] In Odysseus' *apologos*, the issue of the companions is problematized by the inclusion of countering viewpoints, notably by Eurylochus. When he argues that eating the oxen of Helios is reasonable when faced with certain starvation (12.340–51), the situation at Thrinacia seems more complex than either the proem of Odysseus suggest. Eurylochus had earlier pointed out that Odysseus is responsible for losing six companions in the Polyphemus scene (10.431–7). Odysseus has no response then beyond being tempted to run him through with his sword, but a reply of sorts occurs just before the Greeks sail past Scylla. Odysseus then recalls the Polyphemus episode in order to claim credit for preserving (the surviving) companions (12.208–12).

---

[58] Embarassed Homer: Heubeck (1988) 13–16, (1989) 3. Creative: Reinhardt (1996) 72–82; Danek (1998) 250–2, (2012) 18–19; M. L. West (2014) 95–7.
[59] Cf. Hansen (2002) 207–8; Foley (1990) 115–68; S. West (2012); Danek (2016).
[60] Foley (1990) 137–42. On Homeric *in medias res*, see Rengakos (2015) 156.
[61] Foley (1990) 139.
[62] 11.363–9, 17.518–21, 21.406–9; cf. *Il.* 3.221–4.
[63] Cf. de Jong (2001) 221–7, 285–6; Zerba (2009).
[64] Most (1989).
[65] Heubeck (1989, 10) attributes a "controlling hand" to the internal arrangement and intratextual significance of the *apologos*.

A hermeneutics of suspicion might describe Odysseus' presentation of alternative viewpoints as a way for Odysseus to control judgment of his behavior—Eurylochus' overall message in Book 10 is shown to be misguided and cowardly, while in Book 12 his persuasive speech leads to the drowning of all the companions. Homer shares with Odysseus a habit of including opposing voices. A notable example is the speech by Eupeithes that condemns Odysseus for the slaughter of a generation of young nobles, as well as—more relevant to our concerns—the loss of the entire fleet (24.426–37). Eupeithes, "Mr. Persuasive," is effective enough to persuade many relatives of the slain suitors to attack Odysseus' *oikos*-based cohort. That Eupeithes becomes the only casualty of the conflict might be attributed to the poem's generally heavy-handed condemnation of the suitors (as well as the companions). But the inclusion of contradictory narratives might rather be seen as a characteristically Homeric embrace of multi-sided ambiguity.[66] Even if Odysseus strategically controls speech antithetical to his self-conception, and the main narrator similarly manages passages at variance with the *Odyssey*'s ideology, countervailing words once spoken cannot be taken back. Eurylochus' charges at Aeaea potentially ring in our ears when Odysseus loses another six companions to Scylla, as Eupeithes' words might when peace is suddenly established by divine intervention at the end of the *Odyssey*.

Characterization of the companions in the *apologos* correlates intratextually to characterization of the suitors.[67] Though the main narrator and several characters denounce the suitors as villains, even here countervailing material abounds. Notable is Eurylochus' seemingly reasonable offer of compensation to Odysseus in exchange for peace (22.45–59). The audience might wonder why all the suitors must die, including the sympathetic Amphinomus. Odysseus beheads Leodes mid-supplication (22.326–9), and then there is the brutal maiming of Melanthius followed by the hanging of the handmaids (22.465 ff.). For an epic that insistently portrays Odysseus' vengeance as ethically founded, the *Odyssey* is rather generous with problematizing material. The *apologos* and the rest of the poem seem linked not only by correlation of companions and suitors but also by complication of their negative characterization.

Another qualitative aspect of the *apologos* is its ethnographic material.[68] Odysseus' description of the Cyclopes, for example, portrays them as a tribe of exotic humans.[69] In this sense the *apologos* would seem to be the type of ethnographical travel tale that Alcinous requests from his guest: 'Relate where you

---

66 See Burgess (2014b).
67 Bakker (2013) 53–134.
68 Scodel (2005); cf. Burgess (2012).
69 Burgess (2012) 275.

wandered and what lands of men you reached, the people and their well-situated cities, and how many were rough, uncivilized, and unjust, and who were hospitable with a god-fearing mind' (8.72–6). The *Odyssey*'s proem characterizes the wanderings similarly when it states that Odysseus 'viewed the cities of many men and learned of their nature' (1.3). The references to cities has been thought dissimilar from what we find in Books 9–12, leading some Homerists to conclude that the *Odyssey* either mistakenly or allusively contains vestiges of an entirely different wanderings. But in Books 9–12 Odysseus does visit polis-cultures, of a sort, as in the case of the Cicones, Aeolus island, and the Laestrygonians.[70] The *Odyssey*'s polis-visiting phraseology should be viewed as shorthand for the encountering of non-Greek cultures. These cultures exist on a spectrum between the real and the supernatural, and are often a hybrid of both. Polyphemus is a Cyclops with divine parentage, for example, but he is also a human practicing a pastoral lifestyle.

Most Homerists differently describe the world of the *apologos* as a "fairyland" or "enchanted world". Structuralist analysis takes a more anthropological perspective, perceiving the *apologos* as an imagined inversion of Greek culture. Postcolonial interpretation goes a step further by discerning discourse resulting from Greek expansion into the western Mediterranean.[71] These approaches are more insightful than the common dismissal of the *apologos* as otherworldly fantasy. The supernatural characters met by Odysseus are not folktale witches, ogres, and monsters; they are situated within Greek mythological lineage, if often within non-Olympian branches.[72] Odysseus does not wander in a non-heroic world, since other Greek heroes like Heracles and Perseus encounter supernatural *phenomena* when travelling beyond Greek civilization to the edge of the earth and beyond. In Greek myth the cosmos is a unified continuum of Greek civilization, exotic cultures, and far-flung eschatology.

---

[70] E. Cook (1995) 67–8. Odysseus reports to Penelope that Tiresias directed him to travel to 'many cities of men' (on his "inland journey;" 23.268–9). On this passage cf. Burgess (2014c) 118–19; Tsagalis (2008) ch. 4.

[71] Structuralist: Vidal-Naquet (1996); Hartog (2001). Postcolonial: see Burgess (2014a), with bibliography. Greek colonization has often been considered a context for the wanderings (e.g., Adorno and Horkheimer (2002) 39; Heubeck (1989) 15, 22; S. West (2012) 125; M. L. West (2014) 37–8. Linkage of colonization and early blinding images in the West: Dougherty (2003); Lowenstam (2008) 15–17.

[72] For example, Circe and Calypso stem from Titans, and Polyphemus from the monster-producing Phorkys branch. Scylla's mother *Krataiis* (12.124) apparently references Scylla's strength, but non-Homeric sources provided lineage that included parentage by Phorkys or Hecate (E. Cook 1995, 89–90).

The balance of real and supernatural aspects in multiforms of the traditional wanderings might have varied, of course.[73] The journey of Menelaus is relatively anchored in the known geography of the southeastern Mediterranean, but besides meeting the sea-god Proteus, the hero claims to have visited the eschatological Aethiopians, the mysterious Erembi, and a utopian pastoralism of Libya (4.83–9). In his Book 19 lying tale, Odysseus claims that "Odysseus" travelled from Thrinacia to Scheria and on to Thesprotia, a hybrid of the wanderings and the (usually) real-world lying tales (269–9). In his Book 24 lying tale, Odysseus claims he hosted "Odysseus" in his native Sicania, vaguely described (303–14). Eventually the wanderings were localized in the Greek colonial world of Italy and Sicily,[74] and this may have been possible for alternative versions of the wanderings, provided that the bard and his audience had only a dim grasp of its geographical reality.[75] The suitors threaten to send Irus and Odysseus to 'King Echetus, maimer of all men', who sounds like a legendary bogeyman ("King Captor"?).[76] But the *scholia* locate him in Sicily or Epirus, and the real-world aspect of the threat is indicated at 20.382–3, where the suitors suggest that Odysseus and Theoclymenus be sent to Sicilian slavers. In the *Odyssey* these peripheral places are geographically identifiable yet exist at the murky edges of the Greek world, and perhaps might be included in other forms of the wanderings. But I do not think that alternative wanderings of Odysseus ever occurred exclusively in the known Greek world, as suggested by some of the "conspiracy theories" surveyed below. To meet the elemental requirements of the crisis of Ithaca, the wanderings should be long, centrifugal, and beyond the limits of communication within the Greek world.

How stable is traditional characterization of Odysseus?[77] The hero himself declares to the Phaeacians that he is famous for trickery.[78] The *Odyssey*'s etymological linking of the hero's name in the *Odyssey* with a verb of hating,

---

[73] Comparable is the relative weighting of local and Pan-Hellenic content perceived for Homeric and Cyclic epic (Nagy 1990, 70–9). Cf. the issue of relative weighting of pre-colonial and colonial content for nostoi stories: Malkin (1998) 151–3; Danek (2015) 360, 375, 378–9.

[74] See my website "In the Wake of Odysseus".

[75] As seems to be the case at *Theogony* 1011–16, where Circe's sons Agrius and Latinus rule over Tyrsenians within the 'holy islands'. The *Odyssey* refers to Sicily (20.383, 24.211, 307, 366, 89), and perhaps Italian Temesa (1.183–4; see Malkin 1998, 73), but not in the context of the wanderings. At Marks (2008, 101 n. 30) the non-geographial nature of the *apologos* is attributed to pan-Hellenic suppression of local traditions.

[76] 18.84–7, 115–16; 21.307–9, with Russo (1992) 52–3.

[77] Nature and ethos of Odysseus: Philippson (1947); Friedrich (1987); E. Cook (1999); Finkelberg (1995); Danek (1998) 508–9; Scodel (2002) 107–9; M. L. West (2014) 6–11.

[78] 9.19–20; cf. 13.291–5; *Il.* 3.202, 11.430.

ὀδύσσεσθαι, probably suggests that Odysseus is an object of hate because of his deceitful nature.⁷⁹ Outside of Homer, Odysseus indeed is characterized negatively. For Stanford in *The Ulysses Theme*, this was a matter of post-Homeric poets perversely contradicting Homer.⁸⁰ More likely, Homer is the odd man out, suppressing pre-Homeric aspects of the hero. In the *apologos*, Odysseus' trickery is only prominent in the Polyphemus episode. Odysseus portrays himself as more typically enduring, patient, and passive. Occasionally in the *apologos* the hero is curious, as when he seeks out the Cyclops, listens to the Sirens' song, and enjoys viewing shades in the Underworld, conversing with many. This adventurous nature was probably more pronounced in tradition. The hero is described as πολύαινος by the Sirens (12.184), which I would translate as "very storied", a frequent subject of traditional myth.⁸¹ Other epithets, apparently reflecting his mythological nature, emphasize his "much-ness" (πολύτλας, πολυτλήμων, πολυμήχανος, πολύμητις). For many, πολύτλας, πολυτλήμων and τλήμων reflect the endurance of the Homeric Odysseus, but the root may rather indicate his traditional daring.⁸² Then there is πολύτροπος, the *Odyssey*'s initial epithet for Odysseus (1.1), repeated by Circe when she recognizes the hero (10.330). Often this is thought to reference the hero's quick-thinking adaptability, but I prefer "much-travelled".⁸³ The *apologos* recounts survival of adventurous travel, most dramatically exemplified when the "twice-dying" (12.12–22) Greeks travel to Hades and back. Eventually, of course, only Odysseus returns. But the selfish aspect of our sole survivor's presence of mind is relatively repressed in the *apologos*, along with the hero's traditional curiosity.⁸⁴

---

79 19.406; cf. 1.62, 5.340, 423, 19.275. See Clay (1983) 54–132; Sacks (1987) 8–11; M. L. West (2014) 6–7; Kanavou (2015) 90–105. E. Cook (1995, 94–5) links the name with Poseidon's hatred of Odysseus; E. Cook (1999) 151–2 notes that the verb is used by Athena to suggest that Zeus hates Odyssseus (1.62).
80 Stanford (1954) 81–117 (relatively cautious on the Epic Cycle).
81 Odysseus is also described so at *Il.* 9.673, 10.545, 11.430. LSJ: 'much-praised'; Nagy (1979) 240, section 19 n. 1: 'speaker of fables'.
82 Hainsworth (1988) 320 (the original sense may have been "much-daring"); M. L. West (2014) 10; Kanavou (2015) 96 n. 37.
83 M. L. West (2014, 10) notes that the epithet is also used for "the deceitful Hermes" (*Homeric Hymn to Hermes* 13, 439), but this god is also a traveller, in the hymn and generally. Of course, travel is often linked with deceit, as Alcinous recognized (11.363–6). Dispute over the adjective's meaning began in antiquity; see Vergados (2013) 232–3.
84 See especially Danek (2002) 23–5. Finkelberg (1995, 4) well compares Odysseus to Heracles, as the poem seems to do at 8.223–5, 11.601–27, 21.24–9; see Burgess (2012) 272–3. Both have questionable ethics, face challenges with brio, and employ rather non-heroic bow and (poisoned) arrows (1.255–64; see below).

My review of possible variation in the wanderings has recognized flexibility yet argued for traditional consistency in form and content. But could the wanderings simply be re-invented in every telling, so long as the basic elements of duration and sole survival were indicated? In other words, is the journey at sea just a blank slot that needs to be filled? Would detention somewhere far away suffice, as often in South Slavic "homecoming husband" tale type?[85] Such a view would be consonant with oralist theory that stresses the typological make-up of early epic. Leaping from the minutiae of formulae to patterns and themes, Oralists often neglect the specific aspects of particular mythological narratives.[86] Consider Adrian Kelly's portrayal of the lying tales told by Odysseus as multi-forms of an oral narrative.[87] Even if we should put two of the five lying tales to one side because they do not share the Cretan theme of the others, we are not left with anything like a unified story. Motifs that might be deemed typological are shared variously from one lying tale to the other, and the persona adopted by Odysseus changes from story to story, as does the sequence of action. Typology-shuffling is not traditional myth. The returns of Agamemnon, Menelaus, and Odysseus, for example, are comparable *nostoi* from the Trojan War, but distinct in character, place, and plot. Typology allows a thematic comparison between the returns of Odysseus and Agamemnon to arise in the *Odyssey*, but in the end the plots of the two are very different. The wanderings of Odysseus were surely more than a random mix of typical dangers and enticements. The hero's return required certain elements to be functional for the story of Penelope's wooing, and I think Odysseus' *apologos* not only contains these elements but also largely reflects the traditional narrative of his wanderings, if perhaps with the quantitative and qualitative adjustments explored above.

Conspiracy theories

Homerists often portray the *apologos* as extremely untraditional in nature. Since the arguments mix much speculation with little evidence, I deem them "con-

---

85 Athena as Mentes at 1.197–9 suggests that "wild men" detain Odysseus on an island, and Proteus at 4.556–60 informs Menelaus that Calypso detains the hero against his will on her island, as we observe in Book 5.
86 Burgess (2006); revised as chapter 4 of Burgess (2009).
87 Kelly (2008). Cf. Kelly (2012), where non-contextual behavior of Achilles and Thetis at the beginning of *Iliad* 18 is filed under a proposed typology "prospective lamentation". The reductionist mathematics that result do not challenge the plausible Neoanalyst argument that the scene implicitly mirrors the funeral of Achilles (Burgess 2009, 83–5).

spiracy theories".[88] The methodologies are numerous. Analysts saw the *apologos* as an idiosyncratic patchwork of inharmonious components from various sources.[89] Unitarians tend to conclude that various sources were successfully arranged in the *apologos*.[90] In recent times this process is commonly described as agonistic engagement with alternative, equally valid wanderings.[91] Whether plagiarizing, compiling, or under-cutting, the *apologos* is seen as highly idiosyncratic in content.

It would be tiresome to rebut in detail theories that I find implausible, so I will survey the basic outlines of the most popular ones. One might be called the Cretan conspiracy theory. This proposes that the lying tales told by Odysseus (often featuring Crete) reflect a traditional form of the wanderings that occurred within real places of the Mediterranean.[92] The external audience of the *Odyssey* knows that these tales are false, something the main narrator emphasizes at 19.203. But the Cretan theory would have it that these lying tales reflect an original form of the wanderings, deemed false in the *Odyssey* as a form of agnostic subversion. Sometimes a casually postmodern approach is employed to challenge the very possibility of truth in the *Odyssey*. But the *Odyssey* largely backs up the veracity of Odysseus's *apologos*. For example, the main narrator references the Thrinacia episode, Calypso, and the wrath of Poseidon at the beginning of the poem, and soon enough Zeus and Athena are talking about Polyphemus as Poseidon's son (68–75).[93] Would a bard who has invoked a Muse, symbol of tradition, proceed to fabricate a completely novel *nostos*, with authoritative gods complicit in the invention?[94] Above I conceded that a degree of creative manipulation could be applied to traditional myth about the wanderings, but I do not consider outright re-invention likely for the oral performance culture of the

---

[88] With thanks to Brad Hald. Since my own work might often seem to be "much speculation with little evidence," it should be clear that my comments about the excellent scholars mentioned below are not polemical.
[89] Bibliography is reviewed at Heubeck (1989) 3–11.
[90] West (2014) is an example of high quality.
[91] Exemplars, also excellent: Danek (1998), (2002); Tsagalis (2012); Barker and Christensen (2014).
[92] Woodhouse (1930) 126–36 is seminal; Grossardt (1998, 37–43) provides a survey (sceptical except for the Thesprotian theory discussed below); see also Danek (1998) 47–9; Tsagalis (2012) 313–19.
[93] Parry (1994); de Jong (2001) 221–2, 285–6. But on the complexity of the "truth" of the *apologos*, see Zerba (2009).
[94] Cf. Danek (1998) 22: infrequent invocation of the Muse by the *Odyssey* (compared to the *Iliad*) allows innovation. At Danek (2002, 17) the *Odyssey* is described as mostly traditional, but with self-conscious signalling of its deviations from tradition.

Archaic Age. Let us also keep in mind the narrative exigencies of the wanderings: the crisis at Ithaca requires him to be missing for a long time, with no report of his whereabouts. Travel in the known Greek world does not meet these requirements, even if I acknowledged above that the periphery of the Greek world might play a role in some versions of the wanderings.

A relevant theory concerns short alternative readings by Zenodotus at two places in the Telemachy, whereby Telemachus travels to Crete, not Sparta. Variants for other passages about Telemachus travelling to Pylos and Sparta are not provided. Since the variation is indirectly reported by the *scholia*, we are in the dark about Zenodotus' source. But on the supposition that Zenodotus had his reasons, the meager evidence becomes a springboard for alternative Telemachies. The nature of the speculation varies widely. From a textualist perspective, the alternative lines might have been present in a variant manuscript, or even an earlier draft by Homer.[95] From an oralist perspective, the evidence might reflect multiformity of the Homeric epic or its performance tradition.[96] To the extent that the issue does not challenge the traditionality of the *apologos*, I need not express my scepticism at length. But some go on to theorize that Telemachus meets Odysseus at Crete, where he presumably travelled in a lying-tales type of wanderings. I find this unlikely for reasons stated above, notably that news of Odysseus could easily arrive from Crete.[97]

Then there's the Thesprotian conspiracy theory. Count me among the conspirators, for I have argued that the frequent mention of Thesprotia in the *Odyssey*, notably in two lying tales of Odysseus, reflects post-return wanderings of Odysseus (as in the *Telegony* or the "inland journey").[98] But this is not the same as an alternative wanderings. The type of Thesprotian conspiracist I have in mind envisions Odysseus travelling to Thesprotia before he returns. The first such conspiracist was Odysseus himself, who on Ithaca spreads rumors of "Odysseus" in Thesprotia, soon to return to Ithaca, as noted above. He's lying, but thereby the *Odyssey* undercuts an alternative wanderings, the reasoning goes.[99] Odysseus also reports that "Odysseus" travels to Dodona in Thesprotia to seek advice from Zeus about whether to return "openly or secretly"

---

95 Cf. S. West (1988) 43; M. L. West (2014) 106 – 8.
96 Cf. Reece (1994); Tsagalis (2012); Nagy (2017).
97 Rumors of Odysseus arriving at Crete is a theme; e.g. 14.122 – 30, 372 – 85, where Eumaeus reports that rumor-mongers often visit the palace, and that an Aetolian man retailed a Cretan conspiracy yarn to him.
98 Burgess (2014b), (2014c). Thesprotia in lying tales) 14.314 – 33, 19.287 – 99.
99 E.g., Danek (1998) 215 – 25, 286; Marks (2003), (2008) 89 – 92, 102 – 3; Tsagalis (2012) 318 – 19, 341 – 3.

(19.296–9).¹⁰⁰ According to the Thesprotian theory, here we have a more grounded alternative to Odysseus seeking out Tiresias in the Underworld. And if Odysseus is looking for supernatural advice, why not go to the Thesprotian Acheron, well known in later times for necromancy?¹⁰¹ There's more to consider: in Book 1 Athena as Mentes reports that Odysseus once travelled to Ephyra, arguably in Thesprotia (1.257–64), in search of poison, and some suitors wonder if Telemachus is off to gather forces or poison to use against them (2.325–30).¹⁰² Mix and match, and you have a nice alternative wanderings in which the last stage of Odysseus' wanderings is at Thesprotia, where he gathers gifts, seeks advice on how to return, and perhaps considers to even the odds by poison, before getting transportation to Ithaca from the king of Thesprotia. Also, change the timing of the "inland journey," locate it in Thesprotia, and Poseidon is appeased *before* Odysseus returns. One can see how attractive this game is. A more logical and real-world return is hypothesized, one that actually improves on the type of Homeric problems that scandalize Analysts and embarrass Unitarians.

I have not ventured to pronounce on the traditionality of the Phaeacian episode, but if it was invented by Homer, as sometimes suspected, a final Thesprotian episode would make a plausible alternative to the Phaeacian episode.¹⁰³ My analysis does concede the possibility of alternative episodes, as long as the basic elements of duration, distance, and sole survival are met. And the final stage of the homecoming is the issue, not the wanderings at sea. But the secrecy of his return seems less likely if Odysseus were to dawdle in a region well connected with Ithaca, as Odysseus' (false) rumor demonstrates.¹⁰⁴ I am also very loath to accept ancillary sub-proposals to the Thesprotian theory, that Homer invented Odysseus' *catabasis* and/or transposed a pre-return "inland journey" to a time subsequent to the return to Ithaca. One can agree that these alterations would improve the logic and plausibility of the *apologos* without conceding that they therefore must be pre-Homeric. My caution might seem surprising for someone who has dabbled in Neoanalyst theories about the relation between the *Iliad*

---

100 Haller (2013) 272: Odysseus returned openly in an alternative version and raised a local force against the suitors.
101 For this and other theories about origins and location of the Homeric underworld, see Burgess 2016b.
102 See S. West (1981) 174–5.
103 If Scheria is jettisoned, an alternative time/place for a first-person retrospective of the wanderings is needed. For possibilities, cf. Danek (1998) 194; M. L. West (2014) 98.
104 See Malkin (1998) 120–55 on the inter-connectivity of the region. The spatial obscurity of the "inland journey" (Purves 2010, 65–96) and the legendary aspects of "King Echetus" (see above) possibly refer to areas deeper in Epirus than Thesprotia.

and myth about Memnon, which are indisputably speculative in nature. But the story of Memnon *did* exist, as documented not just by the *Aethiopis* but art and literature, and its narrative time was outside the narrative boundaries of the *Iliad*. The Memnon story is neither prototype nor alternative to the story of the *Iliad*; it is an independent episode in the Trojan War to which the *Iliad* potentially alludes.[105] I have also argued recently[106] that the centripetal closure of *Odyssey* acknowledges yet obscures the hero's post-return adventures, as represented by the *Telegony* to some degree; this also is not the same as competitive allusion to alternative versions of Homeric narrative.

Homerists have long suspected that Homer plagiarized the Argonautic story.[107] Apollonius of Rhodes' *Argonautica* shares many travel events with the *apologos*, after all. Sure, the conspiracy theory goes, the *Argonautica* is obviously influenced by the *Odyssey*, but maybe some of the correlations originated in pre-Homeric Argonautic myth. The Argo story features Aeetes, brother of Circe, and therefore would seem to have claim on her and the far east, where Aeaea is situated (as the *Odyssey* eventually lets on).[108] And Circe herself references the journey of the Argo when warning Odysseus of the wandering rocks (12.69–72). But this passage, rather than acknowledging a source, as is commonly claimed, actually distinguishes the journey of the Argonauts from the journey of Odysseus.[109] The two may be open to comparison, as the return of Odysseus is with the return of Agamemnon, but that does not make one the origin of the other. The two journeys may almost nearly intersect at the wandering rocks, but that is no surprise for two heroic journeys venturing into peripheral seas. As for episodes shared between the *apologos* and the *Argonautica*, with time I have come to the conclusion that they all originate with the Odyssean wanderings, though one could suppose that they are independently recur in different stories (indeed, the *apologos* portrays its "otherworld" as rather frequented by humans).[110] That one major character in one story is the sibling of a major char-

---

105 Burgess (2009).
106 Burgess (2014b), (2014c).
107 See M. L. West (2005), with bibliography. Hölscher (1989, 172–8) reveals the weakness of the theory.
108 12.3–4. The unexplained conflation of both east and west in the *apologos* has encouraged belief in its collocation of extraneous and various material. But geographical precision is not required for the wanderings, though its conceptual unity can be explained by reference to Greek mythological cosmography (Burgess 2016b).
109 Burgess (2012) 273.
110 Burgess (2012).

acter in another story should not get us too excited, given the elaborate interconnections of genealogy in Greek myth.

Another tale within the *Odyssey* has sometimes been seen as the prototype of the *apologos:* Menelaus' wanderings in Book 4 (81–91, 351–537). Certainly the two returns correlate to a large degree. Menelaus' journey is a first-person tale that includes ethnographic touring, some of which is eschatological in nature, as noted above. Menelaus also encounters a supernatural prophet, Proteus, and the duration of the journey is long, seven years. For M. L. West and S. West, this is the original wanderings, properly located in the eastern Mediterranean. But Homer gave Odysseus' wanderings to Menelaus out of temporal considerations that occurred to him as he worked on a manuscript of the epic.[111] Even aside from this textualist approach, I do not find the Menelaus conspiracy theory appealing. In my view, the parallels are simply due to typology of *nostoi* and travel tales (Menelaus' tale is very similar to the Egyptian "Tale of the Shipwrecked Sailor," discussed below), perhaps emphasized for intratextual reasons in our *Odyssey*.

A less sensational theory is that Homer has gathered folktales or sea yarns that pre-existed but had never been connected to Odysseus.[112] As seen above, it can be helpful to interpret the *apologos* by (cautious) comparative reference to modern tale types. I also find attractive the notion that landmarks noted by seafarers—the strait of Messina, say—in time became suitable material for heroic myth. Those boarding this hermeneutic vessel, however, may soon find themselves between the Scylla of folkloristics and the Charybdis of localization. I worry about the tone taken toward folktales and sea yarns in discussion of them as raw material of the *apologos*—as if they were subliterary detritus properly segregated from the main narrative and worthy of Homeric inclusion only after buffing and collocation. Such discussions repeat classic Unitarian argument, which was happy to wave vaguely to pre-Homeric material as long as it all could be seen as first packaged together, in an inventive manner, by the master poet.[113] It is problematic in any scenario to suppose that folk material can be suddenly and directly interjected into epic. I prefer to see the pre-Homeric traditional wanderings associated with Odysseus as long containing (say, a few centuries) much material that (from our perspective) might be considered folkloric. The process involved thousands of performances by hundreds of bards, not to

---

111 M. L. West (2014) 29–30, 108–9, 115–16, 163–4.
112 Scott (1916) 125; Woodhouse (1930) 41–53; Reinhardt (1996); Heubeck (1988) 20, (1989) 6, 43; Reece (1993) 123–44. Peradotto (1990, 32–58) explores a binary of myth and folktale in the *apologos*.
113 S. West (1981) 174; Scott (1916) 122: 'not a traditional poem, but a new creation'.

mention non-epic and non-verse oral storytelling of traditional myth. Greek myth changed over time, but its tellers were not trying to re-invent it with every telling. They worked within a shared system of myth and performance, and their competitive spirit was focused on aesthetics, not innovation.

Many look farther back into the distant past for analogues to the wanderings. It has long been recognized that the travel in the *Gilgamesh Epic* is comparable to the Homeric *apologos*.[114] Gilgamesh undertakes a long return journey, away from home and back; he travels under the earth and over a "sea of death"; he encounters fantastic beings, like the Scorpion-man; he is assisted by Siduri, who correlates well to Circe; he travels to meet an otherworld figure, Utnapishtim, who is not only a source of wisdom but provides a long embedded character narrative (on the universal flood), itself comparable to Odysseus' *apologos*. Then there is the Egyptian "Tale of the Shipwrecked Sailor," which features a sole-survivor of a shipwreck who meets a giant divine snake that prophesizes his return and provides him with gifts when he leaves.[115] It is back at home that the sailor tells his travel tale to his master in an embedded first-person narrative. The correspondences to the wanderings of Odysseus and Menelaus are remarkable. A direct link between these ancient narratives and the *Odyssey* is doubtful, but they do provide prototypes for both supernatural travel and first-person narration of it. Detailed correlation should not be sought, to be sure. Utnapishtim tells a travel tale of sorts, but the narrative of Gilgamesh's journey is third-person. The shipwrecked sailor's narrative is comparably embedded in a frame, but in contradistinction to Odysseus, the sailor is not a hero and his adventure is not traditional myth. More apposite for heroic first-person narration would be Nestor's account of his exploits in Pylos (*Il.* 11.670 – 762).[116]

Conclusion

I have proposed that the *apologos* of Odysseus represents a multiform of a traditional tale of Odysseus' wanderings. This pre- or non-Homeric narrative would have existed generally in myth and perhaps predominantly in epic form. Some motifs and narrative devices may have existed in hypothetically pre-Homeric folktales, but it was not the Homeric *apologos* that transformed such material

---

[114] Translation and commentary: George (2000), (2003). For Homeric parallelism, cf. M. L. West (1997) 403 – 15; Burgess (1999); Bakker (2001) 338 – 44; Louden (2011) 180 – 221.
[115] Translation: Allen (2014) 9 – 54; see Louden (2011) 61 – 2.
[116] M. L. West (2014, 97) notes these parallels, though he considers the first person narrative of the *apologos* innovative.

into epic for the first time. Nor need the first-person narrative of the *apologos* be original; the wanderings may have normally been narrated in such a manner, if not exclusively. The traditional wanderings would contain the essential elements of long duration outside Greek civilization, with Odysseus returning as a sole survivor. Its plot was motivated by the wrath of Poseidon after the blinding of his son Polyphemus. Circe as well is traditional as a threat/enticement who becomes a valuable guide. But in accordance with the flexibility of oral composition, different versions of the wanderings may have added or dropped episodes, shuffled their sequence, and complicated their nature (e.g., second arrivals at Aeolia and Charybdis). My argument recognizes that the Homeric *apologos* is probably distinctive in nature, whether in terms of poetics, characterization, theme, and ideology. For example, quantitatively the *apologos* seems to increase Odysseus' fleet and the length of his absence from Ithaca; qualitatively it downplays the curiosity of Odysseus and his responsibility for the loss of his fleet. Though I accept variation within the traditional wanderings, in my analysis the degree of difference between multiforms would be relative minor.

I reject "conspiracy theories" about alternative versions of the wanderings because they argue for extreme variance between the Homeric *apologos* and traditional forms of the wanderings. It is curious that speculation about the radical innovation of the *apologos* is found in all fields of Homeric studies. Analysts see an *apologos* idiosyncratically fragmented from multiple sources. Unitarians stress its invention over tradition. Neoanalysts measure its distinction against sources and rivals. And Oralists by concentrating on typology small and large have neglected what is specific to the myth of Odysseus' return. Instead, the *apologos* is portrayed as a multiform so hyper-agonistic as to be untraditional in content.[117] Lazy clichés of postmodern meta-ness that envision personified poems competitively offering radically different wanderings, or even the "singer" Odysseus contending with Homer, further cloud our sense of the *apologos*' traditionality.

For radical innovation, one needs to turn to later ages not committed to the traditional performance culture of the Archaic Age. When Euripides transformed the Polyphemus episode into a Satyr play, besides making changes necessary for the change of media, he felt free to invent freely. For example, the wrath of Poseidon is ignored, replaced by a past prophecy to Polyphemus that he would be blinded by Odysseus (cf. the prophecy of Telemus, *Od*. 9.507–12) but that Odysseus would suffer a long and difficult wanderings (*Cyclops* 696–700). In Walcott's stage version of the play, it is Ajax's casual curse of Odysseus at Troy

---

[117] Scepticsm about Homer's supposed agonistic spirit: Scodel (2004); Burgess (2004).

that is the cause of the long wanderings (I.1). As subscribers of the Cretan conspiracy have noticed, Dictys brought Odysseus to Crete on his return (6.5). In *True Stories* Lucian amusingly mocks the Phaeacians for believing Odysseus' tale, described as a typically mendacious travel tale (1.3). Zachary Mason in *The Lost Book of the Odyssey* delights with a countless number of Borgesian varieties of the wanderings. But this is all reception of Homer. For the early Archaic Age, a time of oral composition within the frame of longstanding traditions, our default assumption should be that the *apologos* is largely consistent with a traditional myth of the wanderings.

Works cited

Adorno, T. W. and M. Horkheimer. (2002) [1947]. *Dialectic of Enlightenment*. Trans. E. Jephcott. Redwood City, CA.
Allen, J. P. (2014). *Middle Egyptian Literature: Eight Literary Works of the Middle Kingdom*. Cambridge.
Bakker, E. J. (2001). 'The Greek Gilgamesh, or the Immortality of Return', in: M. Païsi-Apostolopoulou (ed.), *Eranos*. Ithaca, 331–53.
–. (2013). *The Meaning of Meat and the Structure of the* Odyssey. Cambridge.
Barker, E. T. E., and J. P. Christensen. (2014). 'Odysseus' Nostos and the *Odyssey*'s Nostoi: Rivalry within the Epic Cycle', in: G. Scafoglio, E. Lelle (eds.), *Studies on the Greek Epic Cycle*, 2 vols., Philologia Antiqua 7–8. Rome/Pisa, vol. I, 87–112.
Bremmer, J. N. (2002). 'Odysseus versus the Cyclops', in" S. des Bouvrie (ed.) *Myth and Symbol I. Symbolic Phenomena in Ancient Greek Culture*. Bergren, 135–52.
Burgess, J. S. (1999). 'Gilgamesh and Odysseus in the Otherworld', *CV/EMC [Mouseion]* 13: 171–210.
–. (2001). *The Tradition of the Trojan War in Homer and the Epic Cycle*. Baltimore.
–. (2004). 'Performance and the Epic Cycle', *CJ* 10: 1–23.
–. (2006). 'Neoanalysis, Orality, and Intertextuality: An Examination of Homeric Motif Transference', *Oral Tradition* 21: 148–89.
–. (2009). *The Death and Afterlife of Achilles*. Baltimore.
–. (2012). 'Belatedness in the *Odyssey*', in: F. Montanari, A. Rengakos, and C. Tsagalis (eds.), *Homeric Contexts : Neoanalysis and the Interpretation of Oral Poetry*. Berlin, 269–90.
–. (2014a). ' "If Peopled and Cultured": Bartram's *Travels* and the *Odyssey*', in: G. R. Ricci (ed.), *Travel, Discovery, Transformation*. New Brunswick, 19–44.
–. (2014b). 'Framing Odysseus. The Death of the Suitors', in: M. Christopoulos and M. Païzi-Apostolopoulou (eds.) *Crime and Punishment in Homeric and Archaic Epic*. Ithaki, 355–72.
–. (2014c). 'The Death of Odysseus n the *Odyssey* and *Telegony*', in: G. Scafoglio, E. Lelle (eds.), *Studies on the Greek Epic Cycle*, 2 vols. Philologia Antiqua 7–8. Rome/Pisa, vol. I, 113–24.
–. (2015). *Homer*. London.

–. (2016a). 'The Origins and Reception of the Trojan Cycle', in: F. Gallo (ed.), *Omero: Quaestiones Disputatae*. Milan, 13–30.
–. (2016b). 'Localization of the *Odyssey*'s Underworld', *Cahiers des etudes anciennes* 53: 15–37.
–. 'In the Wake of Odysseus' website: <http://wakeofodysseus.com>
Calvino, I. (1986). *The Uses of Literature*. Trans. P. Creagh. San Diego.
Clay, J. S. (1997). *The Wrath of Athena*. Lanham.
Cook, E. F. (1995). *The* Odyssey *in Athens*. Ithaca, N.Y.
–. (1999). ' "Active" and "Passive" Heroics in the *Odyssey*', *CW* 93: 149–67.
–. (2014). 'Structure as Interpretation in the Homeric *Odyssey*', in: D. Cairns, R. Scodel (eds.), *Defining Greek Narrative*. Edinburgh, 75–102.
Cook, R. M. (1983). 'Art and Epic in Archaic Greek', *Bulletin antieke bechaving* 58: 1–10.
Currie, B. (2016). *Homer's Allusive Art*.
Danek, G. (1998). *Epos und Zitat*. Vienna.
–. (2002). 'Odysseus between Scylla and Charybdis', in: A. Hurst, F. Létoublon (eds.), *La Mythologie et l'* Odyssée. Geneva, 15–25.
–. (2015). 'Nostoi', in: M. Fantuzzi, C. Tsagalis (eds.), *The Greek Epic Cycle and Its Ancient Reception*. Cambridge, 355–79.
de Jong, I. J. F. (2001). *A Narratological Commentary on the* Odyssey. Cambridge.
Davies, M. (2002). 'The Folk-Tale Origins of the *Iliad* and *Odyssey*', *WS* 115: 5–43.
Dougherty, C. (2003). "The Aristonothos Krater. Competing Stories of Conflict and Collaboration', in: C. Dougherty, L. Kurke (eds.), *The Cultures within Ancient Greek Culture*. Cambridge, 35–56.
Edmunds, L. (2016). *Stealing Helen*. Princeton.
Finkelberg, M. (1995). 'Odysseus and the Genus "Hero"', *G&R* 42: 1–14.
Foley, J. (1990). *Traditional Oral Epic*. Berkeley.
Frame, D. (1978). *The Myth of Return in Early Greek Epic*. New Haven.
Frazer, J. G. (1921). *Apollodorus. The* Library. Loeb Classical Library. Cambridge, MA.
George, A. R. (2000). *The Epic of Gilgamesh*. London.
–. (2003). *The Babylonian Gilgamesh Epic*. 2 vols. Oxford.
Giuliani, L. (2013). *Image and Myth*. Trans. J. O'Donnell. Chicago.
González, J. M. (2013). *The Epic Rhapsode and His Craft*. Washington, DC.
Grethlein, J. (2015). 'Vision and Reflexivity in the *Odyssey* and Early Vase-painting', *Word and Image* 31: 197–212.
Grossardt, P. (1998). *Die Trugreden in der* Odyssee *und ihre Rezeption in der antiken Literature*. Bern.
Hainsworth, J. B. (1988). 'Books V-VIII', in: A. Heubeck, S. West, and J. B. Hainsworth (eds.), *A Commentary on Homer's* Odyssey, vol. I. Oxford, 247–385.
Haller, S. (2013). 'Dolios in *Odyssey* 4 and 24: Penelope's Plotting and Alternative Narratives of Odysseus' *nostos*', *TAPA* 143: 263–92.
Hansen. W. (2002). *Ariadne's Thread*. Ithaca, N.Y.
Hartog, F. (2001). *Memories of Odysseus*. Trans. Janet Lloyd. Chicago.
Heubeck, A., (ed.) (1988–1992). *A Commentary on Homer's* Odyssey. 3 vols. Oxford.
Heubeck, A. (1988). 'General Introduction', in: Heubeck (1988–1992), vol. I, 3–23.
–. (1989). "Books IX-XII', in: Heubeck (1988–1992), vol. II, 3–146.
Hölscher, U. (1989). *Die Odysee. Epos Zwischen Märchen und Roman*. Munich.

Jensen, M. S. (2011). *Writing Homer*. Copenhagen.
Kanavou, N. (2015). *The Names of Homeric Heroes*. Berlin.
Kelly. A. (2008). 'Performance and Rivalry: Homer, Odysseus, and Hesiod', in: M. Fevermann, and P. Wison (eds.), *Performance, Iconography, Reception*. Oxford, 177–203.
–. (2012). 'The Mourning of Thetis: "Allusion" and the Future in the *Iliad*', in: F. Montanari, A. Rengakos, and C. Tsagalis (eds.), *Homeric Contexts: Neoanalysis and the Interpretation of Oral Poetry*. Berlin, 221–68.
Kullmann, W. (1960). *Die Quellen der Ilias*. Hermes Einzelschriften 14. Wiesbaden.
Louden, B. (2011). *Homer's Odyssey and the Near East*. Cambridge.
Lowenstam, S. (2008). *As Witnessed by Images: The Trojan War Tradition in Greek and Etruscan Art*. Baltimore.
Malkin, I. (1998). *The Returns of Odysseus*. Berkeley.
Marks, J. (2003). 'Alternative *Odysseys*: The Case of Thoas and Odysseus', *TAPA* 133: 209–26.
–. (2008). *Zeus in the Odyssey*. Washington DC.
Martin, R. (1989). *The Language of Heroes*. Ithaca.
Mondi, R. (1983). 'The Homeric Cyclopes: Folktale, Tradition, and Theme', *TAPA* 113: 17–38.
Most, G. (1989). 'The Structure and Function of Odysseus' *Apologoi*', *TAPA* 129: 15–30.
Nagy, G. (1979). *The Best of the Achaeans*. Baltimore.
–. (1990). *Pindar's Homer*. Baltimore.
–. (2017). 'Diachronic Homer and a Cretan *Odyssey*', *Oral Tradition* 31: 3–50.
Newton, R. M. (1987). 'The Aristotelian Unity of Odysseus's Wanderings', in: K. Myrsiades (ed.), *Approaches to Teaching Homer's* Iliad *and* Odyssey (New York), 137–42.
Olson, S. D. (1995). *Blood and Iron*. Leiden.
Page, D. L. (1955). *The Homeric* Odyssey. Oxford.
Parry, H. (1994). 'The Apologos of Odysseus: Lies, All Lies?', *Phoenix* 48: 1–20.
Peradotto, J. (1990). *Man in the Middle Voice*. Princeton.
Philippson, P. (1947). 'Die vorhomerische und die homerische Gestalt des Odysseus', *MV* 4: 8–22.
Podlecki, A. (1961). 'Guest-gifts and Nobodies in *Odyssey* 9', *Phoenix* 15: 125–33.
Purves, A. (2010). *Space and Time in Ancient Greek Narrative*. Cambridge.
Reece, S. (1993). *The Stranger's Welcome: Oral Theory and the Aesthetics of the Homeric Hospitality Scene*. Ann Arbor.
–. (1994). 'The Cretan *Odyssey*. A Lie Truer than Truth', *AJP* 115: 157–73.
Reinhardt, K. (1996). 'The Adventures in the *Odyssey*', in: S. Schein (ed.), *Reading the* Odyssey. Princeton, 63–132.
Rengakos, A. (2015). 'Narrative Techniques in the Epic Cycle', in: M. Fantuzzi and C. Tsagalis (eds.), *The Greek Epic Cycle and Its Ancient Reception*. Cambridge, 154–63.
Russo, J. (1992). 'Books XVII-XX', in: Heubeck, West, Hainsworth (1988–1992), vol. III, 3–130.
Sacks, R. (1987). *The Traditional Phrase in Homer*. Leiden.
Sammons, B. (2013). 'Narrative Doublets in the Epic Cycle', *AJP* 134 529–56.
–. (2017). *Device and Composition in the Greek Epic Cycle*. Oxford.
Scodel, R. (2002). *Listening to Homer*. Ann Arbor.
–. (2004). 'The Modesty of Homer', in: C. J. Mackie (ed.), *Oral Performance and Its Contexts*. Leiden, 1–19.

–. (2005). 'Odysseus' Ethnographic Excursions', in: R. Rabel (ed.), *Approaches to Homer, Ancient and Modern*. Swansea, 147–65.
Scott, J. A. (1916). 'The Sources of the *Odyssey*', *CJ* 12: 119–30.
Small, J. P. (2003). *The Parallel Worlds of Classical Art and Text*. Cambridge.
Snodgrass, A. M. (1998). *Homer and the Artists*. Cambridge.
Squire, M. (2009). *Image and Text in Graeco-Roman Antiquity*. Cambridge.
Stanford, W. B. (1954). *The Ulysses Theme*. Oxford.
Touchefeu-Meynier, O. (1968). *Thèmes odysséens dans l'art antique*. Paris.
–. (1992a). 'Odysseus', in: *LIMC* 6.1: 943–70.
–. (1992b). 'Kyklops/Kyklopes', in: *LIMC* 6.1: 154–9.
–. (1997). 'Polyphemus I', in: *LIMC*, vol. 8 suppl.: 1011–19.
Tsagalis, C. (2008). *The Oral Palimpsest: Exploring Intertextuality in the Homeric Epics*. Washington, DC and Cambridge, MA.
–. (2012). 'Deauthorizing the Epic Cycle: Odysseus' False Tale to Eumaeus (*Od.* 14.199–359)', in: F. Montanari, A. Rengakos and C. Tsagalis (eds.), *Homeric Contexts: Neoanalysis and the Interpretation of Oral Poetry*. Berlin, 309–46.
Vergados, A. (2013). *The Homeric Hymn to Hermes*. Berlin.
Vidal-Naquet, P. (1996). 'Land and Sacrifice in the *Odyssey*', in: S. Schein (ed.), *Reading the Odyssey*. Princeton, 33–54.
West, M. L. (1997). *The East Face of Helicon: West Asiatic Elements in Greek Poetry and Myth*. Oxford.
–. (2005). '*Odyssey* and *Argonautica*', *CQ* 55: 39–64.
–. (2014). *The Making of the* Odyssey. Oxford.
West, S. (1981). 'An Alternative Nostos for Odysseus', *LCM* 6:169–75.
–. (1988). 'Books I-IV', in: Heubeck (1988–1992), vol. I, 51–248.
–. (2012). 'Odyssean Stratigraphy', in: Ø. Andersen and D. T. T. Haug (eds.), *Relative Chronology in Early Greek Epic Poetry*. Cambridge, 122–37.
Woodhouse, W. J. (1930). *The Composition of Homer's* Odyssey. Oxford.
Wüst, E. (1935–1937). 'Odysseus', *RE* 17.2: 1905–96.
Zerba, M. (2009). 'Odyssean Charisma and The Uses of Persuasion', *AJP* 130: 313–39.

Jonas Grethlein
The best of the Achaeans? Odysseus and Achilles in the *Odyssey*

As the papers in this volume illustrate, the making of Homeric epic can be approached from various critical angles. While archaeological and epigraphic evidence permits us to assess the role and use of writing in archaic Greece, comparative studies help us understand the dynamics of oral composition and orally-derived traditions. Later Greek literature provides potential clues about the institutional setting in which the *Iliad* and the *Odyssey* may have been performed, whether as a whole or in parts. Finally, the epics themselves shed light on their own performance. Achilles' singing of κλέα ἀνδρῶν in the *Iliad* as well as the entries of Phemius and Demodocus in the *Odyssey* have been seen as an embedded mirror of the performance of the Homeric poems.

The making of the epic has also left traces that are tightly interwoven in the *Iliad*'s and the *Odyssey*'s poetic textures. As Monro pointed out at the beginning of the 20th century, 'the *Odyssey* never repeats or refers to any incident related in the *Iliad*'.[1] This observation first led to the thesis that the *Odyssey* was composed without an awareness of the *Iliad*.[2] However, the monumentality of the *Iliad* and the salience of the Trojan War in the *Odyssey* have made it hard to maintain this view; the systematic avoidance of references to the *Iliad* in the *Odyssey* seems rather to be intended. Moreover, there are numerous passages in the *Odyssey* which apparently allude to the *Iliad* – and perhaps also Iliadic verses that acknowledge the *Odyssey*[3] – through a careful and marked reworking of its language. Drawing on studies in oral poetry, Homerists have argued that, emerging at the same time, both poems influenced each other. In the words of Pietro Pucci:

> The two texts probably evolved simultaneously, each aware of the other, before being fixed in the monumental compositions we now have, and it is likely that during the formative period some passages in each were intentionally revised to corresponding passages in

---

1 Monro (1901) 325.
2 E.g. Page (1955).
3 This is contentious; see Currie (2016) 39–40, who assumes that only the *Odyssey* responds to the *Iliad*.

It is with great admiration that I offer this article to Antonios Rengakos. I have learned a great deal from Antonios' important publications on Homeric epic, ancient historiography and in other fields, and it has been a delightful experience to work with him on various occasions.

https://doi.org/9783110559873-008

the other. Clearly, the *Iliad* and *Odyssey* presume each other, border and limit each other, to such extent that one, as it were, writes the other.⁴

My paper offers a case-study of this kind of interaction between oral poems by exploring the *Odyssey*'s presentation of its main hero against the backdrop of the *Iliad*'s Achilles. Homer not only juxtaposes the two heroes explicitly, he also evokes more subtly specific actions of Achilles in the *Iliad* as a foil to Odysseus' deeds in the *Odyssey*. While some of these allusions have been duly noticed, others still wait to be teased out. As we shall see, the juxtaposition of Odysseus with the Iliadic Achilles does not exhaust itself in its metapoetic significance nor can it be reduced to the antagonism of μῆτις versus βίη.⁵ While some passages strive to cast Odysseus as the greater hero and the *Odyssey* as the superior epic (I), others rather align Odysseus with Achilles (II). This resemblance with Achilles, I contend, gives substance to a view of Odysseus that challenges his positive portrayal. As Eustathius shrewdly observed in his commentary, Homer is *philodysseus* (1878.47); nonetheless, hidden under the narrative surface of the *Odyssey*, notably in the *mnēstērophonia* (III), but also earlier in the *Apologoi* (IV), we can detect a layer that is critical of Odysseus. The evocation of Achilles as a model is crucial to this deviant perspective of Odysseus. My argument thus illustrates the complexity of the kind of intertextuality to which oral composition and tradition gave rise. The interaction of Odysseus with the *Iliad*'s hero implies far more than a competition between the best of the Achaeans and the rivalry of the two monumental poems.

I. Odysseus versus Achilles

Odysseus is explicitly juxtaposed with Achilles three times in the *Odyssey*. Demodocus' first song in Book 8 deals with the 'quarrel of Odysseus and Achilles, son

---

4 Pucci (1987) 18. See also Nagy (1979) 20 – 2, and more recently Tsagalis (2008). Burgess (2006) approaches Homeric intertextuality from an angle that combines oral poetry with neoanalysis. Most recently, Currie (2016) has made a case for the pervasiveness of intertextuality in Homer. Bakker (2013) 157– 69 offers a general reassessment of inter– and intratextuality in the oral tradition of Homeric epic. On the *Odyssey* as responding to the *Iliad*, see also Usener (1990); Rutherford (1991–3); Danek (1998); Rengakos (2002).
5 Nagy (1979) has become the canonical reference. The tendency to combine a diachronic approach to Homer with metapoetic readings continues to thrive. Elmer (2013), for example, interprets scenes of decision–making in the *Iliad* as reflective of the evolvement of the epics. Currie (2016) follows a very different agenda, but he also tends to link intertextual references to other poems to poetic rivalry.

of Peleus' (νεῖκος Ὀδυσσῆος καὶ Πηλεΐδεω Ἀχιλῆος, 8.75). We can leave aside the tricky question of whether Homer simply invents this controversy or alludes to another oral tradition.⁶ What matters for our purposes here is that Odysseus and Achilles are adduced as 'the best of the Achaeans', who are at loggerheads with each other (... ὅ τ' ἄριστοι Ἀχαιῶν δηριόωντο, 8.78). Several modern scholars have adopted the idea of some ancient commentators who note that the quarrel is about how to capture Troy, with Achillean force or with Odyssean ruse.⁷ Even if we do not follow this interpretation, the phrase 'through the designs of great Zeus' (... Διὸς μεγάλου διὰ βουλάς, 8.82) seems to gesture to the beginning of the *Iliad* and to complement the confrontation of the two heroes by a juxtaposition of the two epics.⁸

While the brief summary of Demodocus' song does not give one hero an advantage over the other,⁹ the meeting of Odysseus with Achilles in the *Nekyia* suggests the superiority of the former over the latter. Odysseus first gives Achilles the pride of place. He addresses him as 'by far the greatest of the Achaeans' (ὦ Ἀχιλεῦ, Πηλῆος υἱέ, μέγα φέρτατ' Ἀχαιῶν, 11.478) and closes his speech (11.482–6):

...Ἀχιλλεῦ, οὔ τις ἀνὴρ προπάροιθε μακάρτερος οὔτ' ἄρ' ὀπίσσω·
πρὶν μὲν γάρ σε ζωὸν ἐτίομεν ἶσα θεοῖσιν
Ἀργεῖοι, νῦν αὖτε μέγα κρατέεις νεκύεσσιν
ἐνθάδ' ἐών· τῶ μή τι θανὼν ἀκαχίζευ, Ἀχιλλεῦ.

...Achilles,
no man before has been more blessed than you, nor ever
will be. Before, when you were alive, we Argives honored you
as we did the gods, and now in this place you have great authority
over the dead. Do not grieve, even in death, Achilles.

In his much-quoted response, however, Achilles radically rejects this view of his bliss (11.488–91):

μὴ δή μοι θάνατόν γε παραύδα, φαίδιμ' Ὀδυσσεῦ.
βουλοίμην κ' ἐπάρουρος ἐὼν θητευέμεν ἄλλωι,

---

6 See, for instance, Marg (1956); Rüter (1969) 247–54; Nagy (1979) 42–58; Clay (1983) 97–106, 241–6; Finkelberg (1987); Danek (1998) 142–50.
7 Scholion ad *Od.* 8.75 HQV ad 8.75 E, ad 8.77 BE, and, e.g., Clay (1983) 101–2; de Jong (2001) ad 8.73–82; contra Danek (1998) 146–50.
8 On this and further echoes of the beginning of the *Iliad*, see Clay (1983) 103–4. For the confrontation of the *Odyssey* and the *Iliad*, see Rüter (1969) 253–4; Nagy (1979) 40–1; Clay (1983) 106–7.
9 Pace de Jong (2001) ad 11.482–91.

ἀνδρὶ παρ' ἀκλήρωι, ὧι μὴ βίοτος πολὺς εἴη,
ἢ πᾶσιν νεκύεσσι καταφθιμένοισιν ἀνάσσειν.

O shining Odysseus. Never try to console me for dying.
I would rather follow the plow as thrall to another
man, one with no land allotted him and not much to live on,
than be a king over all the perished dead.

In certain important ways, Odysseus' fate is an inversion of the fate chosen by Achilles. Whereas Achilles traded the option of a happy life at home for eternal fame,[10] Odysseus rejected the immortality offered by Calypso and strives to return to Ithaca.[11] He may praise Achilles and, tossed around by the waves at the shores of Scheria, he may even have uttered the wish that he had died on the battle-field and thereby won glory: 'as I wish I too had died at that time and met my destiny / on the day when the greatest number of Trojans threw their bronze-headed / weapons upon me, over the body of perished Achilleus, / and I would have had my rites and the Achaians given me glory' (ὡς δὴ ἐγώ γ' ὄφελον θανέειν καὶ πότμον ἐπισπεῖν / ἤματι τῶι ὅτε μοι πλεῖστοι χαλκήρεα δοῦρα / Τρῶες ἐπέρριψαν περὶ Πηλεΐωνι θανόντι. / τῶ κ' ἔλαχον κτερέων, καί μευ κλέος ἦγον Ἀχαιοί, 5.308–11).[12] But against this Achilles' bitter words highlight that Odysseus is the luckier of the two: he has escaped death, which no amount of glory can counterweight.[13]

The comparison of Odysseus with Achilles is finally taken up in the second *Nekyia*. When the killed suitors enter the Underworld, they meet the shadows of Agamemnon and Achilles, who are conversing about their fates. Achilles moans about the murder of Agamemnon, who was denied a heroic death at Troy and who as a result does not have a tomb to preserve his glory. Conversely Agamemnon praises Achilles, as he received an elaborate proper burial. The Greeks 'piled up a grave mound that was both great and perfect, / on a jutting promontory there by the wide Hellespont, / so that it can be seen afar from out on the water / by men now alive and those to be born in the future' (ἀμφ' αὐτοῖσι δ'

---

[10] 9.412–6: 'If I stay here and fight beside the city of the Trojans, / my return home is gone, but my glory shall be everlasting; / but if I return home to the beloved land of my fathers, / the excellence of my glory is gone, but there will be a long life / left for me, and my end in death will not come to me quickly.' (εἰ μέν κ' αὖθι μένων Τρώων πόλιν ἀμφιμάχωμαι / ὤλετο μέν μοι νόστος, ἀτὰρ κλέος ἄφθιτον ἔσται· / εἰ δέ κεν οἴκαδ' ἵκωμι φίλην ἐς πατρίδα γαῖαν, / ὤλετό μοι κλέος ἐσθλόν, ἐπὶ δηρὸν δέ μοι αἰὼν / ἔσσεται, οὐδέ κέ μ' ὦκα τέλος θανάτοιο κιχείη).
[11] Cf. Wender (1978) 42–3.
[12] For an Iliadic echo (*Il.* 21.281–3) in these verses, see Usener (1990) 141–7. With Odysseus' wish, compare also Telemachus' words in 1.237–40.
[13] Cf. Wender (1978) 43; Schein (1996) 10–14; Rengakos (2002) 180.

ἔπειτα μέγαν καὶ ἀμύμονα τύμβον / χεύαμεν Ἀργείων ἱερὸς στρατὸς αἰχμητάων / ἀκτῆι ἔπι προὐχούσηι, ἐπὶ πλατεῖ Ἑλλησπόντωι, / ὥς κεν τηλεφανὴς ἐκ ποντόφιν ἀνδράσιν εἴη / τοῖσ', οἳ νῦν γεγάασι καὶ οἳ μετόπισθεν ἔσονται, 24.80–4). Odysseus enters this contest as a third party when Amphinomus reports his return and the slaying of the suitors. Besides evoking the story of the Atreidai as a foil to Odysseus and his family yet another time,[14] Homer here also envisages Odysseus specifically in light of Achilles. In his exchange with Amphinomus, Agamemnon addresses Odysseus directly: 'O fortunate son of Laertes, Odysseus of many devices' (ὄλβιε Λαέρταο πάϊ, πολυμήχαν' Ὀδυσσεῦ, 24.192). This address repeats the formula with which Agamemnon had directed himself to Achilles: 'O fortunate son of Peleus, Achilles, like the immortals' (ὄλβιε Πηλέος υἱέ, θεοῖσ' ἐπιείκελ' Ἀχιλλεῦ, 24.36). The parallel drives home the fact that, whereas Achilles had to renounce his *nostos* to gain *kleos*, Odysseus has been granted both *nostos* and glory.[15] More precisely: Odysseus has gained *kleos* through his *nostos*.

The metapoetic significance is hard to ignore when the *Odyssey* compares the glory of its hero with the fame of the *Iliad*'s champion, Achilles. Parallel to Odysseus who gets the better off Achilles, the *Odyssey* outshines the *Iliad*. Just as the epic makes the hero, the hero makes the epic. And yet, another metapoetic reflection is more pronounced in the second *Nekyia*. Agamemnon mentions song as the medium of Penelope's glory and Clytaemnestra's shame, but when he muses on Achilles' fate, he refers to his tomb as the guarantee of fame. The tomb is placed conspicuously on a promontory so that it announces Achilles' κλέος to 'men now alive and those to be born in the future' (οἳ νῦν γεγάασι καὶ οἳ μετόπισθεν ἔσονται, 24.84). The testimony of the grave, however, is bound to a specific place; it reaches only men 'out on the water' (ἐκ ποντόφιν, 24.83). Odysseus' glory, on the other hand, 'goes up to the heavens', as he himself claims when he discloses his identity at the court of Alcinous (... καί μευ κλέος οὐρανὸν ἵκει, 9.20). The spatial confinement of material bearers of memory is set in implicit contrast with the limitless circulation of song.

A much-discussed passage in the *Iliad* further reflects on the impermanence of material memory.[16] Before the chariot race in Patroclus' funeral games, Nestor gives instructions to his son and describes the turn post (23.326–33):

σῆμα δέ τοι ἐρέω μάλ' ἀριφραδές, οὐδέ σε λήσει.
ἕστηκε ξύλον αὖον ὅσον τ' ὄργυι' ὑπὲρ αἴης

---
14 Cf. D'Arms/Hulley (1946); Hölscher (1967).
15 Cf. Nagy (1979) 39.
16 Cf. Nagy (1983); Lynn-George (1988); Grethlein (2008) 31–2.

> ἢ δρυὸς ἢ πεύκης· τὸ μὲν οὐ καταπύθεται ὄμβρωι,
> λᾶε δὲ τοῦ ἑκάτερθεν ἐρηρέδαται δύο λευκὼ
> ἐν ξυνοχῆισιν ὁδοῦ, λεῖος δ' ἱππόδρομος ἀμφὶς
> ἤ τευ σῆμα βροτοῖο πάλαι κατατεθνηῶτος,
> ἢ τό γε νύσσα τέτυκτο ἐπὶ προτέρων ἀνθρώπων,
> καὶ νῦν τέρματ' ἔθηκε ποδάρκης δῖος Ἀχιλλεύς.

> I will give you a clear mark and you cannot fail to notice it.
> There is a dry stump standing up from the ground about six feet,
> oak, it may be, or pine, and not rotted away by rain-water,
> and two white stones are leaned against it, one on either side,
> at the joining place of the ways, and there is smooth driving around it.
> Either it is the grave-mark of someone who died long ago,
> or was set as a racing goal by men who lived before our time.
> Now swift-footed brilliant Achilleus has made it the turning post.

Nestor is the incarnation of memory, but even he is uncertain about the significance of what may have been a tomb. His uncertainty alerts us to the instability of the commemorative power of tombs. The glory created by stones is not only spatially limited, it is also menaced by the flux of time. Even though a material marker is foregrounded as the medium of Achilles' κλέος, the *Odyssey* obviously confronts the *Iliad* when it contrasts its own hero, his virtues and his life, with the *Iliad*'s protagonist and his fate. Poetic rivalry is an important aspect of the *Odyssey*'s oral intertextuality with the *Iliad* and it has duly attracted much attention in scholarship. It is, however, not the only aspect, as we will now see when we consider implicit references and more subtle allusions to Achilles in the *Odyssey*.

II. Odysseus as Achilles *redivivus*

Passages in which Achilles is conjured up implicitly as a foil to Odysseus cluster together in the execution of the suitors as narrated in Book 22. Odysseus first shoots Antinous and then reveals his identity. The suitors are terrified. In an attempt to avert the impending massacre, Eurymachus claims that the culprit, Antinous, has been punished. Odysseus ought to save the others for they would 'repay in gold and bronze' (χαλκόν τε χρυσόν τ' ἀποδώσομεν..., 22.58) what they have eaten and drunk in his house (22.45–59):

> εἰ μὲν δὴ Ὀδυσεὺς Ἰθακήσιος εἰλήλουθας,
> ταῦτα μὲν αἴσιμα εἶπες, ὅσα ῥέζεσκον Ἀχαιοί,
> πολλὰ μὲν ἐν μεγάροισιν ἀτάσθαλα, πολλὰ δ' ἐπ' ἀγροῦ.
> ἀλλ' ὁ μὲν ἤδη κεῖται, ὃς αἴτιος ἔπλετο πάντων,

Ἀντίνοος· οὗτος γὰρ ἐπήλεν τάδε ἔργα,
οὔ τι γάμου τόσσον κεχρημένος οὐδὲ χατίζων,
ἀλλ' ἄλλα φρονέων, τά οἱ οὐκ ἐτέλεσσε Κρονίων,
ὄφρ' Ἰθάκης κατὰ δῆμον ἐϋκτιμένης βασιλεύοι
αὐτός, ἀτὰρ σὸν παῖδα κατακτείνειε λοχήσας.
νῦν δ' ὁ μὲν ἐν μοίρῃ πέφαται, σὺ δὲ φείδεο λαῶν
σῶν· ἀτὰρ ἄμμες ὄπισθεν ἀρεσσάμενοι κατὰ δῆμον,
ὅσσα τοι ἐκπέποται καὶ ἐδήδοται ἐν μεγάροισι,
τιμὴν ἀμφὶς ἄγοντες ἐεικοσάβοιον ἕκαστος,
χαλκόν τε χρυσόν τ' ἀποδώσομεν, εἰς ὅ κε σὸν κῆρ
ἰανθῇ· πρὶν δ' οὔ τι νεμεσσητὸν κεχολῶσθαι.

If in truth you are Odysseus of Ithaca, come home,
what you have said is fair about all the wickedness done you
by the Achaeans, much in your house and much in the country.
But now the man is down who was responsible for all
this, Antinoos. It was he who pushed this action,
not so much that he wanted the marriage, or cared for it,
but with other things in mind, which the son of Cronus would not
grant him: to lie in wait for your son and kill him, and then
be king himself in the district of strong-founded Ithaca.
Now he has perished by his own fate. Then spare your own
people, and afterward we will make public reparation
for all that has been eaten and drunk in your halls, setting
each upon himself an assessment of twenty oxen.
We will pay it back in bronze and gold to you, until your heart
is softened. Till then, we cannot blame you for being angry.

However, Odysseus harshly rejects this offer (22.61–4):

Εὐρύμαχ', οὐδ' εἴ μοι πατρώϊα πάντ' ἀποδοῖτε,
ὅσσα τε νῦν ὔμμ' ἐστὶ καὶ εἴ ποθεν ἄλλ' ἐπιθεῖτε,
οὐδέ κεν ὣς ἔτι χεῖρας ἐμὰς λήξαιμι φόνοιο,
πρὶν πᾶσαν μνηστῆρας ὑπερβασίην ἀποτεῖσαι.

Eurymachus, if you gave me all of your father's possessions,
all that you have now, and what you could add from elsewhere,
even so, I would not stay my hands from the slaughter,
until I had taken revenge for all the suitors' transgression.

As has been noticed by previous scholars, Odysseus' response is reminiscent of Achilles' rejection of the goods offered by Agamemnon in *Iliad* 9 and the ransom that Priam is willing to pay for Hector's corpse in *Iliad* 22.[17] Context and language

---

[17] Cf. Schein (1999) 352–5; Bakker (2013) 151–2. In *Iliad* 22, Achilles will ultimately extradite

are strikingly similar. Like Achilles, Odysseus shows himself unimpressed by a seemingly generous offer and does not relent in his anger. Both consider material goods, no matter how vast, to be insufficient as a compensation for the harm they have experienced. Neither hero can be appeased; Odysseus as well as Achilles insists on the satisfaction of vengeance.

The linguistic parallel to Achilles' speech in *Iliad* 9 is particularly striking. Achilles is more abundant in his list of things that would fail to soften him, but syntactically Odysseus' refusal is closely modelled on his speech. It repeats *verbatim* one verse (ὅσσα τε νῦν ὕμμ' ἐστὶ καὶ εἴ ποθεν ἄλλ' ἐπιθεῖτε) – and copies the syntactic structure of οὐδ' εἰ... οὐδέ κεν ὥς... πρὶν (*Il.* 9.379–87):

> οὐδ' εἴ μοι δεκάκις τε καὶ εἰκοσάκις τόσα δοίη
> ὅσσά τέ οἱ νῦν ἔστι, καὶ εἴ ποθεν ἄλλα γένοιτο,
> οὐδ' ὅσ' ἐς Ὀρχομενὸν ποτινίσεται, οὐδ' ὅσα Θήβας
> Αἰγυπτίας, ὅθι πλεῖστα δόμοις ἐν κτήματα κεῖται,
> αἵ θ' ἑκατόμπυλοί εἰσι, διηκόσιοι δ' ἀν' ἑκάστας
> ἀνέρες ἐξοιχνεῦσι σὺν ἵπποισιν καὶ ὄχεσφιν·
> οὐδ' εἴ μοι τόσα δοίη ὅσα ψάμαθός τε κόνις τε,
> οὐδέ κεν ὣς ἔτι θυμὸν ἐμὸν πείσει' Ἀγαμέμνων
> πρίν γ' ἀπὸ πᾶσαν ἐμοὶ δόμεναι θυμαλγέα λώβην.
>
> Not if he gave me ten times as much, and twenty times over
> as he possesses now, not if more should come to him from elsewhere,
> or gave all that is brought in to Orchomenos, all that is brought in
> to Thebes of Egypt, where the greatest possessions lie up in the houses,
> Thebes of the hundred gates, where through each of the gates two hundred
> fighting men come forth to war with horses and chariots;
> not if he gave me gifts as many as the sand or the dust is,
> not even so would Agamemnon have his way with my spirit
> until he had made good to me all this heartrending insolence.

As Schein points out, Odysseus' rejection of the rich compensation is somewhat surprising since he is 'consistently represented as concerned with κέρδεα (profits) and the honor (τιμή) associated with them'.[18] Even more poignant is the irony that Odysseus, who in the *Iliad* conveys Agamemnon's offer to Achilles, now himself rejects a similar offer with words reminiscent of Achilles' speech.

It has been shown that 'the *Odyssey*'s final battle, the climax of Odysseus' return, is looking at the *Iliad*'s final battle, the climax of Achilles' return.'[19]

Hector's corpse, but as Schein (1999) 355 observes, 'it is clear that he does not surrender his feelings because of this ransom'.
18 Schein (1999) 352.
19 Bakker (2013) 151.

The arguably most striking parallel occurs between the killings of Leodes in the *Odyssey* and Lycaon in the *Iliad*. In a close reading, Pucci has analyzed the strongly Iliadic vocabulary in which the scene leading to the death of Leodes is couched.[20] The specific parallel to the Lycaon scene is cemented by the pointed repetition of a verse: Leodes addresses Odysseus with the same words that Lycaon uses in the *Iliad*: 'I am at your knees, Odysseus / Achilles. Respect me, have mercy' (γουνοῦμαί σ', Ὀδυσεῦ / Ἀχιλεῦ· σὺ δέ μ' αἴδεο καί μ' ἐλέησον, *Od*. 22.312; *Il*. 21.74). Both plead innocent: Lycaon claims that he does not even have the same mother as Hector, whose killing of Patroclus has infuriated Achilles ('Do not kill me. I am not from the same womb as Hektor, / he who killed your powerful and kindly companion'; μή με κτεῖν', ἐπεὶ οὐχ ὁμογάστριος Ἕκτορός εἰμι, / ὅς τοι ἑταῖρον ἔπεφνεν ἐνηέα τε κρατερόν τε, *Il*. 21.95–6). Leodes asserts that he was not involved in the suitors' crimes, that, in fact, he even tried to dissuade them ('For I claim that never in your halls did I say or do anything / wrong to any one of the women, but always was trying / to stop any one of the other suitors who acted in that way.'; οὐ γάρ πώ τινά φημι γυναικῶν ἐν μεγάροισιν / εἰπεῖν οὐδέ τι ῥέξαι ἀτάσθαλον· ἀλλὰ καὶ ἄλλους / παύεσκον μνηστῆρας, ὅτις τοιαῦτά γε ῥέζοι, 22.313–15).

The circumstances bestow pathos on both deaths, if for somewhat different reasons: Lycaon had already been captured by Achilles before, but while Achilles had sold him as a slave the first time, he will now kill him with no mercy.[21] Lycaon had only eleven days in Troy after his release; the feasting which celebrated his being saved throws into relief his present destiny: Achilles 'drawing his sharp sword struck him / beside the neck at the collar-bone, and the double-edged sword / plunged full length inside' (Ἀχιλεὺς δὲ ἐρυσσάμενος ξίφος ὀξὺ / τύψε κατὰ κληῖδα παρ' αὐχένα, πᾶν δέ οἱ εἴσω / δῦ ξίφος ἄμφηκες, 21.116–18). He then throws Lycaon's corpse into the river Scamander to feed the fish. On the other hand, Odysseus' rejection of Leodes' supplication is put more forcefully by the fact that his victim is a bard and had stood apart from the other suitors, not supporting the siege of Odysseus' court: 'To him alone their excesses / were hateful, and he disapproved of all the suitors' (ἀτασθαλίαι δέ οἱ οἴωι / ἐχθραὶ ἔσαν, πᾶσιν δὲ νεμέσσα μνηστήρεσσιν, 21.146–7). As Pucci noted, the pointed echo and similarity between the two scenes draws our attention to the profound difference between Achilles and Odysseus: whereas Achilles deprives Lycaon of the joy of homecoming and emphasizes the inevitability of death, Odysseus 'murders the innocent Leodes because Leodes prayed that Odys-

---

20 Pucci (1987) 128–38. See also Usener (1990) 131–40.
21 On the killing of Lycaon, see further Grethlein (2006) 130–5; 161–3.

seus might never return... Odysseus, in the garb of Achilles, vindicates the value of homecoming, of life and its pleasures'.²²

Achilles' killing spree in the last third of the *Iliad* is also evoked as a model for the *mnēstērophonia* through a lion simile. Homer frequently compares his heroes with lions, commonly to highlight their courage and manliness.²³ Odysseus has been juxtaposed with a lion before: Menelaus and Telemachus describe Odysseus as a lion, which finds in his home two fawns that a doe has left there (4.333–40 = 17.124–31). The carelessness of the doe and the defenselessness of the fawns illustrate the situation of the suitors, who continue to feast on the goods of Odysseus after his return to Ithaca. When Odysseus leaves the thicket at the shores of Scheria and approaches Nausicaa, Homer compares him with a hungry lion, this time to make tangible Odysseus' destitution and the fright of the Phaeacan girls (6.130–6):

> βῆ δ' ἴμεν ὥς τε λέων ὀρεσίτροφος, ἀλκὶ πεποιθώς,
> ὅς τ' εἶσ' ὑόμενος καὶ ἀήμενος, ἐν δέ οἱ ὄσσε
> δαίεται· αὐτὰρ ὁ βουσὶ μετέρχεται ἢ ὀΐεσσιν
> ἠὲ μετ' ἀγροτέρας ἐλάφους· κέλεται δέ ἑ γαστὴρ
> μήλων πειρήσοντα καὶ ἐς πυκινὸν δόμον ἐλθεῖν·
> ὣς Ὀδυσεὺς κούρῃσιν ἐϋπλοκάμοισιν ἔμελλε
> μείξεσθαι, γυμνός περ ἐών· χρειὼ γὰρ ἵκανε.

> ...and went in the confidence of his strength, like some hill-kept lion,
> who advances, though he is rained on and blown by the wind, and both eyes
> kindle; he goes out after cattle or sheep, or it may be
> deer in the wilderness, and his belly is urgent upon him
> to get inside of a close steading and go for the sheepflocks.
> So Odysseus was ready to face young girls with well-ordered
> hair, naked though he was, for the need was on him;...

The simile in the *mnēstērophonia* is very different from these earlier comparisons: Euryclea finds Odysseus among the corpses of the suitors, 'spattered over with gore and battle filth, like a lion / who has been feeding on an ox of the fields, and goes off / covered with blood, all his chest and his flanks on either / side bloody, a terrible thing to look in the face; so / now Odysseus feet and the hands above them were spattered' (αἵματι καὶ λύθρωι πεπαλαγμένον ὥς τε λέοντα, / ὅς ῥά τε βεβρωκὼς βοὸς ἔρχεται ἀγραύλοιο· / πᾶν δ' ἄρα οἱ στῆθός

---

22 Pucci (1987) 141.
23 Cf. Schnapp-Gourbeillon (1981); Lonsdale (1990). On Odysseus and lion similes, see Moulton (1977) 139–41; Magrath (1982); Friedrich (1981).

τε παρήϊά τ' ἀμφοτέρωθεν / αἱματόεντα πέλει, δεινὸς δ' εἰς ὦπα ἰδέσθαι· / ὣς Ὀδυσεὺς πεπάλακτο πόδας καὶ χεῖρας ὕπερθεν, 22.402–6).[24]

Here the image of the lion expresses neither a hero's fortitude nor his isolation, but his animal-like appearance: Odysseus is covered with blood, besides his hands and feet his cheeks are dripping with blood, just as those of a beast which has chased and eaten another animal. The killing of the suitors is thereby aligned with the licentious chase of a predator. The comparison gains poignancy from an Iliadic echo: Homer also uses the image of a lion to illustrate Achilles' rage on the battle-field after Patroclus' death. Achilles wishes to eat Hector's body raw ('I wish only that my spirit and fury would drive me / to hack your meat away and eat it raw for the things that / you have done to me.'; αἲ γάρ πως αὐτόν με μένος καὶ θυμὸς ἀνήηι / ὤμ' ἀποταμνόμενον κρέα ἔδμεναι, οἷα ἔοργας, Il. 22.346–7) and Apollo states that in Achilles' breast 'there are no feelings of justice, nor can / his mind be bent, but his purposes are fierce, like a lion / who when he has given way to his own great strength and his haughty / spirit, goes among the flocks of men, to devour them' (ἀλλ' ὀλοῶι Ἀχιλῆϊ θεοὶ βούλεσθ' ἐπαρήγειν, / ὧι οὔτ' ἄρ φρένες εἰσὶν ἐναίσιμοι οὔτε νόημα / γναμπτὸν ἐνὶ στήθεσσι, λέων δ' ὣς ἄγρια οἶδεν· / ὅς τ' ἐπεὶ ἄρ μεγάληι τε βίηι καὶ ἀγήνορι θυμῶι / εἴξας εἶσ' ἐπὶ μῆλα βροτῶν ἵνα δαῖτα λάβηισιν, Il. 24.39–43).[25] Whereas Achilles appears as a hungry lion, Odysseus is likened to a lion which has quenched its hunger. Despite this difference, the Achillean model for Odysseus is obvious. Their revenge, the slaughtering of their enemies, is depicted as an act of predation; the lion image expresses that Odysseus and Achilles have transformed heroic warfare into bestial hunting.

Since the model of Achilles is so strong in the *mnēstērophonia*, it is at least possible that Athena's final intervention in the *Odyssey* evokes the intervention of the same goddess in *Iliad* 1. When Athena commands that the battle be stopped, all fighters are intimidated and pause. Only Odysseus, 'with a terrible cry' (σμερδαλέον δ' ἐβόησε …, 24.537), continues to rage. Zeus has to throw a thunderbolt and Athena must address Odysseus personally before he relents. The circumstances in *Iliad* 1 are different: here it is not a battle in full swing, but a quarrel between two men about to escalate, and yet, in both situations the same goddess stops a hero, caught up in his anger, from acting on his impulse. Just as Achilles 'did not disobey / the word of Athena' (… οὐδ ἀπίθησε / μύθωι Ἀθη-

---

[24] This simile is later taken up in direct speech by Euryclea in 23.45–8.
[25] Achilles is also compared with a lion in *Il.* 18.318–23; 20.164–75. In *Il.* 22.262–3, he himself compares his relationship with Hector to that between lions and men and between wolves and lambs. In *Il.* 22.189–93, Achilles is likened to a dog, in *Il.* 19.365–6 the grinding of his teeth evokes the idea of a wild boar. Cf. Grethlein (2005) 261–4.

ναίης. ..., *Il.* 1.220–1), Odysseus 'obeyed her with happy heart' (... ὁ δ' ἐπείθετο, χαῖρε δὲ θυμῶι, 24.545). If we follow through this parallel, then Odysseus' final appearance in the *Odyssey* is projected against the backdrop of Achilles' first entry in the *Iliad*. Placed prominently at the *Odyssey*'s ending, the allusion would give emphasis to Odysseus' Achilles-like comportment.

Homeric scholarship primarily views Odysseus as an antipode to Achilles, who substitutes ruse for force. Nagy's juxtaposition of them as representatives of different kinds of heroism, Achilles the champion of βίη, Odysseus the master of μῆτις, has become a staple in later readings.[26] While this is an important point, it should not detract us from recognizing further facets of the relation between Odysseus and Achilles in the *Odyssey*. As I have tried to show, Odysseus' revenge on Ithaca is closely modeled on Achilles' rage after Patroclus' death. Scholars who have already observed some of the parallels between Odysseus and Achilles in the *Odyssey* argue that the Iliadic foil throws into relief the heroic status which Odysseus recuperates on Ithaca. After traversing the miraculous world of the *Apologoi*, exposed to the threats of various monsters, Odysseus finally becomes an Iliadic hero again when he kills the suitors. Pucci comments on the repetition of verses from the *Iliad*: 'With such repetitions, the *Odyssey* puts Odysseus himself in the foreground – Odysseus as a champion of the Trojan War, inferior neither to Achilles nor to Diomedes.'[27] In a similar vein, Bakker writes: 'The extreme violence with which Odysseus retakes his house is not only a harsh necessity imposed on him by Poseidon ..., who forces him to become just as savage as his son; it also places Odysseus in the rarefied sphere where Achilles obtains immortal κλέος without playing by the rules of the heroic code and without being part of the community of his peers and fellow Achaeans.'[28]

Pucci and Bakker identify a salient point that can be fruitfully combined with Cook's distinction of two sides of Odysseus' heroism.[29] As Cook argues, Odysseus is simultaneously an active hero, who punishes his enemies, and a passive hero, who endures ordeals. It is possible to find aspects of active heroism in the *Apologoi*, for instance when Odysseus blinds Polyphemus, and on Ithaca Odysseus has to handle humiliation at the hands of the suitors as well as physical attacks, but, on the whole, the *Odyssey* follows a trajectory in which the need for passive endurance cedes to the renewed empowerment of Odysseus

---

26 Nagy (1979).
27 Pucci (1987) 136.
28 Bakker (2013) 155.
29 Cook (1999).

as an active hero.³⁰ This dynamic of the *Odyssey*'s plot, the movement from passive to active heroism, is enhanced by the foil of the *Iliad*'s hero, which 'stresses Odysseus' Achillean valor'³¹ in the execution of his revenge plan.

III. The dark side of Odysseus in the *mnēstērophonia*

There is, however, more to the analogies between Odysseus and Achilles. The similarities, I contend, not only stress Odysseus' return to the elevated realm of an Iliadic hero, they also raise crucial questions about the ethical correctness of his actions. Achilles, especially in his rage after Patroclus' death, is, after all, a highly ambivalent heroic model. After Patroclus' death, Achilles is in a liminal state which brings him close to the gods, notably when he is fed nectar and ambrosia, but which also aligns him with beasts.³² His beast-like killing spree is reinforced by the fact that, against Odysseus' advice, he wishes to enter battle before having eaten. He thereby follows the lead of animals, which hunt in order to have something to eat. The *propter hoc* is replaced by a *post hoc*, but the order of first killing/then eating puts Achilles in line with beasts. Achilles himself presents his slaughtering as a perverted sacrifice, which fills the waves of Scamander with corpses: '...and there will not / be any rescue for you from your silvery-whirled strong-running / river, for all the numbers of bulls you dedicate to it/ and drown single-foot horses alive in its eddies. And yet / even so, die all an evil death...' (οὐδ' ὑμῖν ποταμός περ ἐΰρροος ἀργυροδίνης / ἀρκέσει, ᾧ δὴ δηθὰ πολέας ἱερεύετε ταύρους, / ζωοὺς δ' ἐν δίνῃσι καθίετε μώνυχας ἵππους. / ἀλλὰ καὶ ὣς ὀλέεσθε κακὸν μόρον..., 21.130–3). Moreover, when Hector asks him before their duel to agree to a fair treatment of the fallen warrior's corpse, he harshly rejects this idea, saying that 'there are no trustworthy oaths between men and lions, / nor wolves and lambs have spirit that can be brought to agreement / but forever these hold feelings of hate for each other' (ὡς οὐκ ἔστι λέουσι καὶ ἀνδράσιν ὅρκια πιστά, / οὐδὲ λύκοι τε καὶ ἄρνες ὁμόφρονα θυμὸν ἔχουσιν, / ἀλλὰ κακὰ φρονέουσι διαμπερὲς ἀλλήλοισιν, 22.262–4). Perhaps most disturbingly, after his victory, Achilles disregards the ritual of burial and cruelly mutilates Hector's corpse. Sacrifice, contractual agreements and burial are central

---

30 Cf. Grethlein (2017) 177–9.
31 Pucci (1987) 133.
32 Cf. Grethlein (2005). On Achilles' rage after Patroclus' death as a threat to order and civilization, see also Segal (1971); Hammer (2004), ch. 4.

tenets of civilization; Achilles' disdain for them demonstrates the transgressive nature of his rage.

The ambivalent model of Achillean heroism may thus do more than underpin Odysseus' heroic valour. That the Iliadic intertext also serves to question Odysseus' behaviour is evident in the poet's comparison of him with a lion. In addition to coupling Odysseus with Achilles, the simile also uncannily echoes the earlier comparison of Polyphemus with a lion.[33] The Cyclops kills two of Odysseus' companions: 'Then he cut them up limb by limb and got supper ready, / and like a lion reared in the hills, without leaving anything, / ate them, entrails, flesh and the marrowy bones alike' (τοὺς δὲ διὰ μελεϊστὶ ταμὼν ὁπλίσσατο δόρπον· / ἤσθιε δ' ὥς τε λέων ὀρεσίτροφος, οὐδ' ἀπέλειπεν, / ἔγκατά τε σάρκας τε καὶ ὀστέα μυελόεντα, 9.291–3). The later likening of Odysseus to a lion parallels the earlier depiction of one of his fiercest opponents. There is however one difference: unlike Odysseus, Polyphemus eats his victims. Meal and murder are metaphorically blended together in the *mnēstērophonia*,[34] but there is no actual case of cannibalism.

Nonetheless, the parallel between the two lion similes invites disconcerting questions: Is Odysseus' revenge different from Polyphemus' behavior? Is Odysseus not unlike a cannibalistic giant, who tramples on the basic rules of civilization? Odysseus himself aligns the suitors with Polyphemus when he compares his situation as a beggar at his own court with his stay in the Cyclops' cave: 'Bear up, my heart. You have had worse to endure before this / on that day when the irresistible Cyclops ate up / my strong companions, but you endured it until intelligence / got you out of the cave, though you expected to perish.' (τέτλαθι δή, κραδίη· καὶ κύντερον ἄλλο ποτ' ἔτλης, / ἤματι τῶι, ὅτε μοι μένος ἄσχετος ἤσθιε Κύκλωψ / ἰφθίμους ἑτάρους· σὺ δ' ἐτόλμας, ὄφρα σε μῆτις / ἐξάγαγ' ἐξ ἄντροιο ὀϊόμενον θανέεσθαι, 20.18–21). In both cases, he deploys a guest gift to punish a violation of the laws of hospitality, Maron's wine to trick the Cyclops and Iphitos' bow to shoot the suitors.[35] However, the tables can be turned: in entering Poyphemus' cave and eating his food in his absence, Odysseus resembles the suitors, who make use of Odysseus' absence to feast on his supplies. Odysseus' revenge also yields parallels to Polyphemus' crime: just as Polyphemus imprisons the invaders, Odysseus shuts the suitors into his megaron and kills them. The Cyclops closes the entrance of his cave with a massive stone,

---

33 Cf. Bakker (2013) 69–73.
34 See, for example, 20.392–4; 21.428–9. See also the comparison of Odysseus and his bow with a bard and his lyre, whose singing is the 'crowning of the feast' (21.406–9; τὰ γάρ τ' ἀναθήματα δαιτός, 21.430). Cf. Saïd (1979).
35 Cf. Grethlein (2008) 42–3.

'like a man closing the lid on a quiver' (ὡς εἴ τε φαρέτρηι πῶμ' ἐπιθείη, 9.314); in the *mnēstērophonia* it is a real quiver from which Odysseus takes his lethal arrows. How different, after all, is Odysseus from Polyphemus?

Admittedly, the thrust of this question is mitigated when, immediately after the lion simile in Book 22, Odysseus tells Euryclea not to rejoice too ostentaticously for 'it is not piety to glory so over slain men' (οὐχ ὁσίη κταμένοισιν ἐπ' ἀνδράσιν εὐχετάασθαι, 22.412). Nor should we forget that Homer takes pains to cast the suitors as reckless sinners. An impressive lexical arsenal is marshalled to present their courtship of Penelope as a transgression. The suitors are called ἀλεῖται, ὑπερηνορέοντες and ἄγριοι; they are charged with ὕβρις, ἀναιδές, αἴσχεα and ὑπερβασίη. Incisively, the suitors' consumption of Odysseus' goods is couched in vocabulary that suggests murder: βίοτον (κατ-)ἔδειν.[36] Βίοτος primarily means 'life', and metonymically signifies what nourishes life, livelihood. That this phrase helps legitimize the suitors' execution comes to the fore in Telemachus' words in 1.374–80 (2.139–45):

> ἐξιέναι μεγάρων· ἄλλας δ' ἀλεγύνετε δαῖτας,
> ὑμὰ κτήματ' ἔδοντες, ἀμειβόμενοι κατὰ οἴκους.
> εἰ δ' ὕμιν δοκέει τόδε λωΐτερον καὶ ἄμεινον
> ἔμμεναι, ἀνδρὸς ἑνὸς βίοτον νήποινον ὀλέσθαι,
> κείρετ'· ἐγὼ δὲ θεοὺς ἐπιβώσομαι αἰὲν ἐόντας,
> αἴ κέ ποθι Ζεὺς δῶισι παλίντιτα ἔργα γενέσθαι·
> νήποινοί κεν ἔπειτα δόμων ἔντοσθεν ὄλοισθε.
>
> ...that you go out of my palace and do your feasting elsewhere,
> eating up your own possessions, taking turns, household by household.
> But if you decide it is more profitable and better
> to go on, eating up one man's livelihood, without payment,
> then spoil my house. I will cry out to the gods everlasting
> in the hope that Zeus might somehow grant a reversal of fortunes.
> Then you may perish in this house, with no payment given.

Νήποινος refers not only, as elsewhere, to murder, but also to the destruction of Odysseus' livelihood, literally 'the eating of his life' (βίοτον ὀλέσθαι). The phrasing insinuates that the suitors' crime is equivalent to murder, and that consequently their death is the only appropriate response to it. Homer's persuasiveness shows not least in the comments of scholars, who emphasize the reciprocity in Odysseus' dealing with the suitors. Reece, for one, notes that the suitors 'should be prepared to be paid back in the same coin'.[37]

---

36 1.160; 11.116; 13.396, 428; 14.377; 15.32; 18.280.
37 Reece (1993): 179.

One may ask how grave the suitors' offence actually is: the suitors woo Penelope and try to assassinate Telemachus; however, neither endeavour is successful. Doubts about the appropriateness of the killing of the suitors may increase in the light of the fate of the Atreidai, whom Homer repeatedly compares with Odysseus' family. Whereas Orestes follows the so-called law of *talion* when he kills Aegisthus, the murderer of his father, Odysseus requites a material damage with mass murder. As we have seen, Odysseus is offered ample material compensation, but he rejects it with Achillean furor. Seen from this perspective, the *mnēstērophonia* may appear as an excessive act of revenge. That being said, we ought not to project onto the world of archaic epic our repudiation of revenge as nourished by the Christian idea of charity. In archaic Greece, revenge was a legitimate, indeed necessary defence of one's honour.[38] It was not necessarily bound to the measure of the harm one had received. Even later in the classical era, Xenophon considered it a virtue to outdo friends in benefactions and enemies in harm (...ἀνδρὸς ἀρετὴν εἶναι νικᾶν τοὺς μὲν φίλους εὖ ποιοῦντα, τοὺς δ' ἐχθροὺς κακῶς ..., *Mem.* 2.6.35).

And yet, while going out of his way to stigmatize the suitors, Homer embeds in his account voices that present an alternative view of their killing. Before offering compensation, Eurymachus appeals to Odysseus: 'Then spare your own people' (... σὺ δὲ φείδεο λαῶν / σῶν ..., 22.54–5). The men Odysseus is about to slaughter are not random men but Odysseus' own people, some from Ithaca, others from neighbouring islands. Like Odysseus they belong to the local elite and form part of the dense aristocratic network that extends beyond the individual *polis*. The suitor Amphimedon, for example, is a guest-friend of Agamemnon (...ξεῖνος δέ τοι εὔχομαι εἶναι, 24.114). Together with Achilles and Ajax, Odysseus fought against Trojans, in his wanderings he braved monsters, but now he is killing his peers.

The weight of killing one's own people is palpable in the words with which Odysseus reminds his son of their precarious situation after the *mnēstērophonia* (23.118–22):

καὶ γάρ τίς θ' ἕνα φῶτα κατακτείνας ἐνὶ δήμωι,
ὧι μὴ πολλοὶ ἔωσιν ἀοσσητῆρες ὀπίσσω,
φεύγει πηούς τε προλιπὼν καὶ πατρίδα γαῖαν·
ἡμεῖς δ' ἕρμα πόληος ἀπέκταμεν, οἳ μέγ' ἄριστοι
κούρων εἰν Ἰθάκηι ...

---

38 On revenge in ancient Greece in general, see, e.g., Gehrke (1987), in the Homeric epics Wilson (2002).

> For when one has killed only one man in a community,
> and then there are not many avengers to follow, even
> so, he flees into exile, leaving kinsmen and country.
> But we have killed what held the city together, the finest
> young men in Ithaca ...[39]

The damage done by Odysseus is also visible in Agamemnon's comment on the shadows of the suitors, as they enter Hades (24.106–13):

> Ἀμφίμεδον, τί παθόντες ἐρεμνὴν γαῖαν ἔδυτε
> πάντες κεκριμένοι καὶ ὁμήλικες; οὐδέ κεν ἄλλως
> κρινάμενος λέξαιτο κατὰ πτόλιν ἄνδρας ἀρίστους.
> ἦ ὕμμ' ἐν νήεσσι Ποσειδάων ἐδάμασσεν
> ὄρσας ἀργαλέους ἀνέμους καὶ κύματα μακρά,
> ἦ που ἀνάρσιοι ἄνδρες ἐδηλήσαντ' ἐπὶ χέρσου
> βοῦς περιταμνομένους ἠδ' οἰῶν πώεα καλά,
> ἦε περὶ πτόλιος μαχεούμενοι ἠδὲ γυναικῶν;

> Amphimedon, what befell you that you came under the dark earth,
> all of you choice young men, of the same age, nor could one, gathering
> the best men out of all a city have chosen otherwise.
> Was it with the ships, and did Poseidon, rousing a stormblast
> of battering winds and waves towering prove your undoing?
> Or was it on the dry land, did men embattled destroy you
> as you tried to cut out cattle and fleecy sheep from their holdings,
> or fight against them, for the sake of their city and women?

The *Odyssey* describes the killing of the suitors as a just punishment, at the same time it indicates the rupture that the extinction of an entire generation of aristocrats on Ithaca constitutes. The havoc which Odysseus wreaks on the *polis* can only be compared to the consequences of a war or a natural disaster.

The model of Achilles and his excessive violence adds weight to this alternative assessment of Odysseus and his revenge. The main perspective that dominates in the *Odyssey* is certainly positive in explicitly moralist terms: the killing of the suitors is presented as the deserved punishment following from an unbearable transgression. Not least the semantics used for the consumption of Odysseus' goods suggests that Odysseus merely pays back the suitors in kind. And yet, just as some comments alert us to the considerable damage to the *polis*, the foil of berserk-like Achilles makes us wonder about the appropriateness of Odysseus' response. Does Odysseus not go off the rails in his revenge, when

---

[39] Theoclymenus (15.224), an Aetolian (14.380) and one of Odysseus' fictitious Cretan personae (13.259) illustrate the exile of murderers.

he, seemingly out of character, rejects material recompense and rages in a manner which brings him even close to Polyphemus? The Iliadic echoes make the *Odyssey* into more than an adventure story: it becomes a multi-facetted narrative engaged with ethical issues.[40]

IV. Odysseus and the companions: whose ἀτασθαλίη?

The capacity of the *Iliad*'s Achilles to establish a critical perspective on Odysseus is confirmed by an allusion that occurs before the *mnēstērophonia*, in the *Apologoi*. Only one of the men sent to inquire about the smoke ascending from what turns out to be the house of Circe, returns from this mission: Eurylochus; the others Circe has transformed into animals. When Odysseus asks the remaining men to go to Circe's house, Eurylochus vehemently opposes this plan and challenges Odysseus' authority. Odysseus' response is vehement (10.438–42):

> ὣς ἔφατ', αὐτὰρ ἐγώ γε μετὰ φρεσὶ μερμήριξα,
> σπασσάμενος τανύηκες ἄορ παχέος παρὰ μηροῦ,
> τῶι οἱ ἀποτμήξας κεφαλὴν οὖδάσδε πελάσσαι,
> καὶ πηῶι περ ἐόντι μάλα σχεδόν· ἀλλά μ' ἑταῖροι
> μειλιχίοισ' ἐπέεσσιν ἐρήτυον ἄλλοθεν ἄλλος·

> So he spoke, and I considered in my mind whether
> to draw out the long-edged sword from beside my big thigh,
> and cut off his head and throw it on the ground, even though
> he was nearly related to me by marriage; but my companions
> checked me, first one then another speaking, trying to soothe me.

The evocation of Achilles in *Iliad* 1 at the end of the *Odyssey* remains an alluring, but tentative suggestion. Here, in contrast, the comparison is clearly 'intended', as Heubeck notes in his commentary.[41] It is not Athena, but the comrades who appease Odysseus; still, the thought process of whether or not to draw the sword and to kill the man brings both scenes together.

Eurylochus is a shady figure. He behaves cowardly in this scene and later he will talk the Greeks into landing on Thrinacia and ultimately into slaughtering the cows of Helios. Nevertheless, Eurylochus' challenge to Odysseus is a strong one – Odysseus becomes angry not without reason. To bolster his plea, Eurylo-

---

40 Cf. Grethlein (2017) 205–42.
41 Heubeck (1988–92) ad 10.438–42.

chus reminds the comrades of another trial: 'So too it happened with the Cyclops, when our companions / went into his yard, and the bold Odysseus was of their company; / for it was by this man's recklessness that these too perished' (ὥς περ Κύκλωψ ἕρξ', ὅτε οἱ μέσσαυλον ἵκοντο / ἡμέτεροι ἕταροι, σὺν δ' ὁ θρασὺς εἵπετ' Ὀδυσσεύς· / τούτου γὰρ καὶ κεῖνοι ἀτασθαλίῃσιν ὄλοντο, 10.435–7). Odysseus himself admits that he is to blame for the disastrous experience with the Cyclops (9.224–30):

> ἔνθ' ἐμὲ μὲν πρώτισθ' ἕταροι λίσσοντ' ἐπέεσσι
> τυρῶν αἰνυμένους ἰέναι πάλιν, αὐτὰρ ἔπειτα
> καρπαλίμως ἐπὶ νῆα θοὴν ἐρίφους τε καὶ ἄρνας
> σηκῶν ἐξελάσαντας ἐπιπλεῖν ἁλμυρὸν ὕδωρ·
> ἀλλ' ἐγὼ οὐ πιθόμην, – ἦ τ' ἂν πολὺ κέρδιον ἦεν, –
> ὄφρ' αὐτόν τε ἴδοιμι, καὶ εἴ μοι ξείνια δοίη.
> οὐδ' ἄρ' ἔμελλ' ἑτάροισι φανεὶς ἐρατεινὸς ἔσεσθαι.

> From the start my companions spoke to me and begged me
> to take some of the cheeses, come back again, and the next time
> to drive the lambs and kids from their pens, and get back quickly
> to the ship again, and go sailing off across the salt water;
> but I would not listen to them, it would have been better their way,
> not until I could see him, see if he would give me presents.
> My friends were to find the sight of him in no way lovely.

Eurylochus' allegation gains force from the word ἀτασθαλίη. This is the very word with which Homer, prominently in the proem, blames the comrades for their fate and with which, repeatedly throughout the poem, the suitors are chastised. Here, however, the reproach of recklessness is leveled at Odysseus. This is a singular occurrence, and yet it has the capacity to make one wonder about whether the stigmatizing of comrades and suitors is not also a rhetorical strategy of exculpating Odysseus. We should not unduly press this interpretation – it is a vague possibility of reading the *Odyssey* against the grain, but it is noteworthy that another critic of Odysseus blames him for the death of both suitors and comrades in the same sentence. When the relatives of the murdered suitors meet, Eupeithes, the father of Antinous, exclaims (24.426–9):

> ὦ φίλοι, ἦ μέγα ἔργον ἀνὴρ ὅδε μήσατ' Ἀχαιούς·
> τοὺς μὲν σὺν νήεσσιν ἄγων πολέας τε καὶ ἐσθλοὺς
> ὤλεσε μὲν νῆας γλαφυράς, ἀπὸ δ' ὤλεσε λαούς,
> τοὺς δ' ἐλθὼν ἔκτεινε Κεφαλλήνων ὄχ' ἀρίστους.

> Friends, this man's will worked great evil upon the Achaeans.
> First he took many excellent men away in the vessels

with him, and lost the hollow ships, and lost all the people,
and then returning killed the best men of the Kephallenians.

For my argument, it is of particular interest that the implicit evocation of Achilles in *Odyssey* 10 occurs in another context which opens up a critical perspective on Odysseus. While the model of Achilles in the *mnēstērophonia* may instil in the audience doubts about the revenge as a suitable and fairly reciprocating punishment, in the *Apologoi* it raises uncomfortable questions about Odysseus' relation with his comrades. After the quarrel with Agamemnon, Achilles withdraws from the battle and nearly provokes a full defeat of the Greek army. Just as he becomes responsible for the death of numerous soldiers, Odysseus may be more involved in the doom of the comrades than is explicitly stated in the *Odyssey*. The death of six men in the cave is only the immediate consequence of Odysseus' decision to meet the Cyclops. Polyphemus' curse arouses the anger of Poseidon. The storm in front of Scheria is the only intervention of Poseidon that Odysseus mentions in the *Apologoi*, but the narrator and speakers who possess authority such as Teiresias repeatedly name Poseidon's wrath as the cause of Odysseus' troubles. When seen from this perspective, Odysseus takes at least partial responsibility for the death of the men under his command.

    I hope to have shown that the relation between Odysseus and Achilles in Homeric epic is far more complex than the metapoetically charged juxtaposition of βίη versus μῆτις, which Greg Nagy's *The Best of the Achaeans* has made a central creed of Homeric scholarship. There are certainly passages which envisage Achilles and Odysseus along these lines. In the embassy scene of the *Iliad*, for example, Achilles rejects Odysseus' speech with the words 'For as I detest the doorways of Death, I detest that man, who / hides one thing in the depths of his heart, and speaks forth another' (ἐχθρὸς γάρ μοι κεῖνος ὁμῶς Ἀΐδαο πύλῃσιν / ὅς χ' ἕτερον μὲν κεύθηι ἐνὶ φρεσίν, ἄλλο δὲ εἴπηι, 9.312–13). The explicit juxtapositions of the two heroes in the *Odyssey*, however, rather centre on their different fates: whereas Achilles gained κλέος at the expense of his *nostos*, it is the *nostos* that grants Odysseus fame. What is more, Achilles appears not only as Odysseus' antagonist, he is also repeatedly evoked as his model through oral intertextuality. Particularly in the *mnēstērophonia*, Odysseus is depicted against the backdrop of the *Iliad*'s Achilles. Through pointed echoes, his revenge against the suitors evokes Achilles' rage against the Trojans. This implicit alignment raises critical questions about Odysseus: does he become in his revenge as savage as Achilles after the death of Patroclus? Is he as responsible for the death of the comrades as Achilles for the death of the Greeks on the battlefield of Troy? These nagging questions go against the grain of the *Odyssey*, which presents Odysseus as a wily hero, and yet, raised and sustained by the poem's intricate dialogue with the *Iliad*, they make us wonder how good the best of the Achaeans actually are.

Works cited

Bakker, E. J. (2013). *The Meaning of Meat and the Structure of the Odyssey*. Cambridge.
Burgess, J. (2006). 'Neoanalysis, orality, and intertextuality. An examination of Homeric motif transference', *Oral Tradition* 21: 148–89.
Clay, J. S. (1983). *The Wrath of Athena. Gods and Men in the Odyssey*. Princeton.
Cook, E. (1999). '"Active" and "passive" heroics in the *Odyssey*', *CW* 93: 149–67.
Currie, B. (2016). *Homer's Allusive Art*. Oxford.
Danek, G. (1998). *Epos und Zitat. Studien zu den Quellen der Odyssee*. Vienna.
D'Arms E. F. and K. K. Hulley (1946). 'The Oresteia-story in the *Odyssey*', *TAPA* 77: 207–13.
de Jong, I. J. F. (2001). *A Narratological Commentary on the Odyssey*. Cambridge.
Elmer, D. F. (2013). *The Poetics of Consent. Collective Decision Making and the Iliad*. Baltimore, MD.
Finkelberg, M. (1987). 'The first song of Demodocus', *Mnemosyne* 40: 128–32.
Friedrich, R. (1981). 'On the compositional use of similes in the *Odyssey*', *AJP* 102: 120–37.
Gehrke, H.-J. (1987). 'Die Griechen und die Rache. Ein Versuch in historischer Psychologie', *Saeculum* 38: 121–49.
Grethlein, J. (2005). 'Eine Anthropologie des Essens. Der Essensstreit in der *Ilias* und die Erntemetapher in *Il.* 19.221–224', *Hermes* 133: 257–79.
–. (2006). *Das Geschichtsbild der Ilias. Eine Untersuchung aus phänomenologischer und narratologischer Perspektive*. Göttingen.
–. (2008). 'Memory and material objects in the *Iliad* and the *Odyssey*', *JHS* 128: 27–51.
–. (2017). *Die Odyssee. Homer und die Kunst des Erzählens*. Munich.
Hammer, D. (2002). *The Iliad as Politics. The Performance of Political Thought*. Norman.
Heubeck, A. et al. (1988–1992) (eds). *A Commentary on Homer's Odyssey*, 3 vols. Oxford.
Hölscher, U. (1967). 'Die Atridensage in der *Odyssee*', in: H. Singer and B. von Wiese (eds.), *Festschrift für Richard Alewyn*. Cologne, 1–16.
Lonsdale, S. H. (1990). *Creatures of Speech. Lion, Herding, and Hunting Similes in the Iliad*. Stuttgart.
Lynn-George, M. (1988). *Epos. Word, Narrative, and the Iliad*. Houncmills.
Magrath, W. T. (1982). 'Progression of the lion simile in the *Odyssey*', *CJ* 77: 205–12.
Marg, W. (1956). 'Das erste Lied des Demodokos', in: *Navicula Chiloniensis. Studia philologica Felici Jacoby professori Chiloniensi emerito octogenario oblata*. Leiden: 16–29.
Monro, D. B. (1901). *Homer's Odyssey XIII–XXIV*. Oxford.
Moulton, C. (1977). *Similes in the Homeric Poems*. Göttingen.
Nagy, G. (1979). *The Best of the Achaeans. Concepts of the Hero in Archaic Greek Poetry*. Baltimore, MD.
–. (1983). '*Sema* and *noesis*. Some illustrations', *Arethusa* 16: 35–55.
Page, D. L. (1955). *The Homeric Odyssey. The Mary Flexner Lectures delivered at Bryn Mawr College, Pennsylvania*. Oxford.

Pucci, P. (1987). *Odysseus Polutropos. Intertextual Readings in the* Odyssey *and the* Iliad. Ithaca, NY.

Reece, S. (1993). *The Stranger's Welcome. Oral Theory and the Aesthetics of the Homeric Hospitality Scene*. Ann Arbor.

Rengakos, A. (2002). 'Narrativität, Intertextualität, Selbstreferentialität. Die neue Deutung der Odyssee', in: M. Reichel (ed.), *Epea pteroenta. Beiträge zur Homerforschung. Festschrift für Wolfgang Kullmann zum 75. Geburtstag*. Stuttgart, 173–92.

Rüter, K. (1969). *Odysseeinterpretationen. Untersuchungen zum ersten Buch und zur Phaiakis*, ed. Kjeld Matthiessen. Göttingen.

Rutherford, R. B. (1991–3). 'From the *Iliad* to the *Odyssey*', BICS 38: 37–54.

Saïd, S. (1979). 'Les crimes des pretendants, la maison d'Ulysse, et les festins de *l'Odyssée*', in: *Études de Littérature Ancienne I. Homère, Horace, le Mythe d'Œdipe, les Sentences de Sextus*. Paris, 9–49.

Schein, S. L. (1996). 'Introduction', in: S. L. Schein (ed.), *Reading the* Odyssey. *Selected Interpretive Essays*. Princeton, 3–31.

– (1999). 'Homeric intertextuality. Two examples', in: J. N. Kazazis and A. Rengakos (eds.), *Euphrosyne. Studies in Ancient Epic and its Legacy in Honor of Dimitris N. Maronitis*. Stuttgart, 349–56.

Schnapp-Gourbeillon, A. (1981). *Lions, Héros, Masques. Les Représentations de l'Animal chez Homère*. Paris.

Segal, C. (1971). *The Theme of the Mutilation of the Corpse in the* Iliad. Leiden.

Tsagalis, C. (2008). *The Oral Palimpsest. Exploring Intertextuality in the Homeric Epics*. Washington, DC.

Usener, K. (1990). *Beobachtungen zum Verhältnis der* Odyssee *zur* Ilias. Tübingen.

Wender, D. (1978). *The Last Scenes of the* Odyssey. Leiden.

Wilson, D. F. (2002). *Ransom, Revenge, and Heroic Identity in the* Iliad. Cambridge.

Language and Formulas

G. O. Hutchinson
Repetition, range, and attention: The *Iliad*

The approach of this piece may put it rather in the margins of the book as a whole; but even from the margins it is a pleasure to laud Antonios Rengakos for all that he has accomplished and organized. His immense zeal has achieved so much, and with such friendliness and humility.

We do not have the evidence to know how Homer's poems were composed. The search for answers could be thought to have made scholars lay too much emphasis on the poet's production of the works, and not enough on the effect of the works upon the audience or audiences of the time. The effect on the audience is to some extent accessible to us, in that various aspects of that effect are likely to lie open in the text. To be extreme: it would seem perverse to deny that the last book of the *Iliad* more probably moved its audience than made them just laugh. We could allow that if, as seems reasonable, the effect comes about because the poet wishes it, to that degree the poet's realized aims form part of what should in some respects be visible even to us. But how in a practical way the poet came to put the words together seems a matter both less important and less apparent, to be reached if at all by theories.

Parry's extraordinary *L'Épithète traditionnelle dans Homère* was much interested in the response of Homer's audience, as well as in the composition of the poems; but the discovery of what seemed confirmation on the composition, and the hardening of the theory, moved scholarly interest more decidedly on to genesis. One might maintain that phrases in the *Iliad* recur because the poem is orally composed; but it can only be shown that the poem was orally composed if it is shown that such recurrence can only have happened in oral composition. As we shall see at the end, that latter demonstration cannot be made. The claim of oral composition has increasingly raised doubts in recent years, and has not always been subscribed to as supposed; but it will be useful to consider it here as a proposition in itself. (Oral performance is assumed by most, and is not here investigated.) The question that matters for those interested in the impact of the works is what attitudes to the text such a theory requires. If we pursue some features of recurrence, we are likely to enhance our appreciation of the text, and

---

I am very grateful to Professor E. Clarke and Dr E. Troscianko for their exciting talks at a seminar I have run in 2017 on attention; I am grateful to the other participants too. Professor R. B. Rutherford has kindly made comments, and allowed me to read work of his before publication.

will come to points which either present problems for such a theory or create conditions with which it must comply.[1]

It could be thought that on a theory in which repetition in a poem is due to its oral composition, repetition can have no intended impact, because the oral composition is the only cause, and no actual impact, because the audience has heard the phrase so often that it has ceased to notice it. But it cannot be that no repetition is noticed by an audience. The following examples from Murat Žunić's dictated *The Wedding of Omer Bey* must have some rhetorical impact, as must kindred passages in Homer:

> Po plećima od zlata pilići,
> a po prsi od zlata čaprazi. (278–9; compare what precedes)
>
> There were buckles of gold on the shoulders and frog fastenings of gold on the breast.
>
> Zlatno se đulbe' po prsima valja,
> zlatna se peča sjaje nad očima. (347–8)
>
> A golden orb was suspended on the horse's chest, and golden blinkers shone over its eyes.

Cf. e.g. *Il.* 11.632–5 (cf. 11.29–31):

> πὰρ δὲ δέπας περικαλλές, ὃ οἴκοθεν ἦγ' ὁ γεραιός,
> χρυσείοις ἥλοισι πεπαρμένον· οὔατα δ' αὐτοῦ
> τέσσαρ' ἔσαν, δοιαὶ δὲ πελειάδες ἀμφὶς ἕκαστον
> χρύσειαι νεμέθοντο.
>
> The old man also put at the side a most beautiful cup, which he had brought from home. It was pierced with golden studs; it had four handles, and around each fed two golden doves.

In *WOB* 793–8 the numerals change within a pattern, which the audience is bound to observe:

> Da si doš'o prvim pašalijam,
> ja bi' reka' da si nevistica.
> Da si mi drugim doš'o pašalijam,
> ja bi' rek'o da si divičica;

---

[1] Parry (1928); an English translation in Parry (1971), but the character of the work is rather lost, as is the connection with Meillet and others. Parry's theory is refined, in particular, by Hainsworth (1968), and has been developed in interesting directions, for example by Visser (1987) and more recently by Bozzone (2010) and others. On improvisation and alleged claims of it, Kelly (2007, 2–3) defends Lord. (The references in the notes offer the merest hints towards the huge bibliography).

A da si <u>trećim</u> doš'o pašalijam,
ja bi' rek'o da si udovica.

Had you [a man] come as bidden by the <u>first</u> men of the Pasha, I would have called you a virgin bride. Had you come as bidden by the <u>second</u> men of the Pasha, I would have called you a little girl. And had you come as bidden by the <u>third</u> men of the Pasha, I would have called you a widow woman.

In the Homeric examples of τρὶς ... τρὶς ... τὸ τέταρτον the numeral is repeated, then changes. Both repetition and change must be noticed by the audience; in Homer the repetition of τρίς reinforces the same point as the cumulative numerals in Žunić. So *Il.* 16.784–8:

<u>τρὶς</u> μὲν ἔπειτ' ἐπόρουσε θοῶι ἀτάλαντος Ἄρηϊ,
σμερδαλέα ἰάχων, <u>τρὶς</u> δ' ἐννέα φῶτας ἔπεφνεν.
ἀλλ' ὅτε δὴ τὸ <u>τέταρτον</u> ἐπέσσυτο δαίμονι ἶσος,
ἔνθ' ἄρα τοι, Πάτροκλε, φάνη βιότοιο τελευτή·
ἤντετο γάρ τοι Φοῖβος . ..

<u>Three times</u> Patroclus charged against them, matching swift Ares, with a dreadful cry; <u>three times</u> he slew nine men. But when he rushed against them the <u>fourth time</u> like a divine being, then, Patroclus, the end of your life was revealed to you: Apollo encountered you

The passage is likely in the context to evoke 702–11 τρὶς μὲν ... Πάτροκλος, τρὶς δ' αὐτὸν ἀπεστυφέλιξεν Ἀπόλλων κτλ. ('three times Patroclus ..., three times Apollo pushed him away'). In 702–3, as e.g. in *Il.* 8.169–71 τρὶς μὲν μερμήριξε [Diomedes] κατὰ φρένα καὶ κατὰ θυμόν, / <u>τρὶς</u> δ' ἄρ' ἀπ' Ἰδαίων ὀρέων κτύπε μητίετα Ζεύς, / σῆμα τιθεὶς Τρώεσσι, μάχης ἑτεραλκέα νίκην ('three times Diomedes pondered in his heart and soul; but three times Zeus of the wise plans made clamour from the mountains of Ida; he was producing a sign that the Trojans would enjoy victory, which turned deliverance to their side'), the repetition makes a contrast, essential to the story-line, and must all the more be registered by the hearer. One can multiply indefinitely instances of repetition which could not escape notice.[2]

---

2 Cf. Fehling (1969). Text of Žunić from http://enargea.org/cave/BosKrajina/pages/1930k.html; translations considerably adapted from http://enargea.org/cave/BosKrajina/pages/1930kTR.html. I started, in a foolhardy way, from Daničić, *et al.* (1880–1976); I then received invaluable help from Dr K. Vukovic, who also referred me to Škaljić 1973 for Turkish loans (see esp. 513 for *peča*). For the morphology see e.g. Meillet and Vaillant (1952). Cf. http://enargea.org/cave/BosKrajina/pages/1937kCOM1.html#talk for interesting material on relations between Žunić's songs and writing.

At *Il.* 11.656–61 Nestor says τίπτε τὰρ ὧδ' Ἀχιλεὺς ὀλοφύρεται υἷας Ἀχαιῶν, / ὅσσοι δὴ βέλεσιν <u>βεβλήαται</u>; οὐδέ τι οἶδεν / πένθεος, ὅσσον ὄρωρε κατὰ στρατόν· οἳ γὰρ ἄριστοι / ἐν νηυσὶν κέαται <u>βεβλημένοι οὐτάμενοί</u> τε. / <u>βέβληται</u> μὲν ὁ Τυδεΐδης κρατερὸς Διομήδης, / <u>οὔτασται</u> δ' Ὀδυσεὺς δουρὶ κλυτὸς ἠδ' Ἀγαμέμνων· [next line spurious] ('Why does Achilles feel such distress for all the sons of the Achaeans who have been <u>hit</u> by weapons thrown? He knows nothing of how much grief has arisen in the army: the bravest men lie in the ships, <u>hit</u> from afar and <u>assailed</u> from near to. Diomedes, the strong son of Tydeus, has been <u>hit</u>; Odysseus, famed with the spear, and Agamemnon have been <u>assailed</u>.'). The rhetorical organization seems inescapable. Yet the very sequence also stresses that there was more than one way in which harm was inflicted; the patterning draws together three scenes which accumulate woes for the Achaeans, but are elaborately differentiated. Two principles are involved, as in the deaths of the *Iliad*: in them terrible events are heaped up with many repeated phrases but also with continual variety.[3]

We may pass to less indubitable, but still plausible cases, since they expand the discussion. At *Il.* 22.273 and 289 we have the line ἦ ῥα, καὶ ἀμπεπαλὼν προΐει δολιχόσκιον ἔγχος ('so he spoke; he then poised his spear aloft with its long shadow, and hurled it forward'). The line occurs elsewhere too (3.355, 5.280, 7.244, 11.349, 17.516); in those instances, it is always followed by καὶ βάλε(ν) ('and he hit'), and usually by a shield, as in the second instance here (22.290 καὶ βάλε Πηληϊάδαο μέσον σάκος, οὐδ' ἀφάμαρτεν, 'and he hit the shield of the son of Peleus in the middle; he had not missed'). After the first occurrence here, however, Hector evades the spear (274); the listener is likely to notice the unusual twist, which relates to the unusual expansion of the encounter. (The point seems only strengthened by 20.438 ἦ ῥα, καὶ ἀμπεπαλὼν προΐει δόρυ, 'so he spoke; he then poised his javelin aloft and hurled it forward', where the repetition is cut short, and Athene saves Achilles from Hector's spear, in a scene strongly related to the present one.) Even without this notable feature in the first occurrence here, the listener is likely to be aware that the same line is used when Hector throws *his* spear: the patterning looks too obvious for an audience not to notice. We will return to this passage.

Several times in the *Odyssey*, Penelope goes to her upper room and weeps for her husband, until Athene makes her fall asleep: 1.363–4 = 16.450–1, 19.603–4, 21.357–8 … κλαῖεν ἔπειτ' Ὀδυσῆα, φίλον πόσιν, ὄφρα οἱ ὕπνον / ἡδὺν ἐπὶ βλε-

---

[3] In the prologue itself μυρί' 'countless' and πολλάς 'many' are both stressed (but different words from each other). On the meaning of the two passives, see Hainsworth (1993) 295. For repetition and accumulation in narrative hexameter more widely cf. Quint (1993) 50–3; Hutchinson (2008) 71–3, 255.

φάροισι βάλε γλαυκῶπις Ἀθήνη ('then she wept for Odysseus, her dear husband, until bright-eyed Athene cast sweet sleep onto her eyelids'). The recurrence of Penelope's weeping for Odysseus is not something that any responsive listener could fail to be aware of, and is explicitly elaborated e. g. at 19.509–17 (nightingale 518–23), cf. e. g. Plaut. *Stich.* 1–3; the present pair of lines, though it uses elements found elsewhere, is unlikely to have appeared as an entity in poems with a different myth. It seems likely that on some level (we will return to this) the repetition makes an impact on the listener. This seems all the clearer since at one point the poet elaborately expands and changes the moment: Athene makes Penelope fall asleep, she beautifies her, Penelope comments on her delicious sleep and speaks of how she longs, with laments, for Odysseus. ἔνθ' αὖτ' ἄλλ' ἐνόησε θεὰ γλαυκῶπις Ἀθήνη· / κούρηι Ἰκαρίοιο κατὰ γλυκὺν ὕπνον ἔχευεν ... 'ἦ με μάλ' αἰνοπαθῆ μαλακὸν περὶ κῶμ' ἐκάλυψεν. / αἴθε μοι ὣς μαλακὸν θάνατον πόροι Ἄρτεμις ἁγνή / αὐτίκα νῦν, ἵνα μηκέτ' ὀδυρομένη κατὰ θυμόν / αἰῶνα φθινύθω, πόσιος ποθέουσα φίλοιο / παντοίην ἀρετήν, ἐπεὶ ἔξοχος ἦεν Ἀχαιῶν' ('Bright-eyed Athene then set about a different plan. She poured sweet sleep on the eyes of the daughter of Icarius... . "What a soft slumber encompassed me, in my terrible sufferings! If only chaste Artemis would give me such a soft death, at this very moment, so that I would no longer wear my life away grieving in my heart, longing for my dear husband, excellent in every way —for he stood out among the Achaeans"', 18.187–8, 201–5). This further reinforces the basic point. The repetition brings something out about Penelope's unchanging pain: she, unlike Odysseus, remains in the same place. (Contrast e. g. 9.436, where the repetition of 306, if genuine, would mark a different stage within the episode for Odysseus, somewhat as in *Iliad* 22 above.) The repetition of Penelope's tears and her longing connects with the repetition seen later in amorous contexts, a repetition of experience and behaviour: so, through explicit comment rather than verbal repetition, Soph. *Trach.* 103–7, Prop. 1.16.15–16 *ille meos numquam patitur requiescere postes, / arguta referens carmina blanditia* ([door speaking] 'he never lets my posts rest, as he repeats his songs with alluring tunefulness').[4]

There are, then, at least some cases where repetition must make an impact on the audience; repetition can have different effects, and can be on different scales, which can be connected; precise repetition can sometimes yield to pointed variation; range and variety appear to be significant aesthetic principles too. For all the obvious impact of repetition and of accumulation, change and variety

---

[4] Repetition of weeping: cf. e. g. Heitman (2005) 34–5 ('will retire ... in tears ... many more times'). The sequence of beautifications in the poem is a separate matter.

can also be welcome. For Telemachus, Phemius' song on the return of the Achaeans from Troy is acclaimed as new in theme, and novelty is a recommendation in a song (*Od.* 1.351–2). For Penelope, however, the very same song is an example of unwelcome repetition, not on mere aesthetic grounds, but because it connects to her perpetual distress (337–45). Complications can be seen in later works too, as can impulses to variation and range; here it is worth considering poetry and prose after Homer, not as evidence for the Homeric period, but as showing us possibilities outside the modern world. Tacitus affects to think tedious his accumulation of condemnations in trials, and contrasts earlier history, which has a wider range and includes *uarietates proeliorum* ('the varied forms of battles'): *nos saeua iussa, continuas accusationes, fallaces amicitias, perniciem innocentium et easdem exitii causas coniungimus, obuia rerum similitudine et satietate* ('I, on the other hand, am packing together brutal orders, prosecutions without a break, betrayals in friendship, the destruction of innocent people, the same reasons for death; the wearisome likeness of events strikes the mind', *Ann.* 4.33.2). Clearly, however, the reader is supposed to think Tacitus has overcome this challenge. The sequence has impressive elements, and is not wholly removed from the proem to the *Histories* (1.2.1 *tempus adgredior* †*opimum*† *casibus, atrox proeliis, discors seditionibus, ipsa etiam pace saeuum*, 'I am taking on a time … with disasters, hideous in its battles, torn apart in its rebellions, savage even in times of peace'). There, indeed, accumulated imperial deaths and civil wars seem aimed to catch the reader's interest (*quattuor principes ferro interempti; trina bella ciuilia*, 'four emperors were slain by the sword; there were three civil wars'); then again the novelty of disaster evidently excites it (1.2.2 *iam uero Italia nouis cladibus uel post longam saeculorum seriem repetitis adflicta*, 'Italy was oppressed with new sorts of disaster, or sorts repeated only after a long sequence of ages'). Ovid notes that his repetition in the exile poetry could be off-putting, but claims that he has varied his expression; he presents variation as something a poet will aim at, and encountering the same sense twice as normally undesirable for a reader: *Pont.* 3.9.39–48 *cum totiens eadem dicam, uix audior ulli / uerbaque profectu dissimulata carent. / … an, ne bis sensum lector reperiret eundem, / unus amicorum, Brute, rogandus eras? … denique materiae quam quis sibi finxerit ipse / arbitrio uariat multa poeta suo* ('As I say the same things so often, hardly anyone listens to me; my words are ignored and fail of their effect… . Or, to stop the reader encountering the same meaning twice, should you have been the only friend I appealed to, Brutus? . . A poet produces many variations, as he sees fit, in subject-matter he has made up for himself'). Yet he hints at something Iliadic in the piling up of woes: *quae tibi si memori coner perscribere uersu, / Ilias est fati longa futura mei* ('if I should attempt to write to you in full of my distresses, in the record of my poetry, the *Iliad* of my fate will be long indeed', *Pont.* 2.7.33 – 4).[5]

Euripides' frequent repetition of words in anadiplosis is aimed to achieve a heightened pathos, perhaps because such repetition departs from normal sentences. So *Phoen.* 1499 – 503 ἢ τίνα μουσοπόλον στοναχὰν ἐπὶ / δάκρυσι δάκρυσιν, ὦ δόμος, ὦ δόμος, / ἀγκαλέσωμαι, / τρισσὰ φέρουσα †τάδε σώματα† σύγγονα, / ματέρα καὶ τέκνα, χάρματ' Ἐρινύος; ('What tuneful groan shall I summon up to join my tears, tears—oh, the house, the house!—enduring these triple ... of kindred, mother and children, joys to the Erinys?') This partly joins with the pattern of heaped-up deaths in the plot. The same manner of repetition is mocked in the *Frogs*, e.g. 1352 – 5 ὁ δ' ἀνέπτατ' ἀνέπτατ' ἐς αἰθέρα / κουφοτάταις πτερύγων ἀκμαῖς· / ἐμοὶ δ' ἄχε' ἄχεα κατέλιπε, / δάκρυα δάκρυά τ' ἀπ' ὀμμάτων / ἔβαλον ἔβαλον ἁ τλάμων ('But he [the cockerel] flew, flew up into the air on his wingtips so light: to me he left woes, woes. Wretched me, from my eyes I cast down, down, tears, tears.'). Repetition is heavily drawn on for mockery in the play, and there are explicit objections to saying the same thing with two different words: so 1153 – 4 Αἰ... . ἥκω γὰρ εἰς γῆν τήνδε καὶ κατέρχομαι. / Ευ. δὶς ταὐτὸν ἡμῖν εἶπεν ὁ σοφὸς Αἰσχύλος ('Aesch.: " .. I have come to this land and I return." Eur.: The skilful Aeschylus has said the same thing twice'; cf. Pind. *Nem.* 7.104 – 5 ταὐτὰ δὲ τρὶς τετράκι τ' ἀμπολεῖν / ἀπορία τελέθει, τέκνοισιν ἅτε μαψυλάκας 'Διὸς Κόρινθος', 'but to repeat the same things three or four times is hopeless, as when someone barking in vain says to the children, "Corinth belongs to Zeus"'). Particularly objectionable elsewhere in Aristophanes is claiming to be bringing on a new play, and actually bringing on the same old stuff; perpetual novelty is a boast: so *Clouds* 546 – 8 οὐδ' ὑμᾶς ζητῶ 'ξαπατᾶν δὶς καὶ τρὶς ταὔτ' εἰσάγων, / ἀλλ' αἰεὶ καινὰς ἰδέας εἰσφέρων σοφίζομαι, / οὐδὲν ἀλλήλαισιν ὁμοίας καὶ πάσας δεξιάς ('nor do I seek to cheat you by bringing on the same stuff two or three times: in my skill I'm always introducing new types, with no likeness to each other and all of them clever'). Even here, perhaps, the clever, original plays accumulate impressively (καὶ πάσας δεξιάς; cf. *Wasps* 1051 – 9). In Plato, Callicles criticizes Socrates for always saying the same things (cf. *Symp.* 221e4 – 222a), but Socrates welcomes the assertion. It is implied that his repetition suits the importance of his underlying subject-matter: Plat. *Gorg.* 490e9 – 11 ΚΑΛ. ὡς ἀεὶ ταὐτὰ λέγεις, ὦ Σώκρατες. ΣΩ. οὐ μόνον γε, ὦ Καλλί-

---

[5] He is drawing on a familiar expression (κακῶν Ἰλιάς, Ἰλιὰς κακῶν, 'an *Iliad* of woes', cf. MacDowell (2000), 264); but in a poetic context there is clearly a further point (cf. Prcp. 2.1.13 – 14). On Tac. *Ann.* 4.33.2 cf. Hutchinson (1993) 57. For variety as a positive value, see most recently and broadly Fitzgerald (2016).

κλεις, ἀλλὰ καὶ περὶ τῶν αὐτῶν ('Call.: How you always say the same things, Socrates! Socr.: Not only that, Callicles, but I say them about the same things too.').

One element that is likely to be relevant to these different uses and ideas is attention—a concept of much interest in cognitive studies, and one which has a great deal more to give in literary criticism. Ill-judged repetition disinclines the reader or listener to maintain attention, novelty arrests attention with the excitement of the first occurrence. On the other hand, repetition can reinforce and so draw greater attention. Accumulation can absorb the reader or listener into a pattern and a world: a different kind of attention from the sudden burst of newness. What typology should be applied to attention is far from clear: common antitheses are active and passive, goal-driven and stimulus-driven, selective and intensive, focal and automatic; from a different angle, one could imagine adding perfective and imperfective (the latter would include a reader's sustained involvement in a larger entity). But conceptualization becomes more difficult beyond the most sudden and lively grabbing of attention; and any division into two aspects or types is itself a convenient simplification. The complexity of literary experience suggests, like other human evidence, a breadth of phenomena; and one of the most valuable aspects of the concept 'attention' is that it allows an indefinite quantity of degrees. At all events, the combination of likeness and variety winningly combines absorption in a pattern, the interest of divergence from the pattern, immersion in a world and its laws, the fascination of seeing the same in a different guise.[6]

We may now return to the most problematic sort of repetition, that of recurring phrases. It was evidently not an obstacle even for later readers in antiquity: so Aristotle, who does not distribute plaudits lightly, has the highest praise for Homer's λέξις 'expression' (*Poet.* 1459^{b}11–16). But it is a feature which distinguishes archaic hexameter from other types of Greek literature, and creates puzzles for us.[7]

Let us first look at two passages in the *Iliad* (on which we shall concentrate) where spears present themselves frequently. These condense and encapsulate the impact of language about spears in the poem as a whole.

---

[6] Attention: for the conception cf. e.g. Pashler (1998), Lavie, Beck, and Konstantinou (2007); sceptical Anderson (2011; I had written the above before reading him on dichotomies); history: Neumann (1971); Hatfield (1998); Thums (2008); important past treatments: James (1981) 380–433; Husserl (2004); some classical applications: Möller (2013) and Scodel (2014) esp. 55–62 (shifts of 'interest-focus'); applications to post-classical culture and to modern culture: Fischer-Lichte (2006); Koehler (2012); Schneider (2013); Seel (2013) 56–61, 187–90, 218–21.
[7] Recent discussion of epithets: e.g. Latacz (2000) 39–59; De Jong (2012) 25–8, Rutherford (forthcoming), Introduction 5 (b).

Ἀτρεΐδην δ' ἄχος εἷλε βοὴν ἀγαθὸν Μενέλαον·
βῆ δ' ἐπαπειλήσας Ἑλένωι ἥρωϊ ἄνακτι,
ὀξὺ δόρυ κραδάων· ὃ δὲ τόξου πῆχυν ἄνελκε.
τὼ δ' ἄρ' ὁμαρτήδην ὃ μὲν ἔγχεϊ ὀξυόεντι
ἵετ' ἀκοντίσσαι, ὃ δ' ἀπὸ νευρῆφιν ὀϊστῶι.
Πριαμίδης μὲν ἔπειτα κατὰ στῆθος βάλεν ἰῶι
θώρηκος γύαλον· ἀπὸ δ' ἔπτατο πικρὸς ὀϊστός.
ὡς δ' ὅτ' ἀπὸ πλατέος πτυόφιν μεγάλην κατ' ἀλωήν
θρώισκωσιν κύαμοι μελανόχροες ἢ' ἐρέβινθοι
πνοιῆι ὕπο λιγυρῆι καὶ λικμητῆρος ἐρωῆι,
ὣς ἀπὸ θώρηκος Μενελάου κυδαλίμοιο
πολλὸν ἀποπλαγχθεὶς ἑκὰς ἔπτατο πικρὸς ὀϊστός.
Ἀτρεΐδης δ' ἄρα χεῖρα βοὴν ἀγαθὸς Μενέλαος
τὴν βάλεν ἧι ῥ' ἔχε τόξον ἐΰξοον ἐν δ' ἄρα τόξωι
ἀντικρὺ διὰ χειρὸς ἐλήλατο χάλκεον ἔγχος.
ἂψ δ' ἑτάρων εἰς ἔθνος ἐχάζετο κῆρ' ἀλεείνων,
χεῖρα παρακρεμάσας· τὸ δ' ἐφέλκετο μείλινον ἔγχος.
καὶ τὸ μὲν ἐκ χειρὸς ἔρυσεν μεγάθυμος Ἀγήνωρ,
αὐτὴν δὲ ξυνέδησεν ἐϋστρεφεῖ οἰὸς ἀώτωι
σφενδόνηι, ἣν ἄρα οἱ θεράπων ἔχε ποιμένι λαῶν. (*Il.* 13.581–600)

Grief seized Menelaus son of Atreus, good at the war-cry. He moved threateningly against lord Helenus, the hero, shaking his sharp javelin; Helenus drew back his bow. The two of them came together, one desiring to hit his opponent with the sharp spear, the other with an arrow from the bowstring. Then the son of Priam struck with his dart the hollow of Menelaus' breastplate, where it covered the chest; but the piercing arrow flew off. As when from a broad winnowing-fan on the great threshing-floor black-skinned beans or chickpeas leap, thanks to the clear-blowing breeze and the impetus of the winnower, even so from the breastplate of glorious Menelaus the piercing arrow flew far away, straying a long distance. Then Menelaus son of Atreus, good at the war-cry, hit the hand in which Helenus was holding the well-polished bow. The bronze spear was driven into the bow straight through the hand. Helenus withdrew into the mass of his companions, to escape death. He let his hand hang down; the ashwood spear was being dragged along after it. Great-hearted Agenor pulled it from his hand, and bound the hand itself with with a well-twisted bandage from the finest wool, which the helper held firm for the shepherd of men.

ἦ ῥα, καὶ ἀμπεπαλὼν προΐει δολιχόσκιον ἔγχος.
καὶ τὸ μὲν ἄντα ἰδὼν ἠλεύατο φαίδιμος Ἕκτωρ·
ἕζετο γὰρ προϊδών, τὸ δ' ὑπέρπτατο χάλκεον ἔγχος,
ἐν γαίηι δ' ἐπάγη. ἀνὰ δ' ἥρπασε Παλλὰς Ἀθήνη,
ἂψ δ' Ἀχιλῆϊ δίδου, λάθε δ' Ἕκτορα ποιμένα λαῶν.
Ἕκτωρ δὲ προσέειπεν ἀμύμονα Πηλεΐωνα·
'Ἤμβροτες, οὐδ' ἄρα πώ τι, θεοῖς ἐπιείκελ' Ἀχιλλεῦ,
ἐκ Διὸς ἠείδης τὸν ἐμὸν μόρον· ἦ τοι ἔφης γε.
ἀλλά τις ἀρτιεπὴς καὶ ἐπίκλοπος ἔπλεο μύθων,
ὄφρα σ' ὑποδδείσας μένεος ἀλκῆς τε λάθωμαι.
οὐ μέν μοι φεύγοντι μεταφρένωι ἐν δόρυ πήξεις,
ἀλλ' ἰθὺς μεμαῶτι διὰ στήθεσφιν ἔλασσον,

εἴ τοι ἔδωκε θεός. νῦν αὖτ' <u>ἐμὸν ἔγχος</u> ἄλευαι
<u>χάλκεον</u>· ὡς δή μιν σῶι ἐν χροΐ πᾶν κομίσαιο.
καί κεν ἐλαφρότερος πόλεμος Τρώεσσι γένοιτο
σεῖο καταφθιμένοιο· σὺ γάρ σφισι πῆμα μέγιστον.'
ἦ ῥα, καὶ ἀμπεπαλὼν προΐει <u>δολιχόσκιον ἔγχος</u>,
καὶ βάλε Πηλεΐδαο μέσον σάκος, οὐδ' ἀφάμαρτεν·
τῆλε δ' ἀπεπλάγχθη σάκεος <u>δόρυ</u>. χώσατο δ' Ἕκτωρ
ὅττί ῥά οἱ <u>βέλος ὠκὺ</u> ἐτώσιον ἔκφυγε χειρός·
στῆ δὲ κατηφήσας, οὐδ' ἄλλ' ἔχε <u>μείλινον ἔγχος</u>.
Δηΐφοβον δ' ἐκάλει λευκάσπιδα, μακρὸν ἀΰσας·
ᾔτεέ μιν <u>δόρυ μακρόν</u>. ὃ δ' οὔ τί οἱ ἐγγύθεν ἦεν. (Il. 22.273 – 95)

He spoke; he then poised aloft his <u>long-shadowed spear</u>, and hurled it forward. Shining Hector saw it straight ahead of him, and evaded it: he had seen it in advance, and crouched down; the <u>bronze spear</u> flew over him. It stuck in the ground; Pallas Athene snatched it up, and gave it back to Achilles, without Hector the shepherd of men observing. Hector addressed the excellent son of Peleus: 'You missed! It seems, Achilles like the gods, that you had not yet had any news of my doom from Zeus; you claimed you had. But you were being a cunning trickster with words, so that I would become afraid of you and forget my force and valour. You are not going to fix a <u>spear</u> in my back as I flee; instead, drive one into my chest as I surge straight forward—if a god has so granted you. But for now, evade <u>my spear of bronze</u>; I hope you get the whole weapon in your flesh. The warfare would become lighter for the Trojans if you perished; you are their greatest harm'. He spoke; he then poised aloft his <u>long-shadowed spear</u>, and hurled it forward. He hit the shield of the son of Peleus in the middle; he had not missed. But the <u>javelin</u> roamed far from the shield. Hector was enraged that the <u>swift missile</u> had fled from his hand to no purpose. He stood dumbfounded; he had no other <u>ashwood spear</u>. He called for Deiphobus of the white shield, with a shout that carried far, and asked him for a <u>long javelin</u>. But Deiphobus was nowhere near him.

The first thing that should arrest us in these passages is range and variation. If our eyes are not focused on poetic modes of production, we can hardly fail to observe that both passages show two different words for 'spear', ἔγχος and δόρυ, supplemented in the last by βέλος, and that the first shows two different words for 'arrow', ὀϊστός and ἰός. Furthermore, the spear is accompanied by a whole range of different epithets, ὀξύ, ὀξυόεις (different noun), χάλκεον, μείλινον [with the same metrical value as χάλκεον], δολιχόσκιον, χάλκεον again, ὠκύ, μείλινον again, μακρόν. In the first passage there is less range on the arrow, a less frequent weapon in Homer; but elsewhere we find close together 5.393 ὀϊστῶι τριγλώχινι ('the arrow with triple barb'), 395 ὠκὺν ὀϊστόν ('the swift arrow'). (The repetition of πικρὸς ὀϊστός, 'the piercing arrow', after the simile is a special case: the whole phrase ἀπὸ δ' ἔπτατο πικρὸς ὀϊστός, 'the piercing arrow flew far away', is reprised and strengthened after the simile, cf. e. g. 15.676, 685 – 6.) The bow, part of the same weapon, offers a different word and a new epithet. All this range could be held, not merely to avert monotony, but to strengthen our attention towards the weapons. Not that epithets are peculiar to these passages, like ἀνεμοτρεφές 'wind-reared' (11.256; πελώριον 'huge' twice, 5.847, 8.424, both times of divine spears); rather, these passages present an intensified form of what the listener experiences in the Iliadic narrative as a whole. Spears will always be a focus of attention; but in these passages especially the weapons engross it.[8]

In the first passage, the opposition between the spear and the bow and arrow is crucial to the narrative, and is embodied in the explicit contrast intensified by parallel line-end: ὃ μὲν ἔγχεϊ ὀξυόεντι / ἵετ' ἀκοντίσσαι, ὃ δ' ἀπὸ νευρῆφιν ὀϊστῶι (584–5). It is also implicitly present in βῆ δ' ἐπαπειλήσας Ἑλένωι ἥρωϊ ἄνακτι, / ὀξὺ δόρυ κραδάων· ὃ δὲ τόξου πῆχυν ἄνελκε and ἐν δ' ἄρα τόξωι / ἀντικρὺ διὰ χειρὸς ἐλήλατο χάλκεον ἔγχος. (ὀξὺ δόρυ κραδάων is repeated at 20.423; that does not deprive it of relation to its context in the same line 13.583). In the unusual sequence of the second passage, both warriors throw their spears without success; Hector contemplates his spear when Achilles has already missed with his. The plain δόρυ without an epithet is used at 285 for any spear Achilles may have (Hector does not know Athene has returned the same one); emphasis falls rather on the spear he will throw himself, ἐμὸν ἔγχος ... / χάλκεον·, cf. 13.831 (also Hector, to Ajax) αἴ κε ταλάσσηις μεῖναι ἐμὸν δόρυ μακρόν ('if you endure to await my long spear'), note also πᾶν 286, contrast 283. νῦν αὖτ' makes the opposition between their weapons apparent in the language. At the end, however, Hector has no other spear, and Deiphobus, whom he calls on for another, is not there; the idea of the spear has reached an ominous blank. We have, then, already encountered the union of repetition and range, and started to see how attention might be of significance.

Let us now look at the poem more broadly, and consider two protests. 1) What we have seen in these passages is just the accidental effect of scope (an epithet for every slot), and would not have been considered 'range' by a listener sitting through the whole poem; 2) the words recur so often that they cannot attract attention, indeed for the listener they have no meaning. 1) can only really be supported by 2). Otherwise, the listener appears to encounter, for things and

---

[8] One could say that χάλκεον and μείλινον do not have the same metrical value, because mu could in theory lengthen; but Parry (1928, 236) himself regards στεροπηγερέτα 'lightning-gatherer' and νεφεληγερέτα 'cloud-gatherer' as equivalents. For other metrical equivalents cf. e.g. ὀξέϊ δουρί 'sharp javelin' and ἔγχεϊ μακρῶι 'long spear'. In Homer's time, the audience are likely to have taken -σκι- in δολιχόσκιος as 'shadow'; no alternatives were intelligible. On spears and their epithets cf. Paraskevaides (1984, 22–7; Bakker and Van den Houten (1992). More broadly on the issue of economy see Shive (1987).

people that recur frequently in the poem, a set of epithets that range considerably in meaning and in their own linguistic character but together build up an impression of the object or person: the spear mighty, strong, long, with a long shadow (evocative), sharp, swift, bronze, of ash wood, bright, wind-fed, monstrous (different archaeological types too come together to form the impression). Even within the general impression created of heroes by more promiscuous epithets, epithets usually or entirely confined to one hero could be thought to build up a picture. So Hector, particularly menacing from an Achaean perspective, is ἀνδροφόνοιο 'man-slaying' [unique to him, save once of Lycurgus, and commoner for him than the metrical alternative ἱπποδάμοιο 'horse-taming'], θρασύν 'daring' [most often of Hector (and twice of his charioteer; generated by 8.89?); same metrical value as μέγας 'great'], and ὄβριμος 'mighty' [also of Ares, once in the vocative of Achilles]. With the vivid image of his formidable helmet he is κορυθαίολος 'helmet-shaking' [nearly always of Hector, once of Ares] and χαλκοκορυστήν 'bronze-helmeted' [nearly always of Hector, once of Sarpedon; same metrical value as ποιμένα λαῶν]. As the most significant Trojan, he has Πριαμίδηι, Πριάμοιο πάϊς, and υἱὲ Πριάμοιο (all 'son of Priam') most often used of him. Range corresponds to the notion of scope (*extension*) in Parry's approach to production, as repetition corresponds to economy (*simplicité*); but range is much less considered by critics than repetition. In impact, it seems hard to escape a combination of the two.[9]

Let us turn to 2). The idea that the epithets have no meaning for the listener is exceedingly implausible *a priori:* if the spear were short or, say, pink, would it make no difference at all to the listener? Would the last line of the *Iliad* have the same effect with ὣς οἵ γ' ἀμφίεπον τάφον Ἕκτορος ἀνδροφόνοιο ('so did they carry out the burial of Hector slayer of men')? An additional argument may be derived here from the word χαλκός 'bronze', which can denote weapons or ar-

---

[9] Cf. for Parry's terms Parry (1928) 22, 48, 110. For discussion of Hector's epithets see esp. Sacks (1987) 105–75, 201–11, 220–6. Epithets etc. are kept above in one of their original cases. On ὄβριμος one should modify Parry (1928) 112; for θρασύς note [Eur.] *Rhes.* 579 of Hector, where the word is repeated and given an unfriendly twist. κάρτερος 'strong' is used once of Hector (13.125), and of no other hero ornamentally (twice of φάλαγγες, 'battle-lines', incl. 13.127). The idea of accumulated force has some affinities with traditional referentiality. But whereas that important approach, like the idea that everything is formulaic, draws on countless lost poems, it may be preferable to concentrate on the force that can be observed in one Homeric poem, and can be observed to differ in the other (see below). For traditional referentiality, cf. Foley (2002) 109–24 (e.g.); Kelly (2007); Rutherford (forthcoming) Introduction 5 (b). See also Foley (2012) 15, 93–4, Foley and Arft (2015) 84 for Foley's view that 'recurrence' within a poem is purely incidental, without the significance of 'repetition'. On the wider impact of Hector upon the audience, cf. Kozak (2017).

mour (or the material of armour): if the epithets had no meaning for poet and listener, one would expect that the word in either denotation could receive epithets appropriate only to the other. In fact, just ἀτειρής 'which never wears out' is used for both (three times weapons, once armour); the adjective is appropriate to either, and is used in other contexts too. Otherwise, for the denotation of armour we have θεσπεσίοιο 'overwhelming' (special context, 2.457), αἴθοπι 'bright-faced', νώροπα (meaning uncertain); for that of weapons νηλέϊ 'pitiless', ὀξέϊ 'sharp', ταναήκεϊ 'long-edged'. The two groups even seem to be kept more separate than one might expect, in that the bronze of a hook in a simile can be bright—if that is what ἤνοπι would be taken to mean (16.408 ἤνοπι χαλκῶι; also 18.349, Od. 10.360 of a cauldron). One further notes, for example, that cutting, in the *Iliad* always violently, is performed with pitiless bronze (obviously of spears at 13.501 = 16.761), not with its metrical equivalent the bright spear, δουρὶ φαεινῶι. A disappearance of meaning in one of the *Iliad*'s epithets for bronze would only be plausible where the word signified little to the listener through linguistic obscurity; but that would not be through repetition as such.[10]

Much more plausible than complete loss of meaning for generic epithets through repetition would be different degrees of attention. Parry sees only *attention* and *inattention*. At a minimum we could invoke, besides strongly focused attention, a habituated attention. But the situation will be much more complicated. It could reasonably be held that over the poem as a whole the greaves of the well-greaved Achaeans caused the sharp attention of novelty less than if the epithet had occurred only once (though greaves may mean less to us than to the original hearers). But humans can have different degrees of attention towards elements of the same experience, whether simultaneous or close together; a tune may be attended to more intently than a bass-line, though both may be perceived. In language the idea of emphasis may be deployed; but that is less satisfactory, both because it seems to allow for fewer gradations, and because it is closely related to syntactic function. Now, a sentence could make sense without a given epithet, as it could not without a predicative adjective; but that does not

---

10 Suppose the meaning of νώροπα and ἤνοπι was obscure to the audience; in view of the ending, they are likely to have assimilated ἤνοπι and perhaps νώροπα to the most frequent epithet for χαλκῶι, αἴθοπι. Cf. Nordheider (1987); Beck (1997). On ἀτειρής, cf. Coray (2009) 103. For the difference between δουρὶ φαεινῶι and νηλέϊ χαλκῶι cf. Bakker and Van den Houten (1992) 10 – 12. Parry's position on meaning is itself at times more complicated than the obliteration of all sense in the epithet (save the sense of it being an epithet): see (1928) 159—as against 158.

mean that epithets cannot be a centre of attention. The syntactical dispensability of say Ariosto's adjectives does not diminish their potency.[11]

Various possibilities can be conceived. An epithet could draw attention to itself: especially, say, a vivid compound like κορυθαίολος, or λευκώλενος 'with white lower arm'. Even an epithet that drew attention to itself would also, because it described a feature of a person or thing, draw attention to its noun. The association with the noun is strengthened through repetition; κορυθαίολος is used just of Hector, λευκώλενος in the *Iliad* (not the *Odyssey*) mostly of Hera. (Not that the argument is limited to epithets used only of one person.) Attention to the compound in itself is modified but not annulled by repetition. Note, for example, the very early βροδοδάκτυλος 'rosy-fingered' in Sappho fr. 96.8, which must be deliberately turning the epithet from Dawn to Moon, in consciousness of the meaning (note the roses that follow; the colour is apt, cf. Stat. *Ach.* 1.619–20). One might wonder whether it was plausible that any listener ever heard this epithet of Homer's with no sense of meaning. In the even earlier Tyrtaeus fr. 11.7–8 West ἴστε γὰρ ὡς Ἄρεος πολυδακρύου ἔργ' ἀΐδηλα, / εὖ δ' ὀργὴν ἐδάητ' ἀργαλέου πολέμου ('for you know the destructiveness of the works of Ares who brings many tears, and you have thoroughly learned the temper of painful war'), after the preceding lines on hating one's life and loving death like the sun, it is highly improbable that πολυδακρύου carries no meaning: the four lines embody an argument. The improbability is increased still further by the parallelism of Ἄρεος πολυδακρύου and ἀργαλέου πολέμου. This may be partly inspired by *Il.* 17.543–4 ὑσμίνη / ἀργαλέη πολύδακρυς ('battle that is painful and brings many tears'); it is in any case apparent that Tyrtaeus heard meaning in the hexameter phrase πολύδακρυν Ἄρηα ('Ares who brings many tears', *Il.* 3.132, 8.516, 19.318). Compare too the many epithets in Pindar and Bacchylides which only occur once or twice—but obviously aim for an effect inspired by Homeric epithets; so of Zeus ἀργικέραυνος 'of bright lightning' in Homer, once in Pindar, once in Bacchylides (and in fr. dub. 65 (a) 12), ἐγχεικέραυνος 'with lightning spear' twice in Pindar (cf. also for form τερπικέραυνος 'delighting in light-

---

11 Cf. e.g. (all these in front of the noun) *OF* 1.1.1–2 'Le donne, . . . l'arme, . . . le cortesie, l'audaci imprese io canto' ('I sing of the ladies, . . . the weapons, . . . the courtesies, the bold enterprises', 17.89.2–3 'et abbaiando guarda / come negli occhi orribil fuoco gli arda' ('the dog barks and sees how terrible fire burns in the wolf's eyes'), 21.57.4–5 'Oreste, / poi che la madre uccise e il sacro Egisto' ('. . . Orestes, after he had killed his mother and the accursed Aegisthus'), 33.115.7 'almen discaccia le fetide arpie' ('at least chase away the foul-smelling Harpies', 38.84.1–2 'subito s'accenda / la formidabil ira d'ambidui' ('let the dreadful wrath of you both blaze up at once'). Emphasis: e.g. Dik (2007). An objection to this valuable analysis might be, not that it fails to make all words equal (33–4), but that it has too few gradations.

ning' in Homer), κεραυνεγχής 'with lightning spear' once in Bacchylides, φοινικοστερόπας 'of crimson lightning' once each in Pindar and Bacchylides, cf. στεροπηγερέτα 'lightning-gatherer' once in Homer, ἀστεροπητής 'lightning-(thrower)' several times.¹²

Or an epithet might attract less attention in itself, but give weight by its presence to the noun. So perhaps at the alarming moment *Il.* 6.42–4: αὐτὸς δ' ἐκ δίφροιο παρὰ τροχὸν ἐξεκυλίσθη / πρηνὴς ἐν κονίηισιν ἐπὶ στόμα· πὰρ δέ οἱ ἔστη / Ἀτρεΐδης Μενέλαος, ἔχων δολιχόσκιον ἔγχος ('Adrestus himself rolled out of the chariot to by a wheel; he fell on his face, prone in the dust; next to him there stood Menelaus son of Atreus, with a long-shadowed spear'). Just Μενέλαος would have had a weaker effect. Not that the epithet has no meaning; Menelaus' ancestry makes him the more formidable, and Adrestus addresses him as Ἀτρέος υἱέ ('son of Atreus', 46). Likewise, at 6.75–6 εἰ μὴ ἄρ' Αἰνείαι τε καὶ Ἕκτορι εἶπε παραστάς / Πριαμίδης Ἕλενος, οἰωνοπόλων ὄχ' ἄριστος ('if Aeneas and Hector had not been addressed close to by Helenus son of Priam, far the most excellent of augurs') the patronymic adds to the dignity of the introduction—his first appearance. In music, an ornament on a note might draw attention to the note within the line of melody, or it might—as in a long trill—draw attention principally to itself. Different epithets, then, are likely to call forth different kinds and degrees of attention.¹³

In the poem as a whole, the epithets absorb the listener's attention in a world. Parry thinks, it seems, of the non-particularized epithet as not meaning

---

12 For κορυθαίολος or κορυθαίολος cf. Risch (1974) 213–14; Markwald (1991); if adjectival, the compound attracts more notice for its unusual structure. λευκώλενος in the *Iliad* comes 24 times of Hera, once of Helen, three times of Andromache; in the Hesiodic corpus, three times of Hera, once of Persephone; of various characters (as in the *Odyssey*) in Pindar and Bacchylides, and once in each of Hera. Cf. further Hainsworth (1978) 45; Bozzone (2010) 38–40 (Hainsworth's 'indistinct... colour' for θεὰ λευκώλενος Ἥρη, 'the goddess Hera of the white arms', is not about literal colour, but he seems to ignore the impact of literal colour and e.g. Pind. *Pyth.* 3.98–9, note λέχος ἱμερτόν, 'desirable bed'; cf. Steiner (2010) 187–8—though the use of white paint for only female skin on vase-painting is put rather early). It must be through its sensual vividness that λευκώλενος occurs much more often in Pindar and Bacchylides than any other Homeric compound. (Medieval poetry, in a culture where women's whole arms normally remained covered, takes sensuality further: see Harvey 1964.) On Sappho fr. 96.8 cf. Lloyd-Jones (1985) 277 (moon seen from Lesbos in spring), Hutchinson (2001) 181. It will be observed that the present argument is not confined to places where an epithet gains pointed significance from its context.
13 For *Il.* 6.44 and 46 cf. 17.24, where Πάνθου υἷες ἐϋμμελίαι ('Panthous' sons, with their fine ashwood spears') in Menelaus' ironic speech as it were takes up Πανθόου υἱὸς ἐϋμμελίης ('Panthous' son, with his fine ashwood spear') from the narrative (17.9). Agamemnon's close address to the other son of Atreus, 6.55 ὦ πέπον, ὦ Μενέλαε ('dear Menelaus', cf. 17.238), contrasts with Adrestus' Ἀτρέος υἱέ. Graziosi and Haubold (2010) 87, 91 offer a somewhat different approach.

anything specific for the listener, but as matching, by being an epithet, the expected manner of all epic poetry (e.g. 1928, 172). Perhaps they create rather a kind of simplified background, against which the penetrating portrayal of fallible humans stands out. The epithets depict all the fighters straightforwardly as brave, and so forth; in practice, there is none of the warriors who simply stands his ground—what might seem the most basic element in a heroic code, if any existed. So, at the sight of Achilles, Ἕκτορα δ', ὡς ἐνόησεν, ἕλε τρόμος· οὐδ' ἄρ' ἔτ' ἔτλη / αὖθι μένειν, ὀπίσω δὲ πύλας λίπε, βῆ δὲ φοβηθείς ('Hector, when he observed him, was seized with trembling. He dared no long stay where he was, he left the gates at his back, and went off in flight', 22.136–7). Hector has weighed up the options, passing from one to another: Homeric syntax has captured the flow of his thoughts. But now his resolution fails. With supposed support from Deiphobus he stands firm; when he realizes there is no Deiphobus and the gods have called him to his death, he faces the inevitable with courage and thoughts of his renown. Courage and frailty are much more profoundly depicted than in his portrait by epithets. Even Achilles has considered escaping death in Book 9; not long before Book 22 he has dreaded not death but an inglorious death, like that of a boy herding pigs; Poseidon tells him μήτ' ἄρ τι λίην τρέε μήτέ τι τάρβει ('do not at all dread or fear excessively', 21.288). As passages which diverge from a repeated feature stand out, so the exploration of men and women stands out within the environment created by repeated words.

But that environment too is essential to the *Iliad*. Let us allow that many of the repeated phrases come from a tradition; they are still made to build a world that is different from that of other poems in which they come. Pitiless bronze and long-shadowed spears come in the *Odyssey* too, but do not create a similar world; even a poem on fighting that was less long and less limited in earthly space would not have the same impact. One could make similar points about the mini-worlds of similes: they do not have the same impact in the *Odyssey* overall because (among other things) they are less frequent; in a shorter poem on warfare they would not have the same impact because (at least) there would be fewer of them. But the matter is much more complicated.

Consider first the simile we have already seen:

Πριαμίδης μὲν ἔπειτα κατὰ στῆθος βάλεν ἰῶι
θώρηκος γύαλον· ἀπὸ δ' ἔπτατο πικρὸς ὀϊστός.
ὡς δ' ὅτ' ἀπὸ πλατέος πτυόφιν μεγάλην κατ' ἀλωήν
θρώισκωσιν κύαμοι μελανόχροες ἠ' ἐρέβινθοι
πνοιῆι ὕπο λιγυρῆι καὶ λικμητῆρος ἐρωῆι,
ὣς ἀπὸ θώρηκος Μενελάου κυδαλίμοιο
πολλὸν ἀποπλαγχθεὶς ἑκὰς ἔπτατο πικρὸς ὀϊστός.   (13.586–92)

Then the son of Priam struck with his dart the hollow of Menelaus' breastplate, where it covered the chest; but the piercing arrow flew off. As when from a broad winnowing-fan on the great threshing-floor black-skinned beans or chickpeas leap, thanks to the clear-blowing breeze and the impetus of the winnower, even so from the breastplate of glorious Menelaus the piercing arrow flew far away, straying a long distance.

There is some broad connection with the usual language of Homeric narrative, in the epithets μεγάλην, μελανόχροες (similar words in Homer only at *Od.* 16.175, 19.246, of people), λιγυρῆι (used with πνοιῆι or in plural with πνοιῆισιν at *Il.* 5.526, 23.215). But the listener's attention is arrested by words, things, phenomena unusual in the poem. An ἀλωή occurs in other similes (20.496, 21.346), on the shield of Achilles (18.561), even in the narrative of a time before the poem (21.36, cf. 77 (Lycaon)); but beans, chickpeas, a winnowing-fan, and a winnower are surprises, and the graphic image of the beans and chickpeas leaping off the fan both defamiliarizes and contrasts with the arrow flying from Menelaus' breastplate. They take listeners momentarily, and with one part of their attention, into a quite different world.[14]

Not altogether so with lions. They occur again and again, and create a parallel recurring world, in which the impressive lions stand in for the warriors. Lion similes occur in the *Odyssey*, and the fascination of the animals and fights with them is indicated by, say, Attic Late Geometric vase-painting (760–700 BC; e.g. kantharos (LGIb), Copenhagen NM 727, tetrapod stand (LGII), Ker. 407) or the bronze group of man, dog, lion, and prey from Samos (once Samos; c.700 BC). But these similes do not have the same accumulating force in the *Odyssey:* they are fewer, the application is less constantly to fighting in battle. Although there is the occasional repeated simile (*Il.* 17.657–64 = 11.548–55; suspected in 17), the range of prey and opponents in the *Iliad* is extensive: bull, cows, goats, sheep, deer, boar, dogs, and above all men. With extraordinary diversity in language, and considerable diversity in length (e.g. 16.751–3, 20.164–73), related scenes occur, above all the lion confronted with a plurality of men holding weapons. The danger and sometimes death of the lion offer a narrative as momentous, for the instant, as the death of the warriors (from childhood to death 5.554–8; killed by own valour 12.46, 16.753 (cf. 6.407); urge to kill or die in the front of the crowd, 20.172–3, cf. 12.305–6).[15]

---

[14] On unusual words here, see Janko (1992) 119; πτυόφιν is linguistically unusual too. See also Fränkel (1921) 45–6 on the simile, with a different view of the word.

[15] Achilles' likeness to a lion spreads disturbingly beyond the ordinary comparison of strength or courage to inhuman ferocity, so 24.41 λέων δ' ὣς ἄγρια οἶδεν ('he has the savage nature of a

Some phrases recur (11.175–6 = 17.63–4, cf. 18.583), but the range of expression is conspicuous: the men ἰύζουσιν 'yell out' 17.65 (only occurrence of verb in *Iliad*, once in *Odyssey*); dogs and men pursue ἔγχεσι καὶ φωνῆι 'with spears and voice' 17.111 (unexpected combination); the hunger of the lion is not just shown with πεινάων 'being hungry' 3.25, *al.* (only of lions), but described with κρειῶν ἐρατίζων 'longing for meat' 11.551 = 17.660 (only uses of verb in Homer), and implied with 12.299 ὅς τ' ἐπιδευής / δηρὸν ἔηι κρειῶν ('who has long been deprived of meat'), one of three uses of the adjective ἐπιδευής in the *Iliad*. In the two places just mentioned with recurring lines, the first, 11.172–6, shows a lion singling out and devouring a cow from a herd, and gives importance to the cows' perspective, the second, 17.61–7, goes on from that point to the dogs and men surrounding the lion and afraid. As is well known, similes show a much lesser quantity of repeated phrases than the rest of the narrative; in the particular instance of lion similes, repetition and range receive a new configuration again.

There are many elements we have not begun to consider: so the speeches, with their fewer repeated phrases and their forceful sequences of thought; or the gods, and how the foundation created by the divine epithets (often archaic) relates to the lively interactions of the Iliadic deities. But a word must said on the plot. The innumerable scenes of human conflict are shaped by its movements, and its vicissitudinous fluctuations; the fluctuation in part expresses the unpredictability of human affairs, which are subjected to the unseen politics of the divine world. The turns and developments in events express themselves through repetitions. Three times a goddess addresses Zeus, with a first line ending ἔειπες ('you have said') and a closing ἔρδ'· ἀτὰρ οὔ τοι πάντες ἐπαινέομεν θεοὶ ἄλλοι ('Go on, do it; but we other gods do not all approve'): when Zeus pretends to consider sparing Troy altogether near the start of the poem (4.25–9), and when he considers sparing Sarpedon (16.440–4, again Hera, first line the same as in book 4) and then Hector (22.178–81; now Athene instead of Hera, but last three lines the same as in 16; in 16 Hera's speech is extended). The moments are too distinctive to be standard material which blurs in the listener's mind. In addition, Zeus within a few lines of the moment in book 4 fantastically envisages Hera entering Troy and eating raw Priam and Priam's children and all the Trojans (34–6). This will connect at the other end of the poem with Achilles wishing he could eat Hector raw now he has given him his death-wound (22.346–7), and depriving Priam and his wife of the body (348–54), and then the wife of Priam wishing she could eat the liver of raw-eating Achilles

---

lion'), etc.; cf. De Jong (2012) 126. On the simile in 17 cf. Wilamowitz (1916) 150 n. 2, West (2011) 341; but note Heyne (1821) ii.223.

(24.212–13, cf. 207). There are too many links here for the passages not to join together.[16]

We have been looking at repetition and range through the lens of attention, and thinking in particular about attention sharply exacted in a striking moment and about attention as immersion in a world by which the mind is absorbed. It may be asked whether there is any sign that these types of mental event are recognized in the Homeric text. We could hardly demand that our critical terminology should be attested in the very work we are studying; its absence would not even suffice to show that the poet failed to articulate his activity in such a way, all the more in a work which contains little discussion of itself. And we are more interested in audiences. However, if the work does show an awareness of such events, that is evidence for the culture of the time.

It seems as though the *Iliad* attaches much importance to the sorts of attention we have been especially considering. A train of action is often arrested and reversed by εἰ μὴ ἄρ' ὀξὺ νόηcε of a god or hero ('if x had not keenly observed', 3.374, 5.680, etc.; a structurally significant repetition). Both the adverb and the verb are notable; the verb is connected with the mind. A piece of narrative including a simile captures with incomparable vividness the searching of a visual field with intense scrutiny for a particular sight, and the moment of sudden perception. This is more active than the sort of attention we have considered, but is closely related, and shows sharp awareness of some things standing out from their background.

ὣς ἄρα φωνήσας ἀπέβη ξανθὸς Μενέλαος,
πάντοσε παπταίνων ὥς τ' αἰετός, ὅν ῥά τέ φασιν
ὀξύτατον δέρκεσθαι ὑπουρανίων πετεηνῶν,
ὅν τε καὶ ὑψόθ' ἐόντα πόδας ταχὺς οὐκ ἔλαθε πτώξ
θάμνωι ὑπ' ἀμφικόμωι κατακείμενος, ἀλλά τ' ἐπ' αὐτῶι
ἔσσυτο, καί τέ μιν ὦκα λαβὼν ἐξείλετο θυμόν.
ὣς τότε σοί, Μενέλαε διοτρεφές, ὄσσε φαεινώ
πάντοσε δινείσθην πολέων κατὰ ἔθνος ἑταίρων,
εἴ που Νέστορος υἱὸν ἔτι ζώοντα ἴδοιτο.
τὸν δὲ μάλ' αἶψ' ἐνόησε μάχης ἐπ' ἀριστερὰ πάσης ...   (17.673–82)

With these words fair-haired Menelaus left. He gazed in all directions like an eagle, which they say has the keenest sight of birds under the heavens. The swift-footed hare does not escape the eagle's gaze even when it is on high while the hare lies beneath a bush with thick foliage. The eagle darts straight down at him, and swiftly catches him and removes his life. Even so, Menelaus, did your bright eyes then turn in all directions among the

---

16 Speeches: see Lohmann (1970) for their structure; cf. Thomas (1992) 36–7.

mass of your many companions; he hoped to see the son of Nestor still alive. He noticed him most quickly on the left-hand edge of the whole scene of battle ...

A bridge to more absorbed attention comes when characters in mid-speech mark a point out for their listener to attend to now, but store lastingly: ἄλλο δέ τοι ἐρέω, σὺ δ' ἐνὶ φρεσὶ βάλλεο σῆισι ('and I will tell you something else; place it in your mind'). These utterances can be of immense significance: so Patroclus' prophecy of Hector's death (16.851).[17]

The *Iliad* is also much interested in absorbed moods, sometimes intriguingly expressed and sustained by repeated actions (so Achilles with Hector's body, 24.12–18). Achilles' singing (9.186–91) seems to be a continuous experience of delight, which Patroclus does not wish to interrupt, and which is actually interrupted by a sudden event that draws Achilles' wondering attention, as he stands up holding his now forgotten lyre. The *Odyssey* provides still more valuable evidence for the period. The Sirens θέλγουσιν 'enchant' people with song (12.44); Eumaeus tells Penelope about his guest (17.514–21):

οἷ' ὅ γε μυθεῖται, θέλγοιτό κέ τοι φίλον ἦτορ.
τρεῖς γὰρ δή μιν νύκτας ἔχον, τρία δ' ἤματ' ἔρυξα
ἐν κλισίηι, πρῶτον γὰρ ἔμ' ἵκετο νηὸς ἀποδράς·
ἀλλ' οὔ πω κακότητα διήνυσεν ἣν ἀγορεύων.
ὡς δ' ὅτ' ἀοιδὸν ἀνὴρ ποτιδέρκεται, ὅς τε θεῶν ἒξ
ἀείδηι δεδαὼς ἔπε' ἱμερόεντα βροτοῖσι,
τοῦ δ' ἄμοτον μεμάασιν ἀκουέμεν, ὁππότ' ἀείδηι·
ὣς ἐμὲ κεῖνος ἔθελγε παρήμενος ἐν μεγάροισι.

The way that he talks, your dear heart would be enchanted. I kept him with me for three nights, and for three days I held him back in my hut—I was the first person he had come to on escaping from the Thesprotians' ship; but he had not yet finished telling of all his miseries. As when a man gazes at a singer, who has learned from the gods, and sings lovely utterances to mortals, who are intensely eager to hear him when he sings; even so that man enchanted me as he sat by me in my main room.

The experience is prolonged; the continued enchantment (imperfect) is likened to gazing at a singer. The singer's effect is linked to his lovely utterances—the loveliness must include their expression. The rapt state of mind expressed by the verb appears in the *Iliad*, though not of listening to poetry. Gods inflict a tranced state on mortals' minds or hearts (or eyes), which prevents them from

---

[17] Counterfactuals and interruptions: see Nesselrath (1992) 12–18. In 17.679 the listener's attention is heightened, through apostrophe, at the same time as Menelaus'; a spatial dimension is important too (cf. e.g. 20.1–3). Cf. Hutchinson (2010). I am obliged to Professor Rutherford for stressing the apostrophe here.

fighting (12.254 – 5, 13.434 – 9 (Alcathous is still as a stele or a tree), 15.320 – 2): they forget about battle (15.322). One can at least say that the kind of mental phenomenon we have been postulating in listeners fits easily enough with types of experience of which the text is keenly aware.

Are there implications in the picture we have been sketching which affect theories about the composition of the poem? In his first work, Parry mostly saw the formulaic 'système' as no more than helping in the creation of lines ('dans tous les cas où elle [*sc.* la formule] aiderait le poète dans sa versification', 1928, 29, 'faciliter la versification', 191; 175 'les nécessités de la versification' refers to the fixed metre). The learner-poet memorizes the formulae by listening to other poets (70), but there is no special emphasis on the significance of oral composition. Two years later, however, the system is not simply a help to the poet, but an indispensable necessity; it has to be a necessity, or otherwise the poet would find words of his own, which he fails to do 'in every verse and every phrase'. Some specific 'complete [i.e. 'absolute'] need' requires to be found; it is 'oral verse-making' (317). The intoxicating discovery of South Slavic oral poetry has led to some strange propositions.

The argument appears to run:

> *p:* If there are no original lines or phrases in the poem, that can only be because the poet is compelled not to invent.
> *q:* There are no original lines or phrases in the poem.
> So: The poet is compelled not to invent.

The notion *q* that there is no invention in any verse or phrase goes far beyond the evidence, and even plausibility: for instance, the many words unique within the poem make the proposition unattractive. (At Parry 1971, 324, a very limited number of exceptions to *q* is in effect allowed.) Suppose that *q* were correct; what justifies us in saying (*p*) that the poet would have made contributions of his own unless he were powerless to do so? Parry had written eloquently of the attractions of the traditional system for the listeners; those attractions would sufficiently explain why a poet would adhere to the system even without practical compulsion. (The later idea that ability to use it would disappear with literacy is simply based on the modern concomitants of literacy.) The existence, according to Parry, of other written versions of oral poems, such as *Beowulf* (e.g. 1971, 377, from 1933), would only show further the attractions of tradition, beyond the situation of original performance.

Even the idea implied by *p* that one can only improvise with a formulaic system seems far from self-evident. Archias' improvisation of hexameters does not sound as if it relies on a formulaic system (Cic. *Arch.* 18): *quotiens ego hunc uidi, cum litteram scripsisset nullam, magnum numerum optimorum uersuum de eis ipsis rebus quae tum agerentur dicere ex tempore, quotiens reuocatum eandem rem dicere commutatis uerbis atque sententiis!* ('How often have I seen him utter off the cuff a great quantity of excellent lines about the very things that were happening at that moment, without having written a single letter down! How often have I seen him, when called back for an encore, speak of the same topic, changing the words and the thoughts!') Nor would we imagine that Antipater of Sidon had a formulaic system for each of the various metres in which he improvised (*De Orat.* 3.193–4). The boy wonder Sulpicius does not seem to rely on a formulaic system, if we suppose that *uersus extemporales* 'lines composed extempore' means what it seems to (cf. Quint. *Inst.* 10.7.16–19); one can point only to ἐφ' ἁψίδεσσιν Ὀλύμπου ('vaults of the heavens') which occurs twice in the 43 hexameters, and the Homeric μέγαν οὐρανόν ('the great sky') in *IGUR* 3.1336 A 36.[18]

Performance—if a repetition may be indulged—is not the point at issue; Attic tragedy was written and performed. The question is whether the poem was entirely created by improvisation in the course of performing. The proposition that it was has not been proved; one may now see if it is even compatible with the *Iliad* which we have. The text, after all, certainly exists, while theories are theories; the minimum we would require of a theory about the *Iliad* is that it should fit the text. The strongest reasons against the idea lie in aspects we have not examined; once we allow that even some speeches show a striking organization of thoughts into a run of hexameters, we seem beyond the idea of a poet who has to have repeated phrases if he is to survive from line to line. But many of the phenomena we have been considering, even in parts of the poem where there is most repetition, present serious challenges. If a feature is usually presented in a certain recurring way, but sometimes diverges, in say an expanded version, that does not suggest the poet was unable to make a contribution. (He would appear to be doing so unless we postulate a sub-tradition in which the first tradition was already expanded without anyone ever making a contribution ...) It suggests rather that the repetition is valued, but does not have to be adhered to.

If we remove the idea of necessity for the poet, and make the formulae merely helpful in oral composition, we remove the contradiction between the conception of the poet and what the text presents. But without the idea that formulae are necessary for oral composition, we cannot even begin a proof that the poem was orally composed. (That idea is needed to make a start towards *p* above.)

---

18 For Sulpicius see Bernsdorff (1997); Nocita (2000).

There would be no intrinsic contradiction between conception and text in the following notion: that all the poem was orally improvised by a gifted poet who either (a) could create inventive and powerful poetry beyond the formulaic system but found that system helpful or (b) made use of repeated phrases and their system because the tradition was appreciated. Such a notion would merely require extreme belief in what improvisation could achieve. There is a certain tension in (a), but (a) is not self-contradictory. It should be added that writing has not yet come into the discussion; nothing so far said militates against unwritten premeditation and practice, even if the existence, preservation, and indeed performance of the written text present formidable obstacles of their own. Nor is anything implied on the origins of the formulaic system, as opposed to the poems we have.

Oral improvisation could, then, be allowed as a conceivable possibility, but only on condition that it does not lead to excluding features which seem clearly to be part of the text. For example, if it were held that an oral improviser could not see beyond the part of the poem he was on, explicit cross-reference by Diomedes from Book 9 (34–5) to Book 4 (364–412) would exclude oral improvisation rather than oral improvisation excluding the explicit cross-reference. But the purpose of the argument is not to reach a view about oral improvisation. Once it has been granted that theories alleging it should not dominate or dictate our reading of the poem, it may be time to turn our shining eyes, or at least our primary attention, elsewhere: to an understanding of its impact which best fits the text and best captures its multiplicity and power.[19]

Comparative material from other cultures is by no means without significance for this search. In particular, modern dictated poems and mediaeval poems in manuscripts enhance the idea that extensive repetition can form part of a style in narrative poems, and thus that such repetition can seem acceptable, and probably traditional. It also supports the idea that such repetition can have a variety of forces. So in the *Nibelungenlied*, B 33.1958.1, Hagen is called just 'Hagen der helt guot [excellent, admirable] |' (cf. e.g. 7.456.2 [Sîfrit] 'der helt guot |', 37.2195.2 [Rüedegêr] 'der helt guot |'); this is as he kills 'das kint Ortlieben' ('the child Ortlieb') in front of his father. The simpler world of typical phrases is here challenged by the more complex world of the narrated events. The attractions of range appear too, and with little complication from metre, in the *Niebelungendlied*'s less exacting scheme of metre and rhyme: so, for Sîfrit, around 7.456.2 (just mentioned), we have 454.3 'daz Sigelinde kint' ('the child of Siglint'), 456.1 'Sîfride dem vil küenen' ('Sîfrit the exceedingly valiant'), 3 'dem helde' ('the

---

[19] On this cross-reference, cf. Reichel (1994) 217–21; more widely, cf. also Reichel (1998).

hero'), 4 'des starken Sîfrides' ('the strong Sîfrit'), 458.2 'daz Sigmundes kint' ('the son of Sigmunt'), 461.3 'der herre Sîfrit' ('the lord Sîfrit').[20]

Large aspects of the poem, and innumerable small moments, stand to gain from our thinking more about how the poem affected listeners and so thinking proportionally a little less about the processes which preceded performance. The ancient world devoted more scrutiny to Homer than to any other text; the scrutiny was literary as well as philological. We should expand the range and increase the intensity of our literary attention; there will be no shortage of things to look at.

Works cited

Anderson, B. (2011). 'There is no such thing as attention', in: *Frontiers in Psychology* 2, 246. http://dx.doi.org/10.3389/fpsyg.2011.00246.

Bakker, E. J., and van den Houten, N. (1992). 'Aspects of synonymy in Homeric diction: an investigation of dative expressions for "spear" ', *CP* 87: 1–13.

Beck, W. (1997). 'νῶροψ', *LfgrE* iii.432.

Bernsdorff, H. (1997). 'Q. Sulpicius Maximus, Apollonios von Rhodos und Ovid', *ZPE* 118: 105–12.

Bozzone, Ch. (2010). 'New perspectives on formularity', in: S. W. Jamison, H. C. Melchert, B. Vine (eds.), *Proceedings of the 21st Annual UCLA Indo-European Conference, Los Angeles, October 30th and 31st, 2009*. Bremen, 27–44.

Coray, M. (2009). *Homers Ilias. Gesamtkommentar (Basler Kommentar / BK). VI: neunzehnter Gesang (T). 2: Kommentar*. Berlin and New York.

Daničić, D., et al. (1880–1976). *Rječnik hrvatskoga ili srpskoga jezika* (23 vols.). Zagreb.

de Jong, I, J. F. (2012). *Homer: Iliad Book XXII*. Cambridge.

Dik, H. (2007). *Word Order in Greek Tragic Dialogue*. Oxford.

Fehling, D. (1969). *Die Wiederholungsfiguren und ihr Gebrauch bei den Griechen vor Gorgias*. Berlin.

Fischer-Lichte, E., et al. (eds.) (2006). *Wege der Wahrnehmung: Authentizität, Reflexivität und Aufmerksamkeit im zeitgenössischen Theater*. Berlin.

Fitzgerald, W. (2016). *Variety: The Life of a Roman Concept*. Oxford.

Foley, J. M. (2002). *How to Read an Oral Poem*. Urbana and Chicago.

–. (2012). *Oral Tradition and the Internet: Pathways of the Mind*. Urbana.

Foley, J. M., and J. Arft (2015). 'The Epic Cycle and oral tradition', in: M. Fantuzzi and C. Tsagalis (eds.), *The Greek Epic Cycle and its Ancient Reception*. Cambridge, 78–95.

Fränkel, H. (1921). *Die homerischen Gleichnisse*. Göttingen.

Graziosi, B., and J. Haubold (2010). *Homer, Iliad Book VI*. Cambridge.

Hainsworth, J. B. (1968). *The Flexibility of the Homeric Formula*. Oxford.

---

[20] It would be more difficult, though not pointless, to consider different media from the same culture: so the appreciation of repetition suggested by Geometric vases.

–. (1978). 'Good and bad formulae', in B. C. Fenik (ed.), *Homer: Tradition and Invention*, Cincinnati Classical Studies n.s. 2. Leiden, 41–50.
–. (1993). *The Iliad: A Commentary, vol. III: books 9–12*. Cambridge.
Harvey, R. (1964). ' "Mîn arme": a textual crux in Heinrich von Morungen's Tagelied', *PBB* [*Beiträge zur Geschichte der deutschen Sprache und Literatur*], Tübingen series, 86: 266–97.
Hatfield, G. (1998). 'Attention in early scientific psychology', in: R. D. Wright (ed.), *Visual Attention*. New York and Oxford, 3–25.
Heitman, R. (2005). *Taking her Seriously: Penelope and the Plot of Homer's Odyssey*. Ann Arbor.
Heyne, C. G. (1821) [orig. 1802]. Ὁμήρου Ἰλιάς / *Homeri Ilias: cum brevi annotatione* (2 vols.). Oxford.
Husserl, E. (2004). *Wahrnehmung und Aufmerksamkeit: Texte aus dem Nachlass (1893–1912)*, edd. T. Vongehr and R. Giuliani, *Husserliana* Bd. 38, Dordrecht, Text Nr. 1: Vorlesungen Wintersemester 1904/C5, 2. Hauptstück, 'Über Aufmerksamkeit, spezielle Meinung', 68–231.
Hutchinson, G. O. (1993). *Latin Literature from Seneca to Juvenal: A Critical Study*. Oxford.
–. (2001). *Greek Lyric Poetry: A Commentary on Selected Larger Pieces*. Oxford.
–. (2008). *Talking Books: Readings in Hellenistic and Roman Books of Poetry*. Oxford.
–. (2010). "Deflected addresses: apostrophe and space (Sophocles, Aeschines, Plautus, Cicero, Virgil and others)', *CQ* n.s 60: 96–109.
James, W. (1981 [orig. 1890]), *The Principles of Psychology* I. Cambridge, MA, and London.
Janko, R. (1992). *The Iliad: A Commentary, vol. IV: books 13–16*. Cambridge.
Kelly, A. (2007). *A Referential Commentary and Lexicon to Iliad VIII*. Oxford.
Koehler, M. (2012). *Poetry of Attention in the Eighteenth Century*. Basingstoke.
Kozak, L. (2017). *Experiencing Hector: Character in the Iliad*. London.
Latacz, J. (ed.) (2000). *Homers Ilias. Gesamtkommentar. Prolegomena*. Leipzig.
Lavie, N., D. M. Beck, and N. Konstantinou (2007). 'Blinded by the load: attention, awareness and the role of perceptual load', *Philosophical Transactions of the Royal Society B: Biological Sciences*, 36920130205.http://dx.doi.org/10.1098/rstb.2013.0205
Lloyd-Jones, H. (1985). Review of D. E. Gerber (ed.), *Greek Poetry and Philosophy: Studies in Honour of Leonard Woodbury* (Chico, 1984), *Phoenix* 39: 275–80.
Lohmann, D. (1970). *Die Komposition der Reden in der Ilias*. Berlin.
MacDowell, D. M. (2000). *Demosthenes, On the False Embassy (Oration 19): Edited with Introduction, Translation, and Commentary*. Oxford.
Markwald, G. (1991). 'κορυθαίολος', *LfgrE* ii.1490–1.
Meillet, A., and A. Vaillant (1952). *Grammaire de la langue serbo-croate*[2]. Paris.
Möller, M. (2013). *Ciceros Rhetorik als Theorie der Aufmerksamkeit*. Heidelberg.
Nesselrath, H.-G. (1992). *Ungeschehenes Geschehen. 'Beinahe-Episoden' im griechischen und römischen Epos von Homer bis zur Spätantike*. Stuttgart.
Neumann, O. (1971). 'Aufmerksamkeit', in: J. Ritter (ed.), *Historisches Wörterbuch der Philosophie*, Darmstadt, i.635–45.
Nocita, M. (2000). 'L'ara di Sulpicio Massimo: nuove osservazioni in occasione del restauro', *Bollettino della Commissione Archeologica Comunale di Roma* 101 (n.s. 2): 81–100.
Nordheider, H. W. (1987). 'ἦνοψ', *LfgrE* ii.926.
Paraskevaides, H. A. (1984). *The Use of Synonyms in Homeric Formulaic Diction*. Amsterdam.

Parry, M. (1928). *L'épithète traditionelle dans Homère. Essai sur un problème de style homérique*, thèse. Paris.

–. (1971). *The Making of Homeric Verse: The Collected Papers of Milman Parry*, ed. A. Parry. Oxford.

Pashler, H. E. (ed.) (1998). *Attention*. Hove and New York.

Quint, D. (1993). *Epic and Empire: Politics and Generic Form from Virgil to Milton*. Princeton.

Reichel, M. (1994). *Fernbeziehungen in der* Ilias. Tübingen.

–. (1998). 'Narratologische Methoden in der Homerforschung', H. L. C. Tristram (ed.), *New Methods in the Research of Epic / Neue Methoden der Epenforschung*. Tübingen.

Risch, E. (1974^2). *Wortbildung der homerischen Sprache*. Berlin and New York.

Rutherford, R. B. (forthcoming), *Homer:* Iliad *Book XVIII*. Cambridge.

Sacks, R. (1987). *The Traditional Phrase in Homer: Two Studies in Form, Meaning and Interpretation*. Leiden.

Schneider, U. (2013). 'Literatur auf dem Markt: Kommunikation, Aufmerksamkeit, Inszenierung', in: Ph. Theisohn, Chr. Weder (eds.), *Literaturbetrieb. Zur Poetik einer Produktionsgemeinschaft*. Munich, 235–47.

Scodel, R. (2014). 'Narrative focus and elusive thought in Homer', in: D. Cairns and R. Scodel (eds.), *Defining Greek Narrative*. Cambridge, 55–74.

Seel, M. (2013). *Die Künste des Kinos*. Frankfurt am Main.

Shive, D. M. (1987). *Naming Achilles*. New York and Oxford.

Škaljić, A. (1973^3). *Turcizmi u srpskohrvatskom-hrvatskosrpskom jeziku*. Sarajevo.

Steiner, D. (2010). *Homer,* Odyssey, *Books XVII and XVIII*. Cambridge.

Thomas, R. (1992). *Literacy and Orality in Ancient Greece*. Cambridge.

Thums, B. (2008). *Aufmerksamkeit. Wahrnehmung und Selbstbegründung von Brockes bis Nietzsche*. Munich.

Visser, E. (1987). *Homerische Versifikationstechnik. Versuch einer Rekonstruktion*. Frankfurt, Bern, New York.

West, M. L. (2011). *The Making of the* Iliad: *Disquistion and Analytical Commentary*. Oxford.

Wilamowitz-Moellendorff, U. von (1916). *Die Ilias und Homer*. Berlin.

A. C. Cassio
'Authentic' vs. 'artificial': Homeric ΕΠΕΕΣΣΙ(Ν) reconsidered

1. Beside the (half-) inherited ending -σι (< I.– E. *-su),[1] ancient Greek employed for the dative plural of the athematic declension an -εσσι ending which is certainly a secondary creation within Greek. It is attested in Homer and in many other dialects at very different chronological stages;[2] two different, and mutually incompatible, theories have been put forward in order to explain its origin and successful career.[3] Since these endings are well attested in Aeolic inscriptions and Lesbian poetry, the numerous datives of this type found in Homer (φυλάκ-εσσι, λιμέν-εσσι, δυσμενέ-εσσι, βελέ-εσσι ἐπέ-εσσι) are traditionally explained either as Aeolic forms or as artifical extensions of Aeolic forms.[4]

One of the most debated issues concerns the authenticity of the Homeric use of the -εσσι datives for the -s- stems (δυσμενέ-εσσι, βελέ-εσσι ἐπέ-εσσι). In other words: were they ever used in any real Greek dialect or were they a bardic creation? A specific problem is posed by ἐπέεσσι(ν), which is almost universally regarded as artificial – an opinion about which I have serious misgivings. In what follows I shall offer a fresh examinaton of the data and a tentative explanation of the peculiarities of ἐπέεσσι(ν).[5]

2. In Homer, two or three dative plural forms are often attested for the same -s-stem, e. g. δυσμενέσιν, δυσμενέεσσι(ν);[6] νέφεσσι, νεφέεσσι(ν);[7] βέλεσσι(ν), βέλεσιν, βελέεσσι(ν); ἔπεσι(ν), ἔπεσσι(ν), ἐπέεσσι(ν). According to traditonal analysis, βέλεσ-σι and (ϝ)ἔπεσ-σι are the old authentic forms (-s- stem + σι), βέλεσι ἔπεσι

---

1 Rix (1976) § 172.
2 E. g. ἄνδρ-εσσι, ταχέ-εσσι, λεχέ-εσσι (Homer), κυλίκ-εσσιν (Sappho 2.14), πολί-εσσι (IG XI 2, 1, Mytilene, 5th c. BC), τειχέ-εσσι (Skotoussa, Thessaly, 3rd c. BC: Missailidou-Despotidou 1993), Ἀκρ]αιφιέ-εσσι, IG VII 2734 (Akraephia, Boeotia), φυγάδ-εσσι (Olympia, 4th c. BC: Minon 2007, no. 30, 11), τρηματιζόντ-εσσι ('to the dice players': Syracuse, Sophr. 124 K.-A.), Εὐμενίδ-ε(σ)σι, ποτερίδ-ε(σ)σι (Lex Sacra Selinuntina, Jameson et al. 1993).
3 See Cassio (2017) forthcoming.
4 Chantraine (1958) 204 f. Gary Miller (2014) has a completely different (to my mind unacceptable) approach, which will be discussed in § 18.
5 I examined the same problem in Cassio (2006), but in this contribution I offer much new material and a more in-depth explanation of the 'fixity' of ἐπέεσσι.
6 Δυσμενέσσι (– υ – υ) being excluded for metrical reasons.
7 (νέφεσιν(ν) is unattested.

are their degeminated Ionic form, and βελέ-εσσι and ἐπέ-εσσι are either authentically Aeolic or the result of the artificial extension of authentic Aeolic forms.

Not all the -s- stems have Ionic dative plurals in Homer: for instance, λέχεσι(ν), τέκεσι(ν) are unattested, only to be found in post-Homeric texts. Since in what follows the discussion will concentrate on some thorny problems concerning the frequent alternation -εσσι(ν) / -εεσσι(ν), the Ionic forms ἔπεσιν, βέλεσιν etc. will not be discussed in detail. When attested in Homer they are very few and clearly late arrivals in the diction (9 occurrences of ἔπεσι(ν) vs. more than 120 of ἔπεσσι(ν) / ἐπέεσσι(ν)).

3. A special pattern with two variants is well attested in Homer, often, but not exclusively, found in line-final position:

(a) thematic adjective followed by (and referring to) an -s- stem noun, both in the dative plural, with -οισι, -ῃσι ending of the adjective and -σι(ν) ending of the noun, e. g. τρητοῖσι λέχεσ-σι(ν), οἷσι τέκεσ-σι(ν), πολλοῖσι βέλεσ-σι(ν), γναμπτῇσι γένυσ-σι(ν) ('curved jaws'), αὐτῇσι βόεσσι(ν); (b) same pattern, but with -οις / ῃς ending of the adjective, and -εσσι(ν) ending of the noun: e. g. τρητοῖς λεχέ-εσσι(ν), πολλοῖς βελέ-εσσι(ν), αἰσχροῖς ἐπέ-εσσι(ν).

It must be emphasized that in these clusters the adjectives precede the noun and semantically refer to it. This looks obvious at first sight but is not: both word-order and semantic coherence are crucial. For the sake of convenience, in what follows I shall refer to this pattern as *A&N* (adjective plus noun, obviously in the dative plural).

In numerous cases the same *A&N* appears in both the (a) and (b) shape: e. g. at *Od.* 1.440 the ms. tradition is split between παρὰ τρητοῖσι λέχεσσι and παρὰ τρητοῖς λεχέεσσι, and similar oscillations are very common in the Homeric mss. and papyri. Yet no oscillation is possible when ἐπέεσσι(ν) is involved. The ms. tradition invariably offers pattern (b): only αἰσχροῖς ἐπέεσσι(ν), μαλακοῖς ἐπέεσσι(ν), ἀταρτηροῖς ἐπέεσσι(ν), never *αἰσχροῖσιν ἔπεσσι(ν), *μαλακοῖσιν ἔπεσσι(ν) etc. I believe with West (1998: XXXIII) that the bards 'olim certe -οισι ϝέπεσσι dixerant', yet the most obvious later outcome of the *-οισι ϝέπεσσι *A&N*, namely -οῖσιν ἔπεσσι(ν), is never attested.

4. Interestingly enough, from a purely formal viewpoint a sequence -οῖσιν ἔπεσσι is in fact attested in the Homeric text: yet only twice, and in syntactic and semantic structures completely different from those described under (a) and (b): *Il.* 9.113 δώροισίν τ' ἀγανοῖσιν / ἔπεσσί τε μειλιχίοισι and *Od.* 4.597 αἰνῶς γὰρ μύθοισιν / ἔπεσσί τε σοῖσιν ἀκούων. In both cases -οῖσιν and ἔπεσσι are separated by a 'feminine' caesura; at *Il.* 9.113 the adjective ἀγανοῖσιν is linked to the preceding δώροισιν and not to ἔπεσσι, which is qualified by the following μειλιχίοισι,

and at *Od*. 4.597 αἰνῶς γὰρ μύθοισιν ἔπεσσί τε σοῖσιν ἀκούων we find ἔπεσσι preceded by μύθοισιν, a noun, not an adjective, and linked to the following σοῖσιν. In any case, these two examples show that from a purely formal viewpoint a sequence -οῖσιν ἔπεσσι is perfectly possible, and if we decide to reconstruct an *-οισι ϝέπεσσι A&N, an explanation of the ubiquitous presence of -οις ἐπέεσσι is badly needed. Note that the sequence -οῖσιν ἔπεσσι seems to be completely unknown to posthomeric hexameter poetry; probably it was regarded as something 'strange' whose imitation was inadvisable.

5. Horrocks (1997, 205) maintains that in ἐπέεσσι(ν) 'the new dative plural suffix was added to the -*s*- stem type in the epic language in a way unparalleled in surviving "real" Aeolic'. He speaks of 'a characteristically "epic" metrical restoration involving the addition of an extra syllable to the following word when this belongs to the neuter -*s*-stem declension', and calls this 'restoration' hyper-Aeolic.

Horrocks adds: 'Since movable –ν might well have been exploited here [e.g. *ἀταρτηροῖσι ϝέπεσσι might well have been turned into *ἀταρτηροῖσιν ἔπεσσιν], this adaptation [i.e. ἀταρτηροῖς ἐπέεσσιν] must originally have been carried out by Aeolic bards, with later adoption of the resultant forms by Ionic poets. And since Lesbian was the only Aeolic dialect both to prefer 1st/2nd declension dative plurals in –αισι / -οισι (forced by the fact that the corresponding accusative plurals end in –αις / -οις) and to experience relatively early loss of initial /w/ (thus forcing elision of the final –ι of the adjectives above before (ϝ)έπεσσι etc.) it seems, as expected, that we must look specifically to 'late' Asiatic Aeolic for an explanation of at least some of the non-Ionic features of Homer's dialect'.

It seems likely to me (see below, §§ 16 and 17) that the ἀταρτηροῖς ἐπέεσσιν 'adaptation', as Horrocks calls it, of a previous *ἀταρτηροῖσι ϝέπεσσι, was carried out by Lesbian bards; but to my mind what follows is unconvincing. Precisely because in the East Aeolic dialect[8] initial [w] was dropped at an early stage, and the -οισι datives were the local authentic form (see e.g. χρυσίοισιν ἀνθέμοισιν, Sappho fr. 132.1), if we posit a reconstructed *ἀταρτηροῖσι ϝέπεσσι, the expected outcome is *ἀταρτηροῖσιν ἔπεσσιν. If we admit that e.g. ἀθανάτοισιν ἀνάσσει (*Il*. 12.242 etc.) is the Ionic (or East Aeolic), modification of an older *ἀθανάτοισι ϝανάσσει, one cannot see what could prevent *μειλιχίοισι ϝέπεσσι from becoming *μελιχίοισιν ἔπεσσι.

---

8 I prefer to speak of East Aeolic dialect, and not Lesbian dialect, since East Aeolic includes the Aeolic dialect spoken in the mainland opposite Lesbos.

6. The complexity of the problems posed by ἐπέεσσι(ν) is evident from Chantraine's words (1958) 206: 'l'extension de la finale -εσσι aux themes en *s* qui on servi de point de départ au système semble proprement homérique', yet he adds in note 1 that ἐπέεσσι 'semble authentique dans de nombreux passages A 304, [μαχεσσαμένω ἐπέεσσιν], B 75 [ἐρητύειν ἐπέεσσιν] etc..... de même pour δυσμενέεσσι en E 488 [ἀνδράσι δυσμενέεσσιν], Z 453 [ὑπ' ἀνδράσι δυσμενέεσσιν] etc......νεφέεσσι en E 867 [φαίνεθ' ὁμοῦ νεφέεσσιν] etc.'. Chantraine's words are perplexing to the extent that the same form is regarded as authentic in certain cases and artificial in others.

7. The -έεσσι datives were regarded as authentic (with some hesitation) by Witte (1914) 56 and later, without hesitation, by Wathelet (1970) 262f.: 'les datifs en -εεσσι constituent certainement des éolismes avec les finales analogiques -εσσι rattachées au thème'; see also Ruijgh (1995) 53 and Nagy (2011) 169, who re-affirmed the Aeolic origin of the -εσσι (and -έεσσι) datives. Yet in recent times many scholars seem inclined to think that the -έεσσι forms are artificial; see Horrocks (1997) 205 quoted in § 5 ('in a way unparalleled in surviving "real" Aeolic') and Haug (2002) 71 'on trouve donc chez Homère des formes telles que ἐπέεσσι, formation inconnue, semble-t-il, des dialectes éoliens'. Blanc (2008, 263) says 'il a souvent été remarqué que si l'on excepte quelques cas très peu nombreux (cf. τειχέεσσι a Skotoussa)[9] les formes en -έεσσι ne sont pas attestées en dehors de la poésie épique. Cette constatation n'a rien qui puisse surprendre, bien au contraire: la final -έεσσι est une création de la langue épique, et cette création ne se justifie que dans ce cadre', and in Jones (2012) 45 we read 'one Aeolic feature in particular, the -εσσι dative plural, is clearly productive beyond its original distribution, as witnessed in the frequent dative plural ἐπέεσσι. Indeed, this epic creation is the dominant form in Homer'.

The latest verdict on ἐπέεσσι(ν) was passed by Gary Miller (2014, 342f.), in whose opinion the idea 'that -οις ἐπέεσσι must be Aeolic' is an 'erroneous assumption'. His analysis of the data will be dealt with in § 18f.

8. One of the main reasons why -έεσσι is traditionally regarded as artificial is the paucity of its epigraphical attestations in the areas where Aeolic dialects were spoken. Until the late sixties of the last century there was only one isolated ἐτ[έε]σσι found in a short 3rd c. BC inscription from the Troad[10] (incidentally, it was the one that prompted Witte (1914, 56) to regard the -έεσσι datives as au-

---

9 An inscription that will be dealt with below, § 9. (c).
10 See below, § 9 (a).

thentic). Another epigraphical -έεσσι surfaced in 1966 and another in 1993,[11] but it is evident from the passages just quoted that many scholars continue to regard -έεσσι as almost nonexistent in inscriptions.

Another source of scepticism has been the absence of -έεσσι from the fragments of Sappho and Alcaeus: there the dative plural of the -s- stems ends in -εσι(ν) (ἄνθεσιν, στήθεσιν, ὤρεσι), interpreted as genuinely Aeolic by Morpurgo Davies (1976).[12] This opinion elicited the skepticism of Blümel (1982) 262f. and García Ramón (1990) 136 n. 8, who rightly suspected that those datives were lifted wholesale from Homer (Il. 2.89 ἐπ' ἄνθεσιν εἰαρινοῖσιν etc., 6.65 λὰξ ἐν στήθεσι βὰς etc., where they should be interpreted as Ionic forms). ὤρεσι falls especially under suspicion, since it looks like the superficial Aeolicization of Homeric οὔρεσι with metrical lengthening (the authentic form is in fr. 14 L.– P. ἰψήλων ὀρέων). Since we possess only a tiny fraction of Sappho's and Alcaeus' literary production, it seems to me incautious to regard ἄνθεσιν etc. as the standard forms in the Lesbian poets and to exclude the potential presence of -έεσσι(ν) in one or more of their numerous lost poems.

In my opinion, it is time to re-examine in detail the forms transmitted by the inscriptions, two from the Aeolic coast of Asia Minor and one from Thessaly. They go back to Hellenistic times, and are as a consequence much later than Homer, but at least in two cases the text is of such a nature to exclude any poetic embellishment, and it is clear that those datives were in common use. On the other hand, the fact that they appear in inscriptions much more recent than the fixation of the Homeric text is no proof that they were *created* late.

9. -έεσσι Datives in Hellenistic Prose Inscriptions
    (a) Decree of an assembly found in ancient Achilleion, Troad (modern Yeniköy), 3rd c. BC; published by Barth – Stauber 1993, no 129.

ἐκκλησίας ψάφισμ[α
ἐψαφίσθαι τοῖς πο[λίταις
καὶ λαβὴν παραλά[βων
παρεληλυθότωμ πρα[
καὶ δύο <u>ἐτέεσσι</u> τοῖς π[ολίταις
ταῖς δὲ κλῆσις
ποι[

---

11 See below, § 9 (b) and (c)
12 In the frame of her theory, according to which we should postulate a sound change from -ss- to -s- for Common Aeolic.

Decree of the assembly .... decision made by the citizens .... and take from.... past.... in two years the citizens....summons....

There are remarkable traces of East Aeolic dialect that seem to have passed unnoticed.[13] For instance λαβὴν looks like the acc. of Attic- Ionic λαβή at first sight, but the accent is due to the editors; it might just as well be East Aeolic λάβην (= λαβεῖν), e. g. λάβην παρὰ λα[......; τοῖς πο[λίταις should probably be read τοὶς πολίταις, the local accusative plural = Attic τοὺς πολίτας; ταῖς δὲ κλῆσις might well be ταὶς δὲ κλῆσῖς (-ῖς < -ῐνς),[14] Asiatic Aeolic = Attic τὰς δὲ κλήσεις = 'summons' in legal sense; cf. Antipho 6.38 τὰς κλήσεις καλεῖσθαι. Since it is virtually certain that we are before a legal document in the local dialect, it is highly improbable that ἐτέεσσι is a poetic embellishment. It is simply the local dative plural.

(b) Inscription in which Aeolic Kyme (modern *Nemrut-Limanı*, Turkish coast south of Lesbos) honours the benefactress Archippa; one of several inscriptions on a pillar, some in *koiné*, others in the East Aeolic dialect. Probably 160 – 150 BC. The inscription was first published by Bean (1966); the standard modern edition is in Engelmann (1976) no. 13 III; see also van Bremen (2008).

ἔδοξε τᾶι βολλᾶι, γνώμα στραταγῶν καὶ φυλάρχων καὶ τῶν συνέ-
(60) δρων· ἐπειδὴ Ἀρχίππα ἀ Δικαιογένεος .... ἆι διὰ παντὸς εἰσφέρεται πρὸς τὰν πάτριν εὐνοίαι καὶ φιλοδοξίαι οὐθένα καιρὸν παραλείπει τῶν πρὸς φιλαγαθίαν καὶ ἐκτένειαν ἀνηκόντων, ἐφ᾽ οἷς ..... ἀπαντᾶσθαι αὐτᾷ συμβαίνει ἀποδο-
(65) χὰν καὶ εὐχαριστίαν τετιμαμέναι{ν} ἐπιφανέεσσι καὶ ἐνδόξοισι τιμαῖς καὶ ἀξίαισι τᾶς τε τῶν προγόνων ἀρετᾶς καὶ καλοκαγαθίας καὶ τᾶς ἰδίας πρὸς τὸν δᾶμον ἐκτενείας, δι᾽ ἃς καὶ τὰν πάτριν καλλίονα καὶ ἐπιφανεστέραν καθέστακε, ... καὶ ἐγλύκισεν τοῖς τε πο[λί]ταις καὶ τοῖς ἄλλοις τοῖς κατοικῆντας ἐν τᾶι πόλει· δεδόχθαι τῶι δ[ά]μωι· ἐπαινέσαι Ἀρχίππαν ....

The council decided – proposal of the strategoi, the chief officers of the tribes and the members of the council: Since Archippa, daughter of Dikaiogenes, ... full of the benevolence and love for the glory with which she is well disposed towards her fatherland, does not neglect any opportunity concerning goodness and zeal, for which reason she meets with approbation and gratitude and is honoured with honours splendid, grand and worthy of the virtue and goodness of her ancestors and of her benevolence towards the people, through which she made her fatherland more beautiful and splendid, ... and has offered refreshments with sweet wine to the citizens and the other inhabitants of the city .... the people has decided to honour Archippa.....

---

13 In ἐτέεσσι the two square brackets have vanished (ἐτ[έε]σσι in previous editions, Collitz (1884) 118 no. 317.
14 Hodot (1990) 114, who, however, does not discuss this occurrence.

This text is written in an incredibly pompous and convoluted Hellenistic chancery style (with typically hellenistic vocabulary: ἐκτένειαν). It is in fact bureaucratic terminology in an East Aeolic dress. Typical dialect forms are βολλᾶι (probably pronounced βόλλαι) = βουλῆι, πάτριν = πατρίδα, τοὶς πολίταις = τοὺς πολίτας, athematic κατοικῆντας (probably pronounced κατοίκηντας) = Attic κατοικοῦντας. Given the nature of the text, -έεσσι in ἐπιφανέεσσι might be a poetic embellishment, but on the one hand the text does not seem especially indebted to Sappho and Alcaeus: at no. I 16[15] we read a hyper-Aeolic κασίγνōτος not found in the fragments of the two Lesbian poets, and in their text (see § 8) the dative plural of the -s- stems ends in -εσι. On the other hand -φανέεσσι is unknown to Homer and to poetical texts at large. Given the presence of ἐτέεσσι in the previous inscription, I believe that ἐπιφανέεσσι is best interpreted as the standard East Aeolic dative plural.

(c) Hellenistic inscription in Thessalian dialect from Skotoussa (Pelasgiotis): a survey of the city walls and the areas close to the walls, ca. 200 – 180 BC; edited by Missailidou-Despotidou (1993).

> Face A, 1ff. Λειτορεύοντος τοῦ Ἀσκλαπιοῦ Φοξίνοι Ἐμπεδιουννε[ίοι μει]ννός
> Ἑρμαίοι ὑστέρα ἐπ' ἰκάδι, ταγευόντουν Νικοκράτε[....]είοι,
> Μεγαλοκλέαο Κλεοβουλιδαίοι, Ὀρθαγόραο Φιλοκρατείοι,]στράτοι Ἀμφιττολεμείοι... ἐυαφίξατο ἁ πόλις.... lines missing or badly damaged .... γειτνί]ασις πὸτ τοῖς τειχέεσσι καὶ ....
> [some fifty lines are almost illegible]
>
> When Phoxinos, son of Empeddion, was priest of Asklepios on the 22nd day of the month Hermaios, during the office of the tagoi Nikokrates, son of ...., Megalokleas son of Kleboulidas, Orthagoras son of Philokrates, ...stratos son of Amphittolemos, ... the city voted that .... proximity to the city walls and ...

This is an inscription in strictly local Thessalian dialect, containing a description of the walls of Skotoussa and prescribing the destination of the areas close to them. Let us cast an eye over B 45f.: ἄτ τοῖ προύτοι πύργοι τοῖ πὸτ τᾶ πυλίδι τοῖ ἐπιστρέφοντος ποτ τὰν πύλαν τὰν ἐπ' Αὐλοῦνα ἄκαιναι ἒξ καὶ πός, ἄτ τᾶν ὑδραγουγοῦν τᾶν κὰτ τὸ Ἐλένειον ἄκαιναι ἒξ καὶ πός κτλ..... It is difficult to imagine a text more remote from any kind of poetic language than this one; and it is *luce clarius* that τειχέεσσι is the local, and banal, dative plural of τεῖχος. Note that for metrical reasons (- ⏑ – ⏑) τειχέεσσι is absent from Homer and any type of hexameter text, and from classical and Hellenistic poetry at large for that matter.

---

15 Another decree in the East Aeolic dialect belonging to the same group.

10. These inscriptions show that -έεσσι was used in Aeolic speaking areas and that there was nothing especially poetic about it. The fact that the inscriptions are 'late' is not particularly significant in this case. In general, we should not forget that the presence of extremely archaic forms in Hellenistic inscriptions is far from impossible, as shown by ἔασσα (= Attic οὖσα) in an inscription of Aeolic Kyme of the 3rd century BC (Hodot 1990, 27 f.; Cassio 2010). In the specific case under investigation, it is far from difficult to show that the creation of the -έεσσι forms might be ancient, although they are attested in late inscriptions, and that this holds good on any theory of the origin of the -εσσι datives. If one subscribes to Wackernagel's explanation (1903 = 1955), -εσσι took shape at a very remote stage, earlier than our alphabetic inscriptions, when *all* the Greek dialects still had –οισι;[16] 'später wurde -εσσι auf die Neutra, sogar auf die mit sigmatischem Stamm, übertragen'. Now, if the original creation of -εσσι went back to such remote antiquity, one would expect its extension to the neuter and -s- stems to take place in archaic times or even earlier, not centuries later.

This holds equally good if we reason in terms of the alternative explanation, which goes back to Bopp and Brugmann, and which I definitely prefer to Wackernagel's.[17] If the -εσσι datives originated through *falsche Trennung* from γένεσ-σι, λέχεσ-σι, διηνέκεσ-σι secondarily interpreted as γέν-εσσι, λέχ-εσσι, διηνέκ-εσσι, and were used for various consonantal stems (e.g. πόδ-εσσι, Αἰθιόπ-εσσι), their (re-)application in the very -s- stems from which they had started must have been obvious and almost immediate. As a matter of fact, intervocalic *-s- had long been dropped,[18] leaving in the plural a secondary stem in ε-: γένε-α, λέχε-α, δυσμενέ-ες (< *gen-eh-a, *lekh-eh-a, both < *- es-h₂, *dusmen-eh-es < * -es-es). At this point, the endings were attached to the stem precisely as in the consonantal declension: δυσμενέ-ες, δυσμενέ-ων, δυσμενέ-εσσι, δυσμενέ-ας like φύλακ-ες, φυλάκ-ων, φυλάκ-εσσι, φύλακ-ας; λέχε-α λεχέ-ων λεχέ-εσσι like λέγοντ-α λεγόντ-ων λεγόντ-εσσι. The fact that the actual occurrences are late means very little: in many areas inscriptions earlier than the fifth c. BC are extremely rare or non-existent.

---

16 For instance, in Thessalian and Boeotian only -οις is attested from the earliest inscriptions onwards; Wackernagel thought that in these dialects at an earlier stage both -οις and -οισι were in use, at the start with different functions, then becoming functionally interchangeable. 'This is certainly correct' (Morpurgo Davies 1976, 182 n. 6), especially in the light of the Mycenaean data.
17 Cassio (2017) 189–96.
18 Cf. e.g. Mycenaean *pa-we-a* = *φάρϝεhα, nom./acc. plur. of *φάρϝος > Homeric φᾶρος (e.g. *Il.* 24.231 φάρεα λευκά).

11. I suspect that one of the reasons why Homerists are inclined to regard ἐπέεσσι and the like as artificial is their insufficient familiarity with similar forms in inscriptions written in other dialects, not only those of the Aeolic area The -εσσι datives were very common in ancient Sicily (e.g. Sophron fr. 124 K.-A. τρηματιζόντ-εσσι 'to the dice players') and were soon employed for any type of secondary stem ending in ε- as a result of whatever phonetic process: in one of the inscriptions from Entella (Western Sicily, probably 3rd c. BC) the dative plural of ἱππεύς is ἱππέεσσι.[19] In Sicily nominative plurals like ὑπογραφέ-ες or τομέ-ες are very common:[20] starting from a plural stem τομε-[21] we get a nominative τομέ-ες, a genitive τομέ-ων and a dative τομέ-εσσι (Archim. *de lineis spiralibus* p. 60, 24). The mechanism is exactly the same as that of Homeric δυσμενέ-ες (*Il.* 10.100), δυσμενέ-ων (*Il.* 13.263) δυσμενέ-εσσι (*Il.* 16.521). Centuries separate Homer from Archimedes, the origin of the secondary stems is different – but the mechanism is exactly the same: a banal analogical process without any poetic pretensions – yet, once applied to certain stems, enormously convenient for an epic singer, hence its 'poetic flavour' for speakers of Attic-Ionic to whom -εσσι and -εεσσι datives were utterly unfamiliar.

To my mind Chantraine was absolutely right when he said that ἐπέεσσι 'semble authentique dans de nombreux passages' (see § 6). It is probably authentic everywhere. Obviously enough, it is perfectly possible that some -έεσσι endings were artificially added by the epic singers to various stems for metrical convenience; this is especially clear in the case of νέεσσι, based on a νε- stem that can only be Ionic.[22] But nothing entitles us to think that *all* the Homeric datives ending in -έεσσι are artificial. Many of them are likely to have been created in a very natural way in an Aeolic environment, and it was that area that provided the authentic models on which to build new 'poetic' forms.

12. Let us now go back to the specific problem of ἐπέεσσι(ν). West (1998, XXXIII) writes:

> -οις ἐπέεσσιν constanter traditur, non –οισι ἔπεσσι quod Payne Knight aliique inferre voluerunt; contra cum nominibus aliis fere semper invenimus -οισ βέλεσσιν, μελεσσιν τέκεσσιν λέχεσσιν, -ῃσι γένυσσιν, βόεσσιν (La Roche Unt. I 82 sq.).[23] Quod non librariorum inconstantiae tribuerim, verum poetis. Olim certe -οισι ϝέπεσσι dixerant; mox deleto ϝ maluerunt ad ἐπέεσσι Aeolicum confugere quam ad -σιν Ionicum' [i.e. -σιν ἔπεσσι].

---

19 Porciani (2001) 25 (inscription C3, lines 9–10).
20 Biondi (2001). 85.
21 τομέ-ες < *τομή-ες < *τομήϝ-ες.
22 νέ-εσσι < νή-εσσι < *νᾶϝ-; see Chantraine (1958) 206.
23 = La Roche (1869) 82f.

This statement is partly right and partly wrong. To be precise, Payne Knight (1820) reconstructed, and printed systematically, not -οισι ἔπεσσι, but -οισι ϝέπεσσι, with a written digamma. As for the rest, -οις ἐπέεσσιν is certainly the norm, but 'fere semper invenimus -οισι βέλεσσιν, μέλεσσιν τέκεσσιν λέχεσσιν, -ηισι γένυσσιν, βόεσσιν' simply does not fit the facts. The case of βέλεσσι / βελέεσσι is especially clear, since, as we shall see, contrary to what West says, the vast majority of the mss. have not -οῖσι βέλεσσιν but -οῖς βελέεσσι. Besides, saying that 'the bards preferred to take refuge in Aeolic ἐπέεσσιν' ('maluerunt ad ἐπέεσσιν Aeolicum confugere') is certainly right as a given fact, but does not provide an explanation.

Payne Knight's reconstruction -οισι ϝέπεσσι is not printed in modern editions but is almost universally accepted as a proto-form (e.g. Chantraine 1958, 206; Horrocks 1997, 205). The only exception seems to be Gary Miller (2014, 342f.) who reconstructs an old instrumental, e. g. μαλακοῖς ϝέπεσφι (see §§ 18 and 19).

Before examining the specific problems posed by -οις ἐπέεσσι(ν) it might be interesting to cast an eye over two words, λέχος and βέλος, whose dative plurals present problems not identical, but very similar, to those of ἔπος.

13. λέχος

There are only 3 instances of λέχεσσι used in the *A&N* pattern in line-final position. One has no variant: *Il.* 3.391 κεῖνος ὅ γ' ἐν θαλάμωι καὶ <u>δινωτοῖσι λέχεσσι</u> ('in beds decorated with circles'; *δινωτοῖς λεχέεσσι is not attested but theoretically possible). The other instances are: *Od.* 1.440 πασσάλωι ἀγκρεμάσασα παρὰ τρητοῖσι λέχεσσι and 10.12 εὕδουσ' ἔν τε τάπησι καὶ ἐν τρητοῖσι λέχεσσι. This is what one finds printed in modern editions (e.g. von der Mühll 1962; van Thiel 1991), but in many mss. a variant τρητοῖς λεχέεσσι is found (not registered in the apparatuses of the abovementioned editions).[24]

Beside these lines, in which oscillation between -οῖς λεχέεσσι and -οῖσι λέχεσσι is attested or theoretically possible, we have 16 lines in which λεχέεσσιν is metrically necessary and *not interchangeable* with λέχεσσι:

Iliad
3.448: Τὼ μὲν ἄρ' ἐν τρητοῖσι κατεύνασθεν λεχέεσσιν
18.233: κάτθεσαν ἐν λεχέεσσι· φίλοι δ' ἀμφέσταν ἑταῖροι
18.352: ἐν λεχέεσσι δὲ θέντες ἑανῶι λιτὶ κάλυψαν
21.124: ἐνθεμένη λεχέεσσι γοήσεται, ἀλλὰ Σκάμανδρος
22.87: κλαύσομαι ἐν λεχέεσσι φίλον θάλος, ὃν τέκον αὐτή

---

[24] I am grateful to Filippomaria Pontani who provided detailed information on this point. For instance, at *Od.* 10.12 τρητοῖσι λέχεσσι(ν) is found in DGHTX, τρητοῖς λεχέεσσιν in KMP.

22.353: ἐνθεμένη λεχέεσσι γοήσεται ὃν τέκεν αὐτή,
23.25: πρηνέα πὰρ λεχέεσσι Μενοιτιάδαο τανύσσας
24.702: τὸν δ' ἄρ' ἐφ' ἡμιόνων ἴδε κείμενον ἐν λεχέεσσι·
24.720: τρητοῖσ' ἐν λεχέεσσι θέσαν, παρὰ δ' εἷσαν ἀοιδοὺς

Odyssey
1.366: πάντες δ' ἠρήσαντο παραὶ λεχέεσσι κλιθῆναι
3.399 = 7.345: τρητοῖσ' ἐν λεχέεσσιν, ὑπ' αἰθούσηι ἐριδούπωι
10.497: κλαῖον δ' ἐν λεχέεσσι καθήμενος, οὐδέ νύ μοι κῆρ
18.213: πάντες δ' ἠρήσαντο παραὶ λεχέεσσι κλιθῆναι
24.44: κάτθεμεν ἐν λεχέεσσι, καθήραντες χρόα καλὸν
24.295: κώκυσ' ἐν λεχέεσσιν ἐὸν πόσιν, ὡς ἐπεώικει

The numerous 'necessary' λεχέεσσι present some peculiar features: (1) the majority have no epithets, (2) epithets appear in four lines only (actually three, since one is repeated, *Il.* 3.448 Τὼ μὲν ἄρ' ἐν τρητοῖσι κατεύνασθεν λεχέεσσιν, 24.720 τρητοῖσ' ἐν λεχέεσσι θέσαν, παρὰ δ' εἷσαν ἀοιδοὺς, *Od.* 3.399 = 7.345 τρητοῖσ' ἐν λεχέεσσιν, ὑπ' αἰθούσηι ἐριδούπωι), (3) the epithet is invariably τρητός, it is found in the first part of the line and is separated from λεχέεσσι by a preposition or a verb.

What happened? To my mind the less improbable scenario is as follows. The compositional story began with the *A&N* pattern in line-final position, i.e. ἐν... δινωτοῖσι λέχεσσι, ἐν / πὰρ τρητοῖσι λέχεσσι. Once λεχέεσσι was created the bards discovered its usefulness in isolation: words scanning (υ υ – υ) or ending in (υ υ – υ) were extremely suitable to hexameter composition. The most obvious and most useful combination was ἐν λεχέεσσι, which was often used without adectives; if τρητός was added, it was placed before the noun, according to the word order of the original *A&N* τρητοῖσι λέχεσσι. It was the remarkable success of the 'new' λεχέεσσι that caused the (partial) replacement of line-final -οισι λέχεσσι with -οις λεχέεσσι in the mss. tradition of some lines.

14. βέλος

βέλος shows a similar cleavage between (a) the *A&N* pattern, namely -οῖσι βέλεσσιν always interchangeable with -οῖς βελέεσσι, and (b) βελέεσσι metrically necessary and *never* interchangeable with βέλεσσιν.

(a) In the *A&N* instances (attested both in line-final and line-internal position) the mss. often oscillate between -οισι βέλεσσι and -οις βελέεσσι. *Iliad*: 1.42 τίσειαν Δαναοὶ ἐμὰ δάκρυα τοῖσι βέλεσσιν / (no variant, but -οῖς βελέεσσιν theoretically possible); 13.555 Νέστορος υἱὸν ἔρυτο καὶ ἐν πολλοῖσι βέλεσσιν / (-οῖς βελέεσσι Τ); 24.759 οἷς ἀγανοῖσι βέλεσσιν ἐποιχόμενος κατέπεφνεν / (-οῖς βελέεσσι A and the majority of the mss.). Oscillations in the mss. are the order of the day in the *Odyssey*: 3.280 οἷσ' ἀγανοῖσι βέλεσσιν ἐποιχόμενος κατέπεφνε =

5.124 (ἐποιχομένη) = 11.173 (ἐποιχομένη) = 11.199 (ἐποιχομένη) 15.411 (ἐποιχόμενος). A high number of mss. and papyri has ἀγανοῖς βελέεσσι, which is systematically printed by van Thiel 1991 (whereas Von der Mühll 1962 prints ἀγανοῖσι βέλεσσι in all the abovementioned lines).

(b) In numerous cases, completely divorced from the *A&N* system, βελέεσσι(ν) is metrically necessary and unchangeable, never linked to an adjective and immediately joined to a verb. *Iliad*: 5.622 = 13.511 ὤμοιιν ἀφελέσθαι· ἐπείγετο γὰρ βελέεσσι; 11.576 Εὐρύπυλος πυκινοῖσι βιαζόμενον βελέεσσι; 11.589 Αἴανθ', ὃς βελέεσσι βιάζεται, οὐδὲ ἔ φημι; 15.727 = 16.102 Αἴας δ' οὐκέτ' ἔμιμνε· βιάζετο γὰρ βελέεσσιν; 16.108 ἀμφ' αὐτῶι πελεμίξαι ἐρείδοντες βελέεσσιν; 16.639 ἐπεὶ βελέεσσι καὶ αἵματι καὶ κονίηισιν / ἐκ κεφαλῆς εἴλυτο κτλ. 21.278 λαιψηροῖς ὀλέεσθαι Ἀπόλλωνος βελέεσσιν; 22.196 εἴ πως οἱ καθύπερθεν ἀλάλκοιεν βελέεσσι.

The conclusions are very similar to those reached for λέχεσσι / λεχέεσσι. The old form βέλεσσι(ν) was used in the *A&N* pattern, then the advantages of the innovated Aeolic form βελέεσσι(ν) were discovered: the latter form became part of short sentences in which it was closely linked to a verbal form and often placed in line-final position, βιαζόμενον βελέεσσι, ἐρείδοντες βελέεσσιν, ἀλάλκοιεν βελέεσσι, ὀλέεσθαι Ἀπόλλωνος βελέεσσιν. The only dative plural of βέλος attested in Hesiod is βελέεσσι in this position (*Th.* 716 κατὰ δ' ἐσκίασαν βελέεσσι / Τιτῆνας). At some point βελέεσσι replaced βέλεσσι in the *A&N* pattern, to a certain extent in the *Iliad*, almost systematically in the *Odyssey*: the influence of the 'necessary' βελέεσσι linked to verbs in line-final position is evident (καὶ ἐν πολλοῖσι βέλεσσι /) > (βιαζόμενον βελέεσσι /) > καὶ ἐν πολλοῖς βελέεσσι /).

15. ἔπος

The Homeric use of ἔπος poses special problems, also because in the Greek oral epics this word started its career as ϝέπος (if not as *wek^wos*) and at some point lost its initial [w]. As is well known, some complex questions are posed especially by ἔπεσσι(ν) and ἐπέεσσι(ν).

(a) In the *A&N* pattern the -εσσι(ν) and the -έεσσι(ν) forms are only theoretically interchangeable since -οῖς ἐπέεσσι(ν) is the only transmitted form. But according to many it must have started its career as *-οισι (ϝ)έπεσσι. It is an extremely frequent pattern e.g. *Il.* 2.378 ἀντιβίοις ἐπέεσσιν, ἐγὼ δ' ἦρχον χαλεπαίνων (*ἀντιβίοισιν ἔπεσσι possible); 3.38 τὸν δ' Ἕκτωρ νείκεσσεν ἰδὼν αἰσχροῖς ἐπέεσσιν (*αἰσχροῖσιν ἔπεσσι possible); 16.628 ὦ πέπον οὔ τοι Τρῶες ὀνειδείοις ἐπέεσσι (ὀνειδείοισιν ἔπεσσι possible). Editions oscillate between a rendering with or without apostrophe, -οις ἐπέεσσι(ν) and -οισ' ἐπέεσσι(ν).[25]

ἔπεσσι(ν) itself is found more than once in Homer (especially in the *Odyssey*), but mainly in other positions of the line and never in the A&N pattern. The instances are: *Il.* 9.113 δώροισίν τ' ἀγανοῖσιν ἔπεσσί τε μειλιχίοισιν 10.542 δεξιῆι ἠσπάζοντο ἔπεσσί τε μειλιχίοισι; *Od.* 3.264 πόλλ' Ἀγαμεμνονέην ἄλοχον θέλγεσκεν ἔπεσσιν; 4.597 αἰνῶς γὰρ μύθοισιν ἔπεσσί τε σοῖσιν ἀκούων; 4.706 ὀψὲ δὲ δή μιν ἔπεσσιν ἀμειβομένη προσέειπε; 5.96 καὶ τότε δή μιν ἔπεσσιν ἀμειβόμενος προσέειπεν; 9.258 ἀλλὰ καὶ ὣς μιν ἔπεσσιν ἀμειβόμενος προσέειπον; 9.363 καὶ τότε δή μιν ἔπεσσι προσηύδων μειλιχίοισι; 9.376 ἔπεσσι δὲ πάντας ἑταίρους / θάρσυνον; 10.500 καὶ τότε δή μιν ἔπεσσιν ἀμειβόμενος προσέειπον; 16.193 ἐξαῦτίς μιν ἔπεσσιν ἀμειβόμενος προσέειπεν; 17.545 οὐχ ὁράαις, ὅ μοι υἱὸς ἐπέπταρε πᾶσιν ἔπεσσι; 19.214 ἐξαῦτίς μιν ἔπεσσιν ἀμειβομένη προσέειπε, 19.415 χερσίν τ' ἠσπάζοντο ἔπεσσί τε μειλιχίοισι.

Note the remarkable contrast with the *A&N* pattern: when ἔπεσσι is linked to an adjective, the adjective is almost always found *after* the noun, while in the A&N pattern the opposite is the case. Besides, a final ἔπεσσι(ν) / is found only twice, preceded by a verbal form at *Od.* 3.264 ἄλοχον θέλγεσκεν ἔπεσσιν / and by (non-thematic) πᾶσιν at *Od.* 17.545 ἐπέπταρε πᾶσιν ἔπεσσι /: they are different from the the A&N pattern and are probably later developments.

(b) In very many instances ἐπέεσσιν is metrically necessary and unchangeable; it is immediately preceded or followed by a verbal form; adjectives linked to ἐπέεσσιν are rare, and invariably separated from it by a verb. Its most frequent placing is at line-end, but in some cases it appears in the first hemistich. Witte (1914, 50 f.) showed to what extent the -εσσι endings were used in order to create words of the (υ υ- υ) shape: Δολόπεσσι, μακάρεσσι, φυλάκεσσι, πολέεσσι... As a consequence 'Formen wie ἐπέεσσιν eigneten sich für die Verwendung im Hexameter noch besser als ἔπεσσιν' (1914, 56).

Iliad
1.304: Ὣς τώ γ' ἀντιβίοισι μαχεσσαμένω ἐπέεσσιν
1.582: ἀλλὰ σὺ τὸν ἐπέεσσι καθάπτεσθαι μαλακοῖσιν
2.75: ὑμεῖς δ' ἄλλοθεν ἄλλος ἐρητύειν ἐπέεσσιν
3.249: ὄτρυνεν δὲ γέροντα παριστάμενος ἐπέεσσιν
4.233: τοὺς μάλα θαρσύνεσκε παριστάμενος ἐπέεσσιν
4.241: ἔνθ' ἡμεῖς μὲν πάντες ὁμοκλέομεν ἐπέεσσι
12.249: παρφάμενος ἐπέεσσιν ἀποτρέψεις πολέμοιο,
15.210: ἔνθ' ἡμεῖς μὲν πάντες ὁμοκλέομεν ἐπέεσσι
17.215: ὄτρυνεν δὲ ἕκαστον ἐποιχόμενος ἐπέεσσι

---

[25] Von der Mühll prints systematically -οισ' ἐπέεσσι(ν).

21.98: λισσόμενος ἐπέεσσιν, ἀμείλικτον δ' ὄπ' ἄκουσε
22.329: ὄφρά τί μιν προτιείποι ἀμειβόμενος ἐπέεσσιν
23.489: χωόμενος χαλεποῖσιν ἀμείψασθαι ἐπέεσσι
23.492: μηκέτι νῦν χαλεποῖσιν ἀμείβεσθον ἐπέεσσιν
24.771: ἀλλὰ σὺ τὸν ἐπέεσσι παραιφάμενος κατέρυκες

Odyssey
2.189: παρφάμενος ἐπέεσσιν ἐποτρύνῃς χαλεπαίνειν
2.240: ἧσθ' ἄνεω, ἀτὰρ οὔ τι καθαπτόμενοι ἐπέεσσι
2.323: οἱ δ' ἐπελώβευον καὶ ἐκερτόμεον ἐπέεσσιν
3.148: ὣς τὼ μὲν χαλεποῖσιν ἀμειβομένω ἐπέεσσιν
3.345: Νέστωρ αὖ κατέρυκε καθαπτόμενος ἐπέεσσι
4.286: Ἄντικλος δὲ σέ γ' οἶος ἀμείψασθαι ἐπέεσσιν
4.420: ἀλλ' ὅτε κεν δή σ' αὐτὸς ἀνείρηται ἐπέεσσι
6.146: λίσσεσθαι ἐπέεσσιν ἀποσταδὰ μειλιχίοισι
7.341: ὤτρυνον Ὀδυσῆα παριστάμεναι ἐπέεσσιν
8.175: ἀλλ' οὔ οἱ χάρις ἀμφὶ περιστέφεται ἐπέεσσιν
8.396: Εὐρύαλος δέ ἑ αὐτὸν ἀρεσσάσθω ἐπέεσσι
8.415: τούτου, ὃ δή μοι δῶκας ἀρεσσάμενος ἐπέεσσι
10.70: ὣς ἐφάμην μαλακοῖσι καθαπτόμενος ἐπέεσσιν
11.81: νῶι μὲν ὣς ἐπέεσσιν ἀμειβομένω στυγεροῖσιν
11.225: νῶϊ μὲν ὣς ἐπέεσσιν ἀμειβόμεθ', αἱ δὲ γυναῖκες
11.465: νῶϊ μὲν ὣς ἐπέεσσιν ἀμειβομένω στυγεροῖσιν
11.552: τὸν μὲν ἐγὼν ἐπέεσσι προσηύδων μειλιχίοισιν
15.440: σιγῆι νῦν· μή τίς με προσαυδάτω ἐπέεσσιν
18.340: ὣς εἰπὼν ἐπέεσσι διεπτοίησε γυναῖκας
19.155: εἷλον ἐπελθόντες καὶ ὁμόκλησαν ἐπέεσσιν
22.26 = 22.225: νείκειον δ' Ὀδυσῆα χολωτοῖσιν ἐπέεσσι
24.173: ἔνθ' ἡμεῖς μὲν πάντες ὁμοκλέομεν ἐπέεσσι

As I said, Chantraine was certainly right when he suspected that ἐπέεσσι 'semble authentique dans de nombreux passages'. The situation is very similar to that of λεχέεσσι and βελέεσσι, with the important difference that in those words the initial stop was kept for good, whereas that of ϝεπέεσσι was dropped at a certain point. It is extremely likely that παριστάμενος ἐπέεσσι, ἐκερτόμεον ἐπέεσσι, ἐποιχόμενος ἐπέεσσι started their career as παριστάμενος ϝεπέεσσι, ἐκερτόμεον ϝεπέεσσι, ἐποιχόμενος ϝεπέεσσι. Once initial [w] was no longer pronounced, -μενος ἐπέεσσι etc. was obviously interpreted as a metrical lengthening, and even elided verbal forms were used before ἐπέεσσι (e. g. *Od.* 18.111 ἡδὺ γελώοντες, καὶ δεικανόωντ' ἐπέεσσι).

16. At this point it seems necessary to me to draw a tentative picture of what happened, for good or ill. λέχεσσι, βέλεσσι *ϝέπεσσι were obviously in use independently from any *A&N*, but the *A&N*s -οισι λέχεσσι, -οισι βέλεσσι, *-οισι *ϝέπεσσι

must have played a central role in the diction. When the old forms were still used by the singers the 'inverted' *ϝέπεσσι τε μειλιχίοισι was created. Under the pressure of the new -έεσσι forms closely linked to verbs (ἐρείδοντες βελέεσσι, παριστάμενος *ϝεπέεσσι), '-οισι –εσσι' in line-final position tended to be replaced by –'οις –έεσσι'. This may have happened in an area (or under the influence of the dialect of an area) where the inherited system using -οισι for the locative and -οις for the instrumental of the masculine/neuter of the thematic declension had been discarded in favour of a syncretic -οις: a good candidate would be Thessaly (Morpurgo Davies 1976, 182). Yet 'short' forms are well attested in Lesbian poetry,[26] where otherwise the standard datives are in -οισι/-αισι, and Blümel (1982, 246f.) has rightly shown the weakness of explanations assuming that the -οις -αις forms attested in the Lesbian poets are due to Homeric models. As a matter of fact, it was perfectly possible to employ in East Aeolic (and elsewhere) 'la "forme courte" dans une expression où le datif pluriel est déjà marqué dans un autre terme et où la "forme longue" apparaîtrait donc comme redondante' (Hodot 1990, 95 n. 8).[27]

17. The tendency to modify the old *A&N*s, especially in line-final position, by turning "οισι -εσσι" into "-οις –έεσσι" must have been pervasive. It is significant that there is only one line in the whole of Homer, *Il*. 1.42 τίσειαν Δαναοὶ ἐμὰ δάκρυα σοῖσι βέλεσσι, for which no variant *-οις βελέεσσι is attested; otherwise oscillations were (and are in our mss.) the order of the day.

It seems likely to me that the whole "operation" took place in an area where initial [w] was still pronounced but moribund. From this viewpoint, Lesbos might be the perfect locale.[28] If at a certain point a systematic replacement of the "οισι -εσσι" *A&N*s with the "-οις –έεσσι" ones took place, some instances of λέχεσσι and βέλεσσι managed to survive because their initial consonants were irremovable and managed to keep alive (in part) the old system πολλοῖσι βέλεσσι etc.; but if very soon after the change into ὀνειδείοις ϝεπέεσσι initial [w] was deleted, the only possible result was ὀνειδείοις ἐπέεσσι, probably immediately interpreted as an elided ὀνειδείοιο᾽ ἐπέεσσι (μαλακοῖσ᾽ ἐπέεσσι, μειλιχίοιο᾽ ἐπέεσσι are systematically printed by Von der Mühll 1962). In the original *ὀνει-

---

26 Vgl. Sapph. Fr. 44, 12 V. φάμα δ᾽ ἦλθε κατὰ πτόλιν εὐρύχορον οἴλοις, Sapph. Fr. 44, 21 V. ἴ]κελοι θέοι[ς.
27 See also Page (1955) 208 on Alcaeus' συνόδοισί μ᾽ αὔταις; he adds that Archilochus and Anacreon 'the shorter form is invariably followed or preceded by a longer form in agreement with it'.
28 'Die Inkonsequenzen in Schreibung und prosodischer Ausnutzung in den Texten der lesbischen Lyriker lassen die Vermutung zu, daß [w] auch schon im 7. Jhdt. kein lebendiger Laut mehr gewesen ist' (Blümel 1982, 80f.).

δείοισι ϝέπεσσι the old [w] had disappeared and could not work as a "prop" to keep the old A&N alive; the only ἔπεσσι that had been left filled different slots in the line, and were not able to undermine the new shape -οις (or -οισ') ἐπέεσσι in line-final position – my impression is that this position played a crucial role in the whole operation.

18. In Gary Miller (2014, 342 f.) one finds a completely different analysis of the data. He says: 'phrases like -οις ἐπέεσσι are supposedly Aeolic' and proceeds to show why in his opinion they are not Aeolic. It should be noted that his words are not immediately obvious to the non-initiated, since after stating (p. 343) that 'such phrases are... irrelevant to the Aeolic phase hypothesis' he reconstructs a hypothetical and extremely old *-οῖς ϝέπεσφι, which later on 'underwent artificial metrical adaptation / Aeolicization to hexametric -οις ἐπέεσσι', which might seem contradictory at first sight. As a matter of fact, he denies that e.g. μαλακοῖς ἐπέεσσι has anything to do with the supposed Aeolic phase of the epics, but suggests that a very archaic form (which he reconstructs) was Aeolicized at what was probably a "late" stage.

His *pars destruens* is: (i) 'older epigraphic Lesbian still had -οισι –αισι', (ii) 'the type ἐπέεσσι is late Lesbian and Thessalian', (iii) 'older -σι forms remain in Lesbian and Thessalian', (IV) 'the spread of -εσσι is recent', and (v) 'the combination is hyper-Aeolic. Such phrases are therefore irrelevant to the Aeolic phase hypothesis'.

As to his *pars construens*, since μαλακοῖς ἐπέεσσιν and the rest are syntactically instrumentals, and 'the instrumental in Mycenaean ended in -οις, distinct from the dative locative -οιhι ... the phrase in Mycenaean would have been e.g. *μαλακοῖς ϝέπεσφι, a perfect line-final aristophanean as predicted by Nils Berg (1978) and others for an early stage of the dactylic hexameter. This is the relevant instrumental type of phrase that underwent artificial metrical adaptation/Aeolicization to hexametric -οις ἐπέεσσι'.

19. Various objections can be raised against these statements. As to the *pars destruens*, it can be observed that: (i) it is true that older epigraphic Lesbian still had -οισι -αισι, but "short" forms could happily be used if linked to "long" ones (§ 16); (ii) the type ἐπέεσσι is attested in Hellenistic inscriptions but it must have taken shape centuries before the date of the inscriptions themselves (§ 10); (iii) here Gary Miller's argument is far from clear; both -εσσι and -σι are attested in the Aeolic dialects (Blümel 1982, 260 ff.), but one cannot argue that an old *ϝέπεσ-σι was condemned to remain as such forever; (iv) it is possible that the spread of -εσσι was a relatively recent development in the history of the Greek epic, but in any case it was an enormously important development

that shaped the epic hexameter as we have it; (v) the idea that the combination -οις ἐπέεσσι is "hyper-Aeolic" is based on the conviction that ἐπέεσσι is artificial, which seems groundless to me (§§ 10 and 11). -οις ἐπέεσσι may be irrelevant to the Aeolic phase hypothesis, but to my mind it shows, along with the various παριστάμενος ἐπέεσσι and βιαζόμενος βελέεσσι, that at some point the influence on the epics of the Aeolic dialects and their analogical innovations became simply enormous.

As to Gary Miller's *pars construens*, apart from the fact that Berg's theory is controversial and not generally accepted,[29] it is far from clear than the grammar of the oldest Homeric phases was a xerox of Mycenaean grammar. In Homer, a high number of semantically "instrumental" Homeric datives are ancient locatives in Indo-European terms: ὀφθαλμοῖσιν ἰδών, ἴδεν ὀφθαλμοῖσιν "saw with his/her eyes" are very frequent; κερτομίοισι means "with abusing words" (*Il.* 1.539: αὐτίκα κερτομίοισι Δία Κρονίωνα προσηύδα) and in *Od.* 1.56 αἰεὶ δὲ μαλακοῖσι καὶ αἱμυλίοισι λόγοισι / θέλγει the dative λόγοισι and its adjectives are old locatives in an "instrumental" capacity. On the other hand, various -φι(ν) are used as locatives, especially ὄρεσφι, e.g. *Il.* 11.474 Τρῶες ἔπονθ' ὡς εἴ τε δαφοινοὶ θῶες ὄρεσφιν / ἀμφ' ἔλαφον κεραὸν βεβλημένον, 19.376 κοιομένοιο πυρός, τό τε καίεται ὑψόθ' ὄρεσφι. We have seen (§ 15) that a certain number of ἔπεσσι is in fact attested in Homer. Gary Miller should explain why not a single instrumental *ἔπεσφι is attested, while a locatival ὄρεσφι (belonging to the same declension) appears more than once. To my mind his reconstruction has no value.

20. In conclusion, βελέ-εσσι, *ϝέπε-εσσι and the like are probably nothing else but banal analogical formations based on the stems βέλε-, ϝεπε- of βέλε-α ϝέπε-α, βελέ-ων ϝεπέ-ων etc., and have nothing artificial about them. The singers discovered their usefulness first in connection with verbal forms (βιαζόμενος βελέεσσι, παριστάμενος *ϝεπέεσσι), then used them to replace the traditonal -οισι βέλεσσι -οισι *ϝέπεσσι in line-final position. It is not excluded that the traditional forms -οισι βέλεσσι etc. were perceived as "old" and in a way out of fashion. The -εσσι ending is an innovation well attested in the Aeolic dialects, and the role of those dialects in the shaping of the epics is likely to have been far more complicated than any modern scholar has imagined so far. Whatever one may think of the notorious Aeolic phase theory, I feel certain that at a certain point Aeolic forms, old and innovated, were perceived as very prestigious and were accepted in the text. The change of the old "-οισι -εσσι" into the new "-οις -έεσσι" must

---

[29] Hoekstra (1981); see Magnelli (1996).

have taken place in a milieu that looked at the East Aeolic dialect as the dialect of an eminent type of poetry. The change happened at a not terribly ancient date: initial [w] was on the wane, and it should be noted that -οις βελέεσσι, -οις *ϝεπέεσσι created overlength in the final *adonius* of the hexameter, unknown to the old forms -οισι βέλεσσι and -οισι *ϝέπεσσι: this shows that sensitivity to the avoidance of overlength in the final *adonius* had already disappeared, exactly as it happened in the late Ionic layers of composition (Cassio 2016). In any case we owe to these ancient, but not enormously ancient, manipulations some very remarkable formal features of the Homeric text as we have it.

Works cited

Barth, M. and J. Stauber (1993). *Inschriften von Mysia und Troas.* Munich.
Bean, G. E. (1966). 'Two Inscriptions from Aeolis', *Belleten Türk Tarih Kurumu* 30: 528–37.
Berg, N. (1978). 'Parergon metricum: der Ursprung des griechischen Hexameters', *Münch. Stud. Sprachwiss.* 37: 11–36.
Biondi, L. (2001). 'La lingua', Scuola Normale Superiore di Pisa. Pisa, 81–8.
Blanc, A. (2008). *Les contraintes métriques dans la poésie homérique. L'emploi des thèmes nominaux sigmatiques dans l'hexamètre dactylique.* Leuven-Paris.
Blümel, W. (1982). *Die aiolischen Dialekte.* Göttingen.
Cassio, A. C. (2006). 'La Tessaglia, l'isola di Lesbo e i dativi plurali del tipo ἐπέεσσι', in: M. Vetta – C. Catenacci (eds.), *I luoghi e la poesia nella Grecia antica.* Alessandria, 73–84.
–. (2010). 'Il participio del verbo 'essere' in Eolico d'Asia tra filologia e linguistica', in: I. Putzu, G. Paulis, G. Nieddu, and P. Cuzzolin (eds.), *La morfologia del greco tra tipologia e diacronia. Atti del VII Incontro internazionale di linguistica greca (Cagliari 13–15 settembre 2007).* Milan, 25–30.
–. (2016). 'Overlong Syllables in the Epic "Adonius" and the Compositional Stages of Greek Hexameter Poetry', in: F. Gallo (ed.), *Omero. Quaestiones disputatae,* Milan, 31–41.
–. (2017). 'Notes on the Origin and Diffusion of the -εσσι Datives', in: G. K. Giannakis, E. Crespo, and P. Filos (eds.), *Studies in Ancient Greek Dialects: From Central Greece to the Black Sea.* Berlin, 189–96.
Chantraine, P. (1958). *Grammaire homérique, I. Phonétique et morphologie.* Paris.
Collitz, H. (1884). *Sammlung der griechischen Dialekt-Inschriften,* vol. I. Göttingen.
Engelmann, H. (1976). *Die Inschriften von Kyme (Inschriften griechischer Städte aus Kleinasien* 5). Bonn.
García Ramón, J. L. (1990). 'Proportionale Analogie im Griechischen: Der Dativ Pluralis der 3. Deklination in den aiolischen und westgriechischen Dialekten', *Glotta* 68: 135–56.
Gary Miller, D. (2014). *Ancient Greek Dialects and Early Authors. Introduction to the Dialect Mixture in Homer, with Notes on Lyric and Herodotus.* Boston – Berlin.
Haug, D. (2002). *Les phases de l'évolution de la langue épique.* Göttingen.
Hodot, R. (1990). *Le dialecte ionien d'Asie.* Paris.
Hoekstra, A. (1981). *Epic Verse Before Homer.* Amsterdam – Oxford – New York.

Horrocks, G. (1997). 'Homer's Dialect', in: I. Morris – B. Powell (eds.), *A New Companion to Homer*. Leiden – New York – Cologne, 193–217.
Jones, B. (2012). 'Relative chronology and an "Aeolic phase" of epic', in: Ø. Andersen and D. Haug (eds.), *Relative chronology in Early Greek Epic Poetry*. Cambridge, 44–54.
La Roche, J. (1869). *Homerische Untersuchungen*. Leipzig.
Magnelli, E. (1996). 'Studi recenti sull'origine dell'esametro: un profilo critico', in: M. Fantuzzi and R. Pretagostini (eds.), *Struttura e storia dell'esametro greco* II. Rome, 111–37.
Missailidou-Despotidou, V. (1993). 'A Hellenistic Inscription from Skotoussa (Thessaly) and the Fortifications of the City', *Ann. Brit. Sch. Athens* 88: 187–217.
Morpurgo Davies, A. (1976). 'The -εσσι Datives, Aeolic –ss-, and the Lesbian Poets', in: A. M. Davies and W. Meid (eds.), *Studies in Greek, Italic, and Indo-European Linguistics Offered to L. R. Palmer*. Innsbruck, 181–97.
Nagy, G. (2011). 'The Aeolic Component of Homeric Diction', in: S. W. Jamison, H.C. Melchert, and B. Vine (eds.), *Proceedings of the 22nd Annual UCLA Indo-Eureopean Conference*. Bremen, 133–79.
Page, D. L. (1955). *Sappho and Alcaeus*. Oxford.
Payne Knight, P. (1820). *Carmina Homerica, Ilias et Odyssea, ... in pristinam formam... redacta*. London.
Porciani, L. (2001). 'I decreti: testo e traduzione', in: *Da un'antica città della Sicilia. I decreti di Entella e Nakone. Catalogo della mostra*, Scuola Normale Superiore di Pisa. Pisa, 11–31.
Rix, H. (1976). *Historische Grammatik des Griechischen*. Darmstadt.
Ruijgh, C. J. (1995). *D'Homère aux origines protomycéniennes de la tradition épique*, in: J. P. Crielaard (ed.), *Homeric Questions. Essays in Philology, Ancient History and Archaeology, including the Papers of a Conference Organized by the Netherlands Institute at Athens*. Amsterdam, 1–96.
van Bremen, R. (2008). 'The Date and Context of the Kymaian Decrees for Archippe (*SEG* 33, 1035–1041)' *REA* 110: 357–82.
van Thiel, H. (1991). *Homeri Odyssea*. Hildesheim – Zurich – New York.
von der Mühll, P. (1962). *Homeri Odyssea*. Basel.
Wackernagel, J. (1903). 'Zur griechischen Nominalflexion: 2. Der Dativ pluralis auf –εσσι', *IF* 14: 373–5 (= *Kleine Schriften*, Göttingen 1955, vol. II, 967–9).
Wathelet, P. (1970). *Les traits éoliens dans la langue de l'épopée grecque*. Rome.
West, M. L. (1998–200). *Homerus. Ilias*, vol. I, Stuttgard and Leipzig (1998), vol. II, Munich and Leipzig (2000).
Witte, K. (1914). 'Zur Frage der Äolismen bei Homer. Der Dativ des Plurals der dritten Deklination', *Glotta* 5: 48–57.

Christos Tsagalis
ΑΠ'/ΚΑΤ' ΑΙΓΙΛΙΠΟΣ ΠΕΤΡΗΣ: Homeric iconyms and Hittite answers

The term 'iconym' was coined by M. S. Silk in his pathbreaking article 'LSJ and the Problem of Poetic Archaism: From Meanings to Iconyms'.[1] After calling attention to the need for a systematic development of 'literary lexicography', Silk defined an 'iconym' as a purely literary phenomenon pertaining to a word (or less often a group of words) that has lost its denotations with the result that its reader or listener often resorts to mere guesswork with respect to its meaning, as if what matters more is an image triggered by its use. Semantic imprecision and lack of a denotative center are counterbalanced by a set of connotations that do not lead to any given meaning. Iconyms are usually nested in verse, especially elevated verse. The more specialized a given register is within the field of poetry, the greater is the possibility for the survival of iconyms, which have become dictional 'fossils' in the course of time.

Αἰγίλιψ, -ιπος

Here is the relevant entry from LSJ s.v.

> αἰγίλιψ [γι], ιπος, ὁ, ἡ, (expl. by Gramm. from αἴξ, λείπω, cf. Sch. Il. 9.15) *destitute even of goats*, hence, *steep, sheer*, πέτρη Il. 9.15, al. (not in *Od.*), A. *Supp.* 794 (lyr.), Lyc. 1325; also in form αἰγίλιπος, Hsch. (Perh. cognate with Lith. *lipti* 'climb').

The organization of the entry classifies under a sole heading the explanation offered by the ancient Grammarians (on the basis of the verb 'abandon') and the word's etymology by means of a Lithuanian verb meaning 'climb'. The former meaning is supported by archaic and classical examples, while the lemma of Hesychius introduces a further meaning ('high': αἰγίλιψ· ὑψηλὴ πέτρα καὶ πόλις καὶ ἰτέα ὑπὸ Θουρίων; αἰγίλιπος· ὑψηλὸς τόπος) and attests to the existence of two forms, one in –ος and one in –ψ. The LSJ entry, thus, testifies (a) to the 'firm'

---

1 (1983) 303–30.

I would like to express my gratitude to Mary Bachvarova, Ian Rutherford, and Panagiotis Filos for reading a draft of this piece and for making many insightful suggestions, and to Georgios Giannakis for discussing the Hittite material.

https://doi.org/9783110559873-011

belief that the first part of this compound comes from αἴξ ('goat'), and (b) to the compiler's confusion with respect to the etymology of the second part of the compound ('abandon' or 'climb'?). The etymology of Homeric αἰγίλιπος (gen. of αἰγίλιψ; 3x in Hom.: *Il.* 9.15, 13.63, and 16.4) has attracted the interest of ancient scholars too. They interpreted it from αἴξ ('goat') + λιπ- (< λείπω) as 'high', 'steep', forsaken even by goats' (see Σ *Il.* 9.15a),[2] which is clearly based on folk etymology.[3]

Understandably, this meaning was not approved by a significant number of modern scholars, who opted for different etymologies. I begin by offering a survey of the etymologies offerred thus far (1–5), accompanied by comments with respect to each proposed 'solution' to this notorious problem, after which I append my own interpretation (6):

1. Uljanov (in Solmsen 1901, 73 n. 1): αἴξ ('goat') + λιπ- (a stem meaning 'to clamber' that was reconstructed on the basis of Lith. *lìpti* ['to clamber']). According to this etymology, αἰγίλιψ means 'what is climbed by goats'. In this light, Αἰγίλιπα τρηχεῖαν (*Il.* 2.633) means 'steep, Goat-climbed [island's name]' and the formula κατ' αἰγίλιπος πέτρης (*Il.* 9.15, 13.63, and 16.4) means 'Goat-climbed rock'.[4]

The standard etymological dictionaries have reacted either with reservation or with open disapproval to this explanation. Chantraine (*DELG* s.v.) explicitly says that 'with respect to the first part of the compound, it is possible but not absolutely certain, that we are dealing with the word for goat'. Concerning the second part of the compound, he deploys three different suggestions without taking sides: (i) association with Lith. *lìpti* ('to clamber'), (ii) association with the Hesychian gloss ἄλιψ· πέτρα, which probably means 'qu'on peut escalader' (that can be climbed), and (iii) λίψ· πέτρα ἀφ' ἧς ὕδωρ στάζει, which results from a contamination with the family of λείβω ('let flow', 'shed'). Frisk (*GEW*

---

[2] αἰγίλιπος: ὑψηλῆς, ἣν καὶ αἴξ ἂν ἀπολίπηι διὰ τὸ ἄγαν ὑψηλόν (AT) / καὶ δύσβατον· ἐν γὰρ τοῖς κρημνοῖς αἱ αἶγες ὡς ἐπίπαν νέμονται (A).
[3] This is the most widespread interpretation of the word in ancient and byzantine authors and lexica. It is attested in the Atticistic Lexicon of Pausanias s.v., in [Zonaras] s.v., in Photius s.v., and in Eustathius' commentary on the *Iliad* (vol. I, 476.21–22; vol. II, 650.1; vol. III, 796.4).
[4] See also Aesch. *Supp.* 794–6: ἦ λισσὰς αἰγίλιψ ἀπρόσ- / δεικτος οἰόφρων κρεμὰς / γυπιὰς πέτρα ('or a slippery crag, where no goat climbs, lonely, overhanging, impossible to point out', transl. Sommerstein 2008, 391); Lyc. *Alex.* 1324–6: ὁ Φημίου παῖς, Σκῦρος ὧι λυγροὺς τάφους / κρημνῶν ἔνερθεν αἰγίλιψ ῥοιζουμένων / πάλαι δοκεύει τὰς ἀταρχύτους ῥιφάς ('the son of Phemius, whose sad grave / below the roaring precipices, the site of his unburied fall, will long be watched from Scyros, the place too steep even for goats—', transl. by Hornblower 2015, 465 with spelling modifications).

s.v.) calls Uljanov's association of -λιψ with Lith. *lipti* ('to clamber') 'gewiß richtig' but treats the overall interpretation '(nur) von Ziegen erkletterbar' as very doubtful. He then points to the Hesychian gloss ἄλιψ· πέτρα, which he regards as 'truly indispensable' in the etymological analysis of the second part of the compound. Like Chantraine, he takes the other Hesychian gloss (λίψ· πέτρα ἀφ' ἧς ὕδωρ στάζει) as having originated from the compound αἰγίλιψ. Conversely, Beekes (*EDG* s.v.) treats the etymological link with Lith. *lipti* as problematic by claiming that 'the meaning "clamber" for the root *leip-* is secondary to "stick, cleave", and it is far from certain that Greek underwent the same development as in Lithuanian'.

2. Kretschmer:[5] αἰγι- (< αἶγες 'waves') + λιπ- (λέπ-ας 'bare rock', 'crag'). The first part of the compound comes from the metaphorical meaning of αἶγες as 'waves', a use that is not only seen in words like αἰγιαλός, Αἴγιον, Αἰγαῖον, but is also supported by the Hesychian gloss αἶγες· τὰ κύματα, Artemidorus 2.12 (καὶ γὰρ αἶγας τὰ μεγάλα κύματα ἐν τῆι συνηθείαι λέγομεν). Kretschmer sees in λέπ-ας and Latin *lapis* the same vowel analogy that exists between πελιός, πιλνός and *palleo* (with an *a* in Latin for Greek ε, ι). According to this etymological analysis, αἰγίλιψ means 'rock of the waves', i.e. rock hit or washed by the waves.[6]

Kretschmer's etymology, which is mentioned neither by the standard etymological dictionaries (*DELG*, *EWG*, *EDG*) nor by *LfGrE*, is based on the metaphorical meaning of αἶγες as 'waves'. The dating of this metaphor is not a problem, since it must be very old, given a large number of place names associated with it. Although there is nothing in the Homeric uses of the formula κατ' αἰγίλιπος πέτρης that hints to this meaning, there are two later examples deserving our attention: εἰς ἅλα δειμήνασα κατ' [α]ἰγίλιπος θόρε πέτρ[ης (Euph. fr. 415C col. 1, 14 *SH*) and αἰγίλιπος δέ / πέτρου ἀλιβρέκται κεῖσαι ὑπὸ πρόποδι (Perses, *AP* 7.501.3–4). Given that in both cases the αἰγίλιψ πέτρη is situated close to the sea, the meaning 'crag of the waves', i.e. washed or hit by the waves, is possible. But there is a crucial counterargument with respect to the Homeric attestations of the formula αἰγίλιψ πέτρη, i.e. that in two of the three cases (*Il.* 9.15 and 16.4) a 'black fountain' is mentioned. This reference makes much more likely a mountain-context than one pertaining to the sea. In any case, as with (1ii and 1iii) above, the

---
5 (1892) 379.
6 See also Tserepis (1902) 694–5, who follows Kretschmer and classifies αἰγίλιψ under compounds the first part of which determines the second. He claims that this is a case of a possessive compound in the manner of ἁρμα-τροχιή, δημο-γέρων, Ἑλλήσ-ποντος, μητρο-πάτωρ etc.

use of πέτρη seems to be pleonastic, resulting from the incomprehensibility of the metaphor triggered by the secondary and less known meaning of αἰγ-.

3. Hainsworth in the *Cambridge Commentary* on the *Iliad* (ad 9.15) argued that -λιπ- should be associated with two other Hesychian glosses (s.v. ἄλιψ· πέτρα meaning 'rock' and s.v. λίψ· πέτρα ἀφ' ἧς ὕδωρ στάζει),[7] but explicity stated that the root is seen in Lith. *lipti* ('climb'). No comment is offered with respect to the first part of the compound, yet Hainsworth suggests the meaning 'rocky', which (if taken together with πέτρη 'rock') would mean 'rocky rock'.[8] Janko in the *Cambridge Commentary* on the *Iliad* (ad 13.62–65) refers the reader to Hainsworth's note. It seems that Hainsworth interprets αἰγίλιψ as 'goat-rock', i. e. as a rock of goats, which probably means 'climbed by goats' (since he calls the interpretation 'forsaken by goats' 'a pleasant fantasy').

One way or another interpretation (3) arrives at the same conclusion as (1). The only difference between the two etymologies is that in (1i) the word πέτρη is indispensable (goat-climbed rock), whereas in (3) it is pleonastic (goat-rock rock = αἰγίλιψ πέτρη). In the latter case, the bards, being unaware of the word's etymology, added πέτρη.[9] A drawback of this etymological analysis is that αἰγίλιψ seems to be a compound 'mit verbalem Hinterglied', and if indeed λιψ- goes back to a verbal form,[10] then the Hesychian gloss ἄλιψ does not help.

4. αἴξ + λιπαίνω ('goat-feeding'). This meaning has been suggested by Eustathius (307.25: ἡ τὰς αἶγας λιπαίνουσα κατά τινας· διὸ καὶ ἡ Ἰθάκη '-ος' λέγεται εἶναι) and is reported by *LfgrE* s.v. αἰγίλιψ.

---

[7] ἠλίβατος constitutes another etymological conundrum. In Homer it is always attached to πέτρη. In later authors it frequently designates πέτρη but also δρύες, ἄντρον, Τάρταρος, κῦμα. It is treated as meaning 'high', 'steep', 'inaccessible', 'deep' but also 'huge', 'emormous'. Its association to αἰγίλιψ (πέτρη) is very difficult, especially since it is unlikely that its first part is connected to ἄλιψ ('rock'). Chantraine (*DELG* s.v.) is sympathetic to Buttmann's etymology (*Lexilogus* 2.176 ff.) who derives it from *ἠλιτό-βατος (= ἄβατος, δύσβατος) with a dissimilation of the initial syllable of the stem seen in ἀλείτης 'he who is commiting a wrondoing' (see ἤλιτον, ἀλιταίνω, ἀλοιτόν etc.) as in ἠλιτόμηνος ('prematurely born'). Seen from this vantage point, it is unwise to connect to αἰγίλιψ. See Watkins (1995, 145) who derives the first part of the compound (ἠλι-) from the adjective āli- ('high', 'steep', 'lofty'), as in Latin *al-tus*.
[8] See Hornblower (2015) 465.
[9] Hornblower (2015, 465) disproves Hainsworth's interpretation and opts for the traditional view, according to which αἰγίλιψ means 'where no goat climbs').
[10] See Risch (1974²) 194–5.

Eustathius' intrepretation is contrasted by his other comment on the same word in 1041.65, where he endorses the meaning 'forsaken by goats'.

5. αἴξ + λίπτω/-ομαι ('storm-desired', i.e. 'storm-hit' or 'wave-desired', i.e. 'wave-hit' or 'goat-desired', i.e. goat-frequented).[11]

The problem with this interpretation is that λίπτομαι ('to be desired') is not attested before the fifth century BC (the active form occurs even later, e.g. Ap. Rh. 4.813; Lyc. 131). The stem λιψ- is attested in the compound λιψουρία ('desire to urinate') for the first time in Aesch. Ch. 756.

6. A remarkable parallel to the formula ἀπ'/κατ' αἰγίλιπος πέτρης is offered by Luwian šalli lāpani' wāniya ('great saltlick rock face').[12] This expression in Luwian is attested in the phrase 'when they drive (the livestock) from the Ḫulaya river land to the great saltlick rock face (šalli lāpani' < wāniya), they should not take the saltlick rights[13] (< lapanalianza), away from him. They are given to the king of Tarḫuntašša, and he can take the salt (MUN) at any time'.[14] It is part of the so-called Ulmi-Tesub treaty[15] drawn either between Hattusili's son and successor Tudhaliya IV and Kurunta, nephew of Hattusili or by Hattusili himself and Kurunta when the latter was appointed by Hattusili as ruler of Tarḫuntašša, which is situated in a Luwian region. If Ulmi-Tesub and Kurunta are one and the same person (the Luwian name Kurunta being adopted by him after he was alloted Tarḫuntašša), then the treaty 'illustrates the concessions and favours which were conferred upon the young prince'.[16] It describes the common practice of taking animals to a mineral lick or saltlick, i.e. a place where animals are taken to lick essential mineral nutrients. Mineral or salt licks can be either artificial (blocks of salt placed by farmers in pastures for their livestock to lick) or natural (they are often found on rocky surfaces). They provide biome-

---

[11] See Curtius (1879⁵) 367–8; Düntzer (1865) 203–6.
[12] See Watkins (1995) 145 and the Bronze Tablet treaty Bo86 299 (Otten 1988, col. II, 5–8); Also Watkins (1997) 29–35.
[13] In the ancient world salt was regarded as a token of civilized life. As early as the Homeric Odyssey, Tiresias tells Odysseus that, in order to appease Poseidon's anger, he needs to travel to a land where people are ignorant of salt (11.123–5). This area must be an inland location, at a distance from the civilized world of the sea, a word which in Greek (ἅλς) denotes (with different genders) both the sea and salt.
[14] Watkins (1975) 145 n. 19.
[15] Treaties making provisions for the control of natural salt are also known from the Greco-Roman world; see Traina (1992) 365–8 with the relevant sources.
[16] Bryce (1998) 298.

tals for bone, muscle, and other biological subsystems in a variety of animals, of which the mountain goat is only one. Saltlicks are of paramount importance in areas poor in nutrients. Exposed by harsh weather, salty mineral deposits draw animals from a great distance.

One of the concessions decreed by the treaty pertains to salt rights, which in the Near East were a royal monopoly. In the words of Moga,[17]

> [d]ue to the fact that salt production, distribution, and consumption is far from being impeded or restricted nowadays, usually people easily forget how important this element was for ordinary life in ancient times. In the societies of the Near East, the rights for control and extraction over the salt exploitation areas were usually a royal monopoly [...] pasturage activity was basically related to this kind of activity, because of their need to use salt for animal foraging. Besides, the importance of the salt exploitation areas in ancient times was so important that we have evidence in the treaties of the 14th–13th centuries of wars fought beween states in order to ensure control over the resources (i.e. between Siyannu and Ugarit).[18]

The Luwian expression *lāpani' wāniya* ('saltlick rock face')[19] is analogous to the Homeric αἰγίλιπος πέτρης, since both words are juxtaposed and in the same order. Given the uncontestable tautology between *wāniya* and πέτρης ('rock face, cliff'), we may turn our attention to the first part of the Luwian and Greek expressions. With respect to αἰγ-, there are two possibilities: it either refers to 'goat' and the compound means 'licked by goats' or (less likely) to salt (in the sense of salty surface; αιγ- being employed in a loose sense for salty water) and the compound means 'saltlick'. Luwian *lāpani* is cognate with Hittite *lap(h)-* (IE

---

17 Moga (2009) 266.
18 PRU IV: 71–75 = RS 17.335+379+381+235, lines 57–63 and PRU IV: 291 = RS 19.81. See also C. Carusi, 'Recherche sur le sel dans la Méditerranée orientale de l'Age du Bronze Récent', in: A. Figuls and O. Weller (eds.), *La Trobada internacional d'arqeologia envers l'exploatación de la sal a la prehistòria i protohistòria*, Cardona, 6, 7 i 8 de desembre del 2003, p. 265 (*non vidi*; this footnote is taken verbatim from Moga 2009, 266 n. 11).
19 The full form of the expression is *šalli lāpani' wāniya* ('great saltlick rockface'). I side with Watkins (1995, 1997) and Melchert (1990) who adopt this interpretation and not with Beckman (1983[2], 83) and the *CHD*. Watkins (1997) is very convincing on this issue; see especially his observation (p. 32) that the *lapanalli*-men mentioned in a cult inventory (IBoT 2.131 l. 17) can only mean 'saltlick warden or the like' and not 'herdsman (on summer pasture)'. Wardens or guardians of salt in salt-producing areas are well known in both the Greek and Roman world. In a 2nd c. AD inscription from Crete (*SEG* 32, 1982.869) they are called ἁλωροί; in Rome they were coined as *salinatores* (see *OLD* s.v.), a term which was used as the cognomen of M. Livius (Salinator), one of the censors who instituted the *vectigal*, in order to exercise a stronger control on land revenues, some of which came from the marshy and lagoon-like italian coast that was rich in salt. See Traina (1992, 365–75) with ample references and bibliography.

lab[h]-), Greek λάπτω, λαφύσσω, Old English *lapian*, Armenian *lap'em*, Alb. *lap*, Lat. *lambo*, Old High German *laffan*.²⁰ All these verbs mean either 'lick' or 'drink by licking'. Is Greek λέπτω (aor. ἔλαψα, fut. λάψω) and the noun λάψις ('licking') cognate with λιψ-, i.e. the second part of the compound αἰγίλιψ?

With respect to the meaning 'licked by goats', doubts can be raised concerning the selection of just one type of animal (among the many attracted by saltlicks for nutritional reasons) as a compound-producing mechanism.²¹ On the other hand, a single type of animal may be employed as representative of a larger phenomenon. To use just one example, both in English and Modern Greek (as well as in other languages) a dog-fight (σκυλοκαβγάς) is used in the sense of 'brutal conflict', although most animal fights are very brutal. It is not impossible that the goat functioned in this context as representing the larger phenomenon of animal attraction to saltlicks. In fact, we may be dealing here with a type of Indo-European compound like the Sanskrit *Tatpuruṣa*, in which the first component is in a case relationship with the second. For example, a doghouse (a house *for* a dog) and a battlefield (a field *for* battle) are dative compounds. Likewise, αἰγίλιψ may be a lick *for* goats. I revisit this problem in the last section of this piece, when I examine the way this Luwian idiom may have passed into Greek in the shape of a Homeric formula.

But before that there is one important question that needs to tackled: is it possible that the first part of Homeric αἰγίλιψ is not connected to 'goat' but to the metonymical use 'salt' of its secondary meaning 'waves' by means of a process like 'waves' > 'sea' > 'salty water' > 'salt'? Let us then turn our attention to the use of this word as a place name and then to its nuanced treatment by various authors.

The place name Αἰγίλιψ (*Il.* 2.633)

Janko argues that the use of Αἰγίλιπα (qualified as τρηχεῖαν, *Il.* 2.633) as a place name on Ithaca 'is surely invented, since our Ionian bard knew little of Ithake

---

[20] See Puhvel, *HED* vol. 5 s.v. *lapana*- (a 'Luwianism') with all the relevant examples from the Ulmi-Tessub treaty.
[21] In Bo 86/299 ll. 4–5, it is decreed that no goat/sheepherder is allowed to enter the area delineated by the *Hūlaya* river, which is the boundary of the land of *Tarḫuntašša*. The continuation of the text of the treaty shows that this prohibition is made with an eye to the saltlick rights of *Kuruntas* in the land of *Tarḫuntašša*. It seems then that, at least in this particular case, measures were taken against bringing goats and sheep to a saltlick to feed.

but that it is αἰγίβοτος and τρηχεῖα (*Od.* 4.606; 13.242)'. His intepretation is based on the assumption that this place name pertains to the island of Ithaca, which would then have been designated with three names in a single entry in the Catalogue of Ships. This approach goes back to Leaf[22] and is repeated in most modern commentaries. Though a plausible suggestion, I would like to entertain an alternative explanation. With respect to the place name Αἰγίλιψ, ancient testimonia offer contradictory information, Stephanus Byzantius (s.v. Κροκύλειον) opting for a place name on Ithaca, Strabo (10.2) for a place name on the mainland (Acarnania). Visser (1997, 592–594) opts for Strabo's view with strong arguments, taking Αἰγίλιψ to be a rock used as a landmark on the mainland.

The epithet τρηχεῖαν ('steep') modifying Αἰγίλιπα has been conditioned by the way the bards understood the latter. If taken as 'steep' (according to LSJ), then τρηχεῖαν is a pleonasm, though not an awkward one. It does not need to be built on the metonymical meaning of Αἰγίλιπα, it can simply be a general epithet designating a common feature of almost any Greek landscape. The same is the case with the other 'competitive' etymology. If the word means 'sea-washed cliff', then we are again dealing with a pleonastic use of τρηχεῖαν since cliffs are by definition steep. In the case of Αἰγίλιπα τρηχεῖαν we should (tentatively) argue that the bards understood the place name as meaning simply 'of goats', perhaps as a place where goats were nourished (Goat island; see Eustathius' interpretation under [4] above), i.e. a steep, rocky place, a typical Mediterannean Goat-island.

All in all, it seems likely that the incomprehensibility of the etymology of αἰγίλιψ led to a new interpretation and, in fact, to one that was conditioned by its use as adjective or place name.

Goats and waves

In light of the preceding observations, we are faced with an odd situation: a dictional fossil that is anything but transparent on the basis of its etymology has survived the test of time either within a formulaic expression or as a place name. The relevant term has lost its original denotations but has active connotations that are part and parcel of its use.

In cases like this we should draw a clear line between the etymology of the word and the way it is employed. The reason lying behind this approach is that the origins of the word's meaning are not recognisable by its users, with the re-

---

[22] (1900) ad loc.

sult that some of them have interpreted it by recourse to the most widespread meaning of the first part of the compound, i.e. αἴξ ('goat'). In fact, we have examples in which this process is almost guaranteed and, what is ever more remarkable, it applies to the meaning and use of the word αἴξ in the plural ('goats' and 'waves'). The first relevant passage is Herodotus, 8.19–20:

> Νόωι δὲ λαβὼν ὁ Θεμιστοκλέης ὡς εἰ ἀπορραγείη ἀπὸ τοῦ βαρβάρου τό τε Ἰωνικὸν φῦλον καὶ τὸ Καρικόν, οἷοί τε εἴησαν τῶν λοιπῶν κατύπερθε γενέσθαι, ἐλαυνόντων τῶν Εὐβοέων πρόβατα ἐπὶ τὴν θάλασσαν, ταύτηι συλλέξας τοὺς στρατηγοὺς ἔλεγέ σφι ὡς δοκέοι ἔχειν τινὰ παλάμην τῆι ἐλπίζοι τῶν βασιλέος συμμάχων ἀποστήσειν τοὺς ἀρίστους. Ταῦτα μέν νυν ἐς τοσοῦτο παρεγύμνου, ἐπὶ δὲ τοῖσι κατήκουσι πρήγμασι τάδε ποιητέα σφι εἶναι ἔλεγε, τῶν τε προβάτων τῶν Εὐβοϊκῶν καταθύειν ὅσα τις ἐθέλοι (κρέσσον γὰρ εἶναι τὴν στρατιὴν ἔχειν ἢ τοὺς πολεμίους), παραίνεέ τε προειπεῖν τοῖσι ἑωυτῶν ἑκάστους πυρὰ ἀνακαίειν· κομιδῆς δὲ πέρι τὴν ὥρην αὐτῶι μελήσειν ὥστε ἀσινέας ἀπικέσθαι ἐς τὴν Ἑλλάδα. Ταῦτα ἤρεσέ σφι ποιέειν καὶ αὐτίκα πυρὰ ἀνακαυσάμενοι ἐτρέποντο πρὸς τὰ πρόβατα. Οἱ γὰρ Εὐβοέες παραχρησάμενοι τὸν Βάκιδος χρησμὸν ὡς οὐδὲν λέγοντα οὔτ' ἐξεκομίσαντο οὐδὲν οὔτε προεσάξαντο ὡς παρεσομένου σφι πολέμου, περιπετέα τε ἐποιήσαντο σφίσι αὐτοῖσι τὰ πρήγματα. Βάκιδι γὰρ ὧδε ἔχει περὶ τούτων ὁ χρησμός·
>
> φράζεο, βαρβαρόφωνος ὅταν ζυγὸν εἰς ἅλα βάλληι
> βύβλινον, Εὐβοίης ἀπέχειν πολυμηκάδας αἶγας.
>
> Τούτοισι δὴ οὐδὲν τοῖσι ἔπεσι χρησαμένοισι, ἐν τοῖσι τότε παρεοῦσί τε καὶ προσδοκίμοισι κακοῖσι παρῆν σφι συμφορῆι χρᾶσθαι πρὸς τὰ μέγιστα

Themistocles thought that if the Ionian and Carian nations were removed from the forces of the barbarians, the Greeks might be strong enough to prevail over the rest. Now it was the custom of the Euboeans to drive their flocks down to the sea there. Gathering the admirals together, he told them that he thought he had a device whereby he hoped to draw away the best of the king's allies. So much he revealed for the moment, but merely advised them to let everyone slay as many from the Euboean flocks as he wanted; it was better that the fleet should have them, than the enemy. Moreover, he counselled them each to order his men to light a fire; as for the time of their departure from that place, he would see to it that they would return to Hellas unscathed. All this they agreed to do and immediately lit fires and set upon the flocks. Now the Euboeans had neglected the oracle of Bacis, believing it to be empty of meaning, and neither by carrying away nor by bringing in anything had they shown that they feared an enemy's coming. In so doing they were the cause of their own destruction, for Bacis' oracle concerning this matter runs as follows

when a strange-tongued man casts a yoke of papyrus on the sea,
then take care to keep bleating goats far from the coasts of Euboea.²³

To these verses the Euboeans gave no heed; but in the evils then present and soon to come they suffered the greatest calamity.

Standard commentaries explain Bacis' oracle by endorsing a literary interpretation of πολυμηκάδας αἶγας. The epithet πολυμηκάδες is a *hapax legomenon* in Greek literature. It immediately recalls the Homeric expression μηκάδες αἶγες ('bleating goats': *Il.* 11.383, 23.31; *Od.* 8.124, 244, 341). The compound πολυμηκάδες seems to have been formed to fit this particular oracle.²⁴ What should be highlighted here is that while in the narrative immediately preceding the oracle, Herodotus attempts to bridge Themistocles' advice to the Euboeans with the content of the oracle, he utterly fails. First, the oracle refers *exclusively* to goats, whereas Themistocles to cattle in general.²⁵ Second, Themistocles did not advise the Euboeans to keep the animals away from Euboea but to sacrifice them, in order to hinder their use as food by the Persian army.

Primary prophetic speech is context-determined; it is a sign, not a meaning, a sign that needs to be decoded within the context to which it belongs. Oracles attested by means of a literary source, such as Herodotus, are the result of a filtering, often to be attributed to the priests in Delphi, who 'translated' the primordial, exclamatory suspension of prophetic speech into a secondary form of deixis pertaining to polysemy, ambiguity, and homonymy, as they are expressed by *double entendre*, sense pauses, syntactical vagueness with respect to the subject or object, contradictions, animal imagery, *adynata*, kennings, synecdoche, metonymy, etc.²⁶

Herodotus is citing an oracle the deliberate ambiguity of which he does not comprehend. The expression πολυμηκάδας αἶγας 'plays' with the semantic oscillation between 'much-bleating' (πολύ – μηκάομαι) and 'very long' (πολύ –

---

23 Translation by Godley (1920) with slight modifications.
24 The false-etymology from μῆκος is already recorded in the ancient scholia to the *Odyssey* (on 9.124 Dindorf: μηκάδας] ἤτοι μηκωμένας, ἀπὸ τῆς φωνῆς. Q V μηκὴ γὰρ λέγεται ἡ τῶν αἰγῶν φωνή. ἢ ἀπὸ τοῦ ἐπὶ μήκη κίειν, ὅ ἐστι πορεύεσθαι V).
25 This is probably the correct rendering of πρόβατα here, which do not mean exclusively 'sheep'; for this meaning in Herod., see e.g. τὰ λεπτὰ τῶν προβάτων 'small sheep and goats' in 1.33, 8.137.
26 See Christidis (2001) 1024–5. Although not solely devoted to oracular speech, the recent work of Beta (2016) is a valuable contribution to the study of oracles.

μῆκος) paired by the *double entendre* 'goats' and 'waves' (αἶγας).²⁷ Herodotus understands the oracle only in relation to the first widespread meaning of αἴξ, which determines the sense of the *hapax legomenon* πολυμηκάδας, in accordance to the Homeric expression μηκάδες αἶγες ('much-bleating goats').²⁸ Thus, the oracle may have well 'played' with the semantical ambiguity of πολυμηκάδας αἶγας in an attempt cryptically to suggest to the inhabitans of northern Euboea to stay away from the 'very long waves'²⁹ [falling on the shores] of this region of the island.

The same semantical interplay between the two meanings of the word αἴξ ('goat' and 'waves' in the plural) is at work in the following passage from Longus (2.15):

> Ἤλθομεν εἰς τούτους τοὺς ἀγροὺς θηρᾶσαι θέλοντες. Τὴν μὲν οὖν ναῦν λύγωι χλωρᾶι δήσαντες ἐπὶ τῆς ἀκτῆς κατελίπομεν, αὐτοὶ δὲ διὰ τῶν κυνῶν ζήτησιν ἐποιούμεθα θηρίων. Ἐν τούτωι πρὸς τὴν θάλασσαν <u>αἱ αἶγες τούτου</u> κατελθοῦσαι τήν τε λύγον κατεσθίουσι καὶ τὴν ναῦν ἀπολύουσιν. Εἶδες αὐτὴν ἐπὶ τῆι θαλάσσηι φερομένην, πόσων οἴει μεστὴν ἀγαθῶν; Οἵα μὲν ἐσθὴς ἀπόλωλεν, οἷος δὲ κόσμος κυνῶν, ὅσον δὲ ἀργύριον. Τοὺς ἀγροὺς ἂν τις τούτους ἐκεῖνα ἔχων ὠνήσαιτο. Ἀνθ' ὧν ἀξιοῦμεν ἄγειν τοῦτον, πονηρὸν ὄντα αἰπόλον, ὃς <u>ἐπὶ τῆς θαλάσσης νέμει τὰς αἶγας</u> ὡς ναύτης.

> We came into these fields to hunt. Wherefore with a green sallow-with we left our ship tied to the shore while our dogs were hunting the grounds. Meanwhile <u>his goats</u> strayed from the mountains down to the sea, gnawed the green cable in pieces, set her at liberty, and let her fly. You saw her tossing in the sea, but with what choice and rich good laden! What fine clothes are lost! What rare harness and ornaments for dogs are there! What a treasury of precious silver! He that had all might easily purchase these fields. For this damage we think it but right and reason to carry him away our captive, him that is such a mischievous goatherd <u>to feed his goats upon those other goats, to wit, the waves of the sea</u>.³⁰

Another example is offered by the word Αἰγαῖος,³¹ which is employed to designate both *land and sea:* a mountain in Crete (Hes. *Th.* 484: Αἰγαίωι ὄρει), a plain near Crisa in Phocis ([Hes]. *Cat.* fr. 220 M-W: Αἰγαῖον πεδίον), and the Ae-

---

27 Papanastasiou (2000) 407–8; Bowie (2007, 112) suggests that πολυμηκάδας αἶγας may be a reference to the 'many different languages spoken in the Persian army'. This intepretation seems to me very strained, given that it is not supported at all by the context (see 8.19–20).
28 *Il.* 11.383, 23.31; *Od.* 9.124, 244, 341.
29 It is also possible that the pair πολυμηκάδας αἶγας could mean 'much-sounding' waves.
30 Translation by Thornley (1916) 89 and 91.
31 Carruba's suggestion (1995, 7–21) that there was a pre-Greek form *Αἶγα (seen in Hittite *Aḫḫijā*) by which the Greeks designated the coastal Asianic area and the Aegean islands (from which the adjective Αἰγαῖος was formed) and that the root *Αἰγ- and *Aḫḫijā* go back to Indo-European *akw-ā) seems to me far-fetched, a case of mere 'straight-jacketing'. Interestingly enough, Carruba does not discuss at all the meaning 'waves' for αἶγες.

gean Sea as πόντος or πέλαγος or κῦμα (e.g. Ibyc. S151.28 *PMGF*; Aesch. *Ag.* 659; Herod. 2.97.1, 4.85.4 etc.; Eur. *Hel.* 130, 776 *Tr.* 88; Thuc. 1.98.2, 4.109.2; Strabo 1.2.20, 2.5.21, 7.7.4 etc; Plut. *Cimon* 8.5; Paus. 1.1.1, 2.22.1, 5.21.10 etc; Opp. *Hal.* 5.427). The use of both meanings of the stem αἰγ- ('goat' and 'waves' in the plural) for different place names testifies to the fact that they were both current at a very early period. Moreover, the examples offered with respect to the use of Αἰγαῖος for the Aegean Sea show that it was 'initially' connected to the notion of 'stormy sea', in particular with reference to the return of the Greeks from Troy.[32]

A third example is given by the use of the stem αἰγ- in proper names or epithets modifying proper names. Again, the root is attested in both its meanings: Αἰγίπαν ('Goat Pan': 'Erat.' *Catast.* 27; Plut. 19.311b), Αἰγεύς (Theseus' father who alternates with Poseidon in various mythical versions: e.g. Bacch. 17.33–36; Apollod. 3.15.7; Plut. *Thes.* 2c; Paus. 2.33.1), Αἰγαῖος Ποσειδῶν (Pher. 28 *EGM*) and Αἰγαίων θεός (sc. Ποσειδῶν: Callim. *Aet.* fr. 59.6 Pf. = 54i.6 Harder), Αἰγαῖον πέλαγος (through Αἰγεύς), Αἰγαίων (different name of the sea-creature Briareos; see *Il.* 1.403–4: ὃν Βριάρεων καλέουσι θεοί, ἄνδρες δέ τε πάντες / Αἰγαίων', ὃ γὰρ αὖτε βίην οὗ πατρὸς ἀμείνων and Eum. *Tit.* fr. 3 *GEF* where he lives in the sea and is designated as son of Gaia and Pontos).[33]

All three examples show that the stem αἰγ- was contextually determined and that it was employed either with respect to the widespread meaning 'goat' or with the less known meaning 'waves', 'sea'.[34] There is, though, an important consideration that decidedly weakens the appearance of this meaning in the compound αἰγίλιψ. Although the stem αἰγ- in the plural is a secondary meaning for the 'goats of the sea' (waves) and constitutes a metaphor with widespread diffusion and representation in various IE languages,[35] to be tempted to treat it as a direct translation of the Luwian expression 'saltlick' and to equate it with salt on

---

[32] For a review of the relevant cases, see Papanastasiou (2000) 412.
[33] On Agaion/Briareos in Eumelus, see Tsagalis (2017) 26, 47 n. 68, 49, 53–7, 59, 78, 87, 97–8, 108.
[34] A brief note on the semantic field designated by the words αἰγίς, ἐπαιγίζω, καταιγίζω. The word αἰγίς designates the goaskin of Zeus, Athena, and Apollo, but because of its magical force the verbs ἐπαιγίζω and καταιγίζω ('to rush upon') display a variety of uses, since they are applied to the winds (*Il.* 2.148; *Od.* 15.293; see also Aesch. *Sept.* 63), streams, (Opp. *Hal.* 2.125.), dolphins ([Opp.] *Cyn.* 2.583) etc. Again, we see that the stem αἰγ- can express, even within the same family of words, different meanings.
[35] I draw the following examples from Papanastassiou (2000) 409: 'white horses' (British English) and 'white caps' (American English), 'palomas' (= 'doves' in Spanish), 'cavalloni' (= 'white horses' in Italian), 'moutons' (= 'sheep' in French), 'προβατάκια' (= 'small sheep' in Modern Greek) etc.

the basis of the fact that the waves are tautological to the sea and sea water (which is salty) is a precarious intepretive leap requiring the metonymical metamorphosis of a metaphor. And that is, obviously, too much.

Homeric formulas and Hittite rituals

In cases in which the data available from a given language are not completely illuminating, it is advisable to turn our lens to relevant material from other languages, especially (but not exclusively) those belonging to the same family. In this light, I will now follow the path trodden by eminent Indo-Europeanists and examine pertinent cases in Hittite culture that partially share phraseology with the Homeric examples at hand. I begin with a presentation of the 'Homeric' material. The compound αἰγίλιψ is attested 4x in Homer (only in the *Iliad*) and 1x in the *Homeric Hymn to Pan*:

A1. *Il.* 2.632–635:
οἵ ῥ' Ἰθάκην εἶχον καὶ Νήριτον εἰνοσίφυλλον
καὶ Κροκυλεῖ' ἐνέμοντο καὶ Αἰγίλιπα τρηχεῖαν,
οἵ τε Ζάκυνθον ἔχον ἠδ' οἵ Σάμον ἀμφενέμοντο,
οἵ τ' ἤπειρον ἔχον ἠδ' ἀντιπέραι' ἐνέμοντο

Those who held Ithaca and leaf-trembling Neriton,
those who dwelt around Krokyleia and rigged Aigilips
those who held Zakynthos and those who dwelt about Samos,
those who held the mainland and the places next to the crossing.[36]

A2. *Il.* 9.13–15:
ἂν δ' Ἀγαμέμνων
ἵστατο δάκρυ χέων ὥς τε κρήνη μελάνυδρος
ἥ τε κατ' αἰγίλιπος πέτρης δνοφερὸν χέει ὕδωρ·

and Agamemnon
stood up before them, shedding tears, like a spring dark-running
that down the face of a rock impassable drips its dim water.

A3. *Il.* 13.62–65:
αὐτὸς δ' ὥς τ' ἴρηξ ὠκύπτερος ὦρτο πέτεσθαι,
ὅς ῥά τ' ἀπ' αἰγίλιπος πέτρης περιμήκεος ἀρθεὶς
ὁρμήσηι πεδίοιο διώκειν ὄρνεον ἄλλο,
ὣς ἀπὸ τῶν ἤϊξε Ποσειδάων ἐνοσίχθων.

---

[36] All Iliadic translations are from Lattimore (1951) with some spelling modifications. Although, I have printed the translation 'impassable' for αἰγίλιπος, I do not agree with it. This is done only for convenience.

and burst into winged flight himself, like a hawk with quick wings
who from the huge height of an impassable rock lifting
leans to flight to pursue some other bird over the wide land;
so Poseidon shaker of the earth broke away from the Aiantes.

A4. *Il.* 16.2–4:
Πάτροκλος δ' Ἀχιλῆϊ παρίστατο ποιμένι λαῶν
δάκρυα θερμὰ χέων ὥς τε <u>κρήνη μελάνυδρος</u>,
ἥ τε <u>κατ' αἰγίλιπος πέτρης</u> δνοφερὸν χέει ὕδωρ.

Meanwhile Patroclus came to the shepherd of the people, Achilles,
and stood by him and wept warm tears, like a spring dark-running
that down the face of a rock impassable drips its dim water.

A5. *HHymn to Pan* (19) 1–4:
Ἀμφί μοι Ἑρμείαο φίλον γόνον ἔννεπε Μοῦσα,
αἰγιπόδην δικέρωτα φιλόκροτον ὅς τ' ἀνὰ πίση
δενδρήεντ' ἄμυδις φοιτᾶι χοροήθεσι νύμφαις
αἵ τε <u>κατ' αἰγίλιπος πέτρης</u> στείβουσι κάρηνα   4
....
σὺν δέ σφιν τότε νύμφαι ὀρεστιάδες λιγύμολποι   19
φοιτῶσαι πυκνὰ ποσσὶν <u>ἐπὶ κρήνηι μελανύδρωι</u>
μέλπονται, κορυφὴν δὲ περιστένει οὔρεος ἠχώ·

About Hermes' dear child tell me, Muse, the goat-footed, two-horned rowdy, who roams about the wooded fields together with the dance-merry nymphs: along the precipitous crag they tread the summits
....
with him then the clear-singing mountain nymphs tripping nimbly by a dark spring, dance and sing: the echo moans round the mountaintop.[37]

In examples (A2) and (A4),[38] the compressed nature of the fountain simile applies to Agamemnon and Patroclus respectively. The repeated simile associates two characters both reacting to Achilles' refusal to return to battle. From the point of view of cognitive science, visual patterning of this sort is primarily mental: the epic tradition has thematized simile space by making 'the dark spring symbolize in its pictorial metalanguage "distress" in the face of a difficult situation'.[39] This thematization conjures further associations resulting from the traditional language of lament. The default idea 'he cried' is so effectively intensified

---

37 Translation by West (2003) 200.
38 (A1) has already been discussed above; (A3) containing only the imagery of the formula ἀπ' αἰγίλιπος πέτρης has been 'reduced' to a connotative field of such meanings as 'high' (notice περιμήκεος) and 'steep'; (A5) is clearly imitating the Homeric similes but dissociating the two sets of imagery, the rock-face (ἀπ' αἰγίλιπος πέτρης) and the spring (κρήνη μελάνυδρος).
39 Tsagalis (2012) 325.

by its visual representation as a constant flow of water that it is developed into a whole simile which in turn reshapes the specific manifestation of the default idea. The falling of water from a cliff makes a sound (see also e.g. Pi. fr. 52f.1–11 Snell-Maehler: ὕδατι γὰρ ἐπὶ χαλκοπύλωι / ψόφον ἀϊὼν Κασταλίας) that is interpreted as 'heavy groaning' (βαρὺ στενόχων), a formulaic expression of lament that surfaces in both passages where the fountain simile is employed (Il. 9.16; Il. 9.20).[40]

Passages (A1)-(A5) from Homer and the *Homeric Hymn to Pan* should be combined with the imagery of the black-water spring that is also part and parcel of the majority of the examples above:

B1. *Il.* 16.156–62:
> οἱ δὲ λύκοι ὣς
> ὠμοφάγοι, τοῖσίν τε περὶ φρεσὶν ἄσπετος ἀλκή,
> οἵ τ' ἔλαφον κεραὸν μέγαν οὔρεσι δηιώσαντες
> δάπτουσιν· πᾶσιν δὲ παρήϊον αἵματι φοινόν·
> καί τ' ἀγεληδὸν ἴασιν <u>ἀπὸ κρήνης μελανύδρου</u>
> <u>λάψοντες γλώσσῃσιν ἀραιῇσιν μέλαν ὕδωρ</u>
> ἄκρον ἐρευγόμενοι φόνον αἵματος

> And they, as wolves
> who tear flesh raw, in whose hearts the battle fury is tireless,
> who have brought down a great horned stag in the mountains, and then fed
> on him, till the jowls of every wolf run blood, and then go
> all in a pack to drink from a spring of dark-running water,
> lapping with their lean tongues along the black edge of the surface
> and belching up the clotted blood

B2. *Il.* 21.257–64
> ὡς δ' ὅτ' ἀνὴρ ὀχετηγὸς <u>ἀπὸ κρήνης μελανύδρου</u>
> ἂμ φυτὰ καὶ κήπους ὕδατι ῥόον ἡγεμονεύῃ
> χερσὶ μάκελλαν ἔχων, ὀμάρης ἐξ ἔχματα βάλλων·
> τοῦ μέν τε προρέοντος ὑπὸ ψηφῖδες ἅπασαι
> ὀχλεῦνται· τὸ δέ τ' ὦκα κατειβόμενον κελαρύζει

---

40 See Ready (2011) 165–73, especially 172–3; also Σ on *Il.* 9.16a that explain στενάχειν as including δακρύειν which was mentioned before. The simile, though only two verses long is remarkable for its symmetry and aural effects: both lines end in a near-similar sound (υδρος – ὕδωρ); the same verb is repeated in both verses (χέων – χέει) and placed just after the simile's beginning and end (third word from the beginning and second word from the end); blackness is highlighted twice (μελάνυδρος – δνοφερόν); the designation of the place from where water falls is effected by two bisyllabic feminine nouns of the first declension both containing a consonantal cluster 'stop+liquid' and two long η sounds (κρήνη – πέτρη); the liquid ρ is appropriately repeated no less than six times in these two verses either within a cluster or on its own so as to imitate the flowing of tears/water (δάκρυ, κρήνη, μελάνυδρος / πέτρης, δνοφερόν, ὕδωρ).

χώρωι ἔνι προαλεῖ, φθάνει δέ τε καὶ τὸν ἄγοντα·
ὣς αἰεὶ Ἀχιλῆα κιχήσατο κῦμα ῥόοιο
καὶ λαιψηρὸν ἐόντα

As a man running a channel from a spring of dark water
guides the run of the water amongst his plants and gardens
with a mattock in his hand and knocks down the blocks of his channel;
in the rush of the water all the pebbles beneath are torn loose
from place, and the water that has been dripping suddenly jets on
in a steep place and goes too fast even for the man who guides it;
so always the crest of the river was overtaking Achilles
for all his speed of foot

The simile of text (B1) refers to a pack of wolves 'lapping with their lean tongues along the black edge of the surface of a spring with dark water' (ἀπὸ κρήνης μελανύδρου / λάψοντες γλώσσηισιν ἀραιῆισιν μέλαν ὕδωρ).[41] λάψοντες is fut. part. of λάπτω, which (as argued above) is cognate with Hittite *lap(h)-* (IE **lab [h]-*), Old English *lapian*, Armenian *lap'em*, Alb. *lap*, Lat. *lambo*, Old High German *laffan*. All these verbs mean either 'lick' or 'drink by licking'. Here, then, is a case attested in the context of a Homeric simile, of an imagery pertaining to the etymology suggested above (6). Given that the κρήνη μελάνυδρος appears together with the expression κατ' αἰγίλιπος πέτρης in *Il.* 9.13–15 and 16.2–4, we may be dealing with the complementary distribution of the connotations inherent in two separate imageries (the black water spring and the goat-licked rock face), which suggests that λάπτω (aor. ἔλαψα, fut. λάψω) and the noun λάψις ('licking')[42] may be cognate with λιψ-, i.e. the second part of the compound αἰγίλιψ.

But how was this Luwian expression transferred into Greek? There are two possible scenarios. For the sake of a balanced discussion, I will mention both of them, though I am inclined to endorse the second, as will become apparent from what follows.

(a) It is possible that in the formula αἰγίλιψ πέτρη we can trace a process similar to that suggested by Watkins[43] with respect to ἠλίβατος (πέτρη). As it may well be that the first part of the compound (ἠλι-) comes from the Luwian

---

41 In the *RV* (3.33.1), river water flows down in great speed 'like two bright mother cows who lick their calves'. This association does not seem to pertain to the Homeric examples, where the licking concerns the water and not the offspring of the animals. In the example from the *RV* the *tertium comparationis* is the huge size of the cows' tongues. On this example, see West (2007) 275.
42 See Hsch. s.v. λάψοντες (γλώσσηι)· τῶι ἄκρωι τῆς γλώσσης πίνοντες.
43 (1995) 145.

adjective *āli-* ('high', 'steep', 'lofty'), as in Latin *al-tus*, and that 'may have been borrowed, perhaps as a toponym, by Mycenean Greek speakers and transformed into ἀλίβατος (πέτρα Pindar, Aeschylus) and ἠλίβατος (πέτρη Homer)', so it is possible that αἰγίλιψ (πέτρη) that is derived from αἰγ- ('goat') and λάπτ-ω ('lick', 'drink by licking') was borrowed by the Myceneans who had contacts with populations speaking Luwian, perhaps (but not necessarily) by means of a place name, and was later transformed because of its incomprehensibility into 'pertaining to goats', i.e. 'high', 'steep', 'difficult to access'.[44] It may not be accidental that the Bronze Tablet treaty, in which the expression *šalli lāpani' wāniya* ('great saltlick rock face') is attested, concerns the king of the *Tarḫuntašša*[45] that like *Karkamis* (another kingdom of the Luwian south zone) and *Taruwisa/Tru(w)isa* (Troy) were places where Mycenean Greeks had contacts with Luwian populations.

(b) The second scenario is based on the assumption that the way this idiom had penetrated Greek is closely associated with its most typical manifestation in Homeric Greek, i.e. within the environment of a simile. In a path-breaking and admirable balanced article, which Hellenists have rather overlooked, Puhvel has carefully set the methodological framework within which a fruitful exploration of the antecedents of Homeric similes should be developed. Given the importance of Puhvel's approach for my topic, I quote this passage in full:

> Compared to such vague echoings, cultural universals, and diffusional debris (which tend to wash over Hellenism in periodic waves of eastern flotsam like those of the Cyrus Gordon [...], a firm grasp on our topic requires a narrower gauge and straiter gate. We need to compare actual records of adjacent, interacting, perhaps overlapping people, places, and times, in order to determine whether under the surface "noise" of the text there may lurk a *coherent thematic structure still discernible in formulaic petrifaction*.[46] Even if the yield should be meager, such is the only rigorous way of comparing Homeric and Hittite similes. The Iliadic elaborated simile is [...] an innovational extravaganza in its own right, and there is little point in trying to find antecedents or parallels. The simple comparison or embryonic simile, on the other hand, is so basic that thematic matchings are probably random [..] Some may be poetic [...], some hyperbolic (*Iliad* 9.14 δάκρυ χέων ὥς τε κρήνη μελάνυδρος 'shedding

---

[44] It should be noted that, as argued by Watkins (1995) 145 n. 19, in the 'Conjuration of Water and Salt' (a bilingual Hittite-Luwian text of the 14th c. going back to a 15th c. archetype) the place where salt comes from is designated as *āli-* ('high', 'steep', 'lofty') and modifies *unwāni-* ('rock face', 'cliff', 'escarpment'), while the Bronze Tablet treaty of the king of Tarḫuntašša makes provisions that the livestock is driven from the Ḫulaya river to the *šalli lāpani' wāniya* ('great saltlick rock face').
[45] *Tarḫuntašša* derives its name from the storm-god *Tarḫunna* or *Tarḫunta* (Luwian *Tarḫunza*, Palaic *Taru*); see West (2007) 247.
[46] My own emphasis.

tears like a dark-watered spring'; *KUB* VIII 48 I 18 [Gilgamesh] *nu-ssi-kan ishahru parā* PA₅.HI.A-*us mān* [*arser* 'his tears flowed like irrigation ditches']. But there remains a distinct middle ground where precise comparison of Homeric and Hittite similes is possible. This is the well-balanced extended simile, expanded beyond the embryonic but not elaborated out of joint, with both parts in expressional equilibrium. In Hittite this type is common in utterances of analogic magic where verbatim matching of parallels is essential to the efficacy of the procedure.[47]

Puhvel's approach is on the right track, insightful but not overambitious, as it warns us of the various *caveats* of such an undertaking. Having said this, I would like to note that it is really a pity that one of his Iliadic examples ('the dark-watered spring') is cited only partially and not in its fullness. Puhvel is right that the 'shedding tears like a spring' simile is so elementary that it may well be called "universal". In such cases, tracing specific antecedents is almost malpractice, not least because this approach silently adopts the *post hoc ergo propter hoc* fallacy. But we need to draw a line between the embryonic simile and the short one, the abbreviated and elliptical nature of the latter camouflaging its expressive potential and, sometimes, its antecedents. In this light, I suggest that we follow Puhvel's insight concerning the link between certain Homeric similes and Hittite expressions of analogic magic and ritual utterances or spells, which are marked by the same inbuilt parallelism, between the *Wie-Satz* and the *So-Satz* the former, and between its two parts the latter. To make this point clear, let us quote one of Puhvel's examples[48]:

izzan GIM-*an* Im-*anza pittenuzzi n-at-kan aruni parranta pedai kēll-a parnas ēshar papratar* QATAMMA *pittenuddu n-at-kan aruni parranda pedāu*

as the wind sweeps chaff and carries it over the sea, let it likewise sweep the blood-defilement of this house and carry it over the sea (*KUB* XLI 8 II 15–19)

Now, compare *Od.* 5.368–70:

ὡς δ' ἄνεμος ζαὴς ἠΐων θημῶνα τινάξηι
καρφαλέων, τὰ μὲν ἄρ τε διεσκέδασ' ἄλλυδις ἄλληι,
ὣς τῆς δούρατα μακρὰ διεσκέδασ'

as a gale wind scatters a heap of dry chaff and spreads it all over, thus it shattered the long timbers of the raft …

---

47 Puhvel (1991) 23. For analogic magic in Hittite, see Oettinger (1976).
48 (1991) 26.

The internal parallelism between the two parts of the Hittite ritual and the parallelism between the the *Wie-Satz* and the *So-Satz* of the Homeric simile are based not only on their structural scaffoldings but also on repeated phraseology (*n-at-kan aruni* / διεσκέδασ'). It is exactly this dictional reiteration that reinforces the two parallelisms, which pertain not only to situations but also to specific objects or people.

In this light, we may focus our attention on several Hittite rituals using the phraseology pertaining to saltlike imagery, which we have posited as the phraseological antecedent of the Homeric formula ἀπ'/κατ' αἰγίλιπος πέτρης. The first example has been called 'The conjuration of water and salt' and pertains to the Puriyanni, a private household ritual of sympathetic magic to ward off evil. The relevant text is bilingual, the first paragraph being in Hittite, the second in Cuneiform Luwian.[49]

> nu=ššan ANA GAL GIR₄ kuit wātar lāḫuwan
> MUN=ya=kan anda išḫuwān
> n=at=kan É-ri anda papparašzi
> ANA BEL SISKUR=ya=ššan šarā papparašzi
> nu kiššan memai
> ————————————————
> wāarša=tta ÍD-ti [nan]amman
> MUN-ša=pa ālāti uwā[niyati] upamman
> wāarša=tta zīl[a ÍD-i] anda nāwa iti
> MUN-ša=pa=[tta z]ila āli uwāniya nā[wa it]i
>
> (Hittite) The water which is poured into the clay bowl
> and the salt which is shaken in it
> he sprinkles in the house
> and sprinkles on the celebrant
> and speaks as follows:
> ————————————————
> (Luwian) The water is led from the river
> and the salt is brought from the steep rock face;
> the water to the river nevermore will go back
> and the salt to the steep rock face nevermore will go back.

Commenting on this bilingual text Watkins draws attention to 'the rhythmic, grammatically parallel, syntactic strophic style of the Luwian spell, which is clearly verbal art'.[50] Water and salt are here used positively, i.e. as protective devices, that will 'cleanse' the household and keep pollution away.

---

49 I print the text and translation from Watkins (1995) 144–5.
50 (1995) 145.

The second case study concerns a parturition ritual performed when pregnancy comes to an end. In this ritual the Sun-God is invoked, whereafter she comes and has a feast, so that the gods Anzili and Zukki are appeased and the pregnant woman overcomes the suffering of delivery. At a certain point it is stated that 'as the salt of the meadow from the saltlick is not exhausted, [...] and [may] this one [i.e. so the life of the offerand] forever after [not be exhausted]'.[51] Here salt symbolizes permanence.[52]

A third example is offered by the magic ritual of ᶠḪantitaššu (CTH 395.1 A) in Kbo XVI 14 I 20ff.:[53]

> š]e-er-ra-aš-ša-an ZÍD.DA ZÍZ MUN-ya šu-uḫ-ḫa-I nu kiš-an me-ma-i M]UN-an GIM-an UDUᴴᴵ·ᴬ li-li-pa-an-ti nu ú-id-du kụ-u-uš ḫ-u-uk-ma-uš ᵈUTU-uš QA-TAM-MA li-li-pa-iš-ki-id-du nu IGI-zi pal-ši ud-da-na-aš EN-aš ᵈUTU-i kiš-an ḫu-u-uk-zi
>
> On it [the smoking cedarwood, oil, and honey] he sprinkles spelt-meal and salt, and speaks as follows: 'As sheep lick salt, so may the Sun-God come and lick these conjurations'. And for the first time the sacrificer conjures [before] the Storm-God as follows.[54]

This text comes from the *Ritual of Hantitassu of Hurma* that was performed when a person's years 'are mobilized/disturbed'.[55] In this case, salt has negative connotations. It has to be absorbed, 'licked away' by the Sun-God, as happens with sheep that lick and swallow it in a saltlick.

The material we have gathered indicates that salt and salt-licking imagery were used in incantations and spells pertaining to Hittite ritual. We have also adduced evidence from the Hittite Ulmi-Tesub treaty that saltlicks were considered to be important resources indicating wealth and prestige. In this light, I would like to argue that ritual constitutes the performative framework by means of which imagery like a 'saltlick cliff' passed to Greek speakers in geographical areas where the two peoples, Greeks and Hittites, met and communicated. This cultural transmission is especially pertinent to the case of the Homeric simile, which shows traces of borrowings from Hittite ritual.[56]

The antiquity[57] of the expression 'as sheep lick salt' that is attested, as we saw above, in the magic ritual of ᶠḪantitaššu amounts to 'sheeplicked salt'

---

51 Beckman (1983²) 76–7; Moga (2009) 269.
52 See Moga (2009) 269.
53 For its duplicate (KUB XLIII 57 I 20′-24), see Watkins (1975) 182 (= 1994, 481).
54 Text and translation from Watkins (1975) 181 (= 1994, 480).
55 See Bachvarova (2016) 94 n. 71.
56 On this matter, see Puhvel (1991) 21–9.
57 See Watkins (1975) 181–2 (= 1994, 480–1), who argues that Latin and Hittite both offer 'two entirely homologous structures as models of religious and cultural behavior' with respect to two

and, by a small extension indicating the locale of this activity, further to 'sheep-frequented saltlick'. This means that the 'saltlick cliff' of the Hittite Ulmi-Tesub treaty functionally equals 'an animal frequented saltlick rock or cliff', i.e. an αἰγίλιψ πέτρη. Such a process, which must have taken some time, resulted in the semantic defamiliarization of an arcane Hittite idiom that entered epic language as a dictional fossil.

Since the formula αἰγίλιψ πέτρη was incomprehensible to the Ionian bards (having lost its denotative force pertaining to salt-licking), the licking aspect was recontextualized and associated with a familiar imagery (*Il.* 16.156–162), i.e. that of a mountain spring, where animals satisfy their thirst, licking with their tongues the flowing, clean water.[58] The similes in *Il.* 9.13–15 and 16.2–4 may have resulted from the combination of two types of imagery, the saltlick rock to which animals (goats included) are attracted, in order to lick the salt on the mineral surface, and the clean-watered spring where animals drench their thirst. For the Ionian bards αἰγίλιψ πέτρη had lost its original meaning, but (as is the case with iconyms) had preserved some of its connotations: the rock face on which minerals are found, the image of the animals licking, the rural environment.

---

rituals in which salt plays a pivotal role. He also forcefully maintains that on linguistic grounds the utterance 'as sheep lick salt' reinforces the 'antiquity of the presence of salt in the [Hittie] ritual'.

[58] On μελάνυδρος, see Σ *Il.* 9.14: πολύυδρος – τὸ βάθος; Σ *Il.* 16.1: ἡ βαθύυδρος, ᾗι κατὰ τοὺς φυσικοὺς μέλαν ἐστὶ τὸ ὕδωρ; *Suda* s.v.: βαθεῖα, κυρίως δὲ καθαροῦ ὕδατος; Hsch. s.v.: ἐν βάθει τὸ ὕδωρ ἔχουσα An. ἢ πολύυδρος; Eust. *Commentarii ad Homeri Iliadem* 2.649.21: μελάνυδρος μὲν οὖν κρήνη οὐ μόνον διότι καθόλου τὸ ὕδωρ μέλαν εἶναι δοκεῖ μὴ φωτιζόμενον, ἀλλὰ καὶ ὡς ἐκ βάθους ἀνάγουσα τὸ ὕδωρ καὶ ὡς πολύυδρος. See also *Od.* 20.158 (αἱ μὲν ἐείκοσι βῆσαν ἐπὶ κρήνην μελάνυδρον), where Eurycleia commands the female servants to fetch water from a dark-water fountain, i.e. a fountain with a lot of clean water. This intepretation of black water pertains to spring water at large. Given the weeping context of the similes in *Il.* 9.13–15 and 16.2–4 the stress on the darkness of water is clealry aimed to create an analogy with the black tears of Agamemnon and Achilles respectively. Hainsworth (1993, 61 on *Il.* 9.14–15) argues against Fränkel's (1921, 21) association of δνοφερός and μελάνυδρος with Agamemnon's dark mood on the basis of the fact that these epithets do not always have gloomy connotations, but in the context of this visual image Fränkel's observations are correct; see the pairing of the 'neighboring' similes of *Il.* 9.4–8 and *Il.* 9.14–16 (κῦμα κελαινὸν ... / ἔχευεν – δάκρυ χέων ... μελάνυδρος / δνοφερὸν χέει ὕδωρ). The former simile uses wind-water imagery for the distress and desperation of the Achaeans, the latter employs water imagery for the distress and desperation of Agamemnon. As a big black wave casts huge seaweed along the shore, so a black-water spring makes tears pour over Agamemnon's cheeks. The black water falling from a spring situated on a cliff (κατ' αἰγίλιπος πέτρης) is paired to the image of the black wave rising and falling on the shores of the Troad.

Although the multiple examples in various modern languages pertaining to the analogy of tears and fountain or spring suggest that the imagery is almost universal (given the liquid form shared by tears and water), there are interesting parallels between Ugaritic, Hittite, and Homeric usage of the weeping idiom. In the words of West,

> [t]wice in the *Iliad* a hero who is about to make a lachrymose speech is described as standing and shedding tears like a fountain whose water pours down a steep rock-face. In a fragment of the Hittite version of Gilgamesh, Enkidu related his doom-laden dream, and then 'he lay before Gilgamesh, and his tears [flowed] like irrigation channels' before he spoke again. We cannot say whether the simile was in the Akkadian original, but it is paralleled in other Hittite texts.[59]

In the context of a rock face environment it may have been reinforced by the psychological phenomenon of *pareidolia* (< παρά + εἴδωλον) that involves an external stimulus, which the human mind reinterprets (by recourse to a familiar pattern) as something that does not exist. Through the process of formation, weathering, or erosion, rocks and cliffs may come to mimic various recognizable forms such as a human face, a common feature of *pareidolia*. In Jewish tradition, certain rock-salt formations on the eastern shore of the Dead Sea were thought to 'picture' Lot's wife who was turned into a stele of salt because of her lack of faith.[60] Likewise in ancient Greek culture, the weeping rock with Niobe's face (who was punished for her arrogance towards Leto) is a well-known example of this phenomenon.[61]

Works cited

Bachvarova, M. (2016). *From Hittite to Homer: The Anatolian Background of Ancient Greek Epic*. Cambridge.
Beckman, G. M. (1983²). *Hittite Birth Rituals*. Wiesbaden.
Beekes, R. S. P. (2010). *Etymological Dictionary of Greek*, 2 vols. Leiden. Abbreviated as *EDG*.

---

[59] West (1997) 231 and n. 47 for other references in Hittite texts.
[60] See Latham (1982) 70.
[61] *Il.* 24.613–617 (ἣ δ' ἄρα σίτου μνήσατ', ἐπεὶ κάμε <u>δάκρυ χέουσα</u>. / νῦν δέ που <u>ἐν πέτρῃσιν, ἐν οὔρεσιν</u> οἰοπόλοισιν, / ἐν Σιπύλωι, ὅθι φασὶ θεάων ἔμμεναι εὐνάς / νυμφάων, αἵ τ' ἀμφ' Ἀχελώϊον [Ἀχελήϊον quiam ap. Σ (T): Ἀχελήϊον agn. Σ (AD), Aˢ: Ἀκελήϊον West] ἐρρώσαντο, / <u>ἔνθα λίθος περ ἐοῦσα θεῶν ἐκ κήδεα πέσσει</u>). Dué (2010, 291) has argued that the fountain simile in *Il.* 9.14–16 'recalls the iconic lamenter of Greek myth, Niobe, whose example is invoked by Achilles as he and Priam mourn for fathers and sons in the lament-filled *Iliad* 24. Niobe in her grief for her twelve children was transformed into such a weeping rock'.

Beta, S. (2016). *Il labirinto della parola: enigmi, oracoli e sogni nella cultura antica*. Torino.
Bowie, A. M. (2007). *Herodotus:* Histories, *Book VII*. Cambridge.
Bryce, T. (1998). *The Kingdom of the Hittites*. Oxford.
Buttmann, Ph. (1825). *Lexilogus oder Beiträge zur griechischen Worterklärung hauptsächlich für Homer und Hesiod*. 2 vols. Berlin. Abbreviated as *Lexilogus*.
Carruba, O. (1995). 'Aḫḫiyā e Aḫḫiyawā, la Grecia e l'Egeo', in: T. P. J. van den Hout and J. de Roos (eds.), *Studio Historiae Ardens: Ancient Near Eastern Studies Presented to Philo H. J. Houwink ten Cate on the Occasion of his 65th Birthday*. Leiden and Istanbul, 7–22.
Chantraine, P. (1999²). *Dictionnaire étymologique de la langue grecque*. Paris [1st ed. 1968–1980. Abbreviated as *DELG*.
Christidis, A.-Ph. (ed.) (2001). 'Προφητικός Λόγος', in: A.-Ph. Christidis (ed.), *Ιστορία της ελληνικής γλώσσας: Από τις αρχές έως την ύστερη αρχαιότητα*. Thessaloniki, 1022–9.
Curtius, G. (1879⁵). *Grundzüge der griechischen Etymologie*. Leipzig.
Dué, C. (2010). 'Agamemnon's Densely-packed Sorrow in *Iliad* 10: A Hypertextual Reading of a Homeric Simile', in: C. Tsagalis (ed.), *Homeric Hypertextuality. Trends in Classics* 2.2 (2010): 279–99.
Düntzer, H. (1865). 'Homerische etymologien', *KZ* 12: 181–214.
Fowler, R. L. (2000–2013). *Early Greek Mythography*, 2 vols. Oxford. Abbreviated as *EGM*.
Fränkel, H. (1921). *Die homerischen Gleichnisse*. Göttingen.
Frisk, H. (1954–1970). *Griechisches etylomogisches Wörterbuch*, 2 vols. Heidelberg. Abbreviated as *GEW*.
Godley, A. D. (1920). *Herodotus*. Cambridge, MA.
Hainsworth, B. (1993). *The Iliad: A Commentary, vol. III: books 9–12*. Cambridge.
Hornblower, S. (2015). *Lykophron:* Alexandra. *Greek Text, Translation, Commentary, and Introduction*. Oxford.
Janko, R. (1992). *The Iliad: A Commentary, vol. IV: books 13–16*. Cambridge.
Kretschmer, P. (1892). 'Indogermanische accent- und lautstudien', *KZ* 31: 325–472.
Latham, J. E. (1982). *The Religious Symbolism of Salt*. Paris.
Lattimore, R. (1951). *The Iliad of Homer*. Chicago – London.
Melchert, C. H. (1993). 'Review of Otten 1988', *Kratylos* 35: 202–3.
Moga, I. (2009). 'Symbolic Functions of Salt and Related Similes in Oriental Curses and Blessings', *Arheologia Moldovei* 32: 265–71.
Oettinger, N. (1976). *Die militärische Eide der Hethiter*. Wiesbaden.
Otten, H. (1988). *Die Bronzetafel aus Bogazköy: ein Staatsvertrag Tuthalijas IV*. Wiesbaden.
Papanastasiou, G. (2000). 'αἴξ, αἶγες, αἰγαῖος κτλ.', in: *Μελέτες για την ελληνική γλώσσα* Thessaloniki, 406–17.
Puhvel, J. (1991). *Homer and Hittite*. Innsbruck.
–. (2001). *Hittite Etymological Dictionary*. Berlin and New York. Abbreviated as *HED*.
Ready, J. L. (2011). *Character, Narrator, and Simile in the* Iliad. Cambridge.
Risch, E. (1974²). *Wortbildung der homerischen Sprache*. Berlin and New York.
Silk, M. S. (1983). 'LSJ and the Problem of Poetic Archaism: From Meanings to Iconyms', *CQ* 33.2: 303–30.
Snell, B. *et al.* (eds.) (1955–2001). *Lexikon des frühgriechischen Epos*, 25 vols. Göttinger and Oakville, CT. Abbreviated as *LfgrE*.
Solmsen, F. (1901). *Untersuchungen zur griechischen Laut- und Verslehre*. Strasburg.

Sommerstein, A. H. (2008). *Aeschylus:* Persians, Seven Against Thebes, Suppliants, Prometheus Bound. Cambridge, MA and London.
Thornley, G. (1916). *Longus:* Daphnis and Chloe, Loeb Classical Library. Cambridge, MA and London.
Traina, G. (1992). 'Sale e saline nel mediterraneo antico', *La parola del passato* 47: 363–78.
Tsagalis, Ch. (2012). *From Listeners to Viewers: Space in the* Iliad. Washington, DC.
–. (2017). *Early Greek Epic Fragments: Genealogical and Antiquarian Epic.* Berlin.
Tserepis, G. N. (1902). Τὰ σύνθετα τῆς ἑλληνικῆς γλώσσης. Athens.
Visser, E. (1997). *Homers Katalog der Schiffe.* Stuttgart und Leipzig.
Watkins, C. (1975). 'Latin *ador*, Hittite *ḫat-* Again: Addenda to *HSCP* 77 (1973) 187–193', *HSCP* 79: 181–7 (= 1994, [ed. L. Oliver] *Selected Writings: Culture and Poetics*, vol. II: 480–6).
–. (1995). *How to Kill a Dragon: Aspects of Indo-European Poetics.* Oxford.
–. (1997). 'Luvo-Hittite '(*lapan(a)-*', in: D. Disterheft, M. Huld, and J. Greppin (eds.), *Studies in Honor of Jaan Puhvel: Ancient Languages and Philology*, vol. I. Washington DC, 29–35.
West, M. L. (1997). *The East Face of Helicon. West Asiatic Elements in Greek Poetry and Myth.* Oxford.
–. (2003). *Homeric Hymns, Homeric Apocrypha, Lives of Homer.* Cambridge, MA and London.
–. (2007). *Indo-European Poetry and Myth.* Oxford.

Figure 1: Goats climbing rock face to lick salt

Stephanie West
Mysterious Lemnos: A note on ΑΜΙΧΘΑΛΟΕΣΣΑ (*Il.* 24.753)

The epithet ἀμιχθαλόεσσα is among many Homeric terms found puzzling in antiquity and revived by learned Hellenistic poets, a trend most rewardingly explored by our honorand.[1] I offer the following reflections as a gesture, all too inadequate, of appreciation of Antonios Rengakos' long-standing and varied services to Homeric scholarship.

The word occurs once in the *Iliad*, in Hecuba's lament for Hector (24.753): ἐς Σάμον ἔς τ' Ἴμβρον καὶ Λῆμνον ἀμιχθαλόεσσαν ('to Samothrace and Imbros and ἀμιχθαλόεσσα Lemnos'), a fine example of a pattern of verse 'widely attested for Indo-European' consisting of 'three names (or occasionally other substantives), of which the third is furnished with an epithet or other qualification'.[2] It appealed to the composer of the *Hymn to Apollo*, where Lemnos is included in the catalogue of islands which rejected Leto as she roamed round the Aegean (*HHom. to Ap.* 36): Ἴμβρος τ' εὐκτιμένη καὶ Λῆμνος ἀμιχθαλόεσσα ('well-settled Imbros and ἀμιχθαλόεσσα Lemnos'). In both passages the unusual adjective is highlighted by the metrical peculiarity of the breach of Hermann's Bridge, the more striking in that the word could be accommodated in the hexameter without any such licence.[3] It is not attested again before Callimachus who used it of dense fog (ἀμιχθαλόεσσαν . . . ἠέρα fr. 18.8 Pf.),[4] though Antimachus' μιχθαλόεσσα (fr. 46 W., 179 M.; cf. Hsch. μιχθαλόεσσα· ἀλίμενες) should be noted.[5]

'Ist nun ein Wort bei Homer überhaupt nur ein einziges Mal oder doch nur in einheitlichem Gebrauch belegt . . . , so weitern sich die Deutungsmöglichkeiten. Ganz besonders gilt das von attributiv gebrauchten Adjektiven' warns Manu Leumann, whose discussion surveys a wide range of suggestions.[6] The *Iliad* scholia offer two etymologically based explanations, ἀπρόσμικτος, *difficult of access* and ὀμιχλώδης, *misty, foggy.*

---

1 I have in mind particularly Rengakos (1992); (1993); (1994a); (1994b).
2 See further M. L. West (2007) 117–8.
3 For a fascinating discussion of Homeric violations of Hermann's Bridge see Schein (2015) 93–116.
4 Colluth. 209 is a tribute to Callimachus rather than independent testimony.
5 The inclusion of μιχθαλόεσσα in the poetic *onomastikon* of *P.Hibeh* 172 (*SH* 991.65; c. 270–230), where it is listed between two words beginning with alpha, cannot be regarded as an independent occurrence.
6 Leumann (1950) 212–13; 215 n. 8; see further 265, 270, 273, 301.

https://doi.org/9783110559873-012

The first, implying derivation from μείγνυμι, is obviously most unsuitable so far as physical geography is concerned. In Moudros Bay Lemnos offers the finest natural harbour in the North Aegean, used as a base for the British fleet in WW I, and anchorage is feasible at many points elsewhere along the coast.[7] The *Iliad*'s other references do not suggest that its inhabitants were regarded as unfriendly; this interpretation is based simply on an assumed connection between the ethnonym of the indigenous Sinties (1.594) and the verb σίνεσθαι.

The second suggested explanation implies a connection with ὁμίχλη. Many islands are shrouded in early morning mist, as Ithaca is when the Phaeacians leave Odysseus on the shore there (*Od.* 13.187–96). Something more distinctive is implied: 'fog' or 'smog', might seem plausible in view of the connection with Hephaestus, the master smith; διὰ τὰ ἐργαστήρια Ἡφαίστου ('because of Hephaestus' workshops') is suggested in the scholia.[8] Callimachus appears to have so interpreted the epithet when he uses it of the impenetrable darkness which overwhelms the Argonauts off Crete (fr. 18.8).[9] Lemnos' alternative name, Aithaleia ('Sooty'), recorded by Polybius (34.11.4; cf. Steph. Byz. s.v. Αἰθάλη) and shared with Elba, highlights this feature.

A further ancient explanation, by reference to Cypriot usage, κατὰ Κυπρίους εὐδαίμονα Sch. bT, 'fortunate', 'prosperous' i.e. 'fruitful', was cautiously championed by Bowra (1934, 71), but rather on the strength of dissatisfaction with the two other ancient interpretations than with any positive argument; I shall return to this suggestion.[10] The painstaking review of more recent proposals by Bettarini (2003) does not yield any immediately promising interpretation.[11] It may be

---

[7] Admittedly Soph. *Phil.* 220 f. might be taken to support the idea that the island lacked good anchorage; but the point seems rather to be that Philoctetes has been marooned in a particularly bleak spot, its only advantage being the commodious cave described in the prologue (15 ff.) (a passage which Milton surely had in mind at the beginning of *Samson Agonistes* (1–11)). Such isolation, dramatically effective as it is, seems extraordinarily cruel, but Odysseus, if asked, would no doubt have argued that Philoctetes could not remain constantly alert, and might be easily robbed of his priceless weapons if secrecy were not maintained.

[8] So Graf, *Kl.Pauly* 2.1025 s.v. Hephaistos: 'von dunstigem Brodem erfullten'.

[9] Well discussed by Harder (2012) *ad loc.*

[10] Leumann (1950, 273) suggested that what are presented as Cypriot glosses do not necessarily record actual Cypriot usage but often originated in the Cyclic *Cypria*; however, this idea does not seem to have been taken up in subsequent studies of the *Cypria*. He himself commended Doederlein's suggestion of a connection with (pre-Greek) ἀμύγδαλον –η, *almond:* an appealing idea but lacking the support of any other evidence for Lemnian almond production, an unlikely crop in view of the island's general lack of trees.

[11] *LfgrE s.v.;* Bettarini (2003). The webpage of the local tourist office describes the island as 'glowing and windy according to Homer'.

worth concentrating on determining what were or might be regarded as the island's distinctive features when the *Iliad* was composed.

Lemnos, at the intersection of major trade-routes,[12] was the scene of important episodes in an elaborate legendary network,[13] offering the first landfall for the Argonauts on their way eastwards and linking Argonautic and Trojan matters. Thus Jason's son by Hypsipyle, Euneos (named after the good ship Argo)[14] sends wine to the Greeks before Troy (*Il.* 7.456–71), the *Iliad*'s only reference to commisariat arrangements. More alert to commercial opportunities than is generally characteristic of Homeric heroes, he seems to be operating a port of trade, including a slave market to which Trojan captives are sent to be sold into slavery or ransomed and to which merchants from further east are attracted (*Il.* 21.40–1; 78–9; 23.740–7).

The poet of the *Iliad* could assume that the island's name was familiar to his audience, and that those with any interest in geography had a rough idea of the island's whereabouts, near to the mouth of the Black Sea (itself almost certainly still regarded as an inlet of the earth – encircling Okeanos) and convenient for Troy. Lemnos is presented as well known when it is first mentioned in Book 1, as Hephaestus attempts to persuade his mother of the folly of contending with Zeus, recalling how he was thrown out of Olympus, and landed on the island in a very poor state, (1.592–4):

πᾶν δ' ἦμαρ φερόμην, ἅμα δ' ἠελίωι καταδύντι
κάππεσον ἐν Λήμνωι, ὀλίγος δ' ἔτι θυμὸς ἐνῆεν·
ἔνθα με Σίντιες ἄνδρες ἄφαρ κομίσαντο πεσόντα.

All day long I dropped, and at sunset I landed on Lemnos, with little breath left in me; and there Sintian men immediately took care of me after my fall.

The close connection between the Firegod and Lemnos, is thus highlighted at the start of the action, and is recalled with the epithet ἠγαθέη, 'very holy' (*Il.* 2.722; 21.58, 79) which Lemnos shares with Pylos (*Il.* 1.252; *Od.* 4.599), Delphi, and the mysterious Nysaion (*Il.* 6.133). It is not surprising that it is described in the *Odyssey* (8.284) as the god's favourite place on earth. There the Sinties are said to be

---

12 The island was settled already in the fifth millennium BC, though the site which we know as Poliochnoi, 'Europe's oldest city' was almost completely abandoned c. 2000 after a very serious earthquake: see further Bernabò Brea (1964, 1976²); Tiné and Traverso (2001). It would be good to know whether any indication of the town remained visible when it was brought under Athenian control in the fifth century.
13 Painstakingly surveyed by Masciadri (2008).
14 Like many Greek heroic names based on something distinctive about the bearer's father; see further Kanavou (2015) 144–5.

ἀγριόφωνοι, 'rough of speech', like the Carians of Miletus, who are βαρβαρόφωνοι (*Il.* 2.867). The Homeric world does not usually suffer from language barriers; the detail is significant, highlighting the foreignness of the Sintians.[15] We cannot tell whether they were thought to be the island's only human inhabitants at the mythologically dim period of Hephaestus' ejection form Olympos, nor whether they were thought to be still there at the time of the Trojan War. Hellanicus (*FGrHist* 4 F71), who is cited in the *Odyssey* scholia, regarded them as hellenized Thracians (rather than the result of Greek marriages with native women), μιξέλληνες ('semi-hellenes') but this is unlikely to be more than a guess based on geographical proximity. He credited them with technical advances in connection with fire and weapons of war: τούτους ἐκάλουν οἱ περίοικοι Σίντιας, ὅτι ἦσαν αὐτῶν δημιουργοί τινες πολεμιστήρια ὅπλα ἐργαζόμενοι (fr. 71a) ('Their neighbours called them Sinties, because there were among them some craftsmen who made weapons of war'). Their name is thus explained by reference to σίνεσθαι, to harm; Hellanicus was fond of etymologizing explanations.[16] Tzetzes (fr. 71b) expresses in a crudely condensed form his report of the technical advances associated with Lemnos: ἐν Λήμνωι πρώτως εὑρέθη τό τε πῦρ καὶ αἱ ὁπλουργίαι ('in Lemnos fire and the making of weapons were first discovered').[17]

The *Iliad* later refers to another version of Hephaestus' fall from heaven (18.391–405; cf. *HHom. Ap.* 319–20), in which his mother, Hera, is responsible, and Thetis and her sister Eurynome care for him in secret. This looks like the poet's own invention; it explains how Thetis came to have a claim on Hephaestus' kindness.[18] The setting, a cave near the stream of Okeanos (18.402–3), could be reconciled with Lemnos, if we think of the Black Sea as an inlet of the earth-encircling river. That the god was occupied during his convalescence in making trinkets for Thetis and Eurynome is a very appealing idea.

Hephaestus is the only Olympian with a proper job; he is himself a smith, not merely the divine patron of smiths, and when Thetis visits him, he is occupied in his workshop on Olympos[19] As we have seen, one ancient explanation related ἀμιχθαλόεσσα to what we should call smog created by industrial pollution from Hephaestus' workshops, διὰ τὰ ἐργαστήρια Ἡφαίστου. When we consider other terrestrial locations for Hephaestus' smithies (apparently on Olympos

---

15 See further Gera (2011).
16 E.g. fr. 111 Italy from *vitulus*; fr. 125 the Apatouria so named from ἀπάτη. For further examples, see Fowler (2013) 687.
17 Philochorus (*FGrHist* 328 fr. 101) identified them as the Pelasgians of the raid on Brauron related by Herodotus (6.138–40, cf. 4.145.2), but this is just guesswork.
18 So West (2010) 351.
19 On his affinities with the Ugaritic craftsman god Kothar, see West (1997) 57, 384, 388f.

in the *Iliad* (18.146 – 8; 616)), Etna and the Aeolian islands, in particular Lipari, are spectacularly volcanic.[20] But Sicily and the west coast of Italy lay beyond the horizons of the poet of the *Iliad* and his audience.[21]

Eustathius' discussion, almost certainly based not on first-hand observation but on the account of Lemnos given in the lost part of Strabo, Book 7,[22] highlights what he regards as evidence of the island's fiery past, what we might call the scientific basis of the myth of Hephaestus' fall:

τὸ δὲ ἐν Λήμνωι κατενεχθῆναι αὐτὸν (Hephaestus) τῆι μυθικῆι συμβάλλεται π θανότητι ὡς ἀπὸ ἱστορίας. . . . ὅτι πῦρ καὶ ἐκεῖ γῆθεν ἀνεδίδοτό ποτε αὐτόματον . . . προσφυὴς γὰρ πάντως τῶι πυρὶ Ἡφαίστωι τόπος πῦρ τε ἀναβλύζων καὶ ἄλλα σημεῖα ἔχων θερμότητος, οἷον τὴν ἐκεῖ θερμῶν ὑδάτων ἀνάδοσιν, τὸ ψιλὸν τῆς πιότητος.

Investigation[23] contributes to the persuasiveness of the myth of Hephaestus landing on Lemnos . . . in that fire from there too used to issue from the ground of its own accord . . . for the place is by its nature associated with Hephaestus as fire, since besides flames bursting forth it presents other indications of heat, such as the flow of hot springs there, the bareness of the ground and its lack of fertility.

The scholion on *Od.* 8.284 (πολὺ φιλτάτη ἐστὶν ἁπασέων) corroborates this sketch: ἐκεῖσε γὰρ ἀνίενται γηγενοῦς πυρὸς αὐτόματοι φλόγες. We should note the tense of ἀνεδίδοτο ('used to issue'): imperfect. Vestiges of vulcanism still observable in Strabo's time could have faded out by the twelfth century. The stench of sulphur, which lies behind the significant part played by horrible smells in Lemnian legend,[24] nowadays appears to cause no problems. As Ovid's

---

20 See further Harder on Callim. *Aet.* 113e, 11.
21 No special association with Hephaestus is attested for the volcanic islands of the southern Aegean, Thera, Nisyros, and Melos. I have argued that problems arising from submarine eruption around Thera lay behind the decision to consult the Delphic oracle, which eventually led to the colonization of Cyrene; see further West (2012). The catastrophic effects of the Late Bronze Age eruption certainly did not exhaust the volcano's energies, though adequate records of eruptions have been kept only since the seventeenth century. That of 1866 – 1870 attracted the attention of Jules Verne, fuelling an interesting episode in *Twenty Thousand Leagues Under the Sea* (Part II, c.vi), published in 1869. There were several eruptions in the last century. The island's fertility was evidently felt to compensate for the hardships thus caused to the inhabitants, above all from noxious fumes, before the development of the lucrative tourist trade.
22 See van der Valk (1971) i. lxxvf.
23 This seems to me the most likely translation of ἀπὸ ἱστορίας; Eustathius uses ἱστορία with quite a range of meaning. I am most grateful to Antony Makrinos for help with the passage.
24 Above all, the δυσωδία inflicted on the Lemnian women as a result of Aphrodite's anger. The lingering stench of Philoctetes' gangrenous foot might also be supposed to contribute to poor air quality. Quintus Smyrnaeus (9.389 – 91) mentions the horrible tourist attraction of a lake of pus from Philoctetes' wound, more realistically to be regarded as a sulphur pit (solfatara).

Pythagoras well points out (*Met.* 15.340–41), *nec quae sulphureis ardet fornacibus Aetne / ignea semper erit; neque enim fuit ignea semper* ('nor will Etna which blazes with sulphurous furnaces always be fiery, nor indeed has it always been').

Lemnos was evidently already proverbial for vigorous fire when Bacchylides composed his description of young Theseus in *Ode* 18 (= *Dithyramb* 4) 55–6, ὀμμάτων δὲ στίλβων ἄπο Λαμνίαν φοίνισσαν φλόγα ('from his eyes flashes scarlet Lemnian flame'); the poem has been persuasively associated with the Panathenaea of 458 (see further Barron 1980; Maehler 2004: 190 f.). For the audience of Aristophanes' *Lysistrata* (299), in 411, 'Lemnian fire' meant a particularly fierce fire.[25]

Our assessment of Lemnos' vulcanicity in antiquity has been complicated by Walter Burkert's treatment of the island's fire festival, the ritual which brought purification to the island as old fires were extinguished, and after a fireless interval of some days, rekindled with new fire uncontaminated by common use, brought from Delos[26] (Burkert 2011, originally published in 1970). The custom is described by Philostratus, in his *Heroicus*, written c. 215 AD; other features suggest extreme antiquity, but before Lemnos came under Athenian control its new fire cannot have come from Delos, and an indigenous source on the Fire God's own island is an obvious conjecture. Burkert cast doubt on what had been taken to be references in Sophocles' *Philoctetes* (799–801, 986–7) and Antimachus (fr. 46 W., 52 M.) to a source of lively volcanic fire.

The first is particularly important. In his agony Philoctetes longs for death and entreats Neoptolemus for help (*Phil.* 799–801): ἀλλὰ συλλαβὼν / τῶι Λημνίωι τῶιδ' ἀνακαλουμένωι πυρὶ / ἔμπρησον ('Seize me, burn me up, in this fire invoked / famed (?) as Lemnian'). So the MSS. But ἀνακαλουμένωι is problematic. Dawe obelizes it. For Burkert (192) it 'seems to imply a certain ceremony to produce this demoniac fire; it is not always there. Understood in this way the verse turns out to be the earliest testimony to the fire festival at Lemnos . . . . How the fire was kindled in the ritual, may have been a secret. Considering

---

25 This usage appealed to Lycophron. When his Cassandra, in deploring Priam's failure to ensure that the new-born Paris would not survive, wishes that he had consigned both baby and mother to Lemnian fire (*Alex.* 227–8), instead of risking the uncertainties of exposure, she does not mean that they should have made a journey to Lemnos. In Lycophron's characterisation of Ajax (462 f.) as ὁ Λήμνιος πρηστὴρ Ἐνυοῦς, 'the war- goddess's Lemnian hurricane', 'Lemnian' must mean 'fiery', the connection with the actual island is minimal.
26 Cf. Plut. *Arist.* 20.4: after the Persian retreat from Greece Delphi issued instructions that as the current fires had been polluted by the barbarian, they must be extinguished and rekindled from fire brought from Delphi.

the importance of Lemnian craftsmen, the most miraculous method for χαλκεῖς would be to use a χαλκεῖον, a bronze burning-mirror to light a new fire from the sun'. Sophocles was making quite heavy demands on his audience if he expected them to appreciate this brief allusion to Lemnian ritual. There is much to be said for Toup's conjecture ἀνακυκλουμένωι,[27] 'spiralling upwards'; corruption would have been easy under the influence of καλούμενος (797). Philoctetes' later invocation of the island's fire poses no special problems (986–7): ὦ Λημνία χθὼν καὶ τὸ παγκρατὲς σέλας ἡφαιστότευκτον 'O land of Lemnos and all-conquering flame wrought by Hephaestus'.

The image of a more obviously recognizable volcano is suggested by a simile preserved from Antimachus of Colophon's epic, the *Thebais*, from the late fifth / early fourth century (fr. 46 W., 52 M.): Ἡφαίστου φλογὶ εἴκελον, ἥν ῥα τιτύσκει / δαίμων ἀκροτάτηις ὄρεος κορυφῆισι Μοσύχλου ('Like the flame of Hephaestus, divinely created on the topmost peaks of Mosychlos'). Similar comparisons in Homer suggest that the context is a warrior's attack. A violent blaze is indicated.[28] But the reference to the mountain peaks hardly suits the level plateau on the island's isthmus identified as Mosychlos. The passage evidently impressed Eratosthenes: compare (fr. 17 Powell): Ἔκ τέ οἱ ὄσσε / κανθῶν παμφαίνεσκε Μοσυχλαίηι φλογὶ ἶσον ('and the beams of his eyes blazed forth like Mosychlaean flame'). These lines are quoted in the scholia to Nicander's *Theriaca* 472, where a delightful pastoral scene is set within a description of forays by the highly venomous snake Cenchrines (472–3): ἢ Σάου ἠὲ Μοσύχλου ὅτ' ἀμφ' ἐλάτηισι μακεδναῖς / ἄγραυλοι ψύχωσι, λελοιπότες ἔργα νομήων ('while beneath the tall pines of Saüs or Mosychlus the shepherds cool themselves, forsaking the tasks of herdsmen' (trans. Gow and Scholfield)). Nicander was evidently unaware that though Lemnos is fertile, it is practically treeless. The learned reference does not suggest local knowledge; his conception of Mosychlos is likely to owe more to his fellow Colophonian Antimachus than to first-hand observation.

Appreciation of Lemnos' vulcanicity has suffered from Walter Burkert's memorably expressed (and well justified) assault on the long-standing assumption that a graceful, cone-shaped volcano, designated as Mosychlos, was a prominent feature of its landscape. 'The commentators on Homer and Sophocles and the Roman poets clearly speak of a volcano on Lemnos; this volcano was active in literature down to the end of the 19th century, with some scatttered eruptions

---

27 Mentioned by Jebb (1890), but ignored by Dawe and Lloyd-Jones/Wilson.
28 φλογί is a conjecture for πυρί; if the latter is kept, we must read ὅ ῥα. τιτύσκει is apparently used as synonymous with τεύχει.

even in later commentaries on Sophocles' *Philoctetes*, though geographical survey had revealed that there never was a volcano on Lemnos at any time since this planet has been inhabited by *homo sapiens*' (Burkert 2011, 191).[29] But volcanic activity can take other forms, and the careful study by Phyllis Forsyth (1984) brings out the cumulative force of the evidence for its former relevance to Lemnos.[30]

'Nothing is ever ended in the volcanic parts of the sea . . . and the globe is always being worked by subterranean fires' observes Jules Verne's Captain Nemo, by way of introduction to an account of the contemporary eruption at Santorini (1866–70) (*Twenty Thousand Leagues Under the Sea*, Part 2, ch. 6). We happen to know of strange developments off the coast of Lemnos in the late sixth century, such (as Jebb saw)[31] being the implication of Herodotus' account of Onomacritus' attempt to interpolate in the oracles of Musaeus a prediction that the islands off Lemnos would disappear (7.6.3):

> ἐξηλάθη γὰρ ὑπὸ Ἱππάρχου τοῦ Πεισιστράτου ὁ Ὀνομάκριτος ἐξ Ἀθηνέων, ἐπ' αὐτοφώρωι ἁλοὺς ὑπὸ Λάσου τοῦ Ἑρμιονέος ἐμποιέων ἐς τὰ Μουσαίου χρησμὸν ὡς αἱ ἐπὶ Λήμνωι ἐπικείμεναι νῆσοι ἀφανιζοίατο κατὰ τῆς θαλάσσης.
>
> Onomacritus was expelled from Athens by Hipparchus the son of Pisistratus after he was caught red-handed by Lasus of Hermione inserting in the work of Musaeus an oracle to the effect that the islands off Lemnos would vanish beneath the sea.

This fraudulent procedure makes sense only if the event predicted had already happened, or was in progress, and Onomacritus was trying to demonstrate the reliability of Musaeus' predictions, no doubt with an eye on prophecies with a more obvious political relevance.[32]

Some six centuries later Pausanias (8.33.4) records the disappearance of the adjacent island of Chryse, according to some the scene of Philoctetes' disastrous encounter with a horribly venomous snake. Appian (*Mithrid.* 77) mentions this as the venue for an episode in the Third Mithridatic War in 73 or 72, so the island must have been submerged between then and the time when Pausanias was writing. The offhand way in which these geological changes are recorded, being treated as of importance only within the context of political developments or

---

[29] The only geological work which Burkert cites was published in 1885, though general acceptance of the theory of plate tectonics developed in the 1960s has revolutionised vulcanology.
[30] The point attracts surprisingly little interest in modern reference books. It is not mentioned in the entries for Lemnos in Müller (1987) 64–7 and Higbie (2011).
[31] Jebb (1890) 242–5.
[32] This episode implies a written collection of Musaeus' oracles, and, more remarkable, some conception of editorial activity.

as illustrating the instability of human life, should be noted, and may discourage a widespread assumption that in illiterate societies oral tradition would be likely to preserve a memory of major eruptions.[33]

Such impermanent islands attract more attention at their birth than at their disappearance.[34] Strabo (1.3.16) offers a vivid description of the birth of a new islet, Hiera, at Santorini, between Thera and Therasia, in 197/6. Its emergence above the waters from a depth of c. 380 m. represented the elevation to sea level of an already existing submarine structure, the product of earlier, unrecorded eruptions. In the mid-nineteenth century the short-lived island of Ferdinandea, off the south-west coast of Sicily, was the object of intense imperialist rivalry during its sporadic existence.[35] But in a competition between sea and lava flow the sea will win unless lava is produced with unusual force. Icelandic Surtsey, which arose through an incipient crack between the American and Eurasian plates in 1963, has enjoyed unusual success.[36] Fascinating and spectacular as such manifestations of fire in the midst of the sea may be to outsiders, they can be expected to produce noxious (even fatal) fumes, and thus great numbers of dead fish.[37]

Classical Greek and Latin lack a term corresponding to 'volcano', apparently a fifteenth-century Italian or Portuguese coinage.[38] This deficiency did not prevent lively discussion of Etna and the wider implications of its behaviour, along with that of the rather less spectacular volcanoes of the Aeolian islands

---

33 Pliny's account of the eruption of Vesuvius (*Ep.* 6.16; 20) was not composed for its scientific interest, or in the hope that it might suggest measures which would mitigate the effects of similar catastrophes in future, but in response to Tacitus' request for information about the circumstances of his uncle's death.

34 In antiquity this kind of development seems to have been taken as a model for the formation of islands: cf. Pliny *NH* 2.202: *Nascuntur et alio modo terrae ac repente in aliquo mari emergunt, velut paria secum faciente natura quaeque hauserit hiatus alio loco reddente*. ('New lands are also formed in another way [i.e. other than alluviation] and suddenly emerge in a different sea, nature as it were balancing accounts with herself and restoring in another place what an earthquake has engulfed' (trans. Rackham, Loeb)). His list starts with Delos and Rhodes, continuing with Anaphe, Halone, Thera and Therasia. Thus Pindar describes Rhodes growing like a flower from the seabed (*Ol.* 7.54–70)

35 My thanks to Jonathan Prag for directing me to information about this desirable naval base.

36 In the early years of this century an addition to the Canaries seemed imminent, but just failed to break the surface.

37 Was the appealing idea of Hephaestus creating trinkets for Thetis and Eurynome (*Il.* 13. 400–2) suggested by indications of submarine volcanic activity off the coast of Lemnos?

38 See further Goodyear (1984); Hine (2002). ῥύαξ, 'stream', often with reference to a stream of lava, proves a useful term in desriptions of volcanic activity. Latin writers use *mons,/ collis ardens/ flagrans*: see further Foulon (2004).

and the vulcanism of the Phlegraean Fields. Strabo (5.4.5 – 9; 245 – 8) offers much of interest. Vesuvius, which for most of us represents the exemplar volcano thanks to the younger Pliny's description of its dramatic eruption in 79 (*Ep.* 6.16; 20), was supposed to be extinct when Strabo was writing. His enthusiasm for the fertility of the region surrounding Etna and Vesuvius, a well recognized effect of volcanic ash in moderate quantity (i.e. a deposit of less than 20 cms.) [39] might be relevant to the alleged Cypriot use of ἀμιχθαλόεσσα to mean 'prosperous', i.e. fertile. For Eustathius, as for Strabo, Etna is the paradigm. But the forces manifested most spectacularly in eruption from a graceful cone-shaped mountain might take other forms. The Phlegraean Fields well illustrated a less picturesque alternative, as did the Cimmerian Bosporus.[40]

Lemnos, as presented in Homer, was well-situated to be a cross-roads of interaction and exposure to linguistic diversity. The *Odyssey* highlights the alien speech of the native Sinties (8.294). The discovery of a grave-stele with an inscription in a language related to Etruscan (*IG* xii 8.1), to be dated c. 500, might suggest a substantial group settled there, but though a handful of short inscriptions have come to light, no other indications of Etruscan material culture have been found during the century since its discovery.[41] According to Diodorus (10.19), the Etruscans decided to leave from fear of the Persians, and handed over the island to Miltiades.

A curious detail in Herodotus' account of the antecedents to the foundation of Cyrene (4.145) may be relevant. Far back in the past, when the future Spartan kings Eurysthenes and Procles were still boys and their uncle Theras was acting as regent, a group arrived from Lemnos and settling down on Taygetos kindled a fire. When a messenger was sent to investigate, they said they were Minyans and having been expelled from Lemnos by Pelasgians claimed kinship on the strength of the Tyndarids' participation in the Argo's quest. The Spartans accepted this, gave them land, and assigned them to tribes. Herodotus presents this part of his narrative as local Spartan tradition (4.150.1), but we may suspect that his source was elegiac poetry.[42]

Lighting a fire is clearly a significant action, but the Spartans are puzzled by it, and no explanation is given. It has been suggested that the act of kindling a

---

[39] See further Fisher et al. (1997) 232– 44. Too much is of course catastrophic.
[40] 'A land weird enough with its mud volcanoes and marshes to supply the groundwork for a picture of the Lower World ' (Minns 1913, 436).
[41] See further de Simone (1996). I shall resist the temptation to speculate about Sophocles, *Inachus* fr. 270: Τυρσηνοῖσι Πελασγοῖς ('Tyrrhenian Pelasgoi'). My thanks to Christopher Smith for help on this point.
[42] On this point we owe much to Ewen Bowie's studies (Bowie 1986; 2001; 2010)

fire in apparently unoccupied territory, *terra nullius,* could be seen as a claim to possession and settlement, like planting a flag.⁴³ For the immigrants from Lemnos, the fiery (πυρόεσσα) island *par excellence,* their control of their own source of fire independent of the community which they wished to join might be expected to hold a peculiar significance. However, the new arrivals do not integrate successfully. It is an odd coincidence that a substantial contingent move to Thera, an island with an even more vividly volcano past (4.148) than Lemnos.

We should consider the possibility that ἀμιχθαλόεσσα has been borrowed from a language other than Greek, from the speech of one of the other groups familiar with the island The poet who first thought that adapted to Greek declension it might appropriately distinguish Lemnos probably believed he knew what it meant; but study of the practices of twentieth-century oral composers have shown that they are sometines uncertain about the meaning of the terms they use.⁴⁴ Leumann's great book (1950) demonstrated the effects of this kind of uncertainty in our texts of Homer. This may sound like the counsel of despair, and the choice of languages among which we might look for its antecedents is discouragingly wide. But we may be on the wrong track in attempting explanation via Greek etymology.

Before the *Iliad* took shape the island had formed the scene of an immensely important episode in Argonautic poetry and in the prehistory of the Trojan War. In ἀμιχθαλόεσσα, I suggest, the poet alludes to such earlier poetry,⁴⁵ highlighting this subtlety by the unusual metrical effect presented by disregard of the convention we know as Hermann's Bridge. I would like to think that it had once marked what was truly distinctive about the island, the indications of its close association with the Fire God. But what the poet or his audience thought it meant is another question.

Matthew Arnold well wrote 'If Homer's poetry, as poetry, is in its general effect on the poetical reader perfectly simple and intelligible, the uncertainty of the scholar about the true meaning of certain words can never change this general effect'.⁴⁶ But translation is sometimes unavoidable: 'mysterious, uncanny, unchancy' might not be misleading.

---

43 So Malkin (1987) 9, 117. This seems a more persuasive explanation than Calame's suggestion (2003, 115 n. 113) that it represented a sacrifice to Hestia, marking a claim to be returning to the land of their fathers.
44 As is well emphasised by Roger Dawe (1993, 18–19).
45 We perhaps have another reminder of that body of earlier poetry in the old form of patronymic for Philoctetes, Ποιάντιος (*Od.* 3.190).
46 *On Translating Homer* (1861).

Works cited

Barron, J. (1980). 'Bacchylides, Theseus and a woolly cloak', *BICS* 27: 1–8.
Bernabò Brea, L. (1964, 1976²). *Poliochni. Città preistorica nell' isola di Lemnos*, 1,2. Rome.
Bettarini, L. (2003). 'Λῆμνος ἀμιχθαλόεσσα (*Il*. 24.753)', *QUCC* 74: 69–88.
Bowie, E. L. (1986). 'Early Greek Elegy, Symposium and Public Festival', *JHS* 106: 13–35.
–. (2001). 'Ancestors of historiography in early Greek elegiac and iambic poetry', in: N. Luraghi (ed.), *The Historian's Craft in the Age of Herodotus*. Oxford, 45–66.
Bowie, E. L. (2010). 'Historical narrative in archaic and early classical Greek elegy', in: D. Konstan and K. A. Raaflaub, *Epic and History*. Chichester, 145–66.
Bowra, C. M. (1934). 'Homeric Words in Cyprus', *JHS* 54: 54–74.
Burkert, W. (2011). 'Jason, Hypsipyle, and New Fire at Lemnos: A Study in Myth and Ritual', *Kleine Schriften V: Mythica, Ritualia, Religiosa* 2, ed. F. Graf. Göttingen, 186–205 (= *CQ* 20 (1970) 1–16; reprinted with a few addenda in R. Buxton (ed.) 2000, *Oxford Readings in Greek Religion*, Oxford, 227–49; in German 'Neuer Feuer auf Lemnos. Über Mythos u. Ritual', in *Wilder Ursprung: Opferritual u. Mythos bei den Griechen*. Berlin 1990, 60–76).
Calame, C. (2003). *Myth and History in Ancient Greece: The Symbolic Creation of a Colony*. Princeton.
Dawe, R. D. (1993). *The Odyssey. Translation and Analysis*. Lewes, Sussex.
de Simone, C. (1996). *I Tirreni a Lemnos. Evidenza linguistica e tradizioni storiche*. Florence.
Finkelberg, M. (ed.) (2011). *The Homer Encyclopedia*. Oxford.
Fisher, R.V., G. Heiken, J. B. Hulen (1997). *Volcanoes: Crucibles of Change*. Princeton.
Forsyth, P. (1984). 'Lemnos Reconsidered', *EMC* 3: 3–14.
Foulon, E. (ed.) (2004). *Connaissance et représentation des volcans dans l'antiquité*. Clermont-Ferrand.
Fowler, R. L. (2000, 2013). *Early Greek Mythography*, 2 vols. Oxford.
Gera, D. (2011). 'Language in Homer', in Finkelberg 2011: 2.464–6.
Goodyear, F. (1984). 'The "Aetna": Thought, Antecedents, and Style', *ANRW* ii 32.1: 344–63.
Harder, A. (2012). *Callimachus: Aetia*. Oxford
Higbie, C. (2011). 'Lemnos', in Finkelberg 2011: 2.472.
Hine, H. M. (2002). 'Seismology and Vulcanology in Antiquity?' in: C. J. Tuplin and T. E. Rihll (eds.), *Science and Mathematics in Ancient Greek Culture*. Oxford, 56–75.
Jebb, R. C. (1890). *Sophocles: The Philoctetes*. Cambridge.
Kanavou, N. (2015). *The Names of Homeric Heroes*. Berlin and Boston.
Leumann, M. (1950). *Homerische Wörter*. Basel.
Maehler, H. (2004). *Bacchylides: A selection*. Cambridge.
Malkin, I. (1987). *Religion and Colonization in Ancient Greece*. Leiden.
Masciadri, V. (2008). *Eine Insel im Meer der Geschichten. Untersuchungen zu Mythen aus Lemnos*.
Minns, E. H. (1913). *Scythians and Greeks*. Cambridge.
Müller, D. (1987). *Topographischer Bildkommentar zu den Historien Herodots 1: Griechenland*.
OCD: Oxford Classical Dictionary (2012⁴). S. Hornblower, A. Spawforth, E. Eidenow (eds.) Oxford.
Rengakos, A. (1992). 'Homerische Wörter bei Kallimachos', *ZPE* 94: 21–47.
–. (1993). *Die Homertext und die hellenistischen Dichter*. Stuttgart.

– (1994a). *Apollonios Rhodios und die antike Homererklärung*. Munich.
– (1994b). 'Lykophron als Homererklärer', *ZPE* 102: 111–30.
Schein, S. L. (2015). 'A cognitive approach to Greek metre: Hermann's Bridge in the Homeric Hexameter and the interpretation of *Iliad* 24', *Homeric Epic and its Reception*. Oxford, 93–116.
Tiné, S. and A. Traverso (2001). *Poliochni. Die älteste Stadt Europas* (trans. H. E. Langenfass). Athens.
van der Valk, M. (1971). *Eustathii, Commentarii ad Homeri Iliadem pertinentes*. Leiden.
West, M. L. (1997). *The East Face of Helicon. West Asiatic Elements in Greek Poetry and Myth*. Oxford.
–. (2007). *Indo-European Poetry and Myth*. Oxford.
–. (2011). *The Making of the Iliad*. Oxford.
West, S. R. (2012). 'From Volcano to Green Mountain: a Note on Cyrene's Beginnings', *Palamedes* 7: 43–66.

Homeric Hymns

Anton Bierl
'Hail and take pleasure!' Making gods present in narration through choral song and other epiphanic strategies in the *Homeric Hymns to Dionysus* and *Apollo*

The *Homeric Hymns*, a heterogeneous collection of hexametrical hymns dedicated to various gods – most dated between the 7th and 5th centuries BC, some ranging even to the Hellenistic times – are situated in the same orally-based performance tradition as the two monumental Homeric epics, the *Iliad* and the *Odyssey*. They share all the same features, especially formulaic diction set in dactylic metre and the Homeric *Kunstsprache* that, in synchrony, shifts between diachronic stages. Both the *Hymns* and the Homeric epics developed in an evolutionary process. Large-scale festivals and assemblies as occasions for seasonal re-performance, like the Panionia and later the Panathenaea in Athens, were important steps toward monumental growth through rhapsodic regularization and textual fixation between the late 9th and the 6th centuries BC. Literacy, writing technique, and alphabetic record all would have helped to produce a considerably stable transcript, while the rhapsodes re-composed in re-performances their parts taken from the whole story in a relay-arrangement according to the principles of the Lord-Parry school. These methods were refined by modern orality scholarship, narratology, and approaches combining orality with neoanalysis.[1] Since Friedrich August Wolf at the end of the 18th century, the *Hymns* have been commonly read as preludes or προοίμια, songs directed to divinities before shifting to larger epic poems.[2] Direct reference to the *Iliad* and *Odyssey* in the longer *Hymns* – those with a developed story-line – is an important component in their aesthetic appreciation. Thus we can take first steps towards intertextuality, or an awareness of a dialogical relationship between narrative traditions, regardless of the medium of the Homeric Hymn and its grade(s) of literacy.[3] In-

---

[1] On the evolutionary theory, see Nagy (1996, 2003, 2008/09, 2009/10); see the survey by Bierl (2015), esp. 186–91. On the combination of orality with neoanalysis, see Montanari, Rengakos and Tsagalis (2012).
[2] Wolf (1795/1985) 112–13. See e.g. Nagy (1990a) 354–6, 359–60, (2008/09) 227–46; Petrovic (2012) 152; Faulkner (2011a) 17–18.
[3] See Rengakos (2002); Tsagalis (2008, 2011).

deed, much speaks in favour of the influence of writing in some of the later *Hymns*.

Between cult and amusement

It would be wrong to see the *Hymns* only as πάρεργα or epigonic plays of literary imitation. In diachronic perspective, the ὕμνος, or 'song', is much older than the regularized monumental epic that developed from smaller epic episodes taken from a much larger context. This type survives in the later Cyclic epic poems.[4] Hymn as a communal and choral manner of praising the gods is the oldest form of lyric song, coexistent with epics over the centuries. In the *Homeric Hymns* hymn is standardized to a rhapsodic and regularized sub-genre of hexameter poetry performed in παρακαταλογή, the recitation of reduced melody. A prior step is the kitharodic accompaniment of an ἀοιδός who sings a rhapsodic hymn.[5] Early mythical musicians, such as Orpheus or Musaeus, perform theogonies, songs about the birth of the gods and the development of a polytheistic system, to the sound of a lyre. Hesiod's *Theogony* will be the model for the Homeric Hymn. The regularized monumental epic can occasionally imitate and integrate lyric, choric and, of course, theogonic-rhapsodic hymns as well as the Cyclic mode through "diachronic skewing".[6] Eventually only the *Iliad* and the *Odyssey* among monumental literature will be attributed to Homer.

The *Homeric Hymns* are thus an interesting epic sub-genre at the intersection of several diachronic developments and production types. The *Homeric Hymns* can be seen as either preludes to other epic recitations, even to theogonies, or as hymns of theogonic quality in themselves, since, regarded as narrative expansions, they use to revolve around the emergence of the Olympian gods.[7] But as hymns they also overlap with the basic function of cultic hymns of the communal, choral or monodic type, whose main function is to praise and summon the gods. But cultic hymns use to address the gods in the second person directly, whereas *Homeric Hymns* speak about them mostly in the third person.[8] Only at the very end we shift to a direct a farewell address of χαῖρε that emphasizes a reciprocal χάρις-relation between the rhapsodic singer and the god, 'combining

---

4 See Nagy (2008/09) 189–98; Bierl (2012) 120.
5 See Nagy (1990a) 20–30; Bierl (2015) 186.
6 See Nagy (2003) 39–48, (2011) 305–22; Bierl (2015) 186.
7 See Furley (2011) esp. 210–18.
8 See Furley and Bremer I (2001) 41–3.

the ideas of pleasure ("gratification") and beauty ("gracefulness") by way of reciprocity ("graciousness")'.⁹ The greeting means thus also a call to take pleasure.

Hymns have a clear division into three parts: the *invocatio* calls upon the divinity to be invoked and establishes the contact, the middle part gives a detailed praise, predicates the divinity's powers, recalls earlier benefits, describes actions and deeds in longer narrations – Ausfeld calls it the *pars epica* –,¹⁰ and the final prayer asks for help or for the divinity to appear.¹¹ In the *Homeric Hymns* the invocation is lacking. Instead, in a very few verses, the rhapsode declares his intention to sing about the god or goddess or to remember him or her; or he summons the Muse or another deity to praise or to help him to sing about the god. The middle part in each case indeed becomes a *pars epica*, where the focus is on a very detailed narration about typical deeds, honours and episodes, all in the third person. In the long narrations we thus shift to the epic perspective of vivid and objective telling. The end does not provide a concrete objective of prayer, but focuses on the close and intimate relation between the god and the singer, and often declares the intention to shift to another song, or the rest of the present song.¹² In short, *Homeric Hymns* should not be seen as purely literary hymns. The gulf between the secular and the religious, at least for archaic and classical Greek literature, has been closed and deconstructed in the last decades.¹³ Despite the clear focus on narration and entertaining amusement,¹⁴ the *Homeric Hymns* are still close to cultic hymns. The latter have been analysed as gifts or even sacrifices in order to honour the divinities through words.¹⁵ Ivana Petrovic thus emphasized the dedicatory aspect of the *Homeric Hymns*, their nature as private ἀγάλματα, devotional objects, and gifts to the gods.¹⁶ John F. García presented a strong argument for their symbolic function, that is, to recognize the gods via the speech act of summoning their presence through a detailed narration similar to an Anatolian *historiola* or other Near Eastern hymn. The story accomplishes divine presence, a function that the middle part took over in the cultic hymns.¹⁷

---

9 Nagy (2013a) 663. On χάρις as reciprocal relation, see Bierl (2009) 116–25, esp. 118 n. 92.
10 Ausfeld (1903) 505.
11 See Furley and Bremer I (2001) 50–63.
12 See Furley and Bremer I (2001) 41–3; Nagy (2011) 327–9.
13 See e.g. Bierl (2007a).
14 See Clay (2011) 245.
15 See Depew (2000); Calame (2011); Petrovic (2012) esp. 155–69.
16 Petrovic (2012) 155–69, esp. 156, 161–9.
17 García (2002).

The *Homeric Hymns* as epiphanies

In her very influential book, *The Politics of Olympus*, Jenny Strauss Clay rightly stresses that the narratives of the *Homeric Hymns* focus on the emergence of the honours and functions of the single gods in the polytheistic system after the establishment of Zeus' order.[18] Since then we are used to reading the *Hymns* as Panhellenic charter tales shaping the polytheistic apparatus of Olympus. In this vein, the *Hymns* focus on the gods in their making, envisaging them in a highly diversified political system under Zeus's rule. We could say that this amounts to the theogonic function of the *Hymns*.[19] But this dominant view almost eclipsed the presence-assuring,[20] the cultic, and the purely narrative factors. As in a kaleidoscope, we can oscillate between various aspects and functions in our reading of the *Homeric Hymns*: respectively, we can focus on a given *Hymn's* cultic worship, devotional character, creation of a valid divine order as superstructure in heaven, cathartic effect to soothe tensions by listening to magic words that tell about conflicts, crises and their solutions, or simply literary amusement with stories about gods who are all-too-human. Beyond all these very legitimate claims, we should not forget that the *Homeric Hymns* are hardly distinguishable from epic narration. Apart from the very small parts at the beginning and end, they look like an epic episode of the Cyclic phase. But as hymn, like the famous story of Ares and Aphrodite in *Odyssey* 8.266–366, it is, in diachronic terms, one more grade removed.[21] The style is light and fluid, often amusing, sometimes burlesque, dealing with circular episodes of love and friendship.[22]

The presence of the Olympian gods is ubiquitous in Homeric epic. Constituting the superhuman apparatus, the gods watch over the action from the Olympian vantage point, while men on earth act in accordance with them and yet on their own will. In short, both sides co-act and complement each other. Gods and men are in permanent interaction and close contact with each other. Through the rhapsodic song, a historical and anthropological phase is re-actualized when gods were still in direct touch with men. Epic makes the past and thus also the gods present. In χάρις-relations of reciprocity, men –

---

[18] Clay (1989); Clay (2011) 241–4.
[19] See Furley (2011) 210–18; on the *Hymns* as expanding elaborations on episodes of Hesiod's *Theogony*, see Clay (2011) 244.
[20] See Bakker (2005) 136–53; Petrovic (2012) 160–1.
[21] See Nagy (2008/09) 313–42, (2009/10) 79–102; Bierl (2012) 118–21.
[22] See Nagy (2008/09) 187–96, 248–76, 296–300, (2009/10) 88.

both inside the plot and as audience outside – and gods are bound together and experience each other. Moreover, the ἀοιδός, the singer, serves as a medium of the Muses in a performance of narrative remembrance and mimetic re-enactment and re-actualization. In total empathy with the epic heroes, the audience experiences the past in the present by listening to numerous performances and re-performances. Despite the collaboration, the direct contact between men and gods remains problematic. It is a situation in limbo, since epic is situated in a period when men were already clearly separated from gods. In the *Iliad* and *Odyssey* both sides meet only occasionally and hardly directly, since human beings cannot stand in the gods' splendid radiance full of light, and are in danger of their lives being extinguished.[23] Thus gods must conceal their true appearance and take on human shape. Even in these partial scenarios men can sense the divine presence through signs and react with astonishment and fear. Yet epiphanies – or at least the ambivalent allusion to and play with them – are centres of narrative energy and important highlights integrated into the monumental Homeric epic that does not focus entirely on the apparition of the god. As such, epiphanies in Homer remain notoriously vague and contradictory, as has been recently stressed by B. C. Dietrich and others.[24] 'Gods are difficult to see for mortals' (χαλεποὶ δὲ θεοὶ θνητοῖσιν ὁρᾶσθαι *HHymn* 2.111).[25] Since the Greeks think of their gods in anthropomorphic terms, the deities can show themselves only in human disguise; as such, they are no longer real gods. Thus, anthropomorphism prevents men from imagining them in a pure and true form. Therefore the immanent tension between εἶναι and δοκεῖν is mirrored in the verb φαίνεσθαι – the basis of epiphany, derived from ἐπι-φαίνεσθαι –, whose meaning ranges from 'to show oneself'/'appear' to 'seem as if'.

The *Homeric Hymns* seem to reflect the other side of the coin. Since hymns very often call for the presence of particular gods, epiphany plays a central role also in *Homeric Hymns*.[26] Since they revolve completely around the gods, without being integrated into a carrier plot, *Homeric Hymns* aim at making the gods present and alive through narration. In contrast to the cultic hymns or Homeric epic, the special mnemonic capacity of the rhapsodic "I", the performer or even the author, is stressed often right in the beginning, instead of the usual invocation of the god to be praised. Furthermore, the performer only rarely asks for the in-

---

23 For light as a sign of epiphany, see Pfister (1924) 315–16; Richardson (1974) 208–10, 252–3; Bremer (1975) 1–12; Seaford (1996) 236 ad *Ba.* 1082–3; see also the literature cited in Bierl (2004) 51 n. 31. On the typical scene of Homeric epiphany in general, see Turkeltaub (2003).
24 Dietrich (1983). See also Fernández Contreras (1999); Bierl (2004)
25 See *Il.* 20.131 χαλεποὶ δὲ θεοὶ φαίνεσθαι ἐναργεῖς. See also *Od.* 13.312–13; 16.161.
26 See Bremer (1975) 1–12; Vergados (2011) esp. the survey 82–3.

spiration by the Muse (*HHymn* 4, 5, 9, 14, 17, 19, 20, 31, 32, 33). In most cases the rhapsodic or poetic "I" starts with a self-referential expression about his own performance: 'I begin to sing' (ἄρχομ' ἀείδειν *HHymn* 2.1, 11.1, 13.1, 16.1, 22.1, 26.1, 28.1); 'I will/I am going to sing – in the sense of a performative future (ᾄσομαι *HHymn* 6.2; ἀείσομαι *HHymn* 10.1, 15.1, 23.1);[27] 'I sing' (ἀείδω *HHymn* 12.1, 18.1, 27.1); 'I start' – in the sense of a performative future in the subjunctive (ἄρχωμαι *HHymn* 25.1); 'I will remember' – again in the performative future (μνήσομαι *HHymn* 3.1, 7.2). The "I" then comes again to the fore at the end of the Hymn. This is especially marked in *HHymn* 1.17–20, where the "I" includes the whole guild of singers and stresses Dionysus' function as god of poetic song: 'we singers sing of you as we begin and as we end a strain, and none forgetting you may call holy song to mind'. Dionysus is the origin and the inspiration for the performative process of making the god present. On the other side, any proximity to λήθη (forgetting) results in poetic failure. At the beginning and the end of a song the rhapsodes, especially in a song about Dionysus, should mention him and get in touch with him through an act of remembrance as actualization. Usually the "I" says farewell (χαῖρε) to the god(dess) and asks him/her to take pleasure, establishing the χάρις-relation of reciprocity in song. Finally, in the very last line, the rhapsode often utters his performative intention to remember the divinity and another song (αὐτὰρ ἐγὼ καὶ σεῖο καὶ ἄλλης μνήσομ' ἀοιδῆς *HHymn* 2.495, 3.546, 4.530, 6.21, 10.6, 19.49, 28.18, 30.19; for a plural address see *HHymn* 25.7, 27.22, 29.14, 33.19). Or, sometimes he asks the god to lead him (ἄρχε δ' ἀοιδῆς *HHymn* 13.3), to pray in song (λίτομαι δέ σ' ἀοιδῆι *HHymn* 16.5), to seek favour for the song (ἵλαμαι δέ σ' ἀοιδῆι *Hym.* 21.5); or, after starting from the god, the performer announces to switch to another song (σεῦ δ' ἐγὼ ἀρξάμενος μεταβήσομαι ἄλλον ἐς ὕμνον *HHymn* 5.293, 9.9, 18.11). In the majority of cases, *Homeric Hymns* represent an activity of μνήμη, memory. But in a still basically-oral culture, as Egbert Bakker and others have demonstrated, memory is not the process of retrieving saved information that has been archived through a written coding technique.[28] Rather, μνήσασθαι means the act of "total recall", re-actualizing the past.[29] Song, ἀοιδή, is a μνῆμα, or a vivid σῆμα, a product of performance that calls things back to life. The verbal forms μιμνήσκω and μνάομαι (I recall) have been connected with μένος (vigour, vitality, impetus, urge, active thinking).[30] One may compare *manas, manah* in Sanskrit and the Latin *animus*. It is

---

27 On the performative future, see Bierl (2009) 294 n. 77; Calame (2011) 336 n. 9.
28 Bakker (2005) esp. 140 (with n. 14–16).
29 See Nagy (2013a) 48–50.
30 See Boisacq (1916) 625–7, 638, 641; Chantraine (1968) 658, 685, 702–3; Frisk (1970) 206–8, 238–41, 160–1; see also Bierl (2007b) esp. 49–51.

derived from the roots *mna-* and *men-*, being present in the even more expressive verbs of mental endeavour, strife and desire.[31] The exaggerated mental desire can lead to the etymologically related μανία (madness); see μαίνομαι (I am out of mind).[32] To conclude: μιμνήσκειν is the mental activity to call something back to life by activating it in a mental endeavour.

Therefore the *Homeric Hymns* to and about gods are performances designed to make them present in song and narration, to instigate the enactment of their epiphanies in immediacy and vividness. They are not explicitly called to appear, but brought to life and presence in detailed narrations that tell about their central deeds, honours, signs (σήματα), epithets and features. The hymnic performance is a speech act. By singing about remembering the god in song, the divinity becomes alive. This performative act of re-actualization is also a "mind act" and accomplishes the "presentification" as a mental activity.[33] Moreover, Jean-Pierre Vernant has shown that in archaic Greece this act of memory had metaphysical underpinnings. The Greeks called to life the past not as a simple historical antecedent on a temporal axis, but as an origin and source. Thus, they remembered the past in a mythical sense as the ur-essence. They recall nature itself, the model and idea from which everything develops.[34]

This insight applies also for gods. Remembering the god in a setting of the past means calling to mind the deity in its metaphysical idea and original immediacy of existence from which the cosmos derives. Thus the hymns not only attempt to make the gods present but the performance re-actualizes them in their very essence and as metaphysical beings. The god "is treated" as an object observed in the perspective of the third person, but in total recall. Therefore the "I" does not normally recur to direct address in the second person, not following the usual practice of calling names, attributes, and places, of predicating powers and remembering earlier contacts and benefits. The rhapsode does not accumulate titles, explanations, amplifications either. Nor does he describe them in coincidental episodes of their *curricula vitae*. In the longer hymns the "I" just focuses on narratives, telling typical, formative and essential stories. The gods become actual, real and clearly visible, ἐναργεῖς, via epic narration. The *Homeric Hymns* work like slow-motion epiphanies in Homeric narration. Typically the hymnic performances focus on situations where the gods' metaphysical essence

---

31 See μεμοινάω, μενεαίνω, μέμονα.
32 Superseded explanations connect it to 'woman' via μνᾶσθαι (to woo) and derivatives from *μνα- < *βνα- 'woman' = Vedic *gna-* 'wife of a god'; i.e. *guna- *gunna -> γυνή; see Boisacq (1916) 641.
33 See Bakker (2005) 136–53, esp. 151.
34 Vernant (1988) 115.

comes into being, such as stories about the birth and first deeds, arrival and first manifestation, return after retreat and crisis. The quintessential features, also expressed in epithets, are revealed in action and put into practice. Divinities can thus be grasped in a cognitive act and brought to life through song. In the act of singing, the hymn does what it narrates. The gods become accessible and real through performance. In the eyes of a given *Hymn's* audience or recipients, deities become alive in their essence and in their making, being summoned as gods who are part of the polytheistic system that rules the present world order. In endless chains of re-performances each rhapsodic "I" can access these formative situations of the Olympus in the making in order to get the recipient in touch with its quintessential, original and metaphysical existence. In the same way, each rhapsode reconnects to Homer, the model ἀοιδός. After each successful narrative evocation of the deity, the singer finally gets directly in touch with him or her, establishing reciprocity in χάρις. The epic song full of grace pleases the god who has become present. In exchange for this gift the god will recompense the singer with further pleasure. Thus, in the end, the deity will somehow serve as the source of the song that, as an autonomous, creative process, first made him its subject, its theme.

As was said before, we can understand the process of remembering, enacting and revealing the essence of a god in the making through longer narration as an epiphanic act in the wider sense. Therefore, I would like to explore how epiphany, as a motif, plays an important role also within the hymns. The second *Hymn to Dionysus* (*HHymn* 7) is wholly based on the fact that this *kommende Gott* (Hölderlin) came and showed himself (ὡς ἐφάνη 7.2).[35] Furthermore, since the perspective of the singer is so prominent, I will look closely at how epiphany is emphasized through the self-referential integration of music, instruments, singing and dancing in monodic and choral configurations. We thus have a double constellation of a *mise en abyme* to bring the epiphanic aspect to the fore.

Before we go into more detail, I would like to hint at the fact that anthropomorphic blurring also plays a central role in the *Homeric Hymns*. One would expect greater religious clarity given the genre. But since anthropomorphism was the decisive factor for the notoriously vague treatment of epiphanies in the monumental Homeric epics, it likewise influences how gods are made to appear in the *Hymns*. On the one hand, we hear about the essence of the gods; on the other hand, these gods are dangerously close to mortals. They must appear in human guise to communicate with people and to achieve their objectives. Dionysus stands at the shore in the shape of a beautiful ephebe in *HHymn* 7, and De-

---

[35] See Jaillard (2011).

meter acts as a mortal woman in *HHymn* 2 to become the nurse of the young baby Demophon, perhaps a substitute for the loss her child Persephone. Moreover, Aphrodite plays the role of a young girl in order to have sex with a mortal herdsman, Anchises, in *HHymn* 5. Often people, as in the case of Anchises, sense the divine behind the disguise.[35] Thus we have sometimes a subtle and amusing play between recognition and misrecognition, with the situation remaining in limbo and highly vague. Aphrodite must even recur to the lie that she is not a goddess in order to reach her goal, alleging in false fabrications that she came as a mortal girl, abducted by Hermes from the maiden choruses, to marry Anchises (*HHymn* 5.109–43). Since both goddesses became too human they must soon turn to partial epiphanies.[37] In many longer *Hymns* we encounter the typified Homeric scene of gods making themselves manifest through a whole gamut of signs, such as appearing in fuller size, beaming light, glamour, radiance, etc., while mortals evince their usual reaction: trembling, fearing, wondering.[38] Moreover, human instincts dominate even the Olympians. The *Hymn to Aphrodite* (*HHymn* 5) makes the goddess present by showing how her capacity to make other gods, even Zeus, fall in love with mortal humans, turns on herself. Aphrodite thus becomes alive in her essence, in her own erotic passions and sufferings. The most human of all is Hermes, the god who comes dangerously close to transgressing the boundary between gods and men. Even as a god he craves for meat.[39] Thus in the longer *Hymns to Aphrodite* and *Hermes* (*HHymns* 5 and 4), these human – all too human – traits define the narrations. Indeed, the entire *Hymn to Hermes* (*HHymn* 4) makes this god appear in his very essence through a long epiphany, despite the absence of the typical scene of a full epiphany.[40] The *Hymn* shows in detail how the burlesque anti-god triumphs as newly born baby in the form of a rascal and trickster. In comic distortion and in a poetics of reversal, the god becomes alive in his corporeality, trickery, wits, laughter, theft, hunger for meat and inventiveness. We even see him sacrificing and singing about and for the gods. All features speak for a very human behaviour, where the subhuman meets the supra-human and divine.[41] Thus, at least in some of the longer *Hymns*, we encounter the following paradox: the epic hymn makes the metaphysical essence of Olympian gods present, thus coming close to the cultic dimension, while at the same time these gods are envisaged in non-divine situa-

---

36 See *HHymn* 2.159 (Callidice); *HHymn* 5.92–106 (Anchises).
37 See *HHymn* 2.185–90; *HHymn* 5.172–90.
38 See Turkeltaub (2003); Vergados (2011) 82–7.
39 See Versnel (2011) 319–27, 348–70.
40 See Jaillard (2007) 69–98; Vergados (2011) esp. 83–7.
41 See Versnel (2011) 309–77; Vergados (2011).

tions and perspectives. The almost religious quality is counterbalanced by an occasionally rather non-cultic atmosphere where narratives about all too human deities create amusement and ironic detachment. Nonetheless, Hermes or Aphrodite in *HHymns* 4 and 5, for example, become present and gain epiphanic concreteness just in these traits.

Moreover, in some *Hymns* the gods, especially Hermes (*HHymn* 4) and Dionysus (*HHymn* 7), manifest themselves through signs, features, σήματα.⁴² For the disclosure of their true nature, they give signs that require correct decoding and interpretation. Inside the narrated story, figures fail to recognize them, while the outside listener (or reader) clearly understands these markers. When Dionysus strikes back, assuming a terrible (δεινός) nature through metamorphosis into a lion and through the scenic production of a wild bear, he brings forth signs (σήματα φαίνων *HHymn* 7.46). His epiphany proceeds via signs that everybody should realize. But signs bear a certain ambivalence. Like oracular words they are not clear-cut, but hard to recognize by nature. They can only allude to and hint at the higher truth, nodding to enigmatic allegoresis and indirect semiosis.⁴³ In the "traditional referentiality", σήματα can metonymically stay for well known traditional story patterns.⁴⁴ The product of recalling, the μνῆμα, is also a σῆμα, a symbol that has to do with a mental awakening and activation. Something is brought to consciousness, νόος, by the act of becoming aware of or noticing something, νοῆσαι, so that qua homecoming, νόστος, – both words derive from the common root **nes-* –, it can "return to light and life". As a reminder, the σῆμα is encoded according to the model to be decoded later on.⁴⁵

The example of Parmenides describing the nature of "being" through σήματα provides an ideal foil to the revealing process through signs in the *Hymns*. The very abstract but still concrete ἔστιν of veridical quality, 'it is', the only way of thinking, or as the deduced being, the ἐόν, is a pure concept of metaphysical quality. It can only be grasped in a mental process, conceived as a very stable, everlasting, unchanging abstract entity. 'To it many σήματα, road-markers, are ascribed' (ταύτηι δ' ἐπὶ σήματ' ἔασι / πολλὰ μάλ' fr. 8.2–3 DK). It is signalled by reference to primarily negative attributes, expressed with the alpha-privative and substantiated by logic proofs. It is 'uncreated and undestroyable, complete, alone-born, unshakeable and perfectly completed' (ὡς ἀγένητον ἐὸν καὶ ἀνώλεθρόν ἐστιν / οὖλον μουνογενές τε καὶ ἀτρεμὲς οὐδ' ἀτέλεστον fr. 8.3–4). It is a νόημα (fr. 8.34) about the essence of being, told by a goddess, and itself of meta-

---

42 See Vergados (2013) 15–22. On σήματα in general, see Nagy (1990b) 202–20.
43 See Vergados (2013) 15–22, esp. 20–2.
44 See Foley (1999) 115–67 and Bierl (2015) 193.
45 See Frame (1978) 81–115 and 134–52; Nagy (1990b) 218–19, (2013a) 275–8.

physical quality, of ἀλήθεια, truth, and πίστις, certainty. In its static abstraction it can be concretely conceived, compared to a round ball and neatly bound in the chains of cosmic necessity.

Parmenides' sentence, 'The same can be thought of and be' (... τὸ γὰρ αὐτὸ νοεῖν ἐστίν τε καὶ εἶναι fr. 3 DK), is decisive for his understanding. Since one can mentally behold and become aware of it, one can speak about it in rhapsodic form. The metaphysical essence thus becomes evident through pure logic and iconic ἐνάργεια, clarity, in a speech act of rhetoric πειθώ, persuasion. On the contrary, in the *Homeric Hymns* hexametric poetry does not attempt to prove the static and abstract essence of being as eternal truth, but to unfold the dynamic and living essence of anthropomorphic gods through narration. The narrative part is not an abstract, but very vivid and amusing discourse about gods in action. The stories focus on Olympian gods in their making, on their essentials and prerequisites in action. The epic narratives reveal the gods' formative actions, deeds, honours or signs, when they materialize for the first time. In other words, the narrative process sets epithets in action. The features are remembered, dynamically exposed as they emerge. In this way the *Homeric Hymns* amount to an epiphanic disclosure in epic telling. By going back to the very origin and through a dynamic lens the poetic "I" tells about vivid and non-abstract divine personalities immersed in interaction with other figures. In short, the *Hymns* do not map static and metaphysical entities in close-up views, but narrate delightful stories about the essence of real gods in flesh and blood as they come into being. The *Hymns* remember them and bring them back to life in a mental and performative act through narration.

Epiphany and mystery in the *Hymn to Dionysus* (*HHymn 7*)

It is well known that Dionysus bridges dichotomies in a paradoxical manner.[46] He oscillates between all possible polar oppositions, such as man–woman, man–ephebe, god–man–animal, inside–outside, life–death, Greek–Barbarian, quietness–motion, civilization–nature, cosmos–chaos, idyll–violence, happiness–suffering, order–destruction. Euripides summarizes this tension, calling him δεινότατος, ἀνθρώποισι δ᾽ ἠπιώτατος ('most terrible, but to the people most gentle and kind' *Bacchae* 861). In his presence both sides of polar axes, un-

---

[46] The entire paragraph is based on Bierl (2013a) 366–7; on Dionysus as the god of polar oppositions, see Otto (1933); Henrichs (1982) esp. 158; Bierl (1991) 14–20.

derstood as energetic forces in dynamic reciprocation, tend to fuse and blur. Moreover, Dionysus is a god on the move and in constant change. He abounds in vital energy, making everything grow and sprout. His hallmarks are: wine, wild nature, vegetation and animality; madness and ecstasy; underworld and death; mystery cult and afterlife; sex and love; dance, music and performance; mask and costume; fiction, imagination, vision and miracle. Most of all, he always desires to become present. Thus, we see him arriving from outside or even from the realm of the dead, and he wishes to appear, manifesting himself in his manifold forms and signs as the most epiphanic god (ἐπιφανέστατος θεός).[47]

At the beginning of *HHymn* 7, the performer turns his thoughts to Dionysus through the central marker μνήσομαι. The rhapsodic "I" thus is going to "remember" how the epiphanic god *par excellence* produced an epiphany on the promontory close by the sea.[48] In short, the epic singer will make Dionysus present in all his essential qualities and characteristics by telling how the god showed himself in a sudden apparition. Most of all, it is somehow an "epiphany in an epiphany", since *Homeric Hymns* in principle function on the basis of the model of epiphany. Furthermore, I argue that the ritual concepts of epiphany and mystery function as the decisive motors of the *Hymn to Dionysus* and configure its correct understanding.[49] On the one hand, we can identify the mythic model of the arriving god who seeks recognition but meets resistance, captivation and violence. Through miracles the god, freeing himself, warns his opponent by revealing himself, until he finally punishes sceptical, irreligious people and rewards his followers. On the other hand, myth is complemented by ritual, particularly by the practice of the Dionysian mystery cult where the initiates inside the religious circle are opposed to the uninitiated people outside. It is striking that Euripides' *Bacchae* is based on the identical mythic-ritual scenario.[50] While the longer

---

47 See the inscriptions of Antiochia *CIG* III 3979 und *CIG* 1948; on Dionysus' particular presence and tendency to show himself in an epiphany, see Otto (1933) esp. 70–80; Henrichs (2011).
48 Despite some recent interest, *HHymn* 7 has still attracted relatively little critical attention. See now Nobili (2009); Jaillard (2011); Herrero de Jáuregui (2013) on all three *HHymns* to Dionysus (1, 7, and 26).
49 On epiphany in *HHymn* 7, see Jaillard (2011); Herrero de Jáuregui (2013, 240–1) mentions the aspects of mystery and mystic epiphany for *HHymn* 7 only *en passant*; Nagy (2013a, 659–64, esp. 664) associates the *Hymn's* hidden emphasis on salvation with the hero cult.
50 Seaford (1981), (1996) esp. 39–44; with the review by Bierl (1999); on the *Bacchae* as epiphany, see also Wildberg (2002) 149; Bierl (2004) 45; Bierl (2013b) 214–21. On *HHymn* 7 and the Dionysian concept of resistance that constitutes also the *Bacchae*, see Herrero de Jáuregui (2013) 244–6.

Hymns tend to motivate everything in detail, in this *Hymn* of middle length everything seems to be sketchy, unmotivated, fuzzy and indeterminate. But, as Dominique Jaillard has well shown, this is not a flaw, a sign of lack of care in composition, but it reflects the poetic principle of presenting an adequate picture of this god in "iconic force".[51]

After the entrance formula in which the singer wants to fix his mind on Dionysus by "remembering" (1) how the god once suddenly appeared (ὡς ἐφάνη 2) by the shore, the narration evolves directly from this scene. In a pointillist procedure, the singer-narrator sketches the scene: the god appears on the cliff, between sea and land, in the shape of a very young, almost feminine and good-looking man at the very beginning of puberty. As in the *Bacchae*, he thus comes in human disguise. His dark locks are waving in the wind, a purple cloak over his strong shoulders (1–6). A beautiful, anthropomorphic figure – his outfit promises money and wealth, at least for pirates passing by; all of a sudden, they show up, again unmotivated, sailing over 'the wine-coloured sea' (7), that is already associated with the god through this attribute. Economic greed for ὄλβος, wealth and money, is their driving force. By kidnapping rich and beautiful men and selling them into slavery they make their living. Being all too human, they fail to recognize the god. The entire story is based on different degrees of recognition and misrecognition of the god and his prerogatives that thus appear in a blurred perspective. Inside and outside overlap in similar signs. But for the initiated people inside, recognizing and following the god in the process of his epiphany, Dionysus promises higher values, blessedness, happiness and true pleasure in the beyond, whereas the outsiders simply strive for momentary happiness in this life.

The narration plays with boundaries and frames the nucleus by ring-composition. 'Bad destiny' (κακὸς μόρος 8) is waiting for the people resisting to right understanding of the epiphany, or they wish to avoid it (κακὸν μόρον ἐξαλύοντες 51). The pirates quickly 'jump out' (ἔκθορον 9) from the ship to land to catch the young man when they have seen him (ἰδόντες 8). They also jump out (πήδησαν 52) from the deck into the sea, seeing (52) the terrible punishment of their leader. After the ephebe's seizure the pirates are 'happy in their hearts' (κεχαρημένοι ἦτορ 10) in the sight of the proceeds. And the god calls the steersman, the only person on the ship who recognizes him, κεχαρισμένε θυμῷ (55), 'having achieved beauty and pleasure for the god's heart'. Im-

---

51 Jaillard (2011) 150 and 144–50 (also in relation to the famous Exekias Cup). In the past scholars criticized the flamboyant style, the lack of coherence and poetic talent; see Gemoll (1886) 317; Humbert (1936) 169; Allen, Halliday and Sikes (1936) 379.

mediacy and suddenness are the hallmarks of an epiphany.⁵² Therefore the sketchy narration is marked by signals and markers of urgency and speed. The hymn unfolds in a poetics of suddenness. The narrative steps proceed repeatedly 'all of a sudden' or 'quickly'.⁵³

The hymn permanently oscillates between recognition and misrecognition. On the basis of the stranger's look the pirates surmise – the irony of the hymn – that he might be a son of kings stemming from a divine line (11). Instinctively they forebode the revelation of the god's divine origin, but consciously acknowledge his looks only as an economic indicator. Their attempt to bind him fails, his first miracle. The bonds of willow fall automatically off his hands and feet (12–14).⁵⁴ The god does not take any steps of resistance, but nature acts for him. He sits in silence, 'smiling' (μειδιάων), and remains a detached observer (14), just like Dionysus in Euripides' *Bacchae*.⁵⁵ Seizing the god mirrors and inverts the fact that in his cult, his followers are captivated by him. His frontal gaze with 'dark eyes' (15) means erotic attraction and danger. The steersman is the only one who becomes aware of the divine presence, mediating between the outside and inside. He steers the ship and its crew, sailing in the territory of Dionysus, i.e. the 'wine-faced sea' (7),⁵⁶ on a journey towards him. By means of his mental "communication" with the god the steersman warns his comrades. He realizes that the beautiful ephebe is a god, but cannot say which one (17). Since the bonds could not hold him, not even the ship can do so (18). The present and super-human figure in the here and now could be Zeus, Apollo or Poseidon (19–20) – all three are mighty and terrible gods. The steersman thus sees through the disguise, albeit obliquely. Despite his human

---

52 See Bohrer (2015) 11–37, esp. 15.
53 Regarding the repeated markers of urgency in *HHymn* 7, compare esp. αἶψα (9), τάχα (6, 9, 34), αὐτίκα (16, 23) and ἐξαπίνης (50). On Dionysiac δύναμις, see Detienne (1985) 89–98.
54 He is thus Dionysus Λύσιος or Λυαῖος. On his liberating force, see Eur. *Ba*. 497–98 and Seaford (1996) 190 ad loc. On bonds that fall off automatically, see Eur. *Ba*. 444–8. See also Merkelbach (1988) 103–4. On Dionysus and wonder, see Eur. *Ba*. 248, 449, 667, 693, 716. See also Merkelbach (1988) 109–11. On λύγος, willow or *agnus castus*, as an anti-aphrodisiac, see Versnel (1993) 247. To free from the bonds, on the contrary, thus means licence for sexual union. Pharmacological studies indicate that the consumption of a higher dose leads to a higher sexual activity. Therefore λύγος is as ambivalent as Dionysus. The pirates wish to control his erotic radiance, focusing on the economic value of the captivated youth. Yet, ironically, they bring him in touch with the plant so that his sexual appeal and beauty will even be higher.
55 Compare Eur. *Ba*. 439 (laughter; see Seaford 1996, 186 ad loc.; compare *Ba*. 1021), 621–2 (detached observer). On Dionysus' quiet reaction in *Bacchae*, see ἥσυχος (622, 636).
56 On the epithet οἶνωψ, see Jaillard (2011) 143 n. 28. At Eur. *Ba*. 438 the epithet is applied to Dionysus' cheeks.

shape, the young man is not like mortal humans, but rather resembles the gods (20–1). Therefore the steersman pleads with his fellows to release him, leaving him on land. They should not mistreat him. On the boat he might stir up terrible storms, like the god of the sea (22–4). As steersman, he is still mainly concerned with the men's safety at sea. Soon this will shift into the σωτηρία of the initiates.

The leader of the pirates reviles him with hateful words (25), turning the steersman's reproach of being possessed by a supernatural, demonic power (δαιμόνι' 26, see δαιμόνιοι 17) back on him.[57] The steersman should watch the wind and do his job to steer the sailing boat with hissed sails (26–7). The beautiful captive should be 'the concern of the men' (ἄνδρεσσι μελήσει 27), an allusion to the famous expression in the Homeric epic (Il. 6.492).[58] But the words might allude to homosexual penetration of the female-looking ephebe as well.[59] In full irony, the captain predicts that this mysterious man will lead them to foreign and utopic lands far away; after Egypt and Cyprus even to the Hyperboreans and beyond (28–9). This would be a journey to death, soon to extend beyond the range of mortals. Apollo, Dionysus' complementary brother, abides in the far north, in the fabulous land of the Hyperboreans, associated with myths and cults in Delos and Delphi. The leader, full of greed and hope, anticipates that on this journey the stranger will show them his dear friends and brothers, his possessions in the beyond, since a god, δαίμων, caused them to meet this young man (30–1).[60] Ironically, and according to his everyday diction, the leader associates him with the superhuman. The sailors have indeed encountered a god, who will function sometimes as friend and sometimes as adversary. Thus the god will show who is close and dear to him, according to the logic of the in-group of the initiated. Moreover, he will become manifest through his holy attributes.

Without any insight, the leader hoists the sails, and the wind starts blowing (32–3). The ship is sailing full speed over the stormy sea, the ropes are tight (33–4). At this point prediction becomes reality. Then, right away, the second stage of Dionysus' epiphany begins. All of a sudden, θαύματα ἔργα, 'things, deeds of marvel', 'appear' (ἐφαίνετο 34). The verb clearly takes up the phrase ὡς ἐφάνη (2), 'when he appeared', at the beginning. The ἔργα are Dionysian sym-

---

57 On Dionysus as δαίμων, see Eur. Ba. 272.
58 See Prauscello (2007), who thinks that the expression implies that the steersman is somehow effeminate, like the young man. Herrero de Jáuregui (2013) 247 n. 24 suggests that it 'could be understood also as a threatening mockery of the scarce masculinity of Dionysos himself, from the viewpoint of the pirate, similarly to Lycurgus or Pentheus'.
59 On sex in mysteries, see Burkert (1987) 104–6.
60 On Dionysus as δαίμων, see Eur. Ba. 272. On δαίμων in general, see Nagy (2013a) 109–13.

bols, signs or attributes. In a sort of Dionysian semiotics these attributes become alive, direct agents standing for their divine origin: sweet wine of fine smell splashed in the boat (36–7). The reaction to this unexpected presence of the main features of the god is amazement (37). Then, at once, at the top of the sail, on both sides, a vine spreads out, with many grape clusters hanging thereupon. Around the mast black ivy is winding around, teeming with blossoms, the fruit full of beauty and pleasure like the god himself (and his attendant symbols). The benches hold cultic garlands (38–41).[61] The Dionysian, affecting all the senses, takes possession of the ship. It is a series of positive signals, making the ship into a cup, a vessel of his inebriating drink and plants. The positive warning, focusing on epiphanic signs of χάρις, beauty and pleasure, is successful, as far as the crew is concerned. Realizing the miracles and responding with amazement and fear, the pirates are ready for a reversal. They thus start giving loud orders to the steersman to return to the land (42–4). It remains an open question whether they want to flee or to set free the kidnapped young man. Be that as it may, on his element of the sea, the god becomes present through signs that belong to his power on land. In various festivals he is envisaged as arriving from the sea, entering into the cities in triumphant processions.[62] The steersman cannot react since, at this point, Dionysus starts with the third phase of his epiphany, now of a wild, terrible nature. With these manifestations the god intends to punish his opponents and trigger new metamorphic changes (44–53). Dionysus typically turns into a terrible lion to scare everybody with his roaring voice (44–5). In the *Bacchae* Pentheus is also frightened by imaginary monsters and wild beasts.[63] In addition, in the middle of the ship he made a bear with a shaggy neck (45–6). Like a director, he makes this additional beast, another miracle, appear on the imaginary stage, put forward through narration. After all, the singer summarizes the entire epiphanic scene with the expression σήματα φαίνων (46) – thus he made his 'signs appear'. These are the features of the god enacted in a mental and narrative act. Since a god cannot have a direct, full-fledged epiphany, he must recur to signs. The epic singer embeds them into a narrative plot full of beauty and pleasure. They have to be read, decoded and understood by the figures inside and by the recipient. As Dionysus oscillates between positive and negative signs, it makes sense that he does not

---

[61] On ivy and vine as cultic attributes, see Blech (1982) 183–210. On garlands, see Merkelbach (1988) 99.
[62] See Burkert (1983) 200–1.
[63] Agaue believes that she hunted a lion (*Ba.* 1196, 1215) or a beast (1204, 1237) instead of Pentheus; Dionysus is seen as a beast (920), bull (618, 920, 1018) or snake/dragon (1019). On frightening terror in initiation, see Merkelbach (1988) 104.

refrain from making use of his violent side either. As stage director he makes the bear in raging voracity rear up and the lion, his new disguise, on top of the deck, look horrific to them (47–8). The men of the crew, in their terror, thrust themselves into the stern, seeking help from the steersman, who has a heart that is moderate (48–50), thinking of salvation (σαόφρονα θυμόν 49). They stand still in terror and marvel (50). But the lion, all of a sudden, leaps up and seizes (ἕλ' 51) the leader of the pirates (50–1), he who had seized the god (ἑλόντες 9) at the beginning. The opponent will be devoured, but the men under the rule of this leader, in their astonishment and terror, trying to flee from their bad destiny, leap all together out into the divine sea. They turn into dolphins (51–3), the Dionysian and most intelligent "fish" and the animal that brings salvation from the sea.[64]

The jump from the deck means death. But the transformation into dolphins means new life. It emblematizes the entire paradox of Dionysian ritual and its mythic narrative complex, bound to the logic of the mystery. The jump into the sea or into a liquid is a typical motif of mysteries. I only recall the famous sentences on the Pelinna gold-leaves: Ταῦρος ἐς γάλα ἔθορες ('bull, you jumped into milk' OF 485 Bernabé = Graf and Johnston 26a.3, b.3) / αἶψα εἰς γάλα ἔθορες ('quickly, you jumped into milk' OF 486 Bernabé = Graf and Johnston 26a.4) – followed by κριὸς εἰς γάλα ἔπεσες ('ram, you fell into milk' OF 485 and 486 Bernabé = Graf and Johnston 26a.5, b.4).[65] The initiate experiences death only to be reborn again. He dives into the unknown, the wine-coloured sea associated with the god. He flees 'bad destiny' (see κακὸν μόρον ἐξαλύοντες 51) to reach salvation,[66] and thus a good and blessed destiny. We can compare the typically mystic σύνθετον, a summary sentence: ἔφυγον κακόν, εὗρον ἄμεινον ('I fled the bad, I found the better' Dem. 18.259). Furthermore, Eric Csapo and others have pointed out that the myth represents the aetiology of the Dionysian chorus, dancing and leaping around the chorus leader.[67] The ideal chorus leader is the κυβερνήτης, the steersman, the one who steers both the ship and its men through the dangerous sea, likewise the circular chorus. According to Parmenides (fr. 12.3 DK), a female δαίμων 'steers' the cosmos (δαίμων ἣ πάντα κυβερνᾷ), while stars are envisaged as choruses as well.[68] Heraclitus (fr. 41 DK) believes that a certain insight in logos steers all through all (εἶναι γὰρ ἓν τὸ σοφόν, ἐπίστασθαι γνώμην, ὁτέη

---

64 See Burkert (1983) 196–212.
65 For αἶψα and θορεῖν, see also HHymn 7.9.
66 In the Orphic Hymn 74.5 Leucothea is adressed as bringing relief from the 'miserable destiny' at sea (θνητῶν οἴκτρον μέρον εἰν ἁλὶ λύεις).
67 Csapo (2003) esp. 90–4. See also Lonsdale (1993) 93–9.
68 See Csapo (2008).

ἐκυβέρνησε πάντα διὰ πάντων – 'Wisdom is one thing: to know the Thought (Intelligence) by which things are steered through all (ways)', translation M. Marcovich fr. 85). From archaic and early classical times we possess presentations of dolphin dancers and comasts in cyclic formations on vases.[69] Salvation and blessedness come out of the sea. They also derive from the singing and dancing chorus and from the choruses of the Nereids accompanying the dolphins. This applies especially for the μύσται. Csapo cites the beautiful *Orphic Hymn* 24 (Quandt) to the Nereids.[70] Their chorus is accompanied by the chorus of 'wet-domiciled, leapers, winding about the waves, sea-wandering dolphins sea-surge-resounding, blue-flashing' (ὑδρόδομοι, σκιρτηταί, ἑλισσόμενοι περὶ κῦμα / ποντοπλάνοι δελφῖνες, ἁλιρρόθιοι, κυαναυγεῖς *Orphic Hymn* 24.7–8). Comparable sea-leaps are known from Arion and Melicertes, as both are associated with transformation, transport to new territories, and with Dionysian mysteries.[71] Next to Dionysus, both mythic figures were linked to Poseidon and Apollo. This fact might be the reason why the steersman believes that these gods play a role (19–20). According to the famous story told in the *Iliad* (6.131–7), Dionysus, when threatened by Lycurgus, the typical θεομάχος, with violence, takes refuge in the sea, 'diving (δύσεθ') into the wave of the sea', *Il.* 6.136), and the Nereid Thetis receives the frightened god into her bosom, or womb (ὑπεδέξατο κόλπωι / δειδιότα *Il.* 6.136–7). In the *Homeric Hymn* 7 the roles are changed: it is now Dionysus who frightens the pirates so that they jump into the sea.

A further evidence for a link to mysteries is the fact that Dionysus takes pity on the steersman,[72] who as a moderate and wise person has always seen that there is a god behind the stranger. The anonymous steersman expresses the idea of the meaning in a generalized program of action.[73] He is the one who steers, and he both belongs to the group of pirates and does not. Moreover, he stands in strong opposition to their leader (ἀρχός) who does not recognize the divine. Dionysus holds the good steersman back and makes him πανόλβιος (54), a typical quality of initiates. The adjective ὄλβιος, likewise μάκαρ, has a double meaning, according to its occurrence in the unmarked or marked sense respectively. For the uninitiated it simply means 'fortunate' and 'rich', in a sec-

---

[69] See Csapo (2003) esp. 78–90.
[70] Csapo (2003) 93.
[71] See Csapo (2003) 86 with n. 55, regarding Palaemon. See also the *Orphic Hymn* 75.
[72] Pity for the select person, encountering the mystic fears and sufferings with his group – is perhaps another characteristic of mysteries; see Merkelbach (1988) 148, 168, 186, regarding Longus' *Daphnis and Chloe*.
[73] On the lack of names in the context of a general detachment, esp. in local regards, to express the idea Panhellenism, see Herrero de Jáuregui (2013) 242 with n. 21.

ular and material sense. But for initiates, when they have reached deeper knowledge, it bears the meaning of 'happy' or 'blessed'.[74] We can compare the passage to Sappho's recently found Brothers Song, where we encounter a similar discourse about material profit through sea-traffic, that assumes also a mystic meaning.[75] On this basis we can speculate about the narrative setting of pirates and seafaring.[76] It thus becomes evident that the related motifs do not reflect only a historical development, but allude to a deeper mystic subtext. Dionysus makes the steersman 'completely blessed' (54), since he excels everyone else in the group of happy dancers who are leading a blissful existence as Dionysian animals after their transformation. As mammal fish, the dolphins (δελφῖνες) are named after the female uterus, δελφύς. Dionysus' birth from the womb of his mother Semele, impregnated in love by Zeus, is the decisive feature of the god, even in his self-presentation (56–7; see 1, 58). The leap from the womb in an early birth, triggered by Zeus' lightning, is the very first, the original appearance of the epiphanic god. The initiate, so to speak, returns into the sea, the maternal womb. Similar to Dionysus sinking into the bosom or womb of Thetis under the sea (*Il.* 6.136–7), the initiate mentioned in a gold-leaf in Thurii says 'I have sunk beneath the breast/lap of the Lady, the Chthonian Queen' (Δεσποίνας δὲ ὑπὸ κόλπον ἔδυν χθονίας βασιλείας *OF* 488 Bernabé = Graf and Johnston 5.7).[77]

The prominence of a mystic subtext becomes again clear by the fact that the much more detailed narration in Ovid's *Metamorphoses* (3.582–691) makes the context of mysteries explicit. The episode is put in a frame that mentions twice the new Bacchic mysteries (*morisque novi sacra* 3.581 and *Baccheaque sacra* Ov. *Met.* 3.691). In Ovid's first-person narration in front of Pentheus, the steersman is called Acoetes, telling the story about the epiphany of the most present god – *nec enim praesentior illo / est deus* (3.658–9). In the god's body

---

74 See Nagy (2013a) 314–44. For μάκαρ and ὄλβιος in archaic poetry, see De Heer (1968) esp. 28–38, 51–55. For the μακαρισμός, the praise of the blessed condition for those witnessing the mysteries, see *HHymn* 2.480–2; Soph. fr. 837 Radt; Eur. *Ba.* 73–4; in several instances we encounter the mystic terms on the Orphic gold-leaves: τρισόλβιος *OF* 485.1, 486.1; ὄλβιος *OF* 485.7, 488.3, 9, 489.3, 490.3; μακαριστός *OF* 488.9 Bernabé. Ploutos, the personification of riches and wealth, is also involved with mysteries, esp. in the Eleusinian context: see Burkert (1987) 20.
75 See Bierl (2016) 317–23, 334. Compare πανόλβιος with μάκαρες und πολύολβοι (Sappho, Brothers Song 19–20) On Charaxus as programmatic name, containing χαρά, joy, see Bierl (2016) 319 with n. 37. On αἶψα, see Sappho, Brothers Song 24; on storm, see ἐκ μεγάλαν ἀήταν ('from big storms', Sappho, Brothers Song 15); on safety, see Sappho, Brothers Song 11.
76 Regarding Sappho's Brothers Song, see Bierl (2016) esp. 318.
77 The expression might allude to sexual practices; on Sabazius/Dionysus as θεὸς διὰ κόλπου and rites of symbolic sexual union with the god, see Burkert (1987) 106.

of maiden beauty Acoetes recognized the divine (*corpore numen in isto est* 3.612). Moreover, the name Acoetes could allude to the sexual aspects of mysteries. As ἀκοίτης he is the potential lover of the homosexually-marked god. It is well known that erotic practices, remainders of the first encounter with sexuality in puberty initiation, played a certain role in Dionysiac mysteries.[78] Since he is the select and the only person left, his closeness to the god is imagined in a sexual union with him. In Ovid's version also, the choral dimension of the whirling dolphins is made explicit, 'as they play in the form of a chorus' in the water (*inque chori ludunt speciem* 3.685).

In the *Homeric Hymn to Dionysus* everything remains more hidden, in the dark, and enigmatic. The recipient must decipher and interpret the signs that the god makes to appear (σήματα φαίνων 46). Therefore, the sketchy and pointillist poetics is not only a matter of a new technique based on the iconic, on images and the imaginary,[79] but it exerts a direct function in the narration, associated with the decisive feature of the mystic quality that unfolds in epiphany. Dionysus feels pity for the outstanding and select person, who must endure the mystic fears and sufferings together with his group, and saves his life. The steersman of moderate character, possessing sound thought, experiences salvation and blessedness. Choral dance belongs to this elevated state of mysteries. The dolphins, the enthusiasts of music and dance, leap and wind around the ship in the Dionysian element of sea, associated with wine. The steersman, as representative and surrogate of Dionysus, stands in the middle, on the ship, steering their choral movement. But behind him, at a second remove, is Dionysus, the divine chorus leader. He addresses the still frightened steersman with the θάρσει ('Have courage!' 55), a typical code word in the context of mysteries.[80] He continues to address him in the vocative: † δῖ' ἑκάτωρ τῶι ἐμῶι κεχαρισμένε θυμῶι, 'radiant and divine man, affected by a power from afar, who has become beauty and pleasure for my heart' (55). He became divine, since a god reaches his heart, while the god is filled by the pleasure of the new initiate's attitude. The address stands in stark contrast to the beginning, when the pirates were happy in their hearts (κεχαρημένοι ἦτορ 10) in prospect of their anticipated profit, having seized the young man. The reciprocity of χάρις is achieved through the steersman's σαόφρων θυμός ('moderate mind' 49) that pleases the θυμός of the

---

[78] See Burkert (1987) 104–6.
[79] See Jaillard (2011).
[80] See Firmicus Maternus, *De errore profanarum religionum* 22: θαρρεῖτε μύσται. In the context of mysteries, see Joly (1955); Merkelbach (1988) 52, 155, 175. On θάρσει in the relevation of divine identity and epiphany, see *Il.* 24.460; *HHymn* 2.120, 268; *HHymn* 5.193 (in the ironical, playful way).

god (55), but even more so in view of the beautiful chorus. Its leader is the steersman, but even he is driven by a transcendent force. It is Dionysus himself, the hidden and divine chorus leader at the very centre of his whirling chorus. The chorus reaches out to the ship, the entire sea, to the sky to the cosmos. Everything has become a Dionysian σῆμα and thus a μνῆμα, singing, dancing and creating a synaesthesia of choral performance. Sound, sight, smell – all together envelope the god, the origin and destination, in total pleasure. Therefore, in the last step of his epiphany, he finally reveals himself with a solemn self-representation: εἰμὶ δ' ἐγὼ Διόνυσος ἐρίβρομος ὃν τέκε μήτηρ / Καδμηῒς Σεμέλη Διὸς ἐν φιλότητι μιγεῖσα ('I am Dionysus, the one with the very thundering sound, whom as mother bore Semele, daughter of Cadmus, having mixed in love with Zeus' 56–7).[81] In the very first verses of Euripides' *Bacchae* (1–3), itself built on the model of an epiphany, Dionysus, as god coming from afar, somehow resumes these words: Ἥκω Διὸς παῖς τήνδε Θηβαίαν χθόνα / Διόνυσος, ὃν τίκτει ποθ' ἡ Κάδμου κόρη / Σεμέλη λοχευθεῖσ' ἀστραπηφόρωι πυρί. In the self-revelation of the *Homeric Hymn* 7 Dionysus emphasizes his roaring sound, i.e. his acoustic dimension as choral god.[82] By mentioning also Semele and Zeus, he further stresses his epiphanic quality, his birth in a sudden lightning. Dionysus speaks of the mingling in love, the main feature of the hymnic and cosmic dimension of the Orphic prehistory of the hymn.[83] Inside the story, the god of choral dance, mystery and epiphany has finally revealed himself; that is what the performance re-enacted qua song. Thus he is pleased by the beauty of the chorus that has been narrated in its very making, and the chorus leader, whom he kept back and saved. At this point, after the final revelation, the singer shifts to his farewell formula of χαῖρε – 'farewell and find pleasure, son of the nice-looking Semele' (58). Since Dionysus took pleasure in the beauty of song inside the narrative, he should also take pleasure in the performance of the actual song outside the narrative. The performance brought the god to life in his essence, the divine force of song and mysteries. The beauty of the god, the son of Semele with beautiful eyes and responsible for wonderful music and song, radiates grace. In a chain of musical transmission, song is transferred from the divine choral leader Dionysus via the initiated steersman and his chorus of dolphins to the performer of the hymn. Therefore he prays to receive his share of grace also for future song production. In the logic of the χάρις-reciprocity the perform-

---

81 For such self-revelations in later texts, see Merkelbach (1988) 53. For the expression ἐν φιλότητι and love as features of the hymns of the oldest form, see Nagy (2009/10) 88.
82 On the acoustic dimension, see Aillard (2011) 149. On the sound aspect of the epiphanic parodos of the *Bacchae*, see Bierl (2013b).
83 See Nagy (2009/10) 88.

er states his deep loyalty to the god of song and mysteries. He has offered pleasure to the god by telling how the god took pleasure in his chorus, the first initiates of his mysteries, narrated in the very process of their coming into being. The rhapsodic singer is well aware of the fact that this "mind act" of re-enacting the god accomplished the song about the god and made the god thus present. Since the god took pleasure in it, the performer hopes that the god's radiance and beauty will extend this effect to his next epic song and all future performance. As musical follower, he knows very well: 'It is impossible for me, who once has forgotten you, to order a sweet song' (οὐδέ πηι ἔστι / σεῖό γε ληθόμενον γλυκερὴν κοσμῆσαι ἀοιδήν 58–9). This self-referential statement makes Dionysus, the principle of choral song, hymn and mysteries, the very source of the performance, at least in this particular domain. He never asked a Muse or Dionysus to receive inspiration at the beginning of the song. But by remembering him, making him present in a mind and speech act, he is mentally connected with him so that Dionysian grace and beauty automatically enters and vivifies his song.[84]

In the fragmentary *Hymn* 1, as well to Dionysus, obviously focusing on his birth, we have a similar self-referential connection of the performance with the god of music and song. Indeed, in the very end where the hymn shifts to the performative frame and new epic songs, the hymn speaks about the rhapsodic singers in the plural, including the entire guild and all future singers of re-performances. After a prayer for favour ἵληθ' εἰραφιῶτα γυναιμανές (1.16), addressing the god with very marked epithets, the 'insewn' (or 'the one of the shape of the ram') and 'the one maddening women', the performer emphasizes that he is well aware that the singers must mentally connect with their source Dionysus. 'We singers sing of you in the beginning and in the end, and it is impossible to have one's mind disconnect from you as anyone recalls to mind the holy song' (οἱ δέ σ' ἀοιδοὶ / ᾄδομεν ἀρχόμενοι λήγοντές τ', οὐδέ πηι ἔστι / σεῖ' ἐπιληθομένωι ἱερῆς μεμνῆσθαι ἀοιδῆς *HHymn* 1.16–18). Any performer thus reconnects with the god while making him present. The mental connection must be accomplished in the introductory part, where the performer usually speaks about his performative intention to bring the god, in this case the god responsible for song, music and dance, to mind, making him present through a third-person narration. After the narration, the mental contact must be installed again, as it happens here. The god has been pleased by the song, he should take beauty and pleasure in it, the god sewn into the thigh of Zeus but also "sewn" into the texture of the hymn; ὕμνος means 'woven texture' as song and the rhapsodes are the singers

---

[84] See also Nagy (2013a) 659–64, esp. 663–4.

who "sew" songs together (from ῥάπτω, to 'sew, stitch').[85] In the composition in performance or in its written manifestation, the singer puts his song together, picking the decisive features to ensure the god's presence. As the god born by Semele in the most epiphanic birth triggered by lightning and thunder, Dionysus must be sewn into his father's thigh serving as second womb until he can be born as a mature baby. Also, his songs are palimpsests, overlays and mixtures of textual levels, hybrid compositions taken from different traditions and sewn together. Thus the farewell address χαῖρε, the appeal to take pleasure (καὶ σὺ μὲν οὕτω χαῖρε Διώνυσ' εἰραφιῶτα, / σὺν μητρὶ Σεμέληι ἥν περ καλέουσι Θυώνην 1.19–20), is addressed again to Dionysus in his quality as the insewn god and to his real mother, who bears the name Thyone, etymologically associated with "smoke" and "mind", and thus 'energy' in poetic and epiphanic perspective. But the name εἰραφιώτης could perhaps also be linked to εἴρω, 'to put in series', 'knit', thus another hint at the level of composition and performance.

Epiphany and choral festivity in the *Hymn to Apollo*

In the longer Hymns the main gods, to whose honour the hymns are sung, are often in interaction with other Olympian gods. This was not the case in the long *Hymn to Dionysus*, where he acts as a singular and independent figure. But, to some degree, we can put the famous HHymn 3 to Apollo next to HHymn 7. Besides common themes, such as a focus on song, epiphany, arrival, and dolphins, it is well known that both gods exert a complementary function and are in close contact with each other in the complex polytheistic system.

At this point, we must mainly leave aside the long discussion about the *Hymn*'s unity. Much ink has been spilled over an original divide between the Delian and the Delphic part or an original cohesion. Today most critics subscribe to a unitarian view. In this regard, Jenny Strauss Clay's opinion that highlights the Panhellenic ideology and the mythic-narrative coherence is the most influential. As for the other longer *Hymns*, Clay argues that this *Hymn*, fulfilling a specific Panhellenic agenda, narrates the installation of fundamental deeds and honours of Apollo as well, after the establishment of Zeus' order.[86] David Ruhnken was the first scholar who pleaded for the *Hymn*'s separation into two parts, recogniz-

---

85 See Nagy (1996) 64.
86 Clay (1989) 17–94; see also Stehle (1996) 177–96.

ing that lines 165–78 correspond to the typical ending strain.[87] Both parts constitute a coherent entity in themselves, but the Pythian part, despite a prologue, does not have the typical hymnic opening. In a separatist vein, Wilamowitz famously argued that the Pythian part was a later addition, imitating the earlier independent Delian part so that they were put together at a later stage.[88] Another attractive theory has been developed by Richard Martin, who argues that the apparent division reflects a competition of two performers, the first part in the Homeric mode, the second in the Hesiodic mode.[89] But be that as it may, if we focus on later re-performance we realize that both units were artfully put together over a longer period of revisions and adjustments so that our unified single *Hymn*, where it is hardly possible to recognize the stitching seam, perfectly works to demonstrate Apollo's essence. Following an evolutionary model, in which single units grow to a perfect unity over a diachronic chain of compositions in re-performances or orally based re-adjustments, we can just look on how the *Hymn* functions in a neounitarian way.[90]

The two parts correspond also in the microstructure.[91] At the beginning and the end of each part we encounter passages that focus on epiphany and music in a double ring-composition. After all, we can speak of an aesthetics of framing, looping and *mise en abyme* effects. These features serve again to make the god present. Like his complementary brother Dionysus, Apollo is extremely ambivalent, but much less mysterious in blurring binary differences. As the 'God of Afar' (Wilamowitz), Apollo is strangely removed and yet very near. His effect as Loxias is of "oblique" quality in dual polarities. This trait becomes particularly prominent in his oracular speech, giving only signs to decipher (σημαίνειν, see Heraclitus fr. 93 DK).[92] Sometimes he seems rather isolated, speechless and enigmatic, despite his responsibility for assemblies and political council. This means that, as the god of the bow and arrows, Apollo is brutal, violent and frightening, but at the same time, as the god of the lyre and chorality, he is idyllic, giving

---

87 Ruhnken (1749).
88 Wilamowitz-Moellendorff (1916) 440–62; West (1975) pleads for the opposite: the Delian part would be a later composition, imitating the Pythian, put together by Cynaethus of Chios. Burkert (1979) argues that the occasion of the *Hymn* was the Delian-Pythian festival organized by Polycrates in 523/22 BC.
89 Martin (2000); for a history and reassessment, see Chappell (2011). For further literature on the *HHymn* 3, see Förstel (1979); Miller (1986); Martin (2000); Bergren (2008) 131–60; Peponi (2009); Nagy (2008/09) 196–206, (2009/10) 12–20, (2011), (2013b); Olson (2017).
90 See Nagy (2012) esp. 30. On the evolutionary model, see Bierl (2015) 186–91.
91 On a survey of "paired affiliations", see Martin (2000) 409.
92 Fr. 93 DK = 14 Marcovich (translation): 'The Lord whose is the oracle in Delphi neither speaks out nor conceals, but gives a sign (σημαίνει)'.

pleasure and beauty. Heraclitus famous fragment 51 DK οὐ ξυνιᾶσιν ὅκως διαφερόμενον ἑωυτῶι ὁμολογέει· παλίντονος [παλίντροπος] ἁρμονίη ὅκωσπερ τόξου καὶ λύρης ('men do not understand how what is being brought apart comes together with itself: there is a connexion/harmony caused by opposite tensions (v.l. turning back), that of the bow and of the lyre') reflects the complex ambivalence of the god and the palintropic harmony' also reflects the situation of this hymn.[93]

Again at the very beginning, we have the voice of the rhapsodic "I" who wishes to make the god present: Μνήσομαι οὐδὲ λάθωμαι Ἀπόλλωνος ἑκάτοιο – 'I am going to bring to mind and never pass over Apollo, the far-shooter' (HHymn 3.1). The narration immediately shifts with a relative pronoun into a scene of arrival (2–12). The arriving god triggers terrible fear because of his bow. All tremble and spring up when he bends the bow (2–4). Only his mother can unstring it, after which she takes it off her son's shoulders, hangs it on a peg and make her son sit down (5–9). Leto is the main focus of the narration relating how this god came into existence on Delos, another typical scene of a revealing epiphany. But before shifting into the narration about Apollo's birth, the poetic "I" stops to think about the contents of the song to be sung: Πῶς τάρ σ' ὑμνήσω πάντως εὔυμνον ἐόντα; / πάντηι γάρ τοι, Φοῖβε, νομὸς βεβλήαται ἀοιδῆς – 'how shall I sing of you who in all ways are a worthy of a good song? / For everywhere, Phoebus, the whole range of song is fallen to you' (19–20, translation after H. G. Evelyn-White). The whole world is resounding with song about him, the god of music. In reciprocal fashion, he is the subject of good song and therefore songs are sung everywhere about him. But the climax, in this respect, is the rocky and empty island of Delos. Yet it took some time to reach this rather unexpected status. All islands trembled and felt fear, when only thinking about granting his pregnant mother the license to give birth to him (47–8). Since many islands did not grant Leto, on her long trip through the Greek world (29–46), permission, Delos must be praised for her courage for having done so. But first, afraid of the hubristic evildoer Apollo (67) and his violent behaviour, Delos is eager to make an agreement with Leto. As a matter of fact, the rocky island fears that the terrible god could scorn her and make her fall into the sea. Since nobody would care – nobody lives there (78) – Delos demands a temple (80) so that many people can come on θεωρίαι, holy missions, to celebrate annual festivals there (81–82). Leto swears the oath, after which a miraculous birth can take place (83–119). As soon as the baby Apollo has eaten of the

---

93 The translation is based on M. Marcovich (fr. 27). On the 'palintropic harmony', see also Bergren (2008) 154. On a brief survey of Apollo, see Burkert (1985) 143–9.

divine food, all cords cannot hold him any more in his bed. Freeing himself, he at once raises a claim on the κίθαρις (his lyre), the bow and prophecy (127–32): εἴη μοι κίθαρίς τε φίλη καὶ καμπύλα τόξα, / χρήσω δ' ἀνθρώποισι Διὸς νημερτέα βουλήν (131–2). Soon he starts walking through the wasteland, and all gods are amazed (133–5). Wonder is the typical reaction to an epiphany: this is an apparition, not before men, but before his fellow gods, who are quite afraid of this apparently outstanding and exceptional god (2–4). In contrast to the other gods, Apollo is not seen in an anthropomorphic disguise.

Apollo's birth is pure wonder: his paraphernalia triggering astonishment are his bow and his lyre. Music will be the field where he produces marvels on Delos and elsewhere. As a god walking on the heights, always close to Mount Olympus, he looks down to his island where the oaths are quickly fulfilled (140–5). The Delian part ends with two most self-referential passages, where hymnic music is put *en abyme* in order to show the god in his essential nature (146–78). Looking down, he recognizes marvellous choruses. At this point the singer addresses the god directly and speaks about how he takes pleasure (ἐπιτέρπεαι ἦτορ 146) in the first Delian competition: 'there the long-robed Ionians gather in your honour with their children and chaste wives: with boxing and dancing and song' (147–9). Engaging Apollo to facilitate his presence, they please him (μνησάμενοι τέρπουσιν 150) whenever they re-perform the song in the ἀγών (150), the contests taking place at the occasion of the annually recurring festival. Especially through refined and beautiful choral hymns, the performers are mentally linked with the god in a χάρις-relationship of reciprocity from aetiological beginnings. Whenever a stranger would join them and see their grace (151–5), he would say that these dancers are 'immortal and ageless' (151). This means that the performers, connecting with the god and with the original choruses, gain an almost divine status in the eyes of later generations. It is as if they received from Apollo, as they pleased him, all his divine beauty and grace. This potential visitor would himself be delighted in his heart (τέρψαιτο δὲ θυμόν 153), watching the grace (ἴδοιτο χάριν ... εἰσορόων 153–4) of the dancers and the magnificent festival. Moreover, he becomes the ideal emblem of any future audience, enchanted by the choral spectacle and later by the monodic-rhapsodic recitation of the *Hymn* in itself. In this unfolding chain of performances and re-performances in diachrony, Apollo and his Delian Maidens will have their eternal epiphany. Through hymnic song and via his attendants, the god will be present forever; both their fame will never perish (ὅου κλέος οὔποτ' ὀλεῖται 156). Thus, the quintessentially epic ideology of the κλέος ἄφθιτον,[94] the undying glory and memory

---

[94] See Nagy (2013a) 26–31.

of the heroic past, will be transferred to the very presence of the Olympian god and his medium. Moreover, all future re-performers of hymns praising Apollo, the source of their beauty, will have again a model, the Delian Maidens, a form of local Muses, the subject 'of great marvel' and 'never-ending fame' (156):

> πρὸς δὲ τόδε μέγα θαῦμα, ὅου κλέος οὔποτ' ὀλεῖται,
> κοῦραι Δηλιάδες Ἑκατηβελέταο θεράπναι·
> αἵ τ' ἐπεὶ ἂρ πρῶτον μὲν Ἀπόλλωνα ὑμνήσωσιν,
> αὖτις δ' αὖ Λητώ τε καὶ Ἄρτεμιν ἰοχέαιραν,
> μνησάμεναι ἀνδρῶν τε παλαιῶν ἠδὲ γυναικῶν   160
> ὕμνον ἀείδουσιν, θέλγουσι δὲ φῦλ' ἀνθρώπων.
> πάντων δ' ἀνθρώπων φωνὰς καὶ κρεμβαλιαστὺν
> μιμεῖσθ' ἴσασιν· φαίη δέ κεν αὐτὸς ἕκαστος
> φθέγγεσθ'· οὕτω σφιν καλὴ συνάρηρεν ἀοιδή.
>
> And on top of that, there is great thing of wonder, the fame of which will never perish, the Delian Maidens, attendants of the one who shoots from afar.
> So when they sing their hymn in honour of Apollo first and foremost,
> followed in turn by Leto and Artemis, shooter of arrows,
> they keep in mind men of the past and women too,
> as they sing the hymn, and they enchant all different kinds of humanity.
> All humans' voices and rhythms
> they know how to re-enact. And each single person would say that his own voice
> was their voice. That is how their beautiful song has each of its parts fitting in place.
> HHymn. 3.158–64 (translation G. Nagy)

The Deliades are another personified emblem of local and Panhellenic memory, not only making present the god but also the first human performers of the past. As perfect singers they are experts of μίμησις, re-enactment. Through voice they thus re-enact all possible performers who praised the god in the progressive chain of choral competitions. Everyone in this chain, even future rhapsodes performing at the annual Delian festival, would say that they shape their songs on the model of the ideal maiden singers and in full harmony with them.[95]

At this point, at the end of the Delian part, the farewell address goes to Apollo and Artemis (165), and finally to the Delian Maidens (166). They all should take pleasure (χαίρετε δ' ὑμεῖς πᾶσαι 166) in the current song sung by the poetic "I" as well. Now comes the surprise: they should keep him in mind even in the future (ἐμεῖο δὲ καὶ μετόπισθε / μνήσασθ' 166–7) – a very unique phrase. Nor-

---

[95] See Nagy (1990a) 42–5; on the mimesis of the Delian Maidens, see Nagy (2008/09) 198–206; Peponi (2009) esp. 62–8; Nagy (2013b) esp. 227–40; on the choral aesthetics of the entire passage, see Peponi (2009). On the festive poetics and aesthetics, see Bierl (2011) 125–38, esp. 136–7; on "kinesthetic empathy" and audience response, see now Olson (2017) 158–63.

mally it should be the turn of the performer to remember the local Muses and, in the last instance, Apollo himself. But now the Delian Muses should remember him, the rhapsodic "I" – as if he were the god; when someone in later generations should come and ask 'O Maidens, who is for you the most pleasurable of singers that travels here? In whom do you take the most pleasure?' (169–70), they should respond: τυφλὸς ἀνήρ, οἰκεῖ δὲ Χίωι ἔνι παιπαλοέσσηι, / τοῦ πᾶσαι μετόπισθεν ἀριστεύουσιν ἀοιδαί ('It is a blind man, and he lives in Chios, a rugged land, and all his songs will in the future prevail as the very best'. (171–3). At this point, by changing into the first person plural, he speaks in the name of the entire guild of the Homeridae. They, including himself, promise to carry the Delian Maidens' fame all over the world. The listeners of the performance will believe, since it is true and genuine (ἐπεὶ καὶ ἐτήτυμόν ἐστιν 176) (174–6).

This famous end of the Delian part thus highlights the original essence of the god by focusing on the medium in a self-referential manner. The epiphany evolves through the medium and the performance. In a looping effect the god manifests himself at the top of the cascade of hymnic singers. In a diachronic chain of hymns we pursue a long line of performances sung by his Delian attendants; via numerous choral re-performances as perfect re-enactments inspired by these Muses, we finally come to the monodic-rhapsodic hymn, our *Hymn to Apollo*. The text even throws a glance into the future. The god, the origin of song and music, and his Muses will always be praised in further re-performances. But next to the god and the Delian Maidens, now the performer/composer of this perfect *Hymn* comes into the play. With him the first chain of free and fluid performances comes to an end. He claims to have sung the best hymn. Thus, from now on, the local Muses should not re-enact the original performance of the first performer, but this very best version, his own. The Delian Maidens do not need to inspire him, the best rhapsode, but they should, on the contrary, start now with a new chain of tradition. The new "original" derives from an anonymous blind man from Chios (172). In the seal the poetic "I" makes an indirect claim on Homer, the one who 'fits the songs together', from ὁμῶς ἀραρίσκω.[96] But he does not mention him explicitly. As a sort of new origin of the rhapsodic school of the Homeridae in Chios, he seals the tradition, implicitly giving it back to "Homer". From now on, the Delian Maidens can only re-enact this "Homeric" version. The shift to the "we" (174) implies that later rhapsodes of this school will from this point on only re-perform this very best epic song, our *Homeric Hymn to Apollo*. They will sing as if it came from the Delian Maidens, and the

---

[96] See Nagy (2008/09) 206–8.

future listeners will believe it, because it is the customary tradition to give it back to them as the local Muses. However, from this moment on they will only 'imitate' (see μιμεῖσθαι 163) the voice of "Homer". The entire chain and diachronic cascade is hold together by the reciprocal concepts of χάρις (grace and beauty), τέρψις (pleasure) and θέλξις (enchantment). They also unify the performers and the audience in an almost divine experience of festive performativity. At last behind everything Apollo, the origin and essence of song, comes to the fore in an unfolding epiphany of a hymn that continues.

The rhapsodic "I" cannot stop singing about Apollo, mediator of these amazing effects and emotions, and moves into the Pythian part (177–8). The god is addressed, pursuing his way from East to West, from Lycia, Miletus to the Delian festival, and finally to Delphi, where he is celebrated in choruses as well (179–85). The arrival of Apollo in Delphi will be the central theme of the second part of the *Hymn*. But, in the temporal order of events, the song starts from the end, how he leaves the earth from Delphi, arriving on Mount Olympus. The scene stands in parallel to the terrible arrival at the beginning of the *Hymn*, but also in contrast to it, because now it is not the bow, but the lyre that constitutes the atmosphere in heaven. Mount Olympus is ordered in χορεία. As chorus leader and kitharodic singer, Apollo should be the centre, while the gods wish the arriving god to sing and play the lyre. The Muses respond in refrain, singing about the human mortals, while the other gods join into the chorus formation: αὐτὰρ ὁ Φοῖβος Ἀπόλλων ἐγκιθαρίζει / καλὰ καὶ ὕψι βιβάς, αἴγλη δέ μιν ἀμφιφαείνει / μαρμαρυγαί τε ποδῶν καὶ ἐϋκλώστοιο χιτῶνος ('But Apollo plays his lyre stepping high and a radiance shines around him, the gleaming of his feet and close-woven mantle' 201–3). This scene carries again all features of an epiphany. The god of the bow evolved to the model of song, music and choral dance.[97] From his choral competition in Delos he passed over Delphi and the choruses there to finally reach heaven and to establish the choral festivity among the Olympian gods.

Looping back from the end of the chronological order, the narration then focuses on Apollo's arrival in Delphi. Choosing his future attendants, he stages his epiphany in front of Cretan sailors. The scene full of wonder about his apparition as a dolphin on the ship, who leads it to land in Krisa (388–439), bears some traits of outdoing the *Hymn to Dionysus*. From there he guides the Cretans like a radiant star (ἀστέρι εἰδόμενος 441) and gives fire signs (440–5). Human mortals react to the epiphany with cries and fear (445–7). In a last step he appears now in the shape 'of a man, brisk and sturdy, in the prime of his youth, while his

---

[97] See Bierl (2011) 137.

broad shoulders were covered with his hair' (ἀνέρι εἰδόμενος αἰζηῶι τε κρατερῶι τε / πρωθήβηι, χαίτηις εἰλυμένος εὐρέας ὤμους 449–50), very similar to Dionysus, as he appeared on the shore in the *Hymn to Dionysus* (compare νεηνίηι ἀνδρὶ ἐοικώς / πρωθήβηι· καλαὶ δὲ περισσείοντο ἔθειραι / κυάνεαι, φᾶρος δὲ περὶ στιβαροῖς ἔχεν ὤμοις / πορφύρεον *HHymn* 7.3–6). In contrast to the pirates and similar to the steersman in the *Hymn to Dionysus*, the leader of the sailors recognizes the god behind the young man (463–6) addressing a speech to them (451–61). The rhapsode finally tells how the god led his new band of attendants in a choral procession from the shore up to Delphi (514–23). As in the entrance scene at the beginning of the Pythian part (182–7, 201–3), 'Apollo, the son of Zeus, led them, holding a lyre in his hands, and playing sweetly as he stepped high' (ἦρχε δ' ἄρα σφιν ἄναξ Διὸς υἱὸς Ἀπόλλων / φόρμιγγ' ἐν χείρεσσιν ἔχων ἐρατὸν κιθαρίζων / καλὰ καὶ ὕψι βιβάς 514–6). The Cretans followed him and 'chanted "Ie Paean" after the manner of the Cretan paean-singers and of those in whose hearts the heavenly Muse has put sweet-voiced song' (ἰηπαιήον' ἄειδον / οἷοί τε Κρητῶν παιήονες οἷσί τε Μοῦσα / ἐν στήθεσσιν ἔθηκε θεὰ μελίγηρυν ἀοιδήν 517–19). This choral procession to Delphi is then the model for his choral entrance into the Olympus where he will order everything in choruses. On the one hand, in a loop, the impressive beginning of the Pythian part comes to mind (182–206, esp. 182–7, 201–3). On the other hand, moving backward in time, we are reminded of his birth, when he grabbed the lyre (131), and the time shortly afterwards, when Delian choruses were first institutionalised, which mirror Apollo's own chorality (146–64). In the final farewell (545) the god is summoned to take pleasure in this monumental song stitched together in artful loops and rings, itself comparable to the circular dance. In its very performance the original essence of the god comes to the fore. He becomes manifest and present, and by making mental contact with him, the *persona cantans* can call to mind another song (546). Perhaps the new song will be still another re-performance of this perfect composition done by 'the blind man' from Chios (181).

Conclusion

This paper has shown how Dionysus and Apollo, in their idiosyncratic manners which reflect their respective essences, became present through song and performance. In both cases the narration focuses on χορεία in the making, on how both gods became gods linked to music, song and choral dance. The detailed epic narration makes this aspect of the *Hymns* all the more poignant and in this way brings the gods to mind, right before the reader's/listener's inner eyes, in all their glory. Therefore the song is the means to epiphanize the gods, while they themselves, in the inner story, become manifest through music, choral dance and other epiphanic strategies. The epic singer can thus self-referentially allude to his own epic production that itself unfolds in a poetic epiphany.

The Olympian gods can be grasped only in their anthropomorphic quality. Some are closer to men than others. Apollo is perhaps the least human of all. He is power in totality, full of energy, terrible force. Dionysus complements him, blurring the boundaries between men and animals. Through mystery cult men themselves become part of the god. As initiates, μύσται, they become βάκχοι, full of Bacchus. The initiates express their pleasure, happiness and salvation in choruses. As chorus leaders both gods have an effect on poetic production. In his choral and musical aspects Dionysus remains enigmatic, much more hidden, whereas Apollo is made present as an all-mighty force that dominates even the entire cosmos and the Olympus in chorality.

Perhaps it is not by chance that the *Hymn to Hermes* (*HHymn* 4) of a much later date, perhaps from the beginning of the fifth century BC, comes next the *Hymn to Apollo* in the order of the collection. In this song Hermes, the closest god to men, invents the lyre, sings two songs (*HHymn* 4.54–62, 423–33), as *mise en abyme* and again in the dynamics of his epiphany,[98] before giving it to Apollo in exchange for herds and numerous other honours. The vivid but mute tortoise must die to be transformed to the sounding instrument. The lyre is not just there, but must be fabricated. Song thus becomes much more artificial and detached from natural or even supernatural existence. The idea of an absolute origin is thus deconstructed and dissolved in traces that are blurred in the long tradition, just as Hermes blurs his footprints in the sand. In this new perspective it seems as if Apollo lost his original authenticity in respect to a living song culture and as if Hermes, as god of literacy, brought the diachronic chain of performances and re-performances to an end.[99] But this is another story that must be developed elsewhere. This new view seems revolutionary, but even in the *Hymn to Hermes* the rhapsodic "I" attempts to connect with the god to make him present in song and to call him and new song in mind. In the same formulaic diction of the last line as given in the *Hymn to Apollo* (*HHymn* 3.546), he thus ends: αὐτὰρ ἐγὼ καὶ σεῖο καὶ ἄλλης μνήσομ' ἀοιδῆς (*HHymn* 4.580).[100]

---

[98] See Vergados (2013) 4–14. On the lyre, see Jaillard (2007) 167–96.
[99] See Bergren (2008) 131–60.
[100] I can only end by greeting Antonios Rengakos, the good colleague and friend: χαῖρε – 'hail and take pleasure in that!'

Works cited

Allen, W., W. R. Halliday, and E. E. Sikes (1936). *The Homeric Hymns*. Oxford.
Ausfeld, K. F. (1903). 'De Greaecorum precationibus quaestiones', *Jahrbücher für classische Philologie* 28: 503–47.
Bakker, E. (2005). *Pointing at the Past: From Formula to Performance in Homeric Poetics*. Cambridge, MA and London.
Bergren, A. (2008). *Weaving Truth: Essays on Language and the Female in Greek Thought*. Cambridge, MA and London.
Bierl, A. F. H. (1991). *Dionysos und die griechische Tragödie. Politische und 'metatheatralische' Aspekte im Text*. Tübingen.
–. (1999). '*Euripides, Bacchae*. Edited with an Introduction, Translation and Commentary by Richard Seaford, Warminster 1996 (The Plays of Euripides)', *Gnomon* 71: 582–92.
–. (2004). '"Turn on the Light!" Epiphany, the God-Like Hero Odysseus, and the Golden Lamp of Athena in Homer's *Odyssey* (Especially 19.1–43)', *ICS* 29: 43–61.
–. (2007a). 'Literatur und Religion als Rito- und Mythopoetik: Überblicksartikel zu einem neuen Ansatz in der Klassischen Philologie', in: A. Bierl, R. Lämmle and K. Wesselmann (eds.), *Literatur und Religion I. Wege zu einer mythisch-rituellen Poetik bei den Griechen*. Berlin and New York, 1–76.
–. (2007b). 'Mnema und Mneme – Gedanken eines Gräzisten', in: H.-J. Lenger and G. C. Tholen (eds.), *Mnema. Derrida zum Andenken*. Bielefeld, 47–64.
–. (2009). *Ritual and Performativity. The Chorus in Old Comedy*, translated by A. Hollmann. Cambridge, MA and London. http://nrs.harvard.edu/urn-3:hul.ebook:CHS_Bierl.Ritual_and_Performativity.2009
–. (2011). 'Fest und Spiele in der griechischen Literatur', in: A. Chaniotis (ed.), *Festivals and Contests* (= ThesCRA VII). Los Angeles, 125–60.
–. (2012). ''Demodokos' Song of Ares and Aphrodite in Homer's *Odyssey* (8.266–366): An Epyllion? Agonistic Performativity and Cultural Metapoetics', in: M. Baumbach and S. Bär (eds.), *Brill's Companion to Greek and Latin Epyllion and Its Reception*. Leiden and Boston, 111–34.
–. (2013a). 'Dionysos in Old Comedy. Staging of Experiments on Myth and Cult', in: A. Bernabé et al. (eds.), *Redefining Dionysos*. Berlin and Boston, 366–85.
–. (2013b). 'Maenadism as Self-Referential Chorality in Euripides' *Bacchae*', in: R. Gagné and M. G. Hopman (eds.), *Choral Mediations in Greek Tragedy*. Cambridge, 211–26.
–. (2015). 'New Trends in Homeric Scholarship (NTHS)', in: A. Bierl and J. Latacz (eds. / general editor of the English edition S. D. Olson), *Homer's Iliad. The Basel Commentary (BKE)*, transl. by B.W. Millis and S. Strack, vol. I: *Prolegomena*. Berlin and Boston, 177–203.
–. (2016). '"All you Need is Love": Some Thoughts on the Structure, Texture, and Meaning of the Brothers Song as well as on Its Relation to the Kypris Song (P. Sapph. Obbink)', in: A. Bierl and A. Lardinois (eds.), *The Newest Sappho (P. Sapph. Obbink and P. GC inv. 105, Frs. 1–4)*. Leiden, 302–36. open access online: http://booksandjournals.brillonline.com/content/books/9789004314832
Blech, M. (1982). *Studien zum Kranz bei den Griechen*. Berlin and New York.
Bohrer, K. H. (2015). *Das Erscheinen des Dionysos. Antike Mythologie und moderne Metapher*. Frankfurt am Main.

Boisacq, E. (1916). *Dictionnaire étymologique de la langue grecque*. Heidelberg.
Bremer, D. (1975). 'Die Epiphanie des Gottes in den homerischen Hymnen und Platons Gottesbegriff', *ZRGG* 27: 1–21.
Burkert, W. (1979). 'Kynaithos, Polycrates and the Homeric Hymn to Apollo', in: G. W. Bowersock, W. Burkert and M. C. J. Putnam (eds.), *Arktouros: Hellenic Studies Presented to B.M.W. Knox*. Berlin, 53–62.
–. (1983). *Homo Necans. The Anthropology of Ancient Greek Sacrificial Ritual and Myth*, translated by P. Bing. Berkeley.
–. (1985). *Greek Religion. Archaic and Classical*, translated by J. Raffan. Cambridge, MA.
–. (1987). *Ancient Mystery Cults*. Cambridge, MA and London.
Calame, C. (2011). 'The Homeric Hymns as Poetic Offerings. Musical and Ritual Relationships with the Gods', in: Faulkner 2011b, 334–57.
Chantraine, P. (1968). *Dictionnaire étymologique de la langue grecque. Histoire des mots*. Paris.
Chappell, M. (2011). 'The *Homeric hymn to Apollo*. The Question of Unity', in: Faulkner 2011b, 59–81.
Clay, J. S. (1989/2006²). *The Politics of Olympus: Form and Meaning in the Major Homeric Hymns*. Princeton.
–. (2011). 'The *Homeric Hymns* as Genre', in: Faulkner 2011b, 232–53.
Csapo, E. (2003). 'The Dolphins of Dionysus', in: E. Csapo and M. C. Miller (eds.), *Poetry, Theory, Praxis. The Social Life of Myth, Word and Image in Ancient Greece. Essays in Honour of William J. Slater*. Oxford, 69–98.
–. (2008). 'Star Choruses: Eleusis, Orphism and New Musical Imagery and Dance', in: M. Revermann and P. Wilson (eds.), *Performance, Iconography, Reception. Studies in Honour of Oliver Taplin*. Oxford, 262–90.
Depew, M. (2000). 'Enacted and Represented Dedications: Genre and Greek Hymn', in: M. Depew and D. Obbink (eds.), *Matrices of Genre: Authors, Canons, and Society*. Cambridge, MA, 59–79.
Detienne, M. (1985). *Dionysos à ciel ouvert*. Paris.
Dietrich, B. C. (1983). 'Divine Epiphanies in Homer', *Numen* 30: 53–79.
Fernández Contreras, M. A. (1999). 'Las epifanías en la épica homérica', *Habis* 30: 7–17.
Faulkner, A. (2011a). 'Introduction. Modern Scholarship on the *Homeric Hymns*: Foundational Issues', in: Faulkner 2011b, 1–25.
–. (2011b). *The Homeric Hymns. Interpretative Essays*. Oxford.
Förstel, K. (1979). *Untersuchungen zum Homerischen Apollonhymnos*. Bochum.
Frisk, H. (1970). *Griechisches etymologisches Wörterbuch*, II. Heidelberg.
Foley, J. M. (1999). *Homer's Traditional Art*. University Park, PA.
Frame, D. (1978). *The Myth of Return in Early Greek Epic*. New Haven, CT. http://chs.harvard.edu/CHS/article/display/4317
Furley, W. D. (2011). 'Homeric and Un-Homeric Hexameter Hymns. A Question of Type', in: Faulkner 2011b, 206–231.
Furley, W. D. and J.M. Bremer (2001). *Greek Hymns: Selected Cult Songs from the Archaic to the Hellenistic Period. I: The Texts in Translation; II: Greek Texts and Commentary*. Tübingen.
García, J. F. (2002). 'Symbolic Action in the *Homeric Hymns*: The Theme of Recognition', *ClAnt* 21: 5–39.

Gemoll, A. (1886). *Die* Homerischen Hymnen. Leipzig.
Heer, C. de. (1969). *Μάκαρ – εὐδαίμων – ὄλβιος – εὐτυχής. A Study of the Semantic Field Denoting Happiness in Ancient Greek to the End of the 5th Century B.C.* Amsterdam.
Henrichs, A. (1982). 'Changing Dionysiac Identities', in: B. F. Meyer and E. P. Sanders (eds.), *Jewish and Christian Self-Definition,* III. *Self-Definition in the Graeco – Roman World.* London, 137–60 and 213–36.
–. (2011). 'Göttliche Präsenz als Differenz: Dionysos als epiphanischer Gott', in: R. Schlesier (ed.), *A Different God? Dionysos and Ancient Polytheism.* Berlin and Boston, 105–16.
Herrero de Jáuregui, M. (2013). 'Dionysos in the *Homeric Hymns*: the Olympian Portrait of the God', in: A. Bernabé et al. (eds.), *Redefining Dionysos.* Berlin and Boston, 235–49.
–. (2016). '"Trust the God": Tharsein in Ancient Greek Religion', *HSPh* 108: 1–52.
Humbert, J. (1936). *Homère. Hymnes.* Paris.
Jaillard, D. (2007). *Configurations d'Hermès. Une 'théogonie hermaïque'* (Kernos, supplément 17). Liège.
–. (2011). 'The Seventh *Homeric Hymn to Dionysus*', in: Faulkner 2011b, 133–50.
Joly, R. (1955). 'L'exhortation au courage (ΘΑΡΡΕΙΝ) dans les mystères', *REG* 68: 164–70.
Lonsdale, S. H. (1993). *Dance and Ritual Play in Greek Religion.* Baltimore and London.
Martin, R. (2000). 'Synchronic Aspects of Homeric Performance: The Evidence of the *Hymn to Apollo*', in: A. González de Tobia (ed.), *Una nueva visión de la cultura griega antigua hacia el fin del milenio.* La Plata, 403–32.
Merkelbach, R. (1988). *Die Hirten des Dionysos. Die Dionysos-Mysterien der römischen Kaiserzeit und der bukolische Roman des Longus.* Stuttgart.
Miller, A. M. (1986). *From Delos to Delphi: A Literary Study of the* Homeric Hymn to Apollo. Leiden.
Montanari, F., A. Rengakos and C. Tsagalis (2012). *Homeric Contexts. Neoanalysis and the Interpretation of Oral Poetry.* Berlin and Boston.
Nagy, G. (1990a). *Pindar's Homer. The Lyric Possession of an Epic Past.* Baltimore and London. http://nrs.harvard.edu/urn-3:hul.ebook:CHS_Nagy.Pindars_Homer.1990
–. (1990b). *Greek Mythology and Poetics.* Ithaca NY and London. http://chs.harvard.edu/CHS/article/display/5577
–. (1996). *Poetry as Performance: Homer and Beyond.* Cambridge.
–. (2003). *Homeric Responses.* Austin.
–. (2008/2009). *Homer the Classic.* Cambridge, MA and Washington, DC. http://nrs.harvard.edu/urn-3:hul.ebook:CHS_Nagy.Homer_the_Classic.2008
–. 2009/2010. *Homer the Preclassic.* Berkeley and Los Angeles. http://nrs.harvard.edu/urn-3:hul.ebook:CHS_Nagy.Homer_the_Preclassic.2009
–. (2011). 'The Earliest Phases in the Reception of the *Homeric Hymns*', in: Faulkner 2011b, 280–333.
–. (2012). 'Signs of Hero Cult in Homeric Poetry', in: Montanari, Rengakos and Tsagalis 2012, 27–71.
–. (2013a). *The Ancient Greek Hero in 24 Hours.* Cambridge, MA and London. http://chs.harvard.edu/publications
–. (2013b). 'The Delian Maidens and Their Relevance to Choral Mimesis in Classical Drama', in: R. Gagné and M.G. Hopman (eds.), *Choral Mediations in Greek Tragedy.* Cambridge, 227–56.
Nobili, C. (2009). 'L'*Inno Omerico a Dioniso (Hymn. Hom. VII)* e Corinto', *ACME* 62.3: 3–35.

Olson, S. (2017). 'Kinesthetic *Choreia* Empathy, Memory, and Dance in Ancient Greece', *CP* 112: 153–74.
Otto, W. F. (1933/2011⁷). *Dionysos. Mythos und Kultus*. Frankfurt am Main.
Peponi, A.-E. (2009). '*Choreia* and Aesthetics in the *Homeric Hymn to Apollo:* The Performance of the Delian Maidens (lines 156–64)', *ClAnt* 28: 39–70.
Petrovic, I. (2012). 'Rhapsodic Hymns and Epyllia', in: M. Baumbach and S. Bär (eds.), *Brill's Companion to Greek and Latin Epyllion and its Reception*, Leiden and Boston, 149–76.
Pfister, F. 1924. "Epiphanie", *RE* Suppl. IV: 277–323.
Prauscello, L. (2007). '"Dionysiac" Ambiguity: HomHymn 7.27: ὅδε δ᾽ αὖτ᾽ ἄνδρεσσι μελήσει', *MD* 58: 209–216.
Rengakos, A. (2002). 'Narrativität, Intertextualität, Selbstreferentialität. Die neue Deutung der *Odyssee*', in: M. Reichel and A. Rengakos (eds.), *EPEA PTEROENTA. Beiträge zur Homerforschung. Festschrift für Wolfgang Kullmann zum 75. Geburtstag*. Stuttgart, 173–91.
Richardson, N. J. (1974). *The Homeric Hymn to Demeter*. Oxford.
Ruhnken, D. (1749). *Epistola critica I. In Homeridarum Hymnos et Hesiodum, ad L. C. Valckenarium*. Leiden.
Seaford, R. (1981). 'Dionysiac Drama and the Dionysiac Mysteries', *CQ* 31: 252–75.
–. (1996). *Euripides. Bacchae, with an Introduction, Translation and Commentary*. Warminster.
Stehle, E. (1996). *Performance and Gender in Ancient Greece. Nondramatic Poetry in Its Setting*. Princeton.
Tsagalis, C. (2008). *The Oral Palimpsest. Exploring Intertextuality in the Homeric Epics*. Cambridge, MA and London.
–. (2011). 'Towards an Oral, Intertextual Neoanalysis', *TC* 3: 209–44.
Turkeltaub, D. W. (2003). *The Gods' Radiance Manifest: An Examination of the Narrative Pattern Underlying the Homeric Divine Epiphany Scenes*. Diss., Cornell.
Vergados, A. (2011). 'The *Homeric Hymn to Hermes:* Humour and Epiphany', in: Faulkner 2011b, 82–104.
–. (2013). *The Homeric Hymn to Hermes: Introduction, Text and Commentary*. Berlin and Boston.
Vernant, J.-P. (1988). 'Aspects mythiques de la mémoire', in: id. (ed.), *Mythe et pensée chez les Grecs. Études de psychologie historique*. Paris, 109–36.
Versnel, H. S. (1993). *Inconsistencies in Greek and Roman Religion II. Transition and Reversal in Myth and Ritual*. Leiden.
–. (2011). *Coping with the Gods: Wayward Readings in Greek Theology*. Leiden and Boston.
West, M. L. (1975). 'Cynaethus' Hymn to Apollo', *CQ* 25: 161–70.
Wilamowitz-Moellendorff, U. von (1916). *Die Ilias und Homer*. Berlin
Wildberg, C. (2002). *Hyperesie und Epiphanie. Ein Versuch über die Bedeutung der Götter in den Dramen des Euripides*. Munich.
Wolf, F. A. (1795/1985). *Prolegomena ad Homerum sive de operum Homericorum prisca et genuina forma variisque mutationibus et probabili ratione emendandi*. Halle; cited after the adnotated English translation: *Prolegomena to Homer. Translated with Introduction and Notes*, eds. A. Grafton, G. W. Most, and J. E. G. Zetzel. Princeton.

Richard Janko
Tithonus, Eos and the cicada in the *Homeric Hymn to Aphrodite* and Sappho fr. 58

When Sappho's poem on old age (fr. 58 Voigt) was published in 2004, it was not universally welcomed; thus Germaine Greer declared, on the basis of M. L. West's translation, that the new ode was unworthy of the poetess.[1] Perhaps she was repelled by what appears to be its totally pessimistic conclusion: there can be no remedy for old age, since not even the handsome Tithonus, whom the dawn goddess Eos loved, could escape the horrors of senescence. However, I shall argue that her poem is far more elegant in expression and subtle in thought than may at first appear. I shall discuss, firstly, the text of the ode; secondly, its structure; and finally the myth of Tithonus in relation to the version of the story in the *Homeric Hymn to Aphrodite*, in which I shall develop my argument, first advanced in 2005,[2] that the legend that Tithonus was turned into a cicada and therefore able to continue to sing was already known in the north-east Aegean by Sappho's time and was therefore available to both her and her audience, if only they chose to recall it. We can in this respect go beyond the usual scepticism[3] or agnosticism,[4] just as we can be confident that Sappho knew the *Hymn to Aphrodite*.[5] I shall argue that the poem fully measures up to what we

---

1 Stothard (2005).
2 Janko (2005).
3 So Zellner (2008); Edmunds (2009) 65 n. 41, 67 n. 43; Carrara (2011) esp. 103–9.
4 So Geissler (2005) 107 n. 12; Rawles (2006) 7.
5 So Meyerhoff (1984) 187–98; Di Benedetto (1985); Rösler (1985) 161; Nünlist (1998) 54–6; Geissler (2005) 106–7; West (2005) 5 n. 8; Bettarini (2007) 1; Carrara (2011) 85–6 with n. 12.

This paper develops the argument made in the *Times Literary Supplement* on 23 Dec. 2005, 19–20, which I had first advanced in August 2005 at Methymna in a symposium organized by Apostolos Pierris, the publication of which suffered the fate of Tithonus. I thank the participants on that occasion, and especially the cicada in the pine-tree outside, who began to sing right on cue. Its present metamorphosis is owed to the editor's request that I write on the *Hymn to Aphrodite* to honour Professor Rengakos, with whom I had the rare privilege of sharing an office while teaching at the Aristotle University on a Fulbright Fellowship in winter 2017. I also thank Jürgen Hammerstaedt and the conservator of the Papyrussammlung for helping me to study the papyrus in Cologne in 2007. Translations are mine.

https://doi.org/9783110559873-014

already knew of Sappho's oeuvre, and in particular that the myth of Tithonus is not simply 'banal, a weak ending to the poem', as West held.[6]

I. The text of Sappho's Tithonus Ode

My reconstruction below is based on the two articles by Gronewald and Daniel in which it was first published,[7] together with the typically brilliant treatment of it by West,[8] who incorporated some excellent ideas of V. Di Benedetto,[9] and the subsequent efforts to improve it. I have also studied the Cologne papyrus under the microscope. The poem survives in two overlapping papyri, *P.Oxy.* 1787 fr. 1 and *P.Köln* inv. 21351+21376. It is proved to be a complete poem by the fact that the two papyri place different verses before and after it.[10] This is a better explanation for the facts than the idea that it survives in a shorter and a longer version (incorporating the next four lines in *P.Oxy.* 1787 fr. 1), since the latter hypothesis violates Occam's razor by positing an entity unnecessarily. As West showed,[11] in the Oxyrhynchus papyrus the poem that follows began with a priamel, in a fashion known elsewhere in Sappho.

The roll from Oxyrhynchus was presumably a copy of the standard ancient edition of Book IV of Sappho's poems. The Cologne papyrus, however, represents an anthology, because the poem following it is not by Sappho.[12] There are two grounds for thinking that our poem as there transmitted derives from a miscellany. First, it presents the poems in a different arrangement from that in *P.Oxy.* 1787 fr. 1. Secondly, the piece which follows in the Cologne papyrus is definitely not by Sappho, as West deduced from its metre;[13] if it is felt that the presence of a piece by another poet next to this poem undermines the case for Sappho's authorship of the Tithonus ode, its inclusion in the standard ancient edition of her works more than counterbalances that argument. The case for authenticity rests ultimately on both this external evidence and the internal evi-

---

6 West (2005) 6; cf. Rawles (2006, 3), who regards Tithonus as a poor example, as his fate does not illustrate a universal law.
7 Gronewald and Daniel (2004a); (2004b).
8 West (2005) 3–6.
9 Di Benedetto (2004).
10 So Di Benedetto (2004); Luppe (2004) 7–9; West (2005) 3–4. On the question see most recently Nardella (2012).
11 West (2005) 7.
12 Gronewald and Daniel (2004a) 1, (2005); West (2005); Rawles (2006); Hammerstaedt (2009) 18–21.
13 West (2005) 1.

dence of language and thought. Finally, the Cologne papyrus preserves the original usage of ζ that must have been standard in the poet's original manuscripts; in the Alexandrian edition ζ has been replaced in non-initial position by cδ, while ζ is used in initial position for the Lesbian pronunciation of δι-.[14] I have applied the spelling-conventions of the Alexandrian edition, removing both its original use of ζ and the sandhi-effects current in the earlier papyrus (e.g. τὰ]μ φιλάοιδον). The line-numbers used are those of the poem.[15]

× – υ υ – – υ υ – – υ υ – υ – ͡

ὔμμες τάδε Μοίcαν ἰ[ο]κ[ό]λπων κάλα δῶρα, παῖδες,   1
cπουδάcδετε καὶ τὰ]ν φιλάοιδον λιγύραν χελύνναν·
ἔμοι δ' ἄπαλον πρίν] ποτ' [ἔ]οντα χρόα γῆρας ἤδη
κατέcκεθε, λεῦκαι δ' ἐγ]ένοντο τρίχες ἐκ μελαίναν,
βάρυς δέ μ' ὀ [θ]ῦμος πεπόηται, γόνα δ' οὐ φέροιcι,   5
τὰ δή ποτα λαίψηρ' ἔον ὄρχηcθ' ἴcα νεβρίοιcι.

τὰ ⟨νῦν⟩ cτεναχίcδω θαμέωc· ἀλλὰ τί κεν ποείην;
ἀγήραον, ἄνθρωπον ἔοντ', οὐ δυνατὸν γένεcθαι.
καὶ γὰρ π[ο]τα Τίθωνον ἔφαντο βροδόπαχυν Αὔων,
ἔρωι δεδάθειcαν, βάμεν' εἰc ἔcχατα γᾶc φέροιcα[ν,   10
ἔοντα [κ]άλον καὶ νέον, ἀλλ' αὔτον ὔμως ἔμαρψε
χρόνωι πόλιον γῆρας, ἔχ[ο]ντ' ἀθανάταν ἄκοιτιν.   12

Π¹ = *P.Oxy.* 1787 fr. 1 (saec. iii p. C.); Π² = *P. Köln* inv. 21351+21376 (saec. iii a. C.)

edd.: Gronewald et Daniel **1** ὔμμεc τάδε scripsi: ὔμμεc πεδὰ West: φέρω τάδε edd.: γεραίρετε Di Benedetto: νῦν δή μ' ἔτ. vel νῦν μ' ἤδεα Lidov, spatio brevius: τέττιξ ἄτε Livrea | Μοίcαν ἰοκόλ]πων Siebitz **2** cπουδάcδετε West (cπουδάζετε scripserit librarius, cf v. 7): χορεύcατε Di Benedetto: λάβοιcα πάλιν vel ἔλοιcα πάλιν edd.: φίλημμι Lidov, spatio multo brevius | καὶ West: κἀτ Ferrari: δὲ Lidov | τὰ]μ edd. e Π² | φιλάοιδον intellexit Maas **3** ἔμοι Snell: κέκαρφ' edd.: νῦν γάρ μ' Lidov post Di Benedetto | δ' Di Benedetto: μὲν Snell | ἄπαλον edd. | πρίν Di Benedetto: μοι edd. | ποτ' [ἔ]οντα edd. **4** κατέcκεθε West (cf. Hes. fr. 133.4, ἄλφος γάρ χρόα πάντα κατέcχ(εθ)ε): ἐπέλλαβε West, fort. brevius: διώλεcε Di Benedetto, brevius: ὄγμοιc(ιν) vel ὄγμοι δ' ἔνι edd. | λεῦκαι Hunt | δ' Lobel: τ' Hunt | ἐγ]ένοντο Hunt | ἐκ Π¹: ἐγ Π² **5** θ]ῦμος edd. **6** νεβρίοιcι West: νεβρίοιcιν Π¹Π² **7** τὰ ⟨νῦν⟩ supplevi: ⟨ἦ⟩ τὰ Burzacchini et Führer, bene: ⟨ζὰ⟩ τὰ Lindon: ⟨ταῦ⟩τα vel ⟨ὂν δὲ⟩ (i.e. ἀνὰ δὲ) edd.: τὰ ⟨μὲν⟩ West: τά ⟨γ'⟩ ὄν- Tsantsanoglou | cτεναχίcδω West: cτεναχίζω Π²: deest Π¹ | κεν Π¹: κεμ Π² **9** π[ο]τα edd. **10** δεδάθειcαν scripsi: δ‿α‿ειcαμ Π² (deest Π¹): δ' ἐ[λ]άθειcαν Picconi: διελάθειcαν Tsantsanoglou: δε[.]αθειcαμ leg. Hammerstaedt: δέπαc εἰcάμ- edd. | l.tt. δ certa est, tum ε potius quam ιε, tum partem sup. litt. π esse censent edd., ubi tamen Tsantsanoglou λ legit; deinde litt. α mihi certa videtur; dein θ vel c, ο |

---

14 Bowie (1981) 138.
15 Editors's note: since the lunate c is used in the papyrus fragment and the critical apparatus of the Sappho poem, we have decided to keep it throughout R. Janko's piece, so as to avoid having side by side two different types of sigma.

βάμεν' divisit West: εἰcαμβάμεν' edd., quod tamen εἰcομβάμεν' Aeolice scriptum fuerit, ut monuit Blümel | φέροιcα[ν Stiebitz **11** ἔοντα [κ] | ἄλον vel ἔοντ' ἄ[π]αλον edd. **12** πόλιον vel πόλιον edd. | ἔχ[ο]ντ' edd.

Pursue the violet-laden Muses' handsome gifts,
my children, and their loud-voiced lyre so dear to song;
But me – my skin which once was soft is withered now
by age, my hair has turned to white which once was black,
my heart has been weighed down, my knees give no support
which once were nimble in the dance like little fawns.

How often I lament these things. But what to do?
No human being can escape decrepitude.
For people used to think that Dawn with rosy arms,
by love instructed, took Tithonus fine and young
to reach the edges of the earth; yet still grey age
in time did seize him, though *his* consort cannot die.[16]

My reconstruction agrees with those of Di Benedetto and West[17] in seeing a contrast between the girls and the speaker rather than between the actions of singing and dancing, as Lidov suggested.[18] But it differs in four places from what has previously been proposed. In line 1, I have combined elements suggested by West and the first editors. West's ὔμμες forms an excellent contrast with ἔμοι δ', which Di Benedetto rightly desiderated in line 3.[19] But I do not understand West's πεδά. Perhaps it is meant to govern the accusative δῶρα and form a tmesis with cπουδάcδετε, but no compound μεταcπουδάζω is attested. His translation 'Muses' gifts' corresponds to the natural sense of the passage. Accordingly, τάδε, proposed by the first editors, should be retained. The deictic points vividly to the festivities which the performers can see with their own eyes, but which must be left to our own imaginations. One can show that the missing letters fit the spacing by drawing them onto the image of the papyrus.[20] For reasons of spacing I

---

[16] This is a revision of my prior translation (Janko 2005), which is reprinted in Obbink (2009) 14–15, where its authorship is erroneously ascribed to West.
[17] Di Benedetto (2004); West (2005).
[18] Lidov (2009) 84–5, 93–4. He proposes an elided μ' for μοι in line 1, indicating a dative of the possessor without an ἐcτι. The elision is possible in this dialect, but the construction would be found impossibly obscure by readers or listeners. His reading remains possible, but better supplements are needed if it is to be sustained. His objection to τ]ὰν in line 2 can be met by taking it as 'their', i.e. belonging to the Muses.
[19] Di Benedetto (2004).
[20] There is an image of the main portion of the papyrus, *P.Köln* Inv. nr. 21351, at http://www.uni-koeln.de/phil-fak/ifa/NRWakademie/papyrologie/Verstreutepub/21351_ZPE147.html. The left halves of the final five lines are preserved in Inv. nr. 21376, a photograph of which is printed

also prefer West's alternative κατέϲκεθε in line 4 to ἐπέλλαβε, which he printed, and to Di Benedetto's διώλεϲε.²¹ Lastly, I supply the lost syllable in line 6 as νῦν, since this is easier than West's μέν *solitarium*; an indication of time reinforces the contrast between past youth and present age, and νῦν often has the sense of 'as things are' and conveys a sense of resignation to current misfortune.²²

The lacuna in line 10 is the worst *crux* in the poem. It has seemed impossible to think of a feminine passive participle that fills the space, matches the traces, and has the right kind and number of syllables; as West noted, ἔρωτι cannot be read and the obvious aorist passive participle δαμεῖϲαν is one syllable too short. However, scholars' failure to identify such a participle does not mean that none exists, and that we must fall back on the first editor's 'cup' (δέπαϲ), as Carrara holds.²³ At first I sought a present indicative active participle of a contracted verb in -ε-, since its accusative singular feminine would end in -ειϲαν. This is the normal formation in Lesbian dialect: compare ἆδυ φωνείϲαϲ ὐπακούει καὶ γελαίϲαϲ ἰμέροεν (fr. 31.3–5), where φωνείϲαϲ is from φωνέω, or rather φώνημ(μ)ι. But my original idea ἔρωι λαλάγειϲαν 'murmuring with love' proved upon inspection of both the digital photograph and the original not to match the traces, since the second doubtful letter is certainly not Α.²⁴ Hammerstaedt regarded the papyrological basis for textual restoration as δε[ ]αθειϲαμ, observing that the only proposed supplements that match the traces are δέπαϲ εἶϲαν (Gronewald and Daniel), δέμα θεῖϲαν (Danielewicz), δέμαϲ εἶϲαν (Austin), and δέμαϲ εἰϲαμβάμεν' (Livrea).²⁵ Tsantsanoglou has described the traces as follows: 'a Δ is clearly visible. After that, the faint traces of the middle of a vertical are perceptible, apparently an iota, followed by at least two parallel horizontals, most likely an epsilon. The papyrus fragments, as seen in the Web photograph, have to be adjusted as to the size of the gap between them. ... Then, the upper part of the left-hand oblique and, faintly, the foot of the right-hand oblique of a triangular letter, apparently a Λ, are visible, followed by a more or less clear Α with a

---

in ZPE 149 (2004), 1. As the papyrus is mounted, the gap after approximately the sixth letter is too wide; see further the plates in Hammerstaedt (2009). Digital editing of these images, by bringing the separated fragments together, helps to resolve the crux in line 10.

21 Lidov (2009, 94) too prints κατέϲκεθε.
22 For other proposals see Lundon (2007); Hammerstaedt (2009) 25–6.
23 Carrara (2011) 83 n. 6.
24 Bettarini's palaeographical objections (2007, 6) are correct; Carrara's point that the participle should have applied to Tithonus rather than Eos (2011, 104 n. 61) could not have the same force, since, as I show below, the sexual roles in the poem are thoroughly intermingled. Bettarini's own proposal ἄγ[ι]' ἄφειϲαν (2007, 6–7) entails serious difficulties, both metrical, since it demands an unparalleled synizesis, and dialectal, since the correct Lesbian form would be ἄπειϲαν.
25 Hammerstaedt (2009) 26, citing Danielewicz (2006), Austin (2007), and Livrea (2007).

marked serif in its right-hand foot … There follows the left-hand part of a rounded letter.'²⁶ I certainly agree that the initial letter is the usual small Δ with a raised baseline. However, the second letter, once the upright to the left and the horizontals to the right are digitally reunited, is by Occam's razor surely E rather than IE, since we should not posit any more uprights than are necessary (the papyrus is so early that it still uses the angular epigraphic form of E). Like Tsantsanoglou, I perceived traces of a third, triangular, letter, i. e. Λ or Δ, where others have supplied M. The following A is certain, and the last damaged letter is undoubtedly a rounded Θ or C.

On this basis Tsantsanoglou proposed ἔρωι διελάθεισαν, 'pierced by love', from the compound verb διελαύνω; independently, Piccioni proposed ἔρωι δ' ἐ[λ]άθεισαν, 'driven by love', from the simplex ἐλαύνω. These two proposals are much closer than those listed by Hammerstaedt to the traces in the papyrus. Although the scansion of δι(α)- as ζ(α)- is not impossible, since there is the parallel ζάεισαι from δι-άημι,²⁷ to introduce the particle δέ so late in its sentence is extremely difficult, to say the least.²⁸ I now suggest instead ἔρωι δεδάθεισαν, which is syntactically and metrically unproblematic. This hitherto unattested participle is from the old root *δας- seen in the verb *δάημι with the meaning 'to learn, teach', which is based on the root that also underlies the reduplicated present διδάσκω.²⁹ Debrunner showed that the underlying Indo-European root is *d̥ns-, which yielded the aorist δαῆναι < *δας-ῆναι 'to know', future δαήσεαι, and perfect δεδάηκα 'I have learned, I know', as well as the causative present *δι-δάσ-σκω 'I teach', the reduplicated causative aorist active δέδαε < *de-d̥ns-et 'he taught', and the plural noun δήνεα < *déns-es-a 'wiles'.³⁰ The form δεδάθεισαν will be the aorist passive participle corresponding to the third person plural aorist indicative active δέδαον, which is in Hesychius,³¹ and to the more familiar third person singular δέδαε, which appears four times in Homer and again in Hellenistic poetry.³² Here, δεδάθεισαν is in agreement with Αὔων, i.e. 'Dawn, schooled by love'. I find love's gentler approach more appropriate to the poetic

---

26 For further discussion of the traces see Buzzi and Piccioni (2008) 12–13.
27 Tsantsanoglou (2009), citing inc. auct. 35,7 Voigt.
28 Piccioni's parallels (2010, 73–4) do not convince, as her instances of δέ mark the beginnings of new clauses.
29 Chantraine (1968–72) i. 278; Giannakis (1997) 238–40; Beekes (2010) i. 296.
30 Debrunner (1937).
31 δέδαον· ἔδειξαν. ἐδίδαξαν (Hsch. Lex. δ 355 Latte).
32 Od. 6.233 = 23.160, ὃν Ἥφαιστος δέδαεν καὶ Παλλὰς Ἀθήνη / τέχνην παντοίην; 8.448, ἐπὶ δεσμὸν ἴηλε / ποικίλον, ὅν ποτέ μιν δέδαε φρεσὶ πότνια Κίρκη; 20.72, μῆκος δ' ἔπορ' Ἄρτεμις ἁγνή, / ἔργα δ' Ἀθηναίη δέδαε κλυτὰ ἐργάζεσθαι.

context, in which the speaker teaches her charges, than the verb διελαύνω connoting violent compulsion.

II. The Tithonus Ode: structure and meaning

Let us now turn to the poem's structure. It is in stichic verse rather than the stanzas that were used in much of what we know of Sappho's oeuvre. Yet the poem has a very elegant formal structure. The scribe, and West's translation, divides the whole poem into couplets. In an English rendering based on this, Lachlan MacKinnon[33] carefully replicates the twelve lines of the original; these are printed without a break, but the incidence of heavy punctuation divides them into couplets, except for the final four lines. The version by Edwin Morgan published with it divides the poem into six three-line stanzas. In all these versions the last pair of couplets are separated only by a comma or indeed by no punctuation at all.

However, the most natural articulation of the ode divides it into two 'stanzas' of six verses each. I do not expect that we will find 'stanzas' of six verses in other poems in this metre; the poem probably falls into this pattern by accident. However, for convenience within this poem I will refer to them as such. In each stanza the first two lines form a distinct couplet. Lines 1–2 seem to exhort the young people to enjoy themselves, in contrast to the four-line description of the devastating effects of advancing age on the speaker herself. This description, and with it the first stanza, ends with a very brief comparison: her knees used to be as nimble in the dance as fawns'.

The second stanza has an identical structure. The couplet formed by lines 7–8 asks what can be done about old age, and answers that no human can be free of it. Lines 9–12 explain this iron law: 'for' (γάρ) not even Tithonus was immune from it, and *a fortiori* the speaker herself will not be. This mythological illustration is itself equivalent to the brief comparison with which the first stanza ends in line 6

This perfection of form is complemented and diversified by verbal and thematic echoes between the two stanzas. These will have seemed elegant to the ancients, who were less annoyed by verbal repetition than we may be, as Pickering has shown;[34] indeed, they must have held that it intensified the attractive or

---

[33] MacKinnon (2005).
[34] Pickering (2000); id. (2003) 493–5, citing Pausimachus from Philodemus, *De poem.* 1 85–91 Janko.

agreeable features of the repeated words. Repetition troubled them less because the predominant mode of performance of ancient poetry was oral. Provided that the repeated sounds were agreeable, repetition was considered pleasing to the ear. Many of these echoes conform to the circular pattern known as 'ring-composition'. Thus the 'handsome' gifts of line 1 are picked up in line 11 by the 'handsome' Tithonus near the end of the poem. The implicitly immortal Muses in the same line are counterbalanced by the explicitly 'immortal' spouse of the last verse. Just as the speaker was 'once' young (line 3), and her knees were 'once' nimble (line 6), so Tithonus was 'once' snatched by Dawn (line 9); the repetition underscores regret for the passing of youth.[35] 'Old age' has 'grasped' the speaker (line 3), just as Tithonus was 'seized' (line 11) by 'old age' (line 12); the word is also embedded in the privative adjective ἀγήραον in line 7. The speaker's hair has turned 'white' (line 3), while 'grey' old age seizes Tithonus (line 12, since we cannot construe it 'Tithonus grey with time'). The speaker's knees do not 'carry' her (line 5), but Dawn 'carried' Tithonus off (line 10). Finally, references to flowers link line 1 (the 'violet-bosomed Muses') with line 9 (Dawn 'of the rosy forearms').

The crucial contrasts, however, are built into each stanza. The first stanza opposes youth to age. Lines 1–2 and 6 are devoted to youth—the youth of the addressees, and the lost youth of the speaker; these verses frame lines 3–5, which are mostly on old age, with glances at the speaker's once soft skin and dark hair.

The anguished question and answer of lines 6–7 set up a different and more subtle contrast, that between immortality and agelessness, which permeates the second stanza. Old age was, notoriously, something which humans can do nothing to prevent. The phrase 'immortal and ageless' was part of the standard epic diction—the stock description of any divine being in Homer and Hesiod.[36] Line 7 asks how a human being can be 'ageless', and then sets up the terrible contrast between the aging Tithonus and his divine consort, who is duly called 'immortal' in line 12. The standard version of the myth of Tithonus and Eos, from the *Homeric Hymn to Aphrodite* onwards, is of course that the goddess omitted to ask for her lover to have agelessness as well as immortality; thus she was landed with a partner who declined into an endless and horrifying old age from which he could never escape. As Zellner put it, 'even given Dawn's blunder, it would seem that Tithonus had advantages such that he would have been expect-

---

35 On the importance of the contrast between 'then' and 'now' in the poem see Stehle (2009).
36 See Janko (1981). The *Homeric Hymn to Aphrodite* (5) twice replaces the formulaic pattern ἀθάνατον καὶ ἀγήραον ἤματα πάντα with ἀθάνατον τ' εἶναι καὶ ζώειν ἤματα πάντα (221, 240), which reflects exactly the issue that is at stake there, as we shall see in §III below.

ed to have eternal youth, if anyone could. After all, he had an immortal as a lover, and was at the ends of the earth, where marvels are to be found.'[37]

Thus the poem moves from the first stanza's contrast, which is between the addressees' singing and dancing and the aging speaker's inability to join the dance, to the antithesis, in the second stanza, between old age and immortality. Here the speaker is implicitly compared with the aged Tithonus. The comparison suddenly evokes another motif, namely erotic desire. It invites its youthful audience to recognize that the speaker's aged body cannot have the appeal that the young Tithonus had for his lover. But at the same time Dawn is implicitly still married to her aged spouse. The deathless goddess is still his 'consort' the word with which the poem ends. What use could such a divine being possibly have for such a human partner?

Before we address that question, we must note one other peculiarity of the poem. Nowhere does the speaker signal her gender; this ode is unisex. Even though Greek is a highly inflected language, with a separate feminine gender in nouns and adjectives (but not in verbs, unlike Semitic languages), nowhere, in the text as it is plausibly reconstructed, does the speaker indicate her sexual identity, nowhere does she even indicate the sexual identity of the young people whom she is addressing, and nowhere does she signal whether the speaker's and the addressees' desires incline towards others belonging to the same sex, to the opposite sex, or to both. This poem could be performed by a man as easily as by a woman, and addressed to boys or both boys and girls just as easily as to girls. Not even the 'fawns' to which the speaker is compared in line 6 are gendered: the word is a neuter diminutive.[38]

The only passage where genders are differentiated is the comparison with Tithonus. Yet here the gendering of the text is highly complex. The syntax of line 9 is so striking that it suggests that the poet was deeply aware of this question. The use of 'they used to say' (ἔφαντο) to introduce the story of Tithonus and Eos has been controversial; I believe that it can best be understood as serving multiple purposes, which we should welcome in a subtle poem. It has been proposed that (i) it indicates that this story goes back to a time before the young ad-

---

[37] Zellner (2008) 47.
[38] However, this may be less neutral than it appears, since in Thessaly, an area closely related by dialect and tradition to the settlement of Lesbos, girls undergoing puberty-rituals were called 'fawns', just as in Attica they were called 'bears'; for the probable cognate νεβεύω, presumably once *νεβρεύω, means 'to serve Artemis'; see in Πολέμων, ἐπιστημονικὸν ἀρχαιολογικὸν περιοδικόν (Athens, 1929), 1.249 (Larissa) and *IG* 9(2).1123 (Demetrias), second cent. EC; cf. *LSJ*[9] suppl. s.v. I thank Barbara Smith for this information.

dressees were even born;³⁹ (ii) it distances the speaker from believing the myth, particularly if one version of the story, implicit in Homer (*Il.* 11.1–2, *Od.* 5.1–2), was that Eos and Tithonus lived happily ever after, like Zeus and Ganymede;⁴⁰ and (iii), it suggests that going to the ends of the world might be expected to lead to immortality, just as Croesus was taken to the land of Hyperboreans.⁴¹ None of these possibilities conflicts with the others, and they can all be accepted. It has not been noted, however, that ἔφαντο also obscures who does what to whom. The first person mentioned is Tithonus, the second Eos; only at the end of line 10 does it become clear that Eos is the subject and Tithonus the object, since she is carrying him off rather than the converse. But the gender of the possessor is reversed in the last line, where it is Tithonus who 'has' the immortal spouse; this is equally unexpected, since once old age has reduced him to a completely debilitated state he depends entirely on her. This reversal puts the lovers on an equal footing. The complexity of this passage suggests that the lack of gender-markers in the earlier part of the poem is deliberate.

This comparison between the speaker and Tithonus would be completely unproblematic if this poem were held to be the work of a man. Indeed, if a male speaker were addressing a chorus of girls, he could easily flatter his audience by likening them to the goddess. Such addresses by an aged male poet to a chorus of girls are known in archaic Greece, as witness Alcman fr. 26.⁴² In this fragment the speaker complains that he is too old to take part in the dance, and therefore wishes he could become a κηρύλος, i.e. a male halcyon,⁴³ so that he could fly across the waves amongst the (female) halcyons:

οὔ μ' ἔτι, παρσενικαὶ μελιγάρυες ἰαρόφωνοι,
γυῖα φέρην δύναται· βάλε δὴ βάλε κηρύλος εἴην,
ὅς τ' ἐπὶ κύματος ἄνθος ἅμ' ἀλκυόνεσσι ποτήται
νηδεὲς ἦτορ ἔχων, ἁλιπόρφυρος ἰαρὸς ὄρνις.

Maidens of honeyed song and holy voice,
my knees can bear me no longer. Let me be a halcyon,
who flies with his ladies on the spume of the wave,
fearless in heart, a bird that is sacred and blue as the sea.

---

39 I owe this attractive idea to Lardinois (2009) 47.
40 So Meyerhoff (1984) 190; Bettarini (2007) 2–4. Cf. Carrara (2011) 92–3.
41 So Zellner (2008) 47, 50–1, followed by Brown (2011) and Carrara (2011).
42 The comparison, first made by Calame (1983, 474), is also in Lardinois (2009) 51–2. I thank Richard Seaford for making me look again at this poem.
43 One source shows that it was believed that this bird dies having intercourse (*Suda* s.v. κηρύλος, iii. 112 Adler).

The speaker calls his addressees 'maidens'. Although he does not express his gender in the four lines that survive, we infer from the biographical tradition that he is male; the genders in the simile correspond to this difference, since the single male wishes to consort with the plural females. Calame[44] has shown that both Alcman and Sappho composed poetry for choruses of girls to be performed in religious festivals of various kinds, but above all rites of puberty and marriage. They would also have led the performances, or at least represent themselves as doing so. Hence the parallel with Alcman should be highly pertinent.

If, in the Tithonus ode, the speaker is a woman, the situation becomes far more complex, because the genders in the myth are reversed. The speaker compares herself to the male Tithonus; just as she is 'carried' by her youthful knees (line 5), so Eos 'carries' the youthful Tithonus to the ends of the earth (line 10). Conversely, the speaker implicitly compares her audience to the dawn-goddess; yet there is also a comparison between the goddess and the speaker, since the goddess wants to free her companion from old age, just as the speaker wishes she could become free of it.

The fact that the speaker compares herself to Tithonus may seem on the face of it to suggest that the poem is after all by a man, and so not the work of Sappho. Archaic lyricists could and did write in the *personae* of others, even of the opposite sex. Sappho's contemporary and compatriot Alcaeus apparently wrote a poem in which the speaker is a woman (fr. 10B). But that poem is incomplete, and the speaker's identity could have been revealed by a narrator at the end, as in Archilochus fr. 19, where Aristotle[45] tells us that Charon the carpenter is speaking (he could have known this only from the poem itself), or fr. 122, where, as he says in the same passage, a father (Lycambes?) is speaking about his daughter. Likewise, Horace undercuts his *Epod.* 2, the celebration of country life, by revealing at the end that it is spoken by the money-lender Alfius. Horace also wrote a poem with no narrator, in which a male and a female speaker alternates,[46] and in this he no doubt imitates an earlier model. Sappho could certainly have imagined herself into other roles than the biographical; that is, after all, essential to poetry. However, the fact remains that in her oeuvre there is no definite case in which she does this. On the contrary, the narrator identifies herself with the author, giving the name Sappho, in two places. In fr. 1.19 – 20, Aphrodite asks the narrator 'who is wronging you, Sappho?', and in fr. 94.5 the departing

---

44 Calame (1977).
45 Arist. *Rhet.* 3.17, 1418^{b}23.
46 *Od.* 3.9.

girl says to the narrator 'Sappho, I am truly leaving you against my will'.[47] Thus it seems unlikely, if our poem is by Sappho, that the *persona* of the narrator is not also that of the author.

Other explanations for this gender-reversal are possible. First, Sappho could well be using a reversal of gender to indicate her ability to empathise with others. Similar gender-reversals are known in the work of the (presumably male) poet Homer. The most famous case is at *Odyssey* 8.523–31. When Demodocus sings of the fall of Troy, Odysseus, who took part in sacking that city, weeps like a woman who sees her husband killed defending their city. The simile, given in the narrator's voice, is developed at length, so as fully to bring out the woman's misery:

> ὡς δὲ γυνὴ κλαίηιcι φίλον πόcιν ἀμφιπεcοῦcα,
> ὅς τε ἑῆc πρόcθεν πόλιος λαῶν τε πέcηιcιν,
> ἄcτεϊ καὶ τεκέεccιν ἀμύνων νηλεὲc ἦμαρ·
> ἡ μὲν τὸν θνήιcκοντα καὶ ἀcπαίροντα ἰδοῦcα
> ἀμφ' αὐτῶι χυμένη λίγα κωκύει· οἱ δέ τ' ὄπιcθε
> κόπτοντεc δούρεccι μετάφρενον ἠδὲ καὶ ὤμουc
> εἴρερον εἰcανάγουcι, πόνον τ' ἐχέμεν καὶ ὀϊζύν·
> τῆc δ' ἐλεεινοτάτωι ἄχεϊ φθινύθουcι παρειαί·
> ὣc 'Οδυcεὺc ἐλεεινὸν ὑπ' ὀφρύcι δάκρυον εἶβεν.

> As cries a woman fallen about her dear husband,
> who falls before his own citadel, before his own people,
> warding his town and his children from the day of no mercy—
> she, seeing him dying and gasping for breath,
> draping herself over his body keens with a shriek—
> but they with spears from behind beat her back and her shoulders,
> driving her into bondage, so she can have labour and torment;
> her cheeks wither away in pain that needs pity.
> Just so Odysseus shed a pitiful tear from under his brows.

What is so remarkable about this reversal of roles is that Odysseus is himself the attacking warrior whose wiles have caused the kind of destruction that the woman laments. The reversal of aggressor and defender is compounded by the reversal of gender, as if the poetic narrative brings out the complete humanity of the veteran, who, upon hearing the tale of war, is compelled to recognize the terrible losses that it entails both for the victor and for the defeated. Two similar reversals of gender appear in similes uttered by Achilles. At *Iliad* 9.323–5 the warrior compares himself to a mother-bird who toils ceaselessly to bring back morsels for her chicks. Achilles is a famously sensitive hero, who learns to em-

---

47 Sappho is also addressed in damaged contexts at frr. 65.5 and 133.2.

pathise even with the father of his worst enemy; the gender-reversal is one way in which the poet indicates this aspect of his character. He is no less sympathetic towards Patroclus at *Iliad* 16.7–11, even though he disguises his sympathy:

τίπτε δεδάκρυσαι Πατρόκλεες, ἠΰτε κούρη
νηπίη, ἥ θ᾽ ἅμα μητρὶ θέουσ᾽ ἀνελέσθαι ἀνώγει
εἱανοῦ ἁπτομένη, καί τ᾽ ἐσσυμένην κατερύκει,
δακρυόεσσα δέ μιν ποτιδέρκεται, ὄφρ᾽ ἀνέληται·
τῇ ἴκελος, Πάτροκλε, τέρεν κατὰ δάκρυον εἴβεις.

Why are you tearful, Patroclus, resembling an infant
who toddles after her mother, asking to be picked up,
clutching her dress, holding her back in her haste,
looking at her through her tears until she's picked up?
Like her, Patroclus, you're shedding a delicate tear.

Patroclus is derisively likened to a toddler who clings to her mother's skirts asking to be picked up. Yet even here Achilles' own simile turns the gruff warrior into the child's mother.[48] In these cases male speakers in the poetry of a male poet compare themselves to female figures. Thus Sappho could well be doing the same thing in reverse, both to show her ability to empathise with others, and indeed to show that her poetry is as good as any man's.

In addition, Sappho could have written a poem that could be performed by speakers of either gender and to audiences of either or both genders, since this would give it a wider diffusion and hence a greater success. Stehle[49] has shown convincingly how myths like that of Tithonus and Eos, in which a mortal man has intercourse with a goddess, bring into conflict two basic Greek hierarchies, male versus female and divine versus human, and thereby open up a space in which the female partner can occupy a non-traditional, dominant position in the relationship. Stehle noted that Sappho is strongly attracted to this theme, and indeed that she focuses precisely on the moment when the man is weakest, as she does in the case of Tithonus.[50] These are all very valuable explanations, and they can all apply at the same time; the best poetic creativity is of course multiply determined.

However, a further explanation for the reversal of gender in the poem, which I regard as the most important, is that there was in this case a particular purpose to Sappho's self-identification with Tithonus—a detail of his story that could

---

[48] See further Janko (1992) 316–17.
[49] Stehle (1996) 197–210.
[50] Stehle (1996) 193–6, 219–25.

have been known to her entire audience, but which is unknown to all but a few of her new readers of today. Just as the aged poet Alcman wishes in fr. 26 that he could turn into a bird to consort with the dancers, so too, in legend, the aged Tithonus turned into another winged creature, a cicada, that can continue to sing for ever – an ideal image for the aged poetess herself, with her well-attested wish to have her poetry confer glory beyond the grave; Nünlist already suspected, even before the new papyrus completed the damaged verses on Tithonus, that his transformation into a cicada here was an image for the poet.[51] Out of tact or subtlety, Sappho leaves it to her audience to fill in the missing ending of the tale.

III. Tithonus and the *Homeric Hymn to Aphrodite* (5)

Tithonus' name is of obscure origin;[52] Callimachus' name for Dawn, Τιτώ,[53] may seem to suggest an original meaning 'husband of dawn'.[54] According to Homer,[55] he was the son of Laomedon and brother of Priam. Hesiod tells us that, in turn, he begat by the dawn-goddess Eos the Ethiopian Memnon and his brother Emathion.[56] Apollodorus summarises these traditions, adding that his mother was either Leucippe, Strymo the daughter of Scamander,[57] or Placia the daughter of Otreus; his sisters were Hesione, Cilla, and Astyoche, and his half-brother was Bucolion.[58] The earliest attested version of Tithonus' fate is that he was immortalized and lived with Eos, since Homer says that he lives with Eos, from whose bed she rises each day; this must imply that he was immortal and ageless like her.[59] It is not clear, as we shall see, whether this is the oldest form of the story, but I think it most probable. As if to contradict this tradition, Horace in-

---

51 Nünlist (1998) 47, 54–6.
52 von Kamptz (1982, 363–4) records various modern explanations, comparing the Etruscan form *Tinθun* and the Cappadocian place-name *Tintunia*, which, he supposes, might support an Anatolian etymology. Cf. Chantraine (1968–80) ii. 1122 (s.v. Τιτᾶνες).
53 Fr. 21.3 with the notes of Pfeiffer and Harder.
54 W. Brandenstein, 'Tithonos', RE Suppl. vi. 174.
55 Il. 20.236–8; Il. 11.1–2, Od. 5.1–2.
56 Th. 979–80.
57 J. Tzetzes gives the name of Scamander's daughter as Rhoeo or Strymo (schol. ad Lyc. *Alex*. 18, ed. Scheer); the name 'Rhoeo' may come from Hellanicus (see below).
58 *Bibl.* 3.146.1.
59 So, rightly, Meyerhoff (1984) 190, followed by Bettarini (2007) 2–4, and Carrara (2011) 92–3.

sists, from his usual Epicurean perspective,[60] that even Tantalus, Tithonus, Minos, and Euphorbus/Pythagoras all succumbed to our common human lot, which is death:

occidit et Pelopis genitor, conviva deorum,
    Tithonusque remotus in auras
et Iovis arcanis Minos admissus, habentque
    Tartara Panthoidem iterum Orco demissum.[61]

There died both Pelops' father, who'd dined with the gods,
Tithonus, swept into the breezes,
and Minos, let into Zeus' secrets; and Tartarus
holds Panthoides, twice sent to Hell.

The familiar tragic version of Tithonus' fate first appears in two sources: Mimnermus from Smyrna or Colophon, and the *Homeric Hymn to Aphrodite*. Mimnermus, a generation before Sappho's time, cites Tithonus as an example of something to be avoided at all costs—old age. For Mimnermus, even the most handsome man, once youth is gone, is not honoured or loved by boys even if he is their father.[62] Youth is what the poet loves; would that it had lasted longer! It is brief as a dream, whereas 'painful, ugly old age hangs over ones's head, hateful and without honour; it makes a man unrecognizable, harming his sight and his mind once it buries him'.[63] This cult of youth contrasts with the respect for age often expressed in the Homeric poems. Mimnermus continues:

Τιθωνῶι μὲν ἔδωκεν ἔχειν κακὸν ἄφθιτον ⟨οἶτον⟩,
    γῆρας, ὃ καὶ θανάτου ῥίγιον ἀργαλέου.[64]

To Tithonus he gave an evil, immortal ⟨fate⟩,
    old age, more chilling still than painful death.

The poet takes for granted the version of the myth in which Eos asked him for immortality for her spouse and obtained it, but omitted to ask at the same time for eternal youth for him, with disastrous consequences. It is presumably Zeus who 'gave Tithonus an evil, endless fate as his possession, old age, that

---

60 See Frischer (1984).
61 *Odes* 1.28.7–10. See Carrara (2011) 94 n. 32, with discussion of the contortions of the Horatian commentators who tried to emend Tithonus away.
62 Fr. 3 West.
63 Fr. 5 West.
64 Mimnermus fr. 4 West. For the supplement, see Janko (1990); the usual ⟨αἰεί⟩ does not explain why a word fell out, whereas the loss after ΑΦΘΙΤΟΝ of ΟΙΤΟΝ would be easy.

is more chilling than even painful death'; in the myth it was, after all, Zeus who gave him immortality.

The *Homeric Hymn to Aphrodite* is the other early source for this version. The poet brings in Tithonus when Aphrodite, who has terrified her lover Anchises by appearing to him as a goddess after their intercourse, sets out to reassure the Trojan prince, but also to express her chagrin at the limits that Zeus sets to her power. She promises him a child, notes that Anchises' family were always 'close to the gods', and then recounts the story of Ganymede, who was snatched away by Zeus and given eternal youth among the immortals. Zeus gives his grieving father Tros magical horses in recompense (202–17). The following[65] story of Eos and Tithonus, whom she snatched because he was 'like the immortals', has a worse outcome. 'She went to ask the son of Cronus of the dark clouds for him to be immortal and to live for ever. Zeus nodded in agreement and fulfilled her wish. A fool, lady Eos did not think in her mind to ask for youth, and that he *rub off* baneful age' (220–4). As long as youth held Tithonus, he lived happily with Eos by the streams of Ocean at the end of the world (225–7). 'But when the first grey hairs fell from his lovely head and well-bearded chin, lady Eos kept from his bed, but nursed him in her halls with corn and ambrosia, giving him fine clothes' (228–32). The word for 'nurse', ἀτιτάλλω, is normally used of infants and children. The dénouement is grim: 'but when hateful age crushed him completely and he could not move or lift any of his limbs, this seemed to her the best plan. She put him in a chamber, and set on it shining doors. His voice flows ineffably, but there is no strength such as there was before in his bent limbs' (233–8). Aphrodite concludes from this that 'I would not choose for you to be among the immortals and to live for ever in such a state' (239–40). She insists that hateful old age is inevitable for human beings, and will envelop him too (244–5). His consolation is, as she has already told him (196–7), that his son by her will have a continuing line of descendants in the Troad; not even the tree-nymphs who will rear Aeneas are immortal—even they die with their trees, albeit after centuries (257–72). As King showed, Aphrodite's argument in this speech is that old age is inevitable for mortals unless Zeus grants escape from it, and he will not do this for Anchises: 'the story is cut short at a point which must terrify the listening Anchises . . . she thus makes human aging appear almost as the mediating term between Ganymedes and Tithonus; unlike Gany-

---

[65] The combination of these two stories in the same order recurs in Ibycus, fr. 289 Page (τὰ εἰρημένα ὑπὸ Ἰβύκου ἐν οἷς περὶ τῆς Γανυμήδους ἁρπαγῆς εἶπεν ἐν τῆι Εἰς Γοργίαν ὠιδῆι, καὶ ἐπιφέρει περὶ τῆς Ἠοῦς ὡς ἥρπαϲε Τιθωνόν, quoted by schol. ad A. R. 3.114–17); hence I suspect that Ibycus knew this passage of the *Hymn*, just as fr. 282.18–27 proves that he knew Homer's *Iliad* 2.484–92 and Hesiod's *Works and Days* 649–60 (Barron 1969, 134).

medes, Anchises will remain mortal, but unlike Tithonus he will age in a way that is οὐλόμενον' (246).⁶⁶

In many extant versions of the story other than those of the *Homeric Hymn to Aphrodite* and of Mimnermus there is eventually some consolation for Tithonus and his lover. This consolation is that, once his old age has become completely unendurable, Tithonus is turned into a cicada. This variant first appears in the fifth-century historian Hellanicus of Lesbos: 'Day fell in love with Tithonus, the son of Laomedon and brother of Priam, and had by him a son Memnon. When he (i.e. Tithonus) had become spent by a long life, the goddess turned him into a cicada. This is why the poet (i.e. Homer) compares the councillors, his relatives, to cicadas'. It is not clear whether the last sentence belongs to Hellanicus or to the well informed *Mythographus Homericus* who quotes him.⁶⁷

The metamorphosis of Tithonus is usually deemed an accretion to the earlier, tragic form of the myth, since its earliest datable occurrence is later than the *Homeric Hymn to Aphrodite*.⁶⁸ However, this is in fact another among many cases where a later source preserves a very ancient variant of a myth. Kakridis⁶⁹ was the first to argue that the motif of Tithonus' ceaseless (ἄσπετος) voice (*HHymn to Aphr.* 237), which is otherwise unexplained in the *Hymn*, shows that its composer already knew, and even presupposes, Tithonus' metamorphosis into a cicada.⁷⁰ The poet suppressed this story, because it contradicts the argument that Aphrodite needs to make to Anchises; for, although it is a lowly, even ugly, insect, the cicada was believed to have an immortality of a sort, since it was thought to feed on nothing but dew and to be able to rejuvenate itself by shed-

---

66 King (1989) 79–80; cf. Smith (1987) 77–82.
67 Τιθωνοῦ τοῦ Λαομέδοντος, Πριάμου δὲ ἀδελφοῦ, ἠράσθη ἡ Ἡμέρα, ἐξ οὗπερ ἐποίησεν υἱὸν Μέμνονα. μακρῶι δὲ βίωι δαπανηθέντος ἐκείνου μετέβαλεν αὐτὸν ε.ς τέττιγα ἡ θεός. διὸ δὴ αὐτοῦ τοὺς συγγενεῖς δημογέροντας τέττιξιν εἰκάζει ὁ ποιητής (sc. Homerus). ἱστορεῖ Ἑλλάνικος (fr. 140 Jacoby ap. schol. D ad Hom. *Il.* 3.151). Jacoby in his note *ad loc.* thinks Hellanicus is cited only for the genealogy, and is followed by Pfeiffer (1928, 325 n. 1). The D-scholia deriving from the *Mythographus Homericus* are erudite: cf. Kakridis (1930) 26 n. 4; Janko (1986) 51–5.
68 See, for instance, the scepticism of King (1986) 27–30; Edmunds (2009) 65 n. 41, 67 n. 43. Geissler (2005) 107 n. 12, is more circumspect.
69 Kakridis (1930), followed by Davies and Kathirithamby (1986) 126 n. 97, and King (1989) 80. Forbes Irving (1990, 318–19) rejects this on the weak grounds that, when Eos ceases to feed Tithonus, she leaves him to his fate, that the transformation is based on the simile at *Iliad* 3.151 (which I find most improbable), and that the legend that cicadas feed on dew makes them suitable lovers of dawn (this last point proves nothing about the date of the legend). For similar arguments see Carrara (2011) 107.
70 This central point is put backwards by Carrara (2011) 106–7, who implausibly suggests that the cicada's legendary origin was based on the babbling of old Tithonus, neglecting the evidence that Homeric poetry tended to suppress metamorphoses (see next n.).

ding its skin periodically, like a snake. Such a suppression also matches the tendency of more elevated epic compositions like Homer's (and the *HHymn to Aphrodite*) to play down or conceal more egregious types of metamorphosis,[71] and indeed the immortalizations of heroes like Heracles or Achilles that were so prevalent in the Epic Cycle, as Griffin demonstrated.[72] Kakridis added that Eos seems to stop feeding Tithonus once he is locked away, in just the same way as the Greeks believed that the cicada feeds on nothing but dew. Since one late source, which accords with Hellanicus in that it calls the goddess 'Day' rather than 'Dawn', adds that once Tithonus had grown old she used to carry him around in a basket like a baby in a cradle, this detail too may go back to Hellanicus.[73] Tithonus is enclosed just as a cicada is shut in a basket, which was a common prank in Aetolia when Kakridis was a child.[74] With old age the human body shrinks, and if one grew older for ever it would presumably shrink infinitely. Horace hints at this metamorphosis when he writes 'longa Tithonum *minuit* senectus', i.e. 'a long old age *reduced* Tithonus'.[75]

Kakridis rightly argues that the myth of Tithonus was an aetiology for the cicada's extraordinary life and song. Perhaps the story even incorporated the fact only male cicadas sing; this characteristic, familiar to Aristotle and Aelian,[76] was already known to the comic poet Xenarchus, who jokes that they are lucky to have silent wives.[77] In any case, Plato followed in the footsteps of the first myth-makers when he playfully invented a human origin for cicadas: they are men who were so enchanted by the singing of the Muses that they forgot to eat and drink as they sang, and were turned into creatures that could sing with-

---

71 Kakridis (1930) 27–8; cf. Griffin (1977) 40–1. Homer and Hesiod knew of many transformations into birds (Janko 1992 on *Il.* 13.62–5 and 14.290–1). One suspects, for instance, that the surprising array of wild animals that greet Aphrodite on Ida and then mate under her influence (*HHymn to Aphr.* 69–74) is a bowdlerized version of a Near Eastern tradition that Ishtar turns her former lovers into animals (*Epic of Gilgamesh* tablet VI).
72 Cf. Griffin (1977).
73 J. Tzetzes, schol. ad Lyc. *Alex.* 18 Scheer: φασὶ γοῦν ὅτι τὸν Τιθωνὸν τοῦτον σύνευνον ἔσχεν ἡ Ἡμέρα, ἐξ οὗ γεννᾷ Μέμνονα καὶ Ἡμαθίωνα. ἀθάνατον δὲ τὸν Τιθωνὸν ποιήσασα ἐπελάθετο ποιῆσαι καὶ ἀγήρω. γηράσαντα δὲ τοσοῦτον ὡς ἐν ταλάρωι καὶ λίκνωι αὐτὸν περιφερόμενον δίκην βρεφυλλίου καθεύδειν εἰς τέττιγα μετέβαλεν.
74 Kakridis (1930) 31 n. 20; in antiquity crickets commonly suffered this fate, as is attested by a series of epitaphs of crickets that died in their cages (*AP* 7.189, 193–5, 197–8). An epigram of Anyte (*AP* 7.190) shows that it happened to a cicada too (Kakridis 1930, 31–2 with n. 21). Cf. Longus 1.17.4.
75 *Od.* 2.16.30, my emphasis; cf. Kakridis (1930) 32–3. Horace also knows of the variant in which Tithonus was immortalized (*Od.* 1.28.7–10), as we saw above, n. [60].
76 Arist. *HA* 4.7, 532^{b}17, 5.30, 556^{b}11; Ael. *NA* 1.20.
77 εἶτ' εἰσὶν οἱ τέττιγες οὐκ εὐδαίμονες, / ὧν ταῖς γυναιξὶν οὐδ' ὁτιοῦν φωνῆς ἔνι; (fr. 14 K.–A.).

out food or drink until they died, while after death they report to the Muses who among men honours those goddesses.⁷⁸

The *Homeric Hymn to Aphrodite* is intended for an audience that knew of a dynasty in the Troad claiming descent from Aeneas.⁷⁹ One wonders, indeed, whether it originated on Lesbos, since it has elements of Aeolic dialect and shares vocabulary with Sappho, who may imitate it.⁸⁰ Its dating has been highly contested; this proved so difficult to pin down, whether by statistics or by literary arguments, that my own view of the matter has fluctuated. On the one hand, the linguistic data that I compiled point to a date contemporary with Homer's *Odyssey*.⁸¹ However, outliers among the statistics suggest a date contemporary with Hesiod;⁸² there are also many post-Homeric innovations in formulae.⁸³ If the latter data are reliable, the poem's diction has been affected by 'false archaism', i.e. by the poet learning from much older texts which had already received a form fixed by writing. Adopting a different approach, on the basis of literary *imitatio* I concluded that the hymn postdates Hesiod's *Theogony* but is imitated in his *Works and Days* and in the *Homeric Hymn to Demeter*.⁸⁴ However, Faulkner has advanced persuasive arguments that the hymn borrows from both of Hesiod's poems;⁸⁵ if he is right, as now seems to me more likely, its composition must fall between Hesiod and the *Homeric Hymn to Demeter*. Thus it probably antedates Mimnermus, who was active in the late seventh century. In this context, however, the only conclusion that matters is that the *Homeric Hymn to Aphrodite* antedates Sappho, as Mimnermus certainly does, since her contemporary Solon responds to the latter's wish to die at sixty rather than grow old.⁸⁶

It is surely no coincidence that, like Sappho, Hellanicus, who first recounts Tithonus' metamorphosis, was from Lesbos; given Tithonus' genealogy, this tale

---

78 Plato, *Phaedr.* 259a–b.
79 See Faulkner (2008) 3–10, 47–50. On elements of Aeolic dialect in it, see Janko (1982) 176–9.
80 Janko (1982) 169–70, noting the parallels between *HHymn to Aphr.* 12–15 and Sappho fr. 44.12–20, including the rare word κατίνη. For more parallels cf. Carrara (2011) 85 n. 12.
81 This is the conclusion supported, after a careful restudy of the data, by Rodda (2016) esp. 96–101, who, however, acknowledges the complexity of the problem and is concerned that the method of linguistic clustering may not work in this case, and that dialectal influences and 'false archaism' may be involved.
82 Janko (1982) 151–80.
83 Hoekstra (1968) 38–48; Faulkner (2008) 27–31.
84 Janko (1982) 225–8.
85 Faulkner (2008) 35–8, 47–50; his arguments cause me to retract my second thoughts about the value of *exemplum* and *imitatio* for dating the hymn, where I discounted the abundant evidence for its lateness relative to Homer (Janko 2012, 21 n. 3).
86 Solon fr. 20 West.

must have been invented and diffused in the north-east Aegean before it became pan-Hellenic in distribution. Whether or not the explanation of Homer's verse where Priam's councillors, 'good speakers', are compared with cicadas that 'sit on a tree in the forest and let forth a flowing voice'[87] is also owed to Hellanicus, it can hardly be accidental that the councillors belong to Tithonus' family and are stated to be worn out with old age but good speakers; speaking is all cicadas can do.[88] If follows that Homer, too, knew of two versions of the fate of Tithonus, his immortalization and his transformation into a cicada.

No artistic representations of Tithonus' old age have been identified,[89] but his transformation into a cicada is mentioned in many other sources from the fourth century BC onwards. Aristotle's pupil Clearchus of Soli says that 'in accord with his wish Tithonus put off his old age and became a cicada'.[90] Hieronymus of Rhodes in the third century BC shifts the blame from the goddess onto Tithonus, since it is he who makes the flawed request: 'Tithonus asked for immortality from Eos, but not, however, agelessness too. When he began to be troubled because of his advanced age, he asked for death. But as she was unable (sc. to bring this about) she turned him into a cicada, so that she would get continual pleasure from hearing his voice.'[91] The explicit motivation that Eos wished to hear his voice is a new detail, but matches the fact that the *Homeric Hymn to Aphrodite* notes that all that is left of Tithonus, once Eos confines him in his chamber, is his flowing voice (237).[92] The variant that Tithonus was enclosed

---

[87] *Il.* 3.150–1.
[88] So Acosta-Hughes and Stephens (2004) 251–2, who regard the Homeric passage as an important intertext for Callimachus' *Aetia* fr. 1.25–32 (below, n. [98]).
[89] A. Kossatz-Deissmann in Kahil (1997) viii.1: 34–6.
[90] Fr. 56 Wehrli: Τιθωνοῦ γῆρας· ἐπὶ τῶν πολυχρονίων καὶ ὑπεργήρων τάττεται. ἱστορεῖται δὲ ὅτι Τιθωνὸς κατ' εὐχὴν τὸ γῆρας ἀποθέμενος τέττιξ ἐγένετο, ὥς φησι Κλέαρχος ἐν τῶι Περὶ βίων.
[91] Fr. 15a Wehrli, perhaps from his lost *On Poets:* Ἱερώνυμος φηςὶ τὸν Τιθωνὸν αἰτήςαςθαι ἀθαναςίαν παρὰ τῆς Ἠοῦς, οὐ μέντοι καὶ ἀγηραςίαν· ὡς δὲ πολλῶι τῶι γήραι χρώμενος ἐδυςφόρει, αἰτήςαςθαι θάνατον· ἡ δὲ ἀδυνατοῦςα εἰς τέττιγα αὐτὸν μεταβάλλει, ὅπως ἥδοιτο διηνεκῶς τῆς φωνῆς αὐτοῦ ἀκούουςα. Cf. Servius on Vergil *G.* 3.328: *Tithonus, maritus Aurorae, post optatam longissimam vitam in cicadam dicitur esse conversus.* This account is related to a version which adds that, once Tithonus was turned into a cicada, Eos made him immortal (Σ Hom. *Od.* 5.1), as if the goddess could exercise this jurisdiction over insects at least.
[92] After citing Hieronymus, Eustathius offers a similar version, from an unnamed but presumably different source, in which Tithonus' own request again causes the tragic outcome, but he is turned into an incessantly singing cicada because of the endless pleas that he had made to be turned into an animal (*Comm. ad Hom. Il.* 11.1, p. 825,53–61).

in a basket appears in other sources.⁹³ As we saw, the *Homeric Hymn to Aphrodite* replaced this motif by the otherwise unparalleled detail that Eos shuts him in a chamber (236).⁹⁴

By turning into a cicada, Tithonus could finally cast aside his old age, albeit in a way that is only consoling from a very particular point of view, that of a poet. The reason lies in entomology.⁹⁵ The Greeks thought cicadas, like serpents, slough off their old skins or exuvia and are thereby rejuvenated⁹⁶ (in fact neither they nor snakes are made any younger by this process). Strikingly, the word for 'skin' in both cases was γῆρας, the same word as 'old age', as Hesychius records.⁹⁷ Although this usage of γῆρας is first attested of both snakes and insects in Aristotle,⁹⁸ it is already implied by the phrase **ξῦcαι** τ' ἄπο **γῆρας** ὀλοιόν (*HHymn to Aphr.* 224): for the verb ξύω connotes the action of a snake that rubs against a rock to slough off its old skin (γῆρας). This phrase adapts by transposition a formula which occurs in Homer at *Iliad* 9.444–8 (οὐδ' εἴ κέν μοι ὑποcταίη θεὸc αὐτόc / **γῆρας ἀποξύcας** θήcειν νέον ἡβώοντα, / οἷον ὅτε πρῶτον ...), where Phoenix is describing his own hypothetical rejuvenation,⁹⁹ and in the Cyclic *Nostoi* describing Medea's rejuvenation of Aeson (γῆρας ἀποξύcαcα).¹⁰⁰ This phrase is further evidence that the hymnic poet already had in mind the transformation of Tithonus into an animal that can be 'rejuvenated' by casting

---

93 Ath. *Epit.* 2.2 p. 97,3–5, where the detail that he was 'hung' up implies the basket, which is 'hung' up in Suet. Περὶ βλαcφημιῶν 8.3. Suetonius indicates that he knows of Tithonus' transformation into a cicada from sources other than those that speak of the basket; J. Tzetzes knows of both motifs (Σ Lyc. *Alex.* 18 Scheer, from Hellanicus?).
94 King (1986, 73–4) suggests, following Kakridis (1930) 32–3, that Tithonus' fate resembles that of the Cumaean Sibyl, who shrivelled up with extreme age so that Trimalchio could claim to have seen her hanging in a flask at Cumae (Petr. *Sat.* 48.8), with only her voice remaining (cf. Ov. *Met.* 14.101–53).
95 On the cicada, see the exhaustive treatments by Davies and Kathirithamby (1986) 113–33 and Tsagalis (2008) 115–19.
96 Present-day Greeks say that it is so hot that the cicadas are bursting out of their skins —cκάει ο τζίτζικαc (I thank D. Margomenou for this information).
97 The relevant entries are γράπιν· γῆρας τέττιγος ἢ ὄφεως καὶ τῶν ἐκδυομένων (*Lexicon* γ 901 Latte), and ἔcτι δὲ "λεβηρὶc" τὸ τοῦ ὄφεως γῆρας ... τάττουcι δὲ τὴν λέξιν ἐπὶ τέττιγος καὶ cυνόλως ἐπὶ τῶν ἀποδυομένων τὸ γῆρας (γ 1003 Latte).
98 Crabs ἐκδύνουcι τὸ κέλυφος τοῦ ἔαρος, ὥcπερ οἱ ὄφεις τὸ καλούμενον γῆρας (*Hist. An.* 5.17, 549ᵇ26); τὸν αὐτὸν δὲ τρόπον (as in snakes) καὶ τῶν ἐντόμων ἐκδύνει τὸ γῆρας, ὅcα ἐκδύνει, οἷον cίλφη κτλ. (*Hist. An* 7.17, 601ᵃ1–2).
99 I thank Prof. Tsagalis (*per litt.*) for this reference, as for suggesting that Phoenix' name might already bear a relation to the imaginary bird, the phoenix, which was emblematic of rejuvenation.
100 Fr. 6 Davies = 7 Bernabé.

off its old skin. The first undoubted application of the term γῆρας to cicadas is in the prologue to Callimachus' *Aetia*, where the poet wishes that he could become a cicada so that he could cast off his γῆρας.[101]

Sappho too surely knew the myth of Tithonus' metamorphosis, since it was the standard *aition* for the cicada, and originated in her part of Greece. Indeed King proposed[102] that Sappho may have referred to his metamorphosis in an ode in sapphics, fr. 21, which uses the same phrase χρόα γῆρας ἤδη that appears in line 3. However, although it is likely that Sappho here described her 'pitiable' state, with 'trembling' limbs and 'skin now' ruined by 'age' (3–6), it is more convincing to suppose that the masculine subject that 'flies in pursuit' (8) is Love, as Campbell suggested.[103] Nonetheless, the theme would have been attractive to Sappho, since the recollection that Tithonus became an immortal singer evokes the desire for poetic immortality that pervades her work, as West reminded us.[104] Thus the speaker of fr. 55 tells a rival that she will not be remembered after her death as she has no share in the roses of Pieria, the home of the Muses; this implies that the speaker will have a better fate. In fr. 32 the feminine speaker says her works have made her honoured. In fr. 147 the speaker says she will be remembered. In fr. 65 Sappho is addressed by name, presumably by a deity, and told that she is a favourite of Aphrodite and will have great fame across the earth and even in the land of Acheron. As we have seen, in Sappho the speaker and the author are one and the same. These parallels encouraged West to supplement, very plausibly, lines 4–8 of the poem in the new Cologne papyrus that precedes the Tithonus ode, so that the feminine speaker (who is presumably identical with Sappho herself) makes the following claim: 'may it provide me with great glory under the earth, as is right, since I have the favour of the Muses, and may they admire me on all sides, just as now when I am on the

---

101 ἐνὶ τοῖς γὰρ ἀείδομεν οἳ λιγὺν ἦχον / [τέττιγος, θ]όρυβον δ' οὐκ ἐφίλησαν ὄνων. θηρὶ μὲν οὐατόεντι πανείκελον ὀγκήσαιτο / [ἄλλο]ς, ἐ[γ]ὼ δ' εἴην οὐλ[α]χύς, ὁ πτερόεις, / ἆ πάντως, ἵνα γῆρας ἵνα δρόσον ἦν μὲν ἀείδω / πρώκιον ἐκ δίης ἠέρος εἶδαρ ἔδων, / αὖθι τὸ δ' ἐκδύοιμι, τό μοι βάρος ὅσσον ἔπεστι / τριγλώχιν ὀλοῶι νῆσος ἐπ' Ἐγκελάδῳ (fr. 1.25–32). Pfeiffer (1928, 325 n. 7, = *Ausgewählte Schriften* 118–19) rejected any link with the metamorphosis of Tithonus, following Jacoby in denying that Hellanicus recounted it (so too Faulkner 2008, 276), but this seems hypersceptical: for a valuable corrective, and a full survey of ancient beliefs about cicadas, see Tsagalis (2008) 115–19, esp. 118–19. On the cicada in Callimachus see Acosta-Hughes and Stephens (2004) 251–3, and Geissler (2005).
102 King (1989) 86 n. 22.
103 Campbell (1982) 71.
104 West (2005) 2–3, to which I am indebted for this collection of parallels. For a similar argument that the 'open' ending of the poem implies as positive reading, in which the poetess will continue to have an immortal voice, see Geissler (2005) esp. 108–9.

earth they call me the clear-voiced swallow, whenever I take up the *pâktis*, *barbitos* or lyre and sing in the chambers'.[105]

Along the same lines, Stehle has shown that Sappho likes to depict herself as performing in a moment that lies between a remembered memory of happiness and a future point when she is in some way close to divinity;[106] she argues that the metamorphosis of Tithonus into a cicada makes the poem conform to a pattern repeatedly found in Sappho's poems. Stehle rightly concluded: 'there has been debate over whether we should assume that Sappho is alluding to that conclusion of the story. I think that just as in [fr.] 16 V she "finishes" Helen's story with her wish to see her own love again, so it is open to us to construe this poem as Sappho completing Tithonos' story by singing in her old age.'[107] The daring and subtlety with which Sappho leaves her audience to fill in the end of the story against the grain of the initial pessimistic reading to which its argument logically leads,[108] and thereby completely to transform its tone, is matched only by some of the odes of Bacchylides. I have in mind *Od.* 5, in which the myth breaks off abruptly when Heracles is told he can marry Deianeira, or the paean that is *Od.* 17, where we know that Theseus will not only best Minos by escaping from his ordeal in Crete but will also elope with his daughter—an apt riposte to Minos' unwanted attention to Eriboea on the voyage to Crete, which we witness at the start of the poem. What is truly extraordinary about Sappho's poem how powerfully she achieves this effect in a mythic narrative only four lines long.

Works cited

Acosta-Hughes, B. and S. A. Stephens (2004). 'Rereading Callimachus' *Aetia* Fragment 1', *CP* 97: 238–55.
Austin, C. (2007). 'Nuits chaudes à Lesbos: buvons avec Alcée, aimons avec Sappho', in: Bastianini and Casanova, 115–26.
Barron, J. P. (1969). 'Ibycus: to Polycrates', *BICS* 16: 119–49.
Bastianini, G. and A. Casanova (eds.) (2007). *Atti del convegno internazionale di studi 'I papiri di Saffo e di Alceo': Firenze 8–9 giugno 2006*, Studi e Testi di Papirologia n.s. 9. Florence.
Beekes, R. (2010). *Etymological Dictionary of Greek*. Leiden.
Bettarini, L. (2007). 'Note esegetiche sul nuovo Saffo: i versi di Titono', *ZPE* 159: 1–10.

---

105 I translate the text of West (2005) 3.
106 Stehle (2009) 119.
107 Stehle (2009) 127–8. Similarly Clayman (2009) 133.
108 So Zellner (2008), who ably explicates the logic of Sappho's *modus tollens* argument.

Bowie, A. M. (1981). *The Poetic Dialect of Sappho and Alcaeus*. Salem, N.H.
Brown, C. G. (2011). 'To the ends of the earth: Sappho on Tithonus', *ZPE* 178: 21–5.
Burzacchini, G. (2007). 'Saffo Frr. 1, 2, 58 V. tra documentazione papiracea e tradizione indiretta', in: Bastianini and Casanova, 83–114.
Buzzi, S., and F. Piccioni (2008). 'Il "carme della vecchiaia": aspetti paleografici', in: A. Aloni (ed.), *Nuove acquisizioni di Saffo e della lirica greca*. Alessandria, 9–14.
Calame, C. (1977). *Les Choeurs de jeunes filles dans la Grèce antique*. Rome.
–. (1983). *Alcman*. Rome.
Campbell, D. A. (1982). *Greek Lyric: I. Sappho and Alcaeus*, Cambridge, Mass.
Carrara, L. (2011). ' "The very worst that could have been chosen": la funzione dell'*exemplum* di Titono nell'*Inno omerico ad Afrodite*', in: A. Aloni and M. Ornaghi (eds.), *Tra panellenismo e tradizioni locali*. Messina, 81–115.
Chantraine, P. (1968–1980). *Dictionnaire étymologique de la langue grecque*. Paris.
Clayman, D. L. (2009). 'The New Sappho in a Hellenistic Poetry Book', in: Greene and Skinner, 131–46.
Crane, G. (1986). 'Tithonus and the Prologue to Callimachus' *Aetia*', *ZPE* 66: 269–78.
Danielewicz, J. (2006). 'Bacchylides fr. 20 A,12 S.-M. and Sappho, *P.Köln* fr. I–II, 12', *ZPE* 155: 19–21.
Davies, M. and J. Kathirithamby (1986). *Greek Insects*. Oxford.
Debrunner, A. (1937). 'διδάσκω', *Mélanges Émile Boisacq* (Annuaire de l'Institut de philologie et d'histoire orientale 5). Brussels, i. 251–65.
Di Benedetto, V. (1985). 'Il tema del vecchiaio e il fr. 58 di Saffo', *QUCC* 48: 145–63.
–. (2004). 'Osservazioni sul nuovo papiro di Saffo', *ZPE* 149: 5–6.
Edmunds, L. (2009). 'Tithonus in the "New Sappho" and the Narrated Mythical Exemplum in Greek Poetry', in: Greene and Skinner, 58–70.
Faulkner, A. (2008). *The Homeric Hymn to Aphrodite*. Oxford.
Forbes Irving, P. M. C. (1990). *Metamorphosis in Greek Myths*. Oxford.
Frischer, B. (1984). 'Horace and the Monuments: a new interpretation of the Archytas Ode', *HSCP* 88: 71–102.
Führer, R. (2007). 'Zum neuen Sappho-papyrus', *ZPE* 159: 11.
Geissler, C. (2005). 'Der Tithonosmythos bei Sappho und Kallimachos: zu Sappho fr. 58 V. 11–22 und Kallimachos, *Aitia* fr. 1 Pf.', *Göttinger Forum für Altertumswissenschaft* 8: 105–14.
Giannakis, G. K. (1997). *Studies in the Syntax and Semantics of the Reduplicated Presents of Homeric Greek and Indo-European*. Innsbruck.
Griffin, J. (1977). 'The Epic Cycle and the Uniqueness of Homer', *JHS* 97: 39–53.
Gronewald, M. and R. W. Daniel (2004a). 'Ein neuer Sappho-Papyrus', *ZPE* 147: 1–8.
–. (2004b). 'Nachtrag zum neuen Sappho-Papyrus', *ZPE* 149: 1–4.
Greene, E. and M. B. Skinner (eds.) (2009). *The New Sappho on Old Age*. Washington D.C.
Hammerstaedt, J. (2009). 'The Cologne Sappho: its discovery and textual constitution', in: Greene and Skinner, 17–40.
Hoekstra, A. (1968). *The Sub-Epic Stage of the Formulaic Tradition*. Amsterdam and London.
Janko, R. 1981. 'ΑΘΑΝΑΤΟΣ ΚΑΙ ΑΓΗΡΩΣ: the genealogy of a formula', *Mnem.* 34: 382–5.
– (1982). *Homer, Hesiod and the Hymns: Diachronic Development in Epic Diction*. Cambridge.
–. (1986). 'The *Shield of Heracles* and the legend of Cycnus', *CQ* 36: 38–59.
–. (1990). 'Mimnermus fr. 4 West: a Conjecture', *AJP* 111: 154–5.

—. (1992). *The Iliad: A Commentary, volume IV: books 13–16*. Cambridge.
—. (2005). 'Sappho revisited', *TLS*, 23 December: 19–20.
—. (2011). 'πρῶτόν τε καὶ ὕστατον αἰὲν ἀείδειν: relative chronology and the literary history of the early Greek epos', in Ø. Andersen and D.T.T. Haug (eds.), *Relative Chronology in Early Greek Epic Poetry*. Cambridge, 20–43.
Kahil, L. (ed.) (1997). *Lexicon Iconographicum Mythologiae Classicae* VIII.1. Zürich and Dusseldorf.
Kakridis, J. T. (1930). 'ΤΙΘΩΝΟΣ', *Wiener Studien* 48: 25–38.
King, H. (1986). 'Tithonus and the Tettix', *Arethusa* 19: 15–35, reprinted as King (1989), in: T. M. Falkner and J. D. Luce (eds.), *Old Age in Greek and Latin Literature*. New York, 68–89.
Lardinois, A. (2009). 'The New Sappho Poem', in: Greene and Skinner, 41–57.
Lidov, J. (2009). 'Acceptance or Assertion? Sappho's New Poem in its Books', in: Greene and Skinner, 84–102.
Livrea, E. (2007). 'La vecchiaia su papiro: Saffo, Simonide, Callimaco, Cercida', in: Bastianini and Casanova, 149–66.
Lundon, J. (2007). 'Die fehlende Silbe im neuen Kölner Sappho-Papyrus', *ZPE* 160: 1–3.
Luppe, W. (2004). 'Überlegungen zur Gedicht-Ordnung im neuen Sappho-Papyrus', *ZPE* 149: 7–9.
MacKinnon, L. (2005). 'The New Sappho', *Times Literary Supplement*, 15 July 2005.
Meyerhoff, D. (1984). *Traditioneller Stoff und individuelle Gestaltung. Untersuchungen zu Alkaios und Sappho*. Hildesheim.
Nardella, S. (2012). 'Verso una nuova interpretazione dei testimoni del carme della vecchiaia di Saffo', *RCCM* 54: 257–65.
Nünlist, R. (1998). *Poetologische Bildersprache in der frühgriechischen Dichtung*. Stuttgart and Leipzig.
Obbink, D. (2009). 'Sappho Fragments 58–59: Text, Apparatus Criticus and Translation', in: Greene and Skinner, 7–16.
Pfeiffer, R. (1928). 'Ein neues Altersgedicht des Kallimachos', *Hermes* 63: 302–41.
Piccioni, F. (2010). 'Sul "carme della vecchiaia" di Saffo, v. 10', *SIFC* 8: 71–6.
Pickering, P. (2000). 'Verbal Repetition in *Prometheus* and Greek Tragedy Generally', *BICS* 44: 81–101.
—. (2003). 'Did the Greek Ear Detect "Careless" Verbal Repetitions?', *CQ* 53: 490–9.
Rawles, R. (2006). 'Notes on the interpretation of the "New Sappho"', *ZPE* 157: 1–7.
Rodda, M. S. (2016). 'L'*Inno Omerico ad Afrodite* (V) e la cronologia relativa dell'epica arcaica', in: R. Di Donato (ed.), *Comincio a cantare: contributo allo studio degli Inni Omerici*, Pisa, 82–101.
Rösler, W. (1985). Review of Meyerhoff 1984. *GGA* 235: 149–62.
Smith, P. M. (1987). *Nursling of Mortality: A Study of the* Homeric Hymn to Aphrodite. Frankfurt a.M., Bern, and Cirencester.
Stehle, E. (1996). 'Sappho's Gaze: Fantasies of a Goddess and Young Man', in: E. Greene (ed.), *Reading Sappho: Contemporary Approaches*. Berkeley and Los Angeles, 193–225.
—. (2009). '"Once" and "Now": temporal markers and Sappho's self-representation', in Greene and Skinner, 118–30.
Stothard, Sir P. (2005). 'Not Sapphic for Germaine', *The TLS Blog*, 5 Oct. 2005, http://timescolumns.typepad.com/stothard/2005/10/not_sapphic_for.html

Tsagalis, C. (2008). *Inscribing Sorrow: Fourth-Century Attic Funerary Epigrams*. Berlin and New York.
Tsantsanoglou, K. (2009). 'Sappho, Tithonus Poem: two cruces (lines 7 and 10)', *ZPE* 168: 1–2.
von Kamptz, H. (1982). *Homerische Personennamen*. Göttingen.
West, M. L. (2005). 'The New Sappho', *ZPE* 151: 1–9.
Zellner, H. M. (2008). 'Argument in the New Sappho', *Classical Bulletin* 84: 47–55.

List of Contributors

Egbert J. Bakker is the Alvan Talcott Professor of Classics at Yale University. His latest publications include *The Meaning of Meat and the Structure of the* Odyssey (Cambridge, 2013) and *Authorship and Greek Song: Authority, Authenticity, and Performance* (ed. Leiden, 2017).

Anton Bierl is Professor of Greek Literature at the University of Basel. He served as Senior Fellow at Harvard's CHS (2005–2011) and was Member of the IAS, Princeton (2010/11). He is director and co-editor of *Homer's Iliad: The Basel Commentary* and editor of the series *MythosEikonPoiesis*. His research interests focus on Homeric epic, drama, song and performance culture, the ancient novel, Greek myth and religion. His books include *Dionysos und die griechische Tragödie* (1991); *Die Orestie des Aischylos auf der modernen Bühne* (1996); *Ritual and Performativity* (2009); and the co-edited volumes *Literatur und Religion I-II* (2007); *Gewalt und Opfer* (2010); *Intende Lector* (2013); *The Newest Sappho* (2016) and *Time and Space in Ancient Myth, Religion and Culture* (2017).

Jonathan S. Burgess is a Professor of Classics at the University of Toronto. He is the author of *The Tradition of the Trojan War in Homer and the Epic Cycle* (2001), *The Death and Afterlife of Achilles* (2009), and *Homer* (2015), and numerous publications on early Greek epic, reception of Homer, and travel literature.

Albio Cesare Cassio is Professor of Classical Philology at the University of Rome "La Sapienza". After studying Aristophanic comedy for some years he has concentrated on the history of the Greek language in an Indo-European perspective and on the ancient Greek dialects. Included among his publications are: 'Early Editions of the Greek Epics and Homeric Textual Criticism in the 6th and 5th Centuries BC', in: F. Montanari (ed.), *Omero tremila anni dopo* (Rome, 2002); 'The Language of Doric Comedy', in: A. Willi (ed.), *The Language of Greek Comedy* (Oxford, 2002²); *Storia delle lingue letterarie greche* (Milan, 2016, editor and author).

Margalit Finkelberg is Professor of Classics (Emerita) at Tel Aviv University. She is the author of *The Birth of Literary Fiction in Ancient Greece* (OUP, 1998), *Greeks and Pre-Greeks. Aegean Prehistory and Greek Heroic Tradition* (CUP, 2005), *Homer* (TAU, Press 2014; Hebrew), and numerous scholarly articles; a co-editor (with G. G. Stroumsa) of *Homer, the Bible, and Beyond: Literary and Religious Canons in the Ancient World* (Brill, 2003) and the editor of *The Homer Encyclopedia* (3 vols.; Wiley-Blackwell, 2011). She is a member of the Israel Academy of Sciences and Humanities and the recipient of the Rothschild Prize in Humanities for 2012.

Jonas Grethlein holds the Chair in Greek Literature at Heidelberg University and currently directs a project on ancient narrative funded by the ERC. His more recent publications include *The Greeks and their Past* (Cambridge, 2010); *Experience and Teleology in Ancient Historiography* (Cambridge, 2013); *Die Odyssee. Homer und die Kunst des Erzählens* (Munich 2017); *Aesthetic Experiences and Classical Antiquity* (Cambridge, 2017).

Gregory O. Hutchinson is Regius Professor of Greek at the University of Oxford. He has written the following books: *Aeschylus, Septem contra Thebas, Edited with Introduction and Commentary* (Oxford, 1985); *Hellenistic Poetry* (Oxford, 1988); *Latin Literature from Seneca to Ju-*

venal: A Critical Study (Oxford, 1993); *Cicero's Correspondence: A Literary Study* (Oxford, 1998); *Greek Lyric Poetry: A Commentary on Selected Larger Pieces* (Oxford, 2001); *Propertius: Elegies Book IV* (Cambridge, 2006); *Talking Books: Readings in Hellenistic and Roman Books of Poetry* (Oxford, 2008); *Greek to Latin: Frameworks and Contexts for Intertextuality* (Oxford, 2013).

Richard Janko is Gerald F. Else Distinguished University Professor of Classical Studies at the University of Michigan. He studied under John Chadwick at the University of Cambridge and has taught at Columbia, UCLA, and UCL. He is the author of *Homer, Hesiod and the Hymns*, Volume IV of the Cambridge Commentary on the *Iliad*, *Aristotle on Comedy*, *Aristotle: Poetics*, editions of Philodemus' *On Poems* Books 1, 3, and 4, and over eighty articles on Hellenic language, literature, religion and thought. He also edited *Ayios Stephanos, Excavations at a Bronze Age and Medieval Settlement in Southern Laconia*. He is a Fellow of the American Academy of Arts and Sciences and the American Philosophical Society and a Foreign Member of the Academy of Athens.

Franco Montanari is Professor of Ancient Greek Literature at the Università degli Studi di Genova (Italy); Dr. *honoris causa* University of Thessaloniki; Correspondent Member of the Academy of Athens; Foreign Member of The Royal Society of Arts and Sciences in Gothenburg; Member of the Accademia Ligure di Scienze e Lettere. He is the President of the Féderation Internationale des Associations des Études Classiques-FIEC and member of International Council for Philosophy and Humanistic Studies, Societé Internationale de Bibliographie Classique, Centro Studi sui papiri e i documenti antichi 'G. Vitelli' of Florence; Director of the 'Centro Italiano dell'Année philologique' and of the Aristarchus' project (http://www.aristarchus.unige.net). He is the author of the *GI-Vocabolario della lingua greca*, 3rd ed. 2013; English ed. 2015; German ed. forthcoming) and of the *Storia della Letteratura Greca* (1998, new ed. forthcoming; Greek ed. 2008; English ed. forthcoming). He has published more than 230 scientific works.

Ruth Scodel, educated at UC Berkeley and Harvard, is D. R. Shackleton Bailey Collegiate Professor of Greek and Latin at the University of Michigan. Her books include *Credible Impossibilities: Conventions and Strategies of Verisimilitude in Homer and Greek Tragedy* (1999), *Listening to Homer* (2002), *Epic Facework: Self-presentation and Social Interaction in Homer* (2008), (with Anja Bettenworth) *Whither Quo Vadis? Sienkiewicz's Novel in Film and Television*, and *An Introduction to Greek Tragedy* (2010).

Christos Tsagalis is Professor of Greek at the Aristotle University of Thessaloniki. He is the author of the following books: *Epic Grief: Personal Laments in Homer's Iliad* (Walter de Gruyter, 2004), *The Oral Palimpsest: Exploring Intertextuality in the Homeric Epics* (HUP, 2008), *Inscribing Sorrow: Fourth-Century Attic Funerary Epigrams* (Walter de Gruyter, 2008), *From Listeners to Viewers: Space in the Iliad* (HUP, 2012), *Ομηρικές μελέτες: προφορικότητα διακειμενικότητα, νεοανάλυση* (ΙΝΣ, 2016), *Early Greek Epic Fragments: Genealogical and Antiquarian Epic* (Walter de Gruyter, 2017). He has also co-edited with F. Montanari and A. Rengakos the *Brill's Companion to Hesiod* (Brill, 2009) and with M. Fantuzzi *The Greek Epic Cycle and its Ancient Reception* (CUP, 2015).

Martin West, OM, FBA, was a Senior Research Fellow in Classics at All Souls College, Oxford, from 1991 to 2004, when he became an Emeritus Fellow and subsequently Honorary Fellow. He edited various Greek poetic texts and published extensively on Greek literature. Among his most important publications in recent years may be mentioned *Indo-European Poetry and Myth* (Oxford, 2007), *The Making of the Iliad* (Oxford, 2011), *The Epic Cycle: A Commentary on the Lost Troy Epics* (Oxford, 2013), and *The Making of the Odyssey* (Oxford, 2014). When he died in 2015 he was completing an edition of the *Odyssey* to match his Teubner edition of the *Iliad* (Stuttgart, 1998, 2000).

Stephanie West, FBA, is an Emeritus Fellow of Hertford College, Oxford. She has published *The Ptolemaic Papyri of Homer* (Cologne, 1967) and a commentary on *Odyssey* Books 1–4 (Fondazione Lorenzo Valla, 1981 – Oxford, 1988), and articles on a wide range of authors, particularly Herodotus and Lycophron.

Publications by Antonios Rengakos

Books

1. *Form und Wandel des Machtdenkers der Athener bei Thukydides* (Hermes Einzelschriften 48), Stuttgart 1984.
2. *Der Homertext und die hellenistischen Dichter* (Hermes Einzelschriften 64), Stuttgart 1993.
3. *Apollonius Rhodius und die antike Homererklärung* (Zetemata 92), Munich 1994.
4. *Το χαμόγελο του Αχιλλέα: Θέματα αφήγησης και ποιητικής στα ομηρικά έπη*, Athens 2006.
5. *Επινοώντας το παρελθόν: γέννηση και ακμή της ιστοριογραφικής αφήγησης στην κλασική αρχαιότητα*, Athens 2009 (Academy of Athens Award 2010).

Articles

1. 'Zur Biographie des Apollonios von Rhodos', *Wiener Studien* 105, 1992, 39–67.
2. 'Homerische Wörter bei Kallimachos', *Zeitschrift für Papyrologie und Epigraphik* 94, 1992, 21–47.
3. 'Zum Griechenbild in Vergils *Aeneis*', *Antike und Abendland* 38, 1993, 112–24.
4. 'Zeit und Gleichzeitigkeit in den homerischen Epen', *Antike und Abendland* 41, 1995, 1–33.
5. 'Lykophron als Homererklärer', *Zeitschrift für Papyrologie und Epigraphik* 102, 1994, 111–30.
6. 'Fernbeziehungen zwischen den thukydideischen Reden', *Hermes* 124, 1996, 396–417.
7. 'Zur Zeitstruktur der *Odyssee*', *Wiener Studien* 111, 1998, 45–66.
8. 'Το ομηρικό κείμενο κατά την αρχαιότητα', *Φιλόλογος* 93, 1998, 283–300.
9. 'Χρόνος και ταυτόχρονες πράξεις στα ομηρικά έπη', *Φιλόλογος* 98, 1999, 429–41.
10. 'Spannungsstrategien in den homerischen Epen', in: J. N. Kazazis – A. Rengakos (eds.), *Euphrosyne. Studies on Ancient Epic and Its Legacy in Honor of D. N. Maronitis*, Stuttgart 1999, 308–38.
11. 'Zur narrativen Funktion der Telemachie', in: André Hurst – Françoise Létoublon (eds.), *La mythologie et l'Odyssée. Hommage à Gabriel Germain*, Geneva 2002, 87–98.
12. 'The Hellenistic Poets as Homeric Critics', in: F. Montanari (ed.), *Omero tremile anni dopo*, Genova 2002, 143–58.
13. 'Aristarchus and the Hellenistic Poets', *Seminari Romani di Cultura Greca* 3, 2000, 325–35.
14. 'Zu Bakchylides' Erzähltechnik', in: A. Bagordo – B. Zimmermann (eds.), *Bakchylides. 100 Jahre nach seiner Wiederentdeckung*, Munich 2000 (Zetemata 106), 101–12.
15. 'Epic Narrative Technique in Herodotus' *Histories*', *Seminari Romani di Cultura Greca* 4, 2001, 253–70.
16. 'Apollonius Rhodius as a Homeric Scholar', in: Th. Papanghelis – A. Rengakos (eds.), *A Companion to Apollonius Rhodius*, Leiden 2001 (Mnemosyne Suppl. 217), 193–216.
17. 'Αφηγηματικότητα, διακειμενικότητα, αυτοαναφορικότητα. Η νέα ερμηνεία της *Οδύσσειας*', *Φιλόλογος* 110, 2002–2003, 538–62.
18. 'Η κλασική φιλολογία τον 21ο αιώνα', in: A. Rengakos (ed.), *Νεκρά γράμματα; Οι κλασικές σπουδές στον 21ο αιώνα*, Athens 2002, 13–23.

19. 'Tempo e narrazione nelle *Argonautiche* di Apollonio Rodio', in: L. Belloni – L. de Finis – G. Moretti (eds.), *L'officina ellenistica. Poesia dotta e popolare in Grecia e a Roma*, Trento 2003, 1–15.
20. 'Die *Argonautika* und das „kyklische Gedicht". Bemerkungen zur Erzähltechnik des griechischen Epos', in: A. Bierl et al. (eds.), *Antike Literatur in neuer Dichtung* (FS J. Latacz), Leipzig 2004, 277–304.
21. 'Narrativität, Intertextualität, Selbstreferentialität. Die neue Deutung der *Odyssee*', in: Michael Reichel – Antonios Rengakos (eds.), *Epea Pteroenta. Beiträge zur Homerforschung. Festschrift für Wolfgang Kullmann zum 75. Geburtstag*, Stuttgart 2002, 173–91.
22. 'Strategien der Geschichtsdarstellung bei Herodot und Thukydides – oder: Vom Ursprung der Historiographie aus den Geist des Epos', in: V. Borso et al. (eds.), *Geschichtsdarstellung. Medien-Methoden-Strategien*, Cologne 2004, 73–99.
23. 'Ομηρικό, κύκλιο και ελληνιστικό έπος. Παρατηρήσεις στην αφηγηματική τέχνη του αρχαιοελληνικού έπους', *Φιλόλογος* 116, 2004, 225–46.
24. 'Homer and the Historians: The Influence of Epic Narrative Technique on Herodotus and Thucydides', in: F. Montanari – A. Rengakos (eds.), *La poésie épique grecque: métamorphoses d'un genre littéraire* (Entretiens sur l'antiquité classique, vol. 52), Vandoeuvres-Geneva 2006, 183–214.
25. 'Du würdest Dich in Deinem Sinn täuschen lassen. Zur Ekphrasis in der hellenistischen Poesie', in: Chr. Ratkowitsch (ed.), *Die poetische Ekphrasis von Kunstwerkes. Eine literarische Tradition der Großdichtung in Antike, Mittelalter und früher Neuzeit*, Vienna 2006, 7–16.
26. 'Thucydides' Narrative', in: A. Rengakos – A. Tsakmakis (eds.), *Brill's Companion to Thucydides*, Leiden 2006, 279–300.
27. 'Zeit und Erzählung in den *Argonautika* des Apollonios Rhodios', in: J. Althoff (ed.), *Philosophie und Dichtung im antiken Griechenland*, Stuttgart 2007, 43–52.
28. 'The Smile of Achilles, or the *Iliad* and its Mirror-Image', in: M. Paisi-Apostolopoulou – A. Rengakos – C. Tsagalis (eds.), *Άθλα και έπαθλα στα ομηρικά έπη. Από τα πρακτικά του Ι' συνεδρίου για την Οδύσσεια* (15–19/9/2004), Ithaki 2007, 101–10.
29. 'Hesiod's Narrative', in: F. Montanari – A. Rengakos – C. Tsagalis (eds.), *Brill's Companion to Hesiod*, Leiden 2009, 203–18.
30. 'Die Überlieferungsgeschichte der homerischen Epen im Altertum. Eine Skizze', in: *Ἀντιφίλησις. Studies on Classical, Byzantine, and Modern Greek Literature and Culture in honour of J.-Th. Papademetriou*, Stuttgart 2009, 83–91.
31. 'Odyssee', in: A. Rengakos – B. Zimmermann (eds.), *Homer Handbuch*, Stuttgart 2011, 120–49.
32. 'Die Überlieferungsgeschichte der homerischen Epen', in: A. Rengakos-B. Zimmermann (eds.), *Homer Handbuch*, Stuttgart 2011, 167–75.
33. 'Hesiods Erzähltechnik', in: B. Zimmermann (ed.), *Griechische Literatur der Antike, Handbuch der Altertumswissenschaft* VII.1, Munich 2011, 101–10.
34. 'Historiographie', in: B. Zimmermann (ed.), *Griechische Literatur der Antike*, Handbuch der Altertumswissenschaft VII.1, Munich 2011, 326–417.
35. 'Narrative and History: the Case of Thucydides', in: G. Rechenauer – V. Pothou (eds.), *Thucydides – a violent teacher? History and its representations*, Göttingen 2011, 49–60.

36. 'Bemerkungen zum antiken Homertext', in: M. Meier-Brügger (ed.), *Homer, gedeutet durch ein großes Lexikon*, Berlin 2012, 239–52.
37. 'Aethiopis', in: M. Fantuzzi – C. Tsagalis, *The Cambridge Companion to the Epic Cycle*, Cambridge 2015, 306–17.
38. 'Narrative Technique in the Epic Cycle', in: M. Fantuzzi – C. Tsagalis, *The Cambridge Companion to the Epic Cycle*, Cambridge 2015, 154–63.

Edited Books

1. H.-Chr. Günther – A. Rengakos (eds.), *Beiträge zur antiken Philosophie. Festschrift für Wolfgang Kullmann*, Stuttgart 1997.
2. J. N. Kazazis – A. Rengakos (eds.), *Euphrosyne. Studies on Ancient Epic and Its Legacy in Honor of D. N. Maronitis*, Stuttgart 1999.
3. Th. Papanghelis – A. Rengakos (eds.), *A Companion to Apollonius Rhodius*, Leiden (2nd ed., Leiden 2008, *Brill's Companion to Apollonius Rhodius*).
4. M. Reichel – A. Rengakos (eds.), *Epea pteroenta. Festschrift für Wolfgang Kullmann*, Stuttgart 2002.
5. A. Rengakos (ed.), *Νεκρά γράμματα: Η Κλασική Φιλολογία τον 21ο αιώνα*, Athens 2002.
6. A. Rengakos (ed.), *W. Kullmann, Realität, Imagination und Theorie Kleine Schriften zu Epos und Tragödie in der Antike*, Stuttgart 2002.
7. A. Rengakos – A. Tsakmakis (eds), *Brill's Companion to Thucydides*, Leiden 2006 (Choice Outstanding Academic Title for 2007).
8. F. Montanari – A. Rengakos (eds.), *La poésie épique grecque: métamorphoses d'un genre littéraire* (Entretiens sur l'antiquité classique, vol. 52), Vandoeuvres-Geneva 2006.
9. Hans-Christian Günther – Antonios Rengakos (eds.), *Heidegger und die Antike* (Zetemata 126), Munich 2006.
10. M. Paisi-Apostolopoulou – A. Rengakos – C. Tsagalis, *Άθλα και έπαθλα στα ομηρικά έπη. Από τα πρακτικά του Ι' συνεδρίου για την Οδύσσεια* (15–19/9/2004), Ithaki 2007.
11. J. Grethlein – A. Rengakos (eds.), *Narratology and Interpretation* (Trends in Classics Supplementary Volumes, vol. 4), Berlin 2009.
12. F. Montanari – A. Rengakos – C. Tsagalis (eds.), *Brill's Companion to Hesiod*, Leiden 2009.
13. S. Matthaios – F. Montanari-A. Rengakos, *Ancient Scholarship and Grammar. Archetypes, Concepts, and Contexts* (Trends in Classics Supplementary Volumes, vol. 9), Berlin 2011.
14. A. Rengakos – B. Zimmermann (eds.), *Homer Handbuch*, Stuttgart 2011.
15. F. Montanari – A. Rengakos – C. Tsagalis (eds.), *Homeric Contexts* (Trends in Classics Supplementary Volumes, vol. 12), Berlin 2012.

Edited Books in Translation

1. Wolfgang Kullmann, *Η πολιτική σκέψη του Αριστοτέλη*, Athens 1996.
2. *Επιστροφή στην Οδύσσεια. Δέκα κλασικές μελέτες*, Thessaloniki 1998 (with J. N. Kazazis and D. I. Iakov).

3. J. Latacz, *Όμηρος. Ο θεμελιωτής της ευρωπαϊκής λογοτεχνίας*, Athens 2000 (trans. E. Sistakou).
4. J. Latacz, *Η Τροία και ο Όμηρος. Ο δρόμος για τη λύση ενός παλιού αινίγματος*, Athens 2001, (trans. I. Kerametsi – D. Skourellos).
5. H.-G. Nesselrath, *Εισαγωγή στην Αρχαιογνωσία, I. Αρχαία Ελλάδα*, Athens 2001 (with D. I. Iakov).
6. I. Συκουτρής, *Μελέτες και άρθρα. Τα γερμανόγλωσσα δημοσιεύματα*, (with D. I. Iakov), vol. 1, Athens 2001.
7. M. Fantuzzi – R. Hunter, *Ο Ελικώνας και το Μουσείο. Η ελληνιστική ποίηση από την εποχή του Μεγάλου Αλεξάνδρου έως την εποχή του Αυγούστου*, (with Th. Papanghelis), Athens 2002 (trans. D. Koukouzika – M. Noussia).
8. G. S. Kirk et.al., *Ομήρου Ιλιάδα, κείμενο και ερμηνευτικό υπόμνημα*:
Vol. I (with D. I. Iakov): Books 1–4, (trans. E. Tsiringakis), Thessaloniki 2003.
Vol. II: Books 5–8, (trans. Ph. Philippou), Thessaloniki 2003.
Vol. III: Books 9–12, (trans. M. Kaisar), Thessaloniki 2004.
Vol. IV: Books 13–16, (trans. R. Chameti), Thessaloniki 2003.
Vol. V: Books 17–20, (trans. M. Kaisar), Thessaloniki 2003.
Vol. VI: Books 21–24, (trans. M. Noussia), Thessaloniki 2005.
9. A. Heubeck et.al., *Ομήρου Οδύσσεια, κείμενο και ερμηνευτικό υπόμνημα*:
Vol. I: Books 1–8, (trans. M. Kaisar), Athens 2004.
Vol. II: Books 9–16, (trans. R. Chameti), Athens 2005.
Vol. III: Books 17–24, (trans. Ph. Philippou), Athens 2005.
10. S. Hornblower, *Θουκυδίδου Ιστορίαι, κείμενο και ερμηνευτικό υπόμνημα*:
Vol. I: Books 1–3, (trans. Ph. Petika), Thessaloniki 2006.
Vol. II: Books 4–5.24, (trans. Ph. Philippou), Thessaloniki 2006.
Vol. III: Books 5.25–8.109 (trans. Ph. Petika, M. Kaisar, K. Dimopoulou), Thessaloniki 2011.
11. George A. Kennedy (ed.), *Αρχαία ελληνική και ρωμαϊκή κριτική*, Thessaloniki 2008.
12. F. Montanari, *Ιστορία της Αρχαίας Ελληνικής Λογοτεχνίας*, Thessaloniki 2008 (with D. I. Iakov).
13. B. Powell – I. Morris (eds.), *A New Companion to Homer. Εγχειρίδιο Ομηρικών Σπουδών*, Athens 2009.
14. D. Asheri – A. Lloyd – A. Corcella (eds.), *Ηροδότου Ιστορίαι, κείμενο και ερμηνευτικό υπόμνημα*:
Vol. I: Books 1–2, Thessaloniki 2010.
Vol. II: Books 3–4, Thessaloniki 2010.
15. A. Rengakos – A. Tsakmakis, *32 Μελέτες για τον Θουκυδίδη* (*Brill's Companion to Thucydides*), Thessaloniki 2011 (with C. Tsagalis).

General Index

accumulation   7, 148–150, 152
Achilles   4–6, 43–50, 52–55, 57, 59, 62–65, 67–73, 76–89, 121–134, 136–138, 140, 148, 154–156, 160–162, 164, 204, 206, 212, 278–279, 284
– and Agamemnon   49, 82, 84, 109, 148, 203
– and Odysseus   4, 6, 65, 99, 107, 109, 129, 140
– and Patroclus   52, 72, 85, 204
Aeolus   100–103, 106
Aethiopians   81–82, 107
Agamemnon   21, 43–50, 53–54, 64–65, 76, 80–82, 84–86, 89, 109, 113, 124–125, 127–128, 136–137, 140, 148, 159, 203–204, 211
Ajax   37, 47, 60, 65, 116, 136, 155, 220
Allen   17–18, 23, 25, 115, 243
Antilochus   34
apologos/Apologoi   4, 6, 95–96, 100–101, 103–117, 122, 132, 133, 140
Aristarchus   16, 25–26, 77, 85–86.
Aristophanes of Byzantium   16, 26
artificiality   7
attention   4, 7, 18, 20, 33, 37, 87–88, 126, 129, 145, 152, 155, 157–159, 161, 163–164, 167–168
audience   5–9, 52, 59, 73, 75, 78–83, 85–86, 89–90, 95, 104–105, 107, 110, 140, 145–149, 155–157, 163, 217, 219–221, 225, 235, 238, 256–257, 259, 275–277, 279–280, 285, 289
authenticity   7, 171, 261, 268

Briseis   43–45, 48–50, 54

Calypso   100–101, 103, 106, 109–110, 124
Charybdis   96, 100–101, 103–106, 114, 116
choral festivity   253, 259
cicada   8–9, 267, 280, 283–284, 286–289
Circe   6, 20–21, 96, 100–101, 103, 106–108, 113, 115–116, 138

compensatory lengthening   15
concordance interpolation   20
conspiracy theories   4, 95, 107, 109–116
Crete   110–111, 117, 196, 201, 216, 289
Cyclic/'cyclic'   33, 95, 101, 107, 216, 232, 234, 248, 287

desis   54
devotional objects   233
dialects
– Aeolic   7, 171–180, 182, 185–188, 270, 285
– Doric   7
– Ionic   20, 172–173, 175–176, 179, 188
dictation (theory)   51
Diomedes   34, 44, 47, 132, 147–148, 157
Doloneia   14
double motivation   80
doublet   73, 101, 103

Egypt   13, 128, 243
embassy (to Achilles)   4–5, 43, 45, 47–50, 53–54, 84–85, 89, 140
epiphany   9, 235, 238–246, 249–251, 253–256, 258–259, 261
Eurynome   218, 223

fairyland   106
fate   4–6, 21–22, 52, 66–68, 72, 75, 78–81, 85, 87–88, 102, 124–127, 136, 139–140, 151, 267–268, 280–281, 283–284, 286–288
festivals
– Delian   31, 253–254, 256–260
– Panathenaia   29
– Panionian   30–31
fixity   7, 59, 78, 171
formula/formulaic
– diction   5, 8, 32, 59, 172, 185, 231, 245, 261, 274, 285
François Vase   33–35

gifts   5, 22, 44–46, 48–50, 54, 77, 112, 115, 128, 233, 270, 274
Gilgamesh (hero)/*Gilgamesh* (epic)   115, 208, 212, 284

Hector   4–6, 47, 49, 52–54, 57, 60–74, 81–82, 84–88, 127–129, 131, 133, 148, 154–156, 158–160, 162, 164, 215
– and Achilles   5, 43, 45, 48, 68–69, 71–73, 85–86, 121–124, 131–133, 140, 211
– and Paris   62–63, 72
Hephaestus   8, 77, 216–219, 221, 223
Hermann's Bridge   8, 215, 225
Hipparchus   29–30, 222

"iconic"   243
iconym   7–8, 191, 211
improvisation   7, 76–77, 146, 165–167
in medias res   104
incantations   8, 210
incoherencies   51
intertextuality   2, 6, 58–59, 122, 126, 140, 231

kommende Gott,   238

Laestrygonians   100–101, 106
Lemnos   7–8, 215–225
Lesbos   30, 44, 159, 173, 176, 185, 275, 283, 285
Lotus-Eaters   100–101
Ludwich   17–19, 23, 25
lysis   54

Menelaus   5, 21–22, 34, 60, 64–66, 69, 73, 78, 84, 95, 100, 107, 109, 114–115, 130, 153, 159, 161, 163–164
metamorphosis   6, 9, 203, 240, 267, 283–285, 288–289
metapoetics   5, 89
Mimnermus   281, 283, 285
"mind act"   237, 252

mnēstērophonia   122, 130–131, 133–136, 138, 140
monumental composition   5, 57, 59, 121

Neoanalysis   59, 87

Odysseus   4, 6, 19–26, 34–35, 46–47, 49–50, 65, 76, 78, 82, 89, 95–97, 99–117, 121–140, 148–149, 195, 216, 278
– and Achilles: *see* Achilles and Odysseus
– wrath   76–77, 81, 84, 112
old age   9, 273–277, 281–284, 286–287, 289
oraliture   96–98
overdetermination   80

Pan-Hellenic   107
Panathenaic regulation   37
pars epica   233
Patroclus   5, 33–35, 47–50, 52–55, 59, 63, 67, 70–71, 78–80, 84–88, 98, 125, 129, 131–133, 140, 147, 164, 204, 279
performance   4–5, 7, 9, 29–31, 33, 35–36, 58–60, 63, 73, 75, 82, 89–90, 97, 110–111, 114–116, 121, 145, 165–168, 231, 235–238, 242, 251–254, 256, 258, 260–261, 274, 277
persona cantans   260
piecemeal revelation   69
Pisistratus   29, 31, 222
poetic grammar   5, 59, 73
Polyphemus   6, 22–24, 96–104, 106, 108, 110, 116, 132, 134–135, 138, 140
presentification   237
pronunciation   15, 269
prophecy   19, 26–27, 47, 72, 79, 85–86, 102, 116, 164, 256

rage   6, 63, 71, 73, 75, 131–134, 138, 140
range   1–2, 7, 16, 59, 149–150, 154–156, 161–163, 167–168, 215, 219, 235, 245, 255
re-enactment/re-enacting   9, 235, 251–252, 257–258
rejuvenation   287
remembering   237–238, 243, 252

repetition 5, 7, 57–60, 62, 73, 101–102, 129, 132, 146–152, 154–158, 162–163, 166–168, 273–274
revenge 4, 50, 54–55, 127, 131–134, 136–137, 140
rhapsodic "I" 235–238, 241–242, 255, 257–259, 261
ritual 8, 71, 87, 133, 203, 208–211, 220–221, 242, 247, 275
– conjuration of water and salt 209
rock face 7–8, 195–196, 206–207, 209, 211–212

saltlick 7–8, 195–197, 202, 207, 210–211
Sappho 8–9, 158–159, 171, 173, 175, 177, 249, 268–269, 273, 277–281, 285, 288–289
Siduri 115
sign (σῆμα) 14, 43, 53, 83, 147, 163, 200, 235, 237, 239–243, 246, 250, 254, 259
simile 5, 8, 60–63, 70–73, 81, 103, 130–131, 134–135, 154, 157, 160–163, 204–212, 221, 277–279, 283
Sinties 216–218, 224
spell 8, 50, 208–210
sulphur 8, 219

Telemachus 19, 22, 80, 111–112, 124, 130, 135–136, 150
telescopic 4, 57, 73
Thesprotia 107, 110–112

Thetis 46, 52, 69–70, 72, 76–77, 79, 81–84, 86–87, 109, 218, 223, 248–285
Thrinacia 100–104, 107, 110, 138
Tiresias 19–20, 102–103, 106, 112, 135
Tithonus 8–9, 257–268, 271, 273–277, 279–289
"total recall" 237
traditional referentiality 5, 58, 156, 240
traditional tale 6, 115
transmission 14–15, 30–31, 35–36, 58, 210, 251

Ungenauigkeitsprinzip 85
Utnapishtim 115

van Thiel 17–18, 23, 25, 180, 182
variation 7, 34, 99, 103, 109, 111, 116, 149–150, 154
vase paintings 34, 96, 98–99, 103
Venetus A 3, 16, 18
volcano/volcanic 219–225
Von der Mühll 17–18, 20, 25, 182–183, 185

Wackernagel 15, 178
wanderings 99, 101
wrath 80
– of Achilles 5–6, 43, 45–50, 53–64, 57, 59, 64, 66, 70–73, 75, 77, 79–82, 86–87, 109, 122, 125–128, 130–132, 137–138, 140, 156, 160–161
– of Poseidon 88, 101–103, 110, 116, 140

Index of Principal Homeric Passages

Iliad
1.1–6	75	4.517	78
1.213–14	82	5.280	148
1.220–21	132	5.393	154
1.252	217	5.395	154
1.285–303	43	5.526	161
1.293–303	43	5.554–8	161
1.304	183	5.613	78
1.363–4	148	5.680	163
1.396–406	77	5.847	155
1.403–4	202	6.42–4	159
1.423–4	81	6.75–6	159
1.515–16	82	6.133	217
1.517–20	83	6.325–31	65, 68
1.522–27	83	6.407	161
1.582	183	6.506–11	60
1.590–3	77	6.512–14	61
1.592–4	217	7.244	148
1.594	216	7.350–1	66
2.75	183	7.357–60	66
2.155	78	7.466–71	217
2.299–330	78	8.89	156
2.377–80	44	8.169–71	147
2.557–8	37	8.424	155
2.631–7	100	8.473–7	47
2.632–5	203	8.473–8	84
2.633	192, 197	8.516	158
2.722	217	9.1–78	43
2.867	218	9.13–15	203, 206, 211
3.25	137, 162	9.14	207, 211
3.132	158	9.14–15	60, 211
3.249	183	9.14–16	211–212
3.351–4	84	9.15	191–4
3.355	148	9.16	205
3.373–82	78	9.20	125, 205
3.374	163	9.30–50	44
3.448	180–1	9.34–5	167
4.25–9	162	9.51–79	44
4.39–54	84	9.121–61	44
4.163–8	84	9.186–91	164
4.233	183	9.189–95	89
4.234–9	84	9.307–429	45
4.241	183	9.312–13	140
4.364–412	167	9.336	45, 49
		9.379–87	128

Passage	Page	Passage	Page
9.410–20	52	15.320–2	165
9.432–605	46	15.676	154
9.436	149	15.685–6	154
9.606–19	46	16.1–100	48
9.608	78	16.2–4	204, 206, 211
9.618–19	46	16.4	60, 70, 192–193
11.1–2	63, 276, 280	16.7–11	279
11.29–31	146	16.60–73	48
11.172–76	162	16.71–3	48
11.175–76	162	16.83–6	48–49
11.256	155	16.156–62	211
11.349	148	16.408	157
11.383	200–201	16.433–8	86
11.548–55	161	16.440–4	162
11.551	162	16.441	79
11.609	53	16.450–1	148
11.609–10	48	16.538–40	68
11.632–5	146	16.685–90	79
11.656–61	148	16.693	78
11.670–762	115	16.702–11	147
11.780–791	53	16.707–9	78
11.794–803	48	16.751–73	161
12.44	164	16.753	161
12.46	161	16.761	157
12.231–6	67	16.776	59
12.249	183	16.784–8	147
12.254–5	165	16.851	164
12.299	162	17.61–7	162
12.305–6	161	17.63–4	162
13.1–9	90	17.65	60, 162
13.7–9	88	17.111	162
13.62–5	194, 203, 284	17.122	70
13.63	192	17.201–8	69
13.434–9	165	17.215	183
13.501	157	17.270–3	88
13.584–5	155	17.514–21	164
13.586–92	160	17.516	148
13.602	78	17.543–4	158
13.636–7	84	17.657–64	161
13.831	155	17.660	162
14.242–62	77	17.673–82	163
15.62–71	86	17.693	70
15.69–71	84	18.1–64	59
15.210	183	18.21	70
15.213–17	84	18.26	59
15.263–8	60	18.119	78
15.269–70	61	18.130–3	70

Index of Principal Homeric Passages — 307

18.146–8	219	21.288	160
18.151–2	87	21.346	161
18.165–8	87	21.357–8	148
18.185–6	87	22.22–4	63, 71
18.187–8	149	22.87	180
18.201–5	149	22.104	65
18.203–21	85	22.114	66
18.233	180	22.114–21	65
18.285–6	68	22.117	66
18.349	157	22.136–7	160
18.352	180	22.178–81	162
18.356–67	88	22.179	79
18.391–405	218	22.185	88
18.402–3	218	22.258–66	71
18.561	161	22.262–4	133
18.583	162	22.273	148
18.616	219	22.274	148
19.40–300	49	22.289	148
19.137–44	49	22.290	148
19.140–1	49	22.329	184
19.145–53	49	22.346–7	131, 162
19.154–97	50	22.353	181
19.199–300	50	22.358–60	72
19.318	158	22.362–3	72
19.509–17	149	23.25	181
19.518–23	149	23.31	200–201
19.603–4	148	23.215	162
20.20–30	88	23.287–616	34
20.164–73	161	23.489	184
20.172–3	161	23.492	184
20.301	88	23.740–7	217
20.423	155	24.12–18	164
20.438	148	24.39–43	131
20.496	161	24.207	163
21.36	161	24.212–13	163
21.40–1	217	24.702	181
21.58	217	24.720	181
21.74	129	24.753	215
21.77	161	24.771	184
21.78–9	217	24.804	74
21.79	217		
21.95–6	129	*Odyssey*	
21.98	184	1.1	103
21.116–18	129	1.7–9	104
21.124	180	1.245–8	101
21.130–3	133	1.257–64	112
21.257–64	205	1.325–7	95

1.337–44	89	9.213–15	97
1.337–45	150	9.224–30	139
1.346–7	19	9.291–3	134
1.347–9	80	9.314	135
1.351–2	150	9.349	97
1.366	181	9.355–6	97
1.374–80	135	9.362–7	97
1.394–6	101	9.454	97
2.189	184	9.485–6	23
2.240	184	9.516	97
2.323	184	9.534–5	102
2.325–30	112	10.70	184
3.148	184	10.74–5	102
3.345	184	10.330	108
3.399	181	10.330–2	103
4.81–91	114	10.360	157
4.83–9	107	10.431–7	104
4.286	184	10.435–7	139
4.333–40	130	10.438–42	138
4.351–537	114	10.457–9	103
4.420	184	10.490–3	103
4.599	217	10.496–502	20
4.606	198	10.497	181
5.1–2	63, 276, 280	11.81	184
5.308–11	124	11.114–15	102
5.368–70	208	11.129–31	102
6.130–6	130	11.225	184
6.146	184	11.370–6	89
7.341	184	11.465	184
8.37–103	89	11.478	123
8.72–6	106	11.478–91	46
8.73–82	95, 123	11.482–6	123
8.75	123	11.488–91	123
8.78	123	11.552	184
8.82	123	11.601–26	37
8.124	200	12.12–22	108
8.175	184	12.69–72	113
8.244	200	12.184	108
8.284	217, 219	12.208–12	104
8.294	224	12.340–51	104
8.341	200	12.389–90	103
8.396	184	13.187–96	216
8.415	184	13.242	198
8.486–98	89	13.341–3	102
8.499–520	95	13.581–600	153
8.523–31	278	15.440	184
8.533–43	89	16.175	161

Index of Principal Homeric Passages — **309**

16.247–51	101	268	250
18.213	181	480–2	249
18.340	184	495	236
19.155	184	Apollo (3)	
19.203	110	1	236, 255
19.246	161	2–4	256
20.18–21	134	2–12	255
20.382–3	107	5–9	255
21.146–7	129	19–20	255
21.346–7	101	29–46	255
22.26	131, 184	36	215
22.45–59	105, 126	47–48	255
22.54–5	136	61–82	255
22.61–4	127	67	255
22.273–95	154	78	255
22.312	129	80	255
22.313–15	129	83–119	255
22.326–9	105	127–32	255
22.402–6	131	131	260
22.412	135	131–2	255
23.118–22	136	133–5	255
23.177–80	24	140–5	255
23.326–33	125	146–64	260
24.36	125	146–78	256
24.44	181	147–9	256
24.80–4	125	150	256
24.106–13	137	151	256
24.114	136	151–5	256
24.173	184	153	256
24.192	125	153–4	256
24.295	181	156	256–257
24.303–14	107	158–64	257
24.426–9	139	163	259
24.426–37	105	165	257
24.537	131	166	257
24.545	132	166–7	257
		169–70	258
Homeric Hymns		171–3	258
Dionysus (1)		172	258
16	252	174	258
1–18	252	174–6	258
17–20	236	175	22
19–20	253	177–8	259
Demeter (2)		179–85	259
1	236	182–7	260
111	235	182–206	260
120	250	201–3	260

319–20	218	9	243–244, 247, 250
388–439	259	10	243
440–5	259	11	244
441	259	12–14	244
445–7	259	14	244
449–50	260	15	244
463–6	260	16	244
451–61	260	17	244–245
514–16	260	18	244
514–23	260	19–20	244, 248
517–19	260	20–1	245
545	260	22–4	245
546	236, 240, 261	23	244
Hermes (4)		25	245
54–62	261	26	245
423–33	261	26–7	245
530	236	27	245
580	261	28–9	245
Aphrodite (5)		30–1	245
12–15	285	32–3	245
69–74	284	33–4	245
193	250	34	244–245
196–7	282	36–7	246
202–17	282	37	246
220–4	282	38–41	246
221	274	42–4	246
224	287	44–5	246
225–7	282	44–53	246
228–32	282	45–6	246
233–8	282	46	246, 250
236	287	47–8	247
237	283, 286	48–50	247
239–40	282	49	247, 250
240	274	50	244, 247
244–5	282	50–1	247
257–72	282	51	243, 247
293	236	51–3	247
Aphrodite (6)		52	243
21	236	54	248–249
Dionysus (7)		55	243, 250–251
1	243, 249	56–7	249, 251
1–6	243	58	249, 251
2	236, 238, 243, 245	58–9	252
3–6	260	Artemis (9)	
6	244	9	236
7	244	Aphrodite (10)	
8	243	1	236

6	236	5	236
Athena (11)		Zeus (23)	
1	236	1	236
Demeter (12)		To the Muses and Apollo (25)	
1	236	1	236
Mother of Gods (13)		7	236
1	236	Dionysus (26)	
3	236	1	236
Heracles the Lionheart (15)		Artemis (27)	
1	236	1	236
Asclepius (16)		22	236
5	236	Athena (28)	
Hermes (18)		1	235
1	236	18	235
11	236	Hestia (29)	
Pan (19)		14	235
1–4	204	To Earth Mother of All (30)	
49	236	19	235
Apollo (21)		To the Dioscuri (33)	
1	236	19	236

www.ingramcontent.com/pod-product-compliance
Lightning Source LLC
Chambersburg PA
CBHW051629230426
43669CB00013B/2234